EDUCATION CENTRE
ROYAL INFIRMARY, Bl

GW01018586

KNOWLEDGE IN
ORGANIZATIONS

WLD
14/9/10

BLACKBURN, HYNDBURN AND RIBBLE VALLEY
HEALTH AUTHORITY

EDUCATION CENTRE
LIBRARY

ACC. No.

CLASS No. 302.35
658.4038 SPA

BLACKBURN EDUCATION CENTRE
LIBRARY

TB01112

AUTHOR: SPARROW John

TITLE: Knowledge in Organizations

(555)

EDUCATION CENTRE LIBRARY
ROYAL INFIRMARY, BLACKBURN

KNOWLEDGE IN ORGANIZATIONS

Access to Thinking at Work

JOHN SPARROW

SAGE Publications
London • Thousand Oaks • New Delhi

TR01112

© John Sparrow, 1998

First published 1998

All rights reserved. No part of this publication may be
reproduced, stored in a retrieval system, transmitted or utilized
in any form or by any means, electronic, mechanical,
photocopying, recording or otherwise, without permission in
writing from the Publishers.

SAGE Publications Ltd
6 Bonhill Street
London EC2A 4PU

SAGE Publications Inc.
2455 Teller Road
Thousand Oaks, California 91320

SAGE Publications India Pvt Ltd
32 M-Block Market
Greater Kailash – I
New Delhi 110 048

British Library Cataloguing in Publication data

A catalogue record for this book is available
from the British Library

ISBN 0 8039 7828 6
ISBN 0 8039 7829 4 (pbk)

Library of Congress catalog card number 97–062254

Typeset by Mayhew Typesetting, Rhayader, Powys
Printed in Great Britain by The Cromwell Press Ltd,
Trowbridge, Wiltshire

EDUCATION CENTRE
LIBRARY
ACC. No. 990368
CLASS No. 302.35
658.4038 SPA

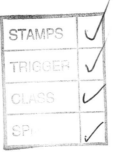

STAMPS ✓
TRIGGER ✓
CLASS ✓
SPI ✓

Contents

List of Figures

List of Tables

Preface

This book provides a framework to help individuals reflect on their own practices at work, and to help organizations understand and promote sharing of the considerations that influence employee thinking and action.

Chapter 1 presents a series of arguments that show that a new form of management is emerging. This management by perception requires much greater recognition of organizational participants' thinking in their decisions. The broad competencies and personality 'required' for this more perceptive approach are considered.

Chapter 2 shows how the knowledge that people use in the course of their action is a dynamic combination of particular kinds of mental material, configured into particular forms of thought, being processed using particular types of thinking. Five different kinds of mental material, two forms of thought and three types of thinking are identified. The potential value of this framework for considering one's own practices and organizational knowledge is discussed.

Chapter 3 addresses the role that physical representation plays in the access to perceptions.

Chapter 4 reviews a comprehensive set of techniques for working with propositional and imagistic forms of thought.

Chapter 5 reviews a range of techniques that can be used to induce different types of thinking. Three different types of thinking may occur at work. An individual's decisions and actions are different when they are made in the course of casual musing (autistic thinking), focused reasoning or prevailing mood. By inducing each of these particular types of thinking, we can gain insights into facets of knowledge that might otherwise elude us.

Chapter 6 shows how specific techniques can be used to focus on different kinds of mental material. One can tease out the mental models that are used in decision-making by invoking an emphasis in thinking that highlights semantic understanding. Similarly one can focus on the memories that one has of particular episodes, *per se*, as opposed to principles. It is also possible to surface some of the non-conscious influences on decision-making and action. Techniques that focus on both skilled and tacit subconscious mental material are presented, together with a range of approaches for highlighting and appreciating unconscious influences on practice.

As a whole, this book offers a framework within which to consider knowledge in individual decision-making and action. It provides a long-needed rationale for the use of particular techniques for knowledge elicitation at work.

Acknowledgements

I would like to take the opportunity to thank Gordon Robinson for suggesting and Roger Baty for insisting that I write the book; Kay Jones for winning space in my diary, and Cath Eden for continuing to find it, so that I could work on the book.

I extend my thanks to all of the people in organizations that have participated in studies with me, together with undergraduate, Masters and Doctoral students who have worked with me to surface key issues.

Finally I would like to thank my wife Marianne and children Jennie, Christie and James for their efforts in proofreading, commenting and generally being patient.

1

The Need to Work with Perceptions

Working with other people has always been a significant requirement for managers. In recent years there have been significant changes in the nature of the information and teams with which managers work. Managers need to work with 'softer' information than in the past and have to ensure that the understanding of team members is sufficient to ensure their commitment and uptake of empowerment opportunities. It has become increasingly apparent that there are significant difficulties in achieving these objectives. The nature of everyday conversation and the forums where employees interact are not sufficient to ensure the necessary interchange of views for effective teamworking. The skills that managers have in these regards have been acquired through formal management education/development, learning through experience and the prevailing 'construction' of management at work.

This book will argue that managers and teamworkers are in danger of being overtaken by developments and need to acquire expertise in securing more comprehensive insights into the bases of each other's decisions and actions. There needs to be a recognition that insights into each other's perceptions are necessary in modern organizations. There needs also to be an evaluation of the adequacy of current organizational discourse for securing the necessary insights. This chapter will outline some of the recent and continuing developments in organizational practices that necessitate more extensive mutual insight at work. It will go on to define a new, general form of management that recognizes working with the views of others as its defining characteristic. This is management by perception. The chapter concludes with an assessment of some of the skills that will be required in managing by perception.

The demands of modern management

Many aspects of management are being questioned as organizations adapt to the needs of the current world of business. By examining some of the emerging constructions of management in organizations, some of the limitations in current management expertise can be highlighted. It will be suggested that there is a clear pattern in the developments in management that have been taking place in recent years. The implications for management in the future can be considered by exploring several trends.

A movement from an emphasis on decision outcomes to a greater appreciation of decision process

Business operations are managed in terms of particular outcomes. These indicators provide information about the state of the business, but they rarely inform us of the actions necessary to correct any problem. For this to happen we need to understand the processes involved and not just the outcomes achieved. In detecting a failure to achieve an outcome we cannot assume that the problem can necessarily be rectified. In designing a machine so that it is effective in reliably producing a particular component we have not necessarily addressed how readily the machine can be maintained or modified. The measurements we use to guide our activities need to recognize all of the processes involved. Only then can any developments be mapped onto the current system and specific needs for modification identified.

But how well do organizations understand their processes? In production processes, perhaps those people with the appropriate technical expertise may understand the functional contribution of each machine or step in the process. In a similar way, when it comes to human operations, if the job is tightly defined then the 'contribution' of each person can quite readily be counted. But how do we cope when we start to consider how flexible the person is? How capable is the person of dealing with the full spectrum of different situations that need to be faced? What impact is the person having on customers above and beyond the immediate encounter?

We could try to legislate for each possibility and measure and seek to control performance against each unique outcome situation. Or we could begin to accept that understanding the processes involved can enable us to design processes that are capable of dealing with the necessary spectrum of variations, and that we do not need to worry about constant outcome assessment. In fact, in uncertain times we may not be clear about the future outcomes. We can, however, design processes that can deal with this uncertainty and are capable of producing acceptable outcomes.

Just as we need to understand the adaptability of an 'intelligent machine' – to understand what it can sense, perceive, remember and do – so we need to understand the adaptability of our human colleagues. How do they actually go about achieving their outcomes? What are they finding difficult? What is unnecessarily complicated or stressful? The need for this understanding has been felt for many years. Movements such as the quality of working life (QWL) attempted to show the importance of recognizing these factors within the design of physical work (Kochan et al., 1986). But now work is becoming more cognitive; that is, the contribution of people lies increasingly in their flexibility rather than their reliability. Prescribing and controlling the detail of interactions with customers is not an approach that the customer wants. If we are to produce systems that can adapt to a changing world of individual customer demands, we need to understand people's thinking and the processes of their decisions, not just the outcomes.

Recognizing that decision processes involve more than logic

The notion of decision processes in organizations being driven by rationality is recognized to be unrealistic. As Levinson (1994) notes, 'despite efforts to make organizational decisions rational and to attenuate individual differences by structure, policies, procedures, and technical proficiency, in the last analysis organizational direction, function, and activity are based on human judgement. Feelings, therefore, are its fundamental currency' (p. 29). People, groups and organizations do not operate on a 'rational' basis. They each have preferences (skills) for dealing with information of particular types and in particular ways. They may be aware of some of these preferences operating, but in many ways both they and others in the organization often lack an understanding of the processes they are actually adopting. Indeed, Argyris (1986) argues that managers have become so skilled at *not* facing decisions that they cannot learn as one might hope. Organizations effectively promote 'skilled incompetence', he feels, by having defensive 'routines' that prevent learning, for example managers can develop the 'skills' to avoid upset and conflict at meetings, and thereby impede the processes necessary for a 'searching' discussion.

Assertions concerning the absence of pure rationality in organizational decision-making have been made by a number of writers since Simon (1947) studied and reported how actual decisions are made. The alternative 'bounded rationality' model demonstrates 'satisficing' as opposed to optimizing because of time pressures, disagreements over goals and incomplete information. There is a large body of studies into management decision strategies and styles (Cohen et al., 1972; Janis and Mann, 1977; Isenberg, 1984). Hickson et al. (1986) identified three ways in which organizations can 'make' strategic decisions. The decision process can be described as constricted, sporadic or fluid, depending on the level of complexity facing decision-makers in a topic, and the level of political activity aroused. The particular process that the decision underwent could be influenced by the complexity and politicality of the context and topic.

The turning of a blind eye to many of these phenomena is dysfunctional for organizations. But are there ways in which these 'actual' processes of decision-making can be acknowledged and addressed? This would not be to minimize them because they are potentially 'confounding' the rational decision. Recognizing interests, rather than denying them, is likely to produce more effective decisions overall. Some of the processes of allowing individuals and groups to identify and reflect on not just their particular way of seeing a situation, but also their more general 'preferences' for managing problems, are discussed throughout this book.

Recognizing the centrality of perceptions and misperceptions in organizational decision-making

There is overwhelming evidence to show that employees in different cultures, industries, organizations and departments come to think differently.

There are discernible differences in the basic ways that they view problems/ issues. In considering one's own thinking, and that of other participants, it can be useful to consider the extent to which it is bounded because of the particular society one lives in. Chikudate (1991), for example, identified clear differences between Japanese and American employees' views of supervisors. Japanese employees may see supervisors as 'company friends' with whom they socialize on a frequent and continual basis. American employees placed supervisors in the category of 'authority figures', with whom socializing is not as common. Abramson et al. (1993) found that Canadian employees preferred fast decisions and rushed to closure on collecting data, whereas the Japanese resisted quick decision-making and had a need for obtaining larger amounts of data. Canadians also tended to minimize relationship-building, manifesting a decision-making style that favoured analytical and impersonal factors, in contrast to the Japanese emphasis on feeling.

Cultural differences in mindset are evident within the same society. Yu (1995), for example, reports how different cultural assumptions guide the ways in which Chinese and American co-workers conceptualize their jobs. Significant differences were found in how the two sets of workers view the role of managers, good service and compensation. Rhinesmith (1992) suggests that it may be possible to develop a 'global' mindset, that can embrace workforce diversity and multicultural teams.

There is some evidence that organizational culture is, in part, a product of the particular industry within which the organization operates (Chatman and Jehn, 1994). Phillips (1994) identified distinct assumption sets within two industries concerning conceptualizations of membership, competition, the origins of 'truth', the purpose of work and the nature of work relationships. Abrahamson and Fombrun (1994) suggest that value-added networks linking organizations into collectivities both induce and reflect the existence and persistence of some form of 'macroculture'.

It is also possible to identify differences between the cultures that characterize different organizations in the same sector. Smart and Hamm (1993), for example, demonstrate 'clan', 'ad-hocracy', 'hierarchy' and 'market' cultures in educational colleges. Miller (1994) shows how basic differences in organizational values influenced the overall frequency of environmental scanning, and whether oral, written and electronic sources of information were used. Ansoff and McDonnell (1990) postulate three kinds of 'filter' that affect the information available to managers about the world: the surveillance, mentality and power filters. These refer respectively to the ability to sense the world comprehensively, the relevance/priorities attached to particular data, and the willingness to face (rather than refuse to recognize) any threat to current conceptions. In individual psychological terms these are the 'sensitivity' of a physical sensory mechanism, the 'current mindsets', and the 'effort' put into integrating disconfirming evidence with previous information in one's mind. In organizational terms they are the particular measures or assessments made by different 'departments' in the organization, the beliefs and values of different groups of co-workers concerning the demands and capability of different resources to cope with, or resolve the situation, and the influence of the 'interests' of each of the different 'sections' in the organization.

The particular view that a manager may have about a situation will be determined in part by that manager's position within the organization. The perception held may depend on the functional specialism or department (Dearborn and Simon, 1958), the management level (Ireland et al., 1987) and the particular organization's filter systems (Ansoff and McDonnell, 1990). Organizations are going to vary in their relative possession of each of the perceptual filters. Because of these perceptual capabilities, it is clear that it is possible for there to be a self-perpetuating element in misperception. Glaister and Thwaites (1993) draw attention to how the response that an organization may make to its perception of a situation in turn affects how it is then capable of seeing future situations, that is, its previous coping strategy can over time function as its blinkers. An organization can therefore develop a particular set of perceptual mechanisms that determine how the entire organization operates and develops. The sorts of information that are being processed can engender particular capabilities and beliefs.

Workgroups can often have particular 'mindsets'. This may be a function of the degree of diversity within the team. This has been studied in management teams, for example. When viewed as an information-processing system, a senior management team's 'potential' can be argued to lay in the 'total' expertise that they can bring to bear (Sparrow, 1994). If a team consists of very like-minded people (perhaps accused of being 'a bunch of clones'!), they could be held to have less expertise than a more diverse team. Of course, for this argument to hold, one must make the assumption that senior management teams are all basically made up of 'equally competent' people. It is just their areas of expertise that differ. Studies have demonstrated links between the diversity of teams and organizational effectiveness. Bantel and Jackson (1989), for example, identified a significant correlation between top team diversity (in terms of age, length of service, functional background and education) and the innovation record of the companies. Wiersema and Bantel (1992) demonstrated a relationship between the same sort of indicators of team diversity with 'effective diversity decisions'. They also identified that the overall relationship is not linear. If team diversity is 'too large' then effectiveness is reduced. The suggestion is that this may be because of communication strain and conflict.

The measures of diversity used in large statistical studies are inevitably rather basic and indirect. These studies tell us little about the process of decision-making and how team differences figure. More 'micro' studies have been conducted to 'expose the complex relationship between the strategic information that managers are presented with and their resulting actions by researching, modelling, understanding and extending the minds of strategic managers' (Sparrow, 1994, p. 159). Perceptions are operationally defined in these studies, as the 'models' that managers have of the business and economic world. The research focuses on the causal arguments that people use in outlining their decisions. Differences in the nature and form of managers' conceptions of the dynamics of their industry, and degree of emphasis on revenue and short term performance, were identified by Calori et al. (1992). Kriger and Solomon (1992) identified significantly different fundamental mindsets concerning the degree of decision-making autonomy that is considered 'appropriate' within subsidiaries. They showed how the approach used in managing subsidiaries within multinationals is influenced by basic beliefs about the value of a general corporate strategy as opposed to empowerment. A senior management team's cognitive maps of competitive positioning may lag behind developments in a marketplace, and yet they may attempt to use these 'old' models. Situations of rapid change mean that different managers will adapt their models differently. There is evidence to suggest that this can increase the diversity of thinking of managers in the same environment, and needs to be recognized in strategic decision-making teams (Reger and Palmer, 1996).

It is of course not just perceptions of the outside environment that are subject to mindsets. The views that workgroups hold about each other depend on available data, subjective preferences and willingness to reconsider a view held about another person. Wohlers et al. (1993) showed how the level of agreement in views among managers depended on the amount of overlap in work roles, respective races and ages. Similarly, London and Wohlers (1991) identified that being of the same gender had a bearing. The nature of areas of homogeneity and heterogeneity need to be better understood. What is clear is that employees who interact with each other have similar interpretations of organizational events and that employees who are members of different interaction groups attach qualitatively different meanings to similar organizational events (Rentsch, 1990). K. Daniels et al. (1994) identify quite high degrees of diversity in managers' mental models, especially as functional and company boundaries are crossed. Walker et al. (1995), in studying executives' selective perception, confirmed that 'executives with customer experience (sales and marketing) would perceive changes in the demand for an organization's products and services', 'executives with experience in R&D would perceive changes in competitors' product designs' and 'executives with customer experience or operations experience are more perceptive of changes in the development, performance and satisfaction of employees' (p. 964). They also note that functional background does not seem to affect assessment of the organization's external environment. Rather, it is perceptions of the organization's own effectiveness that are affected by background. Even here, the influence of functional background depends on the area in which perceiving occurs. Judgements may not be held strongly (and not voiced) in areas where one's expertise is more limited. In areas where one has insight one is 'attuned' to 'see' problems and shortcomings. The 'same' problem can therefore be 'seen' differently, if there are elements of several 'areas' present.

Can these (perhaps complementary) perspectives be captured? Wohlers et al. (1993) showed that close involvement between managers (in a way that draws particular attention to the personal needs, aspirations and views of the other person) reduces mutual misperceptions of their individual views. Of course, such participation is dependent on feelings of 'participative safety' (West, 1990). What might be needed therefore is a situation where managers want to see each other's views *per se* rather than want to know another's view because they may have some specific purpose in mind, and knowing the other person's position may help them.

Avoiding treating implementation as an afterthought

Seeing the decision process in a broader organizational context with 'producers' and 'players' (Bryant, 1989) means that the separation of 'solution selection' from 'implementation' stages in decisions becomes questionable. Piercy (1989) draws attention to some of the ways in which managers can address the views of others in considering the implementation issues 'within' a decision. Argyris (1993) argues that in solving problems and making decisions it is inadequate to seek information about *the* alternative decision 'outcomes'. Rather, the necessary research is a process that explores events as they unfold. 'Actionable knowledge' is not information in the abstract. It is knowledge that is integrated with the steps and skills needed (by all) for something to be done. For example, in working within a small team to decide on a particular course of action, feelings of trust, altruism and tender-mindedness may be created. The notion that these considerations could be 'excluded' from a decision process is not tenable. Team members are not a nuisance factor that can be excluded from *the* decision. This is just a 'convenient' objectification of the process. The participants and their views and actions *are* the decision.

Challenging an overemphasis on the value of rationality

The 'acceptance' that organizational decision processes involve more than strict logic has led some writers to question the 'supremacy' of logic among decision-making considerations and approaches. Bowles (1993) refers to two competing basic and implicit mindsets within Western organizations that can be contrasted. He highlights the distinction made by Habermas (1970) between the 'purposive rational action' of organizations based on the engineering, behavioural and financial sciences and a notion of 'communicative or symbolic interaction'. When operating within a 'Logos' mindset, the organization invents a view where it is meaningful to regard objects as separate from each other and legitimizes the management of the interrelationship in terms of the logic of self-interested control. Under an 'Eros' mindset, complementarity, reciprocity and mutual recognition structure the social relations. Not only is the gulf between these values wide, but Bowles maintains that many of the initiatives which 'aim to redress the current excesses of organizational life are largely dictated by Logos, and thus tend to reinforce those things they purport to address' (p. 1288). He is pessimistic about the prospect of organizations 'letting go' of such a fundamental belief set. Is it possible to challenge the overemphasis on the rational?

Acceptance of chaos

The challenge to the assumption of the supremacy of logic in decision-making is echoed in recent work on the science of prediction. Decision-making of all kinds rests on some assumptions about our ability to predict the future. In recent years, mathematicians have demonstrated that in many situations, a decision's sensitivity to initial conditions may mean that events cannot be predicted. Small initial variations can have major effects on long-term outcomes. Again, the notion of the sense in attempting to predict chains of objective events in 'abstract' is being challenged. A greater relative emphasis on short-term contingency decisions as opposed to long-term planning is needed. Rather than recording 'inputs' and 'outcomes' of pre-vious decisions in the hope that they may be applicable, effort needs to be placed on recording 'positions' on the issues. This information is more reusable.

Jennings and Wattam (1994) suggest that managers will have to learn to operate in 'a less secure world requiring a high tolerance of ambiguity and a capacity for imaginative, flexible and speedy responses' (p. 277). They will need to develop more dynamic agendas of strategic issues and view decision-making as a continuous exploratory experimental process with 'learning groups of managers surfacing conflict, engaging in dialogue, publicly testing assertions' (p. 278). In this they echo Stacey (1992) in considering the essence of managing chaos. This is in contrast to a conception of manage-ment decisions as attempts to develop a 'vision' that can be secured through initial logical analysis and subsequent consensus-forming forces. As Stacey (1991) notes, 'if we were able to achieve this equilibrium and there were no further changes in the market, it would stay there – its structures, systems and common cultures would see to that. Unfortunately, the markets keep changing and so the organization has to keep adapting' (p. 319). Mintzberg (1994) concludes that old-style strategic planning did not work because 'the form (the "rationality" of planning) did not conform to the function (the needs of strategy making)' (p. 415).

Improving decision processes

Increases in the involvement of stakeholders in decision processes may lead to improved decision-making. Drummond (1992) reports that 50 per cent of management time can be spent dealing with the consequences of bad decision-making, for example retrieving projects behind schedule, defending others' mistakes and concealing one's own failures. She believes an answer lies in the basic mindset within organizations concerning what is meant by the effectiveness of a decision. There is a basic drive to produce something that 'will do'. Management is seen as 80 per cent action and 20 per cent thought. Implementation is separated from the decision.

Drummond advocates total quality in decision-making. She suggests a more thorough 'process capability' that places emphasis on getting 80 per cent of the idea right first. Genuine exploration of the decision, to determine what the decision actually is, can come from proactive communication with subordinates to confront ambiguity and fuzziness. Systematic analysis can reveal unrealistic time scales and reduce subsequent buck-passing. Identifying the 'true' requisite resources rather than groupthink and the ignoring of disconfirming data is required. Realistic assessments concerning whether the actions can be taken need to question project-management skills, need to distinguish between enthusiasm and a commitment that carries the devotion of time, need to use hard evidence and analyse what it will take including the politics, that is, the number of moving parts that have to be managed.

For there to be quality in the information-gathering process, Drummond believes that there needs to be a shared responsibility in defining what is needed to reach an effective decision. In particular, rigorous attempts need to be made to identify any assumptions. She suggests that specific tools (such as cause and effect analysis and 'what if?' questioning) should be used rather than more traditional common-sense approaches.

Recognizing that organizational capability requires organizational learning

Enhancing the decision-making process can play a large role in coping with change. Much of the discussion concerning the modern trading environment refers to the turbulence and need for continuous change. As a result, one of the keys to competitive advantage is the ability to adapt rapidly to changing circumstances. In the case of individuals, this is what we mean by intelligence. We are referring to the ability of a person to apply previous experience, and to acquire new understanding, that is, to learn. The capability of a person therefore lies in part in their current competencies and ability to develop. Terms such as learning, acquisition, retention, maintenance, search and retrieval of information are proving to be useful ways of viewing organizations *per se*. Several authors suggest that the learning capability of organizations can be assessed (Pedler et al., 1991; Jenlink, 1994; Dibella et al., 1996).

What does this mean for managers? Burgoyne (1995) believes that we need to develop means whereby 'meta-dialogue' is promoted, sharing and reaching understanding of the ways in which beliefs under discussion in dialogue can be believed to be true and useful. Managers (and other organizational participants) need to understand basic notions of epistemology (the study of knowledge), that is, how we can come to know.

Some conclusions about the emerging construction of management

Figure 1.1 depicts the eight themes outlined above. It seems clear that there is an underlying pattern in these observations concerning the limitations inherent within the current construction of management. A new form of management and manager is indicated. The image suggests that addressing each of these limitations implies a movement in management in a particular direction. It suggests that a 'veil' will be lifted from much of the information that is circulating within organizations. If managers are to understand how an organization can be helped to cope with uncertainty, they have to understand how the organization really functions, and how it learns. A key to this understanding is an appreciation of how people actually behave and learn within organizations. This is, therefore, quite distinct from considering how they 'ought' to behave, or what logic or common sense tells us they may do. It is working with the information that other organizational participants are using in their decision-making. It is about trying to see the ways in which they are putting information together to make sense of situations. It would be convenient if this understanding could be gleaned by observing each other or asking each other what is guiding our decisions and actions. In fact, the sort of perceptual information that is guiding decisions is not necessarily conscious. It is soft and vague. It requires some new skills if it is to be surfaced. It requires some new skills if it is to be entertained. It requires some new skills if it is to be managed.

If we are to understand and promote organizational learning, we will need to manage differently (Senge, 1990; Pedler et al., 1991). Organizations can be seen to be generating and dissipating information. They are a cause as well as a consequence of information generation and dissipation. Managers need to understand 'the stimuli, agents and semiotics, tacitly or explicitly' and create a 'positively reinforcing' information generation/dissipation cycle (Ramaprasad and Rai, 1996).

Management education and processes of socialization affect management practice. Management education's emphasis on the 'sciences' of management manifests a drive for certainty and non-recognition of the value of ambiguity. Boyd and Wild (1993) have argued that there are pressures within organizations to show rationality. Supervisors and managers will describe their actions to show how they have used the rational (for example project management) approaches to achieve successful outcomes rather than their actual use of informal knowledge and action. This leads to an increased belief in such approaches and 'evidence' of their success in managing uncertainty. The authors, in contrast, press for education for uncertainty. They suggest that the strategies of risk analysis, project planning, procedures, information systems, contracts and insurance produce formality, hierarchy, control management and poor learning. They propose a greater emphasis on thinking and reflecting, learning how to learn, self-development, a focus on people and sociotechnical systems in management education.

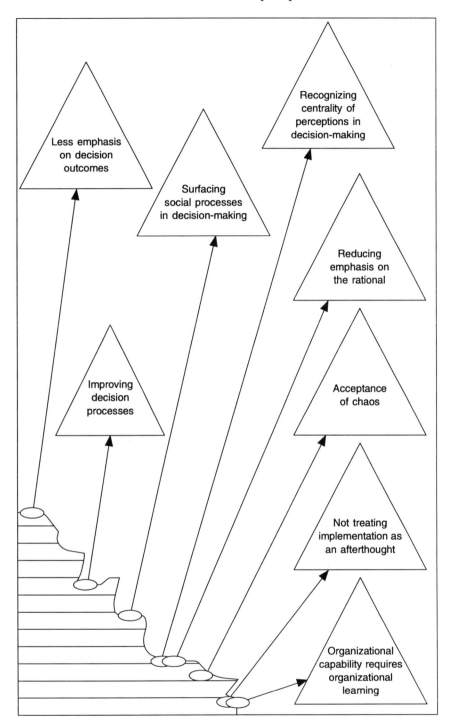

Figure 1.1 *Eight directions in management, or one?*

The ways in which organizations construct work roles and expectations and socialize are captured well by Warr and Conner (1992). Their study shows how 'working styles' are shaped in young people in the first year of employment. It reveals a progressive reinforcement of a working style emphasizing planning, working out, finding out for oneself, being systematic etc. This is at the clear expense of the alternative style emphasizing cooperativeness, trust and interpersonal dealings.

Overall, it would seem that we 'train' people into egocentric working styles with an overemphasis on the intellectual, and expectations to use the toolkit of 'rational' management. The fact that people are actually succeeding through the adoption of the alternative style needs to be acknowledged and addressed.

Management by perception

Formal meetings are often primarily aimed at giving opportunities for 'expertise' to be transacted. These 'views' are not the only consideration now. We need information about others' models. It is not their 'input' in the sense of what it adds to the solution that is important, it is our understanding of them in relation to the issue at hand.

Change management has the hallmarks of a discipline in its own right because management was seen as making decisions in abstract, and then implementing them. The 'right' decision was made and then 'the' solution's adoption needed to be secured. Decisions were made with the 'input' of those that had something to contribute. In the main this was seen as expertise. The notion of involving people in anything other than an expert capacity seemed unnecessary. At best it might be seen as having some 'representation' from different quarters. Involvement was rarely a goal in its own right.

Management by exception is a system where managers design systems which are considered to be running adequately until a problem occurs. This exception is then reported to management in *their* terms, that is, using reports which describe the problem in the language of the system which management has developed.

Management by perception involves management in building models of situations as they are perceived by different stakeholders. The process of making these different perspectives explicit within organizations leads to an increase in shared understanding. Organizations then have more powerful predictive models of people (including employees, customers and competitors) and situations. They can also develop greater mutual insight among participants, and create a greater flexibility in workgroups and the organization as a whole. The result of this is genuine continuous improvement in organizational systems. Managers can have effective models of situations as they are experienced by others.

Many recent management initiatives are processes which emphasize the development and incorporation of other people's motivation and knowledge. Team building (Smith, 1980b), creating commitment (Martin and Nicholls, 1987) and total quality management (James, 1991) all advocate greater explicit recognition of other participants' perceptions. Morgan (1993) describes his concept of 'imaginization' as being about seeing and understanding situations in new ways, finding new images for new ways of organizing, the creation of shared understanding, personal empowerment, and developing capacities for continuous self-organization.

Sinetar (1991) goes further and suggests that what is indicated is a twenty-first-century mind. She puts a case for the desirability of three attributes of mind: autonomy, positive self-valuation and learning resourcefulness. The decision-making approach of such minds, she suggests, should have characteristics of being non-dualistic, experimental, intuitive, objective, having positive mental energy and vision and resolving paradox in a blend that means that their perceptual field is 'illumined'.

There is, it seems therefore, an emerging consensus about many of the characteristics that may be required of managers in the future. There are many different ways of categorizing the sets of skills that managers may require within future organizational forms and modes of operation. One of the most influential perspectives has been put forward by Senge (1990). The strategies and tools required to build a learning organization are drawn from five disciplines. These are personal mastery, mental models, shared vision, team learning and systems thinking. Senge et al. (1994) have assembled a collection of tools that can help managers work more effectively in these terms.

As regards the implications for managing, the general need for mutual insight draws a distinction between managing by exception (Harter and Bass, 1988; Bass and Avolio, 1989) and managing by perception. When practising management by exception, a manager 'only takes action when things go wrong and standards are not met' (Hartog et al., 1997, p. 22) and 'actively seeks deviations from standard procedures'. Management by exception places an emphasis on:

(a) reporting systems and control
(b) firefighting
(c) reactive management
(d) internal orientation within organizations
(e) the elimination of 'limitations' in culture.

It involves seeing the world in certain terms and managing it accordingly. There is a 'singular' view of 'appropriate' behaviour and performance.

Management by perception is based on:

(a) heightened internal sensitivity
(b) development of mutual understanding
(c) the multiplicity of models which explain
(d) greater external orientation
(e) openness to learning.

Figure 1.2 outlines some of the language that might be used to contrast conventional management with management by perception. It describes the behaviour of traditional management in terms of its conceptions of goals, its way of looking at situations (pre-existing models), the styles of behaving and the evidence that tends to be used in guiding management decisions. A set of terms that might be associated with the notion of management by perception is presented as a constellation.

It is worth the effort to consider as many different contra-indicated words within each cell. It is not that the approaches of conventional management are 'wrong'. It is important to reflect on the fact that they are only *one* of the many approaches that can be adopted. For example, if we examine some of the considerations associated with managers' pre-existing models we can see that it is suggested that they are determined in part through the prevailing social constructions, that is, the expectations that guide the definition of management and the reinforcement of this construction. It is possible to consider what these determinants might be, and to explore the implications of releasing one's thinking from them. The constraints on personal exploration may, however, figure here. The tramline thinking that can go with systematization may need to be confronted. Perhaps creativity tools (Rickards, 1990) might be adopted more than they are at present. In examining styles of behaviour we might examine what lies behind some of the adversarial hallmarks and consider alternatives. It is also worth questioning goals and evidence.

Some competence, attitude and personality implications

It seems clear that the expectations and practices that prevail within organizations educe certain styles of management. These in turn can contribute to the prevailing culture. Together these considerations can create an environment where particular attributes are elicited from managers and can in turn become the attributes 'required' to be successful. It is useful to consider these expectancies in two ways. First, we can examine the language that can be used to capture the overall expectations of managers, that is competencies. Secondly, we can examine the more specific aspects of individuals that impinge on their interaction with others, that is, personality.

The broad competencies 'required' of managers

Woodruffe (1992) provides a valuable definition of a competency when he describes it as 'the set of behaviour patterns that the incumbent needs to bring to a position in order to perform its tasks and functions with competence' (p. 17). This definition captures the socially constructed nature of competencies. They are the approaches that are required for the defined tasks and functions. Any listing or categorization of competencies inherently reflects the social and cultural context.

There are some useful frameworks that can be used to consider 'current' expectations of management. There are lists of competencies that are argued

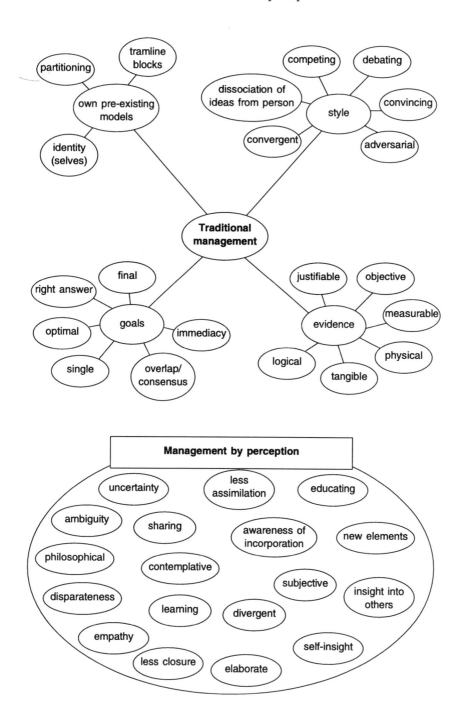

Figure 1.2 *Language of traditional management and management by perception*

to transcend particular organizations (e.g. Dulewicz, 1989) and competency lists developed within major organizations (e.g. Glaze, 1989). There is a discernible degree of homogeneity between all of these 'lists'. They all seek to address the approaches used by managers in their thinking and communication. The labels for these concepts include strategic visioning, organizational drive, persuasion, analytical reasoning skills, managing interaction etc. As Woodruffe (1992) notes, there is a danger that systems derived from the past may miss changes implied by developments in the organization and its environment. What might these changes be? Is there any pattern of changes emerging?

Woodruffe (1992) highlights a key competency of the future as 'changeability'. He cites observations from Pascale (1990) concerning some Japanese companies orchestrating tension rather than driving to reduce ambiguity, and Lorenz (1988) about managers needing to deal with the tight–looseness of network organization. Guptara (1988) highlights abilities to gather information informally on people, curiosity and tolerance of national and cultural differences. Sissons (1989) argues that managers will need to establish frameworks of creativity rather than control.

Another emerging theme in the competency literature concerns the skills of 'emotional labour'. Drawing on the work of Hochschild (1983), Anderson (1993) discusses some of the inadequacies of conventional task and job analyses to reveal the demands placed on people to manage their 'feelings and present a positive image to customers or clients' (p. 10). He suggests that opportunities will need to be established which invite 'job holders to reflect critically on their own attitudes to their work' (p. 14). Even when the demands are identified, he suggests that 'managers and trainers tend not to dwell too long on the negative aspects of the work they are preparing people to perform and, hence, formal training courses may only incidentally acknowledge the difficult feelings a job may evoke' (p. 10). These competencies need to be identified and developed.

McCrimmon (1995) argues that attempts to identify and develop competencies work best in contexts where rationality and planning are possible. He suggests, however, that the movement towards organizational contexts that are determined by evolutionary forces and require a more entrepreneurial response questions much of the basis of current competency frameworks. He contrasts situations where organizational success is achieved through product variation and some successes with researched and planned outputs. The entrepreneurial response is one of being pulled by external circumstances, acting first, being exploratory and letting responses emerge. This is in sharp contrast to the traditional approaches where *a priori* reasoning leads to firmer decisions and plans. As a result, future competencies might be more about knowledge creation rather than the 'efficient use of very standardized routine knowledge' (p. 5) and aimed at organizational self-renewal rather than the efficient and effective 'delivery' of products and services. McCrimmon (1995) asserts that 'organizations which want to be truly creative will have to re-examine the rational model of thinking, deciding, acting and organizational functioning' (p. 6). The focus will not be on the individuals themselves but on organizations managing their environment, focusing on the broad values that they want to create, experimenting, learning and self-renewing. Management will need to change. The broad directions of these changes seem clear.

The changes in competencies and 'new' competencies in general appear to have a pattern. They concern the overall 'fluidity' of modern life, that is, the ability to work flexibly and dynamically with others in a work team in ways that are both externally and internally sensitive and responsive. This may mean working with a different kind of information that is fundamentally interpersonal and that is subtle and latent. This book is about how information of this kind is stored in people's minds, how it can be surfaced, communicated, assimilated and used in decision-making at work. It is about how to address the 'surveillance', 'mentality' and 'power' filters outlined earlier. It addresses how to increase the sensitivity of our management 'senses' – how to 'get at' some of the information that we have up to now failed to sense. It considers how we can surface and recognize our own and others' mental sets. It explores the issues surrounding the 'engagement' or energy required to 'take on board' these insights and use them in decision-making. It is about enhancing management perception.

A general willingness to consider loose qualitative information

One of the clearest experiences of anybody working in management education concerns the whole issue of tolerance of ambiguity and a willingness to work with soft qualitative information, as opposed to dismissing it as 'opinion' or something to do with 'the culture', and thereby enigmatic and unusable. Many managers initially prefer to work with 'hard information'. Indeed, many will hang on to poor indicators knowing that they are inaccurate or misleading! People are seen in a dehumanized way as the manager 'gets their views'. What is generated is not the same as 'real information', it is just 'some opinions' that might affect some of the minor aspects of implementation. Appreciating the true value of others' perceptions is difficult, but essential. Schein (1993) suggests that the use of data obtained during clinical and consulting work needs to be legitimated as valid research data, if the deeper dynamics of organizations are to be understood. Mercier (1994) suggests that the hermeneutic tradition of taking context and past history into account in understanding the basis of institutional characteristics is necessary for understanding organizations.

An example of how a particular manager came to derive real value from in-depth insights into the perceptions of others may be of value here. Bill worked in a medium-sized engineering company in the West Midlands. The company was floundering and yet seemed unable to make any strategic decisions. Several studies had been undertaken and sensible recommendations made, but they never seemed to be taken up. It was apparent that the managing director believed that 'giving someone the job of sorting production out' was the answer. The problem was that two people had already been designated, and had failed. A third engineering manager was appointed. Bill thought that it would be useful to see how his new boss tackled the job, and persuaded him to let him hold a weekly 'interview' where his boss could talk about his efforts in the week and his thinking at the time. Bill elected to use an unstructured interview approach to see if any patterns were evident in the transcripts.

The weeks went by. The boss's actions and thoughts were recorded. The record showed how the key people were 'sounded out', 'some analysis' was done, a tentative 'plan' was arrived at, the 'initial approach' was figured out, and how gradually the engineering manager felt that the 'constraints' were too great, he 'looked for allies', his confidence fell, he became frustrated. As the weeks wore on, it became clear that his boss was struggling to cope, psychologically, with the 'pressures'. Sadly, he could not continue, and had to take several months off work.

Bill's interviews had been terminated. The transcripts had been made. Clearly they were for Bill's eyes only. Were they of any use? What about the morality of seeing and dwelling on how somebody crumbled in a job? It was all very personal and emotional. It could easily have been dismissed as a failed venture. But Bill recalled how many times his boss had kept saying, 'The last guy found this too!', and he felt that if the organization was to learn, he should analyse the tapes and at least see whether there were some general lessons. Qualitative data analysis takes time. But Bill thought it was worth it. His insights into the 'induction' process, and the need for mentoring support of new managers were immensely valuable. The aspects of the job that turned out to be the most difficult were surprising. A report was prepared. None of the 'material' was quoted, but the graphical depictions of the changing balance of the various 'categories' of issues at different points in the first few months of a manager's job were revealing and valuable.

It is rare to find managers being prepared to pore over the precise words of others (unless it is a policy or procedure statement that they are trying to 'live with'!). It is even rarer to work with emotion as the key issue. It can be of value, even in a harsh practical engineering company environment, but it takes a willingness to work with such information.

The personality 'required' of future managers

The movement to more perceptual management is echoed in general calls for more balanced management. The values and processes within organizations in the past have 'created' a need for a particular approach to management. In turn, 'successful' managers have been those that fit this bill. The attributes drawn out by the work context have led to individuals with particular personality profiles tending to be more successful. Kinder and Robertson (1995) report significant correlations between particular competencies and particular dimensions of personality. Using the Occupational Personality Questionnaire (Saville and Holdsworth, 1990) the traditional management competencies of Analysis, Planning and Organizing, Decision Making, Managing Staff, Resilience and Business Sense had significant correlations with personality scales such as Conceptual, Critical, Data Rational, Forward Planning, Decisiveness, Controlling, Optimism and Achievement. Competencies such as Creativity, Communication and Adaptability were significantly associated with the OPQ scales Innovativeness, Conceptual, Change Orientation, Persuasiveness and low scores on Traditionality. If there are movements in the demands placed on managers in the directions indicated earlier in this chapter, then there may be a discernible pattern of movements in associated personality dimensions.

There is value in considering within a framework the overall 'language' of personality attributes associated with management by perception. Psychologists have, in recent years, reached a high degree of agreement on basic frameworks for considering individual differences in personality. Two of these frameworks will be used here to summarize some of the relative emphases within current social constructions of management in relation to those that might be associated with management by perception. The two frameworks are referred to as 'The Big Five' (Digman, 1990; Barrick and Mount, 1991) and the Myers Briggs Typology (Myers, 1989). While the two frameworks have separate histories and purposes, many of the terms used in each framework can be recognized in the other.

Although psychologists have recognized for many years that the vocabulary that can be used to describe individual differences can be extremely large, they have also sought to find pattern in the human behaviour (and the associated assessment terms) that most succinctly captures human personality. From the last 50 years of research, a 'five factor model' has now been recognized as the most reasonable representation. While there are still some debates about its adequacy and legitimacy (Bentall, 1993), there is a great deal of evidence for its utility (Deary and Matthews, 1993). The 'big five' dimensions of personality are the degrees of extraversion, openness, agreeableness, conscientiousness and neuroticism that a person has. The related Myers Briggs terms are extraversion, intuition, feeling and judging, respectively. There is no parallel conception to neuroticism within the Myers Briggs framework. There is no single psychometric test of the 'big five' dimensions that is universally accepted. Jung's typology of the decision-making preferences that people develop (see, for example, Read et al., 1961) has been incorporated in the development of the Myers Briggs Type Indicator personality questionnaire (Myers, 1989). This questionnaire (MBTI) is one of the most widely used approaches to examine management thinking.

INTROVERSION   When one considers the degree of extraversion in a person's thinking, Deary and Matthews (1993) include facets such as warmth, gregariousness, assertiveness, activity, excitement-seeking and positive emotions in their conception. In Myers Briggs terms, Keirsey and Bates (1984) refer to hallmarks of sociability rather than territoriality; interaction rather than concentration; breadth rather than depth; extensiveness rather than intensiveness; multiplicity of relationships rather than limited relationships; expenditure of energies rather than conservation of energies; and interest in external events rather than interest in internal reaction. Extraversion has been associated with a greater readiness to respond but with poorer vigilance and problem-solving. Overall, management by perception might place less emphasis on an 'extravert' attitude where managers 'live it, then understand it' and more emphasis on an 'introvert' attitude with a preference to 'reflect' on information and to model.

OPENNESS AND INTUITION   Openness as a dimension of personality refers to the extent to which a person seeks to move beyond their current conceptions. It is the extent to which they are open to fantasy, aesthetics, feelings, ideas and values. Some writers regard it as an 'intellectual' factor, that is, a correlate of intelligence. Others have noted a relationship with divergent thinking. Goldberg (1993), for example, uses the term 'imagination' rather than openness. Costa and McCrae (1993) suggest that openness is related to many constructs in the psychological literature. These include intuition, flexibility, low dogmatism, private self-consciousness, artistic interests, thoughtfulness, experience-seeking and sentience (that is, emphasizing the known, being alert, cognizance).

Keirsey and Bates (1984) regard MBTI differences between those people whose thinking preference is based on intuition rather than sensing as the source of the most miscommunication, misunderstanding, vilification, defamation and denigration. They feel that it places the widest gulf between people. The suggestion is that the sensing type seems sensible, basing judgements on the experience they have had. They notice the actual state of affairs and the detail within it. Intuitive types focus on the future. They scan or glance. Rather than work with the 'real', they find appeal in the metaphor and enjoy vivid imagery. There are indications that such people may appear flighty, impractical or unrealistic. Keirsey and Bates (1984) refer to emphases in the intuitive type on hunches rather than experience, the future rather than the past, being speculative rather than realistic, inspiration rather than perspiration, the possible rather than the actual, head in the clouds rather than down to earth, fantasy rather than utility, fiction rather than fact, ingenuity rather than practicality. Management by perception would seem to place a greater emphasis on openness and intuition than does current management.

AGREEABLENESS AND AN EMPHASIS ON FEELING   O'Roark (1987) highlights the fact that the majority of individuals in management interact first and up-front with an objective 'cause and effect' judgement process that reflects their preference for a 'thinking' rather than a 'feeling' approach towards coming to conclusions. Keirsey and Bates (1984) refer to the thinking preference where people place emphasis on the objective/impersonal rather than the personal, principles rather than personal impact, dispassion rather than emotion. They suggest that formal schooling develops an emphasis on concepts such as policy, law, critique, analysis and allocation, rather than persuasion, intimacy, social values, extenuating circumstances, humanity, harmony and appreciation. It is interesting to note in the second list of qualities much of the language of effective change management and approaches is associated with the feminization of management (Sparrow and Rigg, 1993). Operating with and through people can benefit from a degree of agreeableness. This is a major dimension of personality. A more perceptual form of management may well call for this orientation.

MOVING AWAY FROM AN OVEREMPHASIS ON CONSCIENTIOUSNESS AND A NEED TO CLOSE DOWN DECISIONS   The fourth dimension of personality of relevance here is that associated with will, determination or conscientiousness. It refers not just to a notion of motivation but also to a fundamental preference to finalize and move on. It is associated with an unease about leaving things 'in the air'. It is a preference to close down rather than to conduct further analysis. For Keirsey and Bates (1984) it is placing an emphasis on outcomes rather than process, concluding rather than becoming aware. This preference to come to judgements may mean that the person is seen as someone who jumps to conclusions, is driven or overly task oriented. On the other hand, those that place more emphasis on perceiving may be accused of being indecisive, purposeless, procrastinating and blocking decisions. The problem for managers of the future, however, may be that little will be settled, planned or completed; rather, a great deal will remain tentative and pending, with options open.

O'Roark (1987) reports the traditional predominance of a preference for judging in managers. The issue here seems not to be reducing the drive of managers, therefore, so much as facilitating their exploration of options and implications. There is a related concept that can capture more of this orientation. Tolerance for ambiguity has been considered by Norton (1975). He developed a general measure of ambiguity tolerance that extends across a person's basic beliefs or philosophy, their approach towards interpersonal communication, projection of public image, problem-solving style, social behaviours, habitual behaviours, job preferences and art taste. People with low tolerance for ambiguity find the deliberate losing of clarity or focus 'pointless' or 'unrealistic'. They feel that 'sticking to the facts' is justifiable rather than 'just opinion'. This has the effect of hiding differences. It is a comforting delusion. Since people 'shouldn't' behave in 'illogical' ways, they 'need' tight control or procedures. These ensure predictability and comfort again.

Subsequent research by others has revealed some interesting associations with work behaviour. The seeking of feedback about one's actions may be an attempt to reduce uncertainty (Ashford, 1986). Bennett et al. (1990) showed that tolerance for ambiguity plays a role in people's decisions to seek feedback. General concerns about success and operating in an information-poor environment can be more acute for those with lower tolerance for ambiguity. There is an associated increase in attempts to secure confirmation of the impact of actions. As Boyd and Wild (1993) note, the quest for models and project-planning tools is in part a comforting process. Investing such procedures with beliefs about their utility and accuracy can make construction managers feel more in control and less exposed. The willingness to take the perspective of others and to involve them in the decision-making process then appears to be associated with basic dimensions of personality. The prevailing conception of management elicits these behaviours. It is not therefore a matter of a single dimension of personality assuming greater importance in the movement towards management by perception. There are implications for several aspects of personality. There are some important links between openness, perceptiveness and participation, for example.

Wall and Lischeron (1977) suggest three facets of participative decision-making. These are power sharing, interactions among co-workers and information exchange. Tett and Jackson (1990) examined some of the correlations between these aspects of participation and the personality of managers. They found that power sharing was lower among managers with a higher need for dominance or autonomy. Interactions among co-workers were greater for managers with higher needs for affiliation or social recognition. Information exchange was lower for managers with higher scores on their measure of 'cognitive structure'. This is effectively a measure of intolerance of ambiguity. It assesses a need to impose structure onto events. Participation was not however correlated with a measure of openness. The particular measure they used assesses the acceptance of others, openness to new ideas and the acceptance of dissent. Overall, it seems that more perceptual management will place less emphasis on the 'judging' preference.

REDUCING NEUROTICISM   The last of the big five personality factors (Digman, 1990) of relevance to management does not, as noted, have a parallel measure in the Myers-Briggs framework. Neuroticism refers to the basic adaptation of a person to the environment and the extent to which the person is anxious, hostile, depressed, self-conscious, impulsive and vulnerable (Deary and Matthews, 1993). There may be tendencies in a person to become swamped by their own confusion. They may feel forced to take actions that have been insufficiently thought through to reduce their feelings of confusion. Very often there is a desire to put a buffer between ourselves and awareness of our feelings. Coping may result in or reflect psychological addiction. The term addiction can be applied to any substance or process that has taken over our lives and over which we are powerless. Have managers adopted routines that buffer them from being swamped? Have these routines become something they have ceased to control? Perhaps the comfort of apparent rationality in accounting information, project-management tools and so on is part of a ritual rationalism. Here, organizations go through the motions of considering options as a ritual, but with no

Table 1.1 *Addictive behaviours in organizations*

Characteristic	Example
Denial	Constant assertion of problems being temporary
Confusion	Busy trying to figure out what is going on
Self-centredness	Those for us or against us
Dishonesty	Wheel and deal. Act as if you know what you are doing
Illusion of control	A quest to secure control
Frozen feelings	Out of touch with own feelings
Ethical deterioration	Spiritually bankrupt, lying, grabbing etc.

intention to be guided by the results. That there are dysfunctional behaviours that organizations actually encourage seems undeniable. Schaef and Fassel (1988), for example, refer to organizations manifesting many of the behaviours of an addict. Table 1.1 lists examples of addictive behaviours in organizations.

Have we evolved a definition of management and organization that is neurotic? How could this be remedied? In such instances people and organizations need to ask searching questions of themselves. They need to surface these routines and practices. They need to learn less maladaptive approaches. They need to look and consult within and work out more appropriate approaches. Could a more perceptual form of management reduce the neuroticism of an organization?

Techniques for securing insights into each other's perceptions

In seeking to get closer to each other's perceptions at work, we may find that we need to do more than ask each other what information we are using in the course of our decisions. We need to be able to appreciate each other's 'thinking'. Managers may need to understand how people think and what information they utilize in the course of their decisions. This book reviews tools and techniques that have been developed in order to gain insight into people's thinking. It demonstrates that many managers are beginning to use quite powerful techniques to capture the knowledge within their organizations. The next chapter considers what we mean by the term knowledge and what might be involved in its 'capture'.

2

Knowledge and its Capture

Defining knowledge

We have established that we need to have insight into what lies behind each others' decisions and actions at work. It seems that we need to understand the 'knowledge' that organizational participants 'have' in order to perform their jobs. Knowledge is one of those words that we use frequently and quite loosely. On closer inspection it is a term that is not really broad enough to cover all of the aspects of mental material that are used as sources of information in a particular decision or action. We often feel more comfortable believing that a person makes decisions on the basis of their knowledge rather than their opinion. It is as if we feel that knowledge is the mental material that is more factual and true, and that there is some other source of mental material that is more biased or prejudiced. We need a term that refers to knowledge and opinion.

We often feel that we need to distinguish between a person's use of their knowledge and their skills in a task. Somehow skill, because it involves rapid and frequently physical responses, is seen as different from knowledge. We need an even broader term in order to embrace factual knowledge, opinion and skill. We may also find it difficult to regard the term knowledge as appropriate to describe the mental material and processes involved when one makes a decision on the basis of unconscious processes. So we need a term that can embrace all of these sources of information in decisions/actions.

And yet the term knowledge can also be too broad for our purposes. When we say that a person has used 'knowledge' in order to perform a task, we know that we mean the person has used 'some' of their knowledge. Which 'bits' were used and 'how' are critical questions. We accept that our desire to establish the knowledge that a person used in a task does not mean that we need to elicit 'all' of their knowledge. In this sense, we need a term that refers to the aspects of knowledge that are invoked in particular circumstances.

In seeking to understand the views, decisions or actions of others we need to be able to establish the 'knowledge' specifically involved. If we examine what lies behind some actions we can see more clearly how we might define the term knowledge for organizational purposes. Let us suppose for a moment that you are asked to divide a cake into four equal pieces. You may know that a full circle is 360 degrees. You may know that 360 divided by four is 90. You may know that cutting four 90-degree angles (right angles) into the centre of the cake will produce the four slices. When observed cutting the cake, you may be asked what 'knowledge' you are using. You may be asked what you know about cakes, angles, division etc. You may refer to your knowledge of geometry. We might also realize that you must have known something more about cakes and knives in order to have used them appropriately. We may explore more closely how you achieved the task. But what if you were seen to cut the cake into two halves, and then cut each half in turn, into halves, to produce four quarters. Perhaps your approach was based on your understanding of fractions rather than geometry. Although you know the geometry, and the geometry could guide the execution of the task, in fact you used some basic insights into fractions. If we believe that the explanation for your actions lies in your grasp and deployment of geometry, we would be wrong. We need therefore to access the material that is used actively in the course of a decision and not material information that one has knowledge of.

But what if you could be seen laying the knife across the cake, and moving the angle of your hand over the knife until the position of them both in relation to each other seemed right. If we wanted to understand you and what lay behind your approach to cake-cutting, would it be relevant to probe what you know about fractions or right angles? Perhaps none of that material was being used in your execution of the task. Perhaps you were using some sort of visualization of the pieces as you moved your knife and hand around. Perhaps you were not using any propositions about cakes and pieces at all. Perhaps you were 'thinking' visually. We may need to recognize that it is not only verbal or numerical propositions that we use in decisions, but various 'imagistic' forms of thought. Perhaps you could be seen going up to the cake and casually (but expertly) cutting it into four pieces. If you were asked about what guided you in cutting the cake, you may not even be aware. You may have just executed the task automatically. You may be a skilled cake-cutter, who doesn't have to 'compute' what to do.

Perhaps there are some aspects of our knowledge that are 'in the practice' itself, and not conscious or rule driven. Imagine if we observed you in the course of cutting several cakes on different occasions. In observing you on one particular occasion, we notice that you appear to be taking much longer than usual. Your whole approach appears to be more 'studied'. You take time and care, and you examine each piece very carefully before you pass it out to the particular individuals to be served. You appear not to be using your skills at all. What might you have 'known' about the second situation/ context that led you to adopt a different strategy? Perhaps these pieces were going to people where equal-size pieces was more of a consideration in your mind. Here we find that it is knowledge about the consequences of actions in a particular situation that can lie behind a performance.

Imagine a final cake. This time you are observed undertaking quick, slipshod, inaccurate cuts. Indeed, you cut the cake so hurriedly that each piece is damaged. What may be happening here? Perhaps you are angry and this has affected the way you have 'processed' the particular information involved in the task. Perhaps our moods can lie behind our actions.

Taken together, these accounts of what lies behind decisions and actions tell us that we need to elicit knowledge in particular ways. The knowledge that was used on the different occasions was the product of accessing particular mental material, configuring it into particular forms (perhaps spatial forms or perhaps as some geometric or algebraic propositions), and processing it in particular ways.

Individual cognition is a dynamic process, with no easy distinctions between knowledge and information-processing. If we are to understand an individual's decisions and actions, we need to establish their thinking on particular occasions. Knowing is an active process that is mediated, situated, provisional, pragmatic and contested (Blackler, 1995). We need to understand the culturally located systems through which people achieve their knowing, the changes within such systems, and the processes through which new knowledge is generated. We need to recognize that these organizational factors cannot be regarded as simple, singular, determining 'cultures'. We need to view people's behaviour in organizations being situated within fragmented, polyvocal (having several voices), polysemous (having multiple meanings) and polydiscursive struggles (Boje, 1994).

Overall, we need to understand that the actions in organizations may be the result of different kinds of knowledge being practised. We cannot equate knowledge with the education and experience that organizational participants have had. We cannot regard it as the facts and opinions that people have. We have to establish far more of what lies behind each other's perceptions and actions. We need to explore three elements in the decision-making process:

1   We need to appreciate that different kinds of mental material are being used in decisions. We need to be clearer about the meanings of terms such as facts, experiences, skills and unconscious influences.
2   We have to consider how the material is being configured, by seeing what forms of thought the person is using.
3   We have to look at the ways in which the different kinds of mental material and forms of thought are being processed. What type of thinking is taking place? Is it a reasoning process? Is it a set of musings? Is it a 'coloured' (e.g. depressed, frustrated etc.) view of things?

Kinds of mental material

Many years of study by psychologists have revealed that human beings process several different kinds of mental material in their decision-making. The collective term for these different bases of organizing mental material is 'schema', a term coined by Bartlett (1932). A schema has been defined formally as 'a mental framework or outline which refuses to be sharply defined consciously, is in the order of a set or attitude, but less definite, and functions as a kind of vague standard, arising out of past experience, and placing any fresh experience in its appropriate context and relation' (Drewer, 1972). A more general definition is to regard schemas as 'experience organized in fairly well-defined patterns' (Abercrombie, 1960, p. 54). Particular experiences or pieces of learning may be stored within different schemas. Five different kinds of mental material (schemas) can be distinguished. These are semantic understanding, episodic memories, skills, tacit feel and unconscious tendencies. Let us consider these kinds of mental material in a hypothetical personnel selection decision.

SEMANTIC UNDERSTANDING   Some of our decisions may be heavily influenced by the 'facts' that we have. We may decide, for example, not to appoint a particular person because he or she has 'not got the necessary mathematical ability to do the job, and that is what you need'. This kind of mental material is referred to as 'semantic understanding'. Semantics is a branch of philosophy concerned with meanings. Our formal education develops much of this semantic understanding, but it is important to note that the concepts that we use are also derived from our own experiences and our own labelling processes.

A concept is a term that comes from logic. It is a kind of category into which things are (metaphorically) put, on the basis of some common factor or classification system. There may be agreement on the definition of an 'asset'. There may be a body of knowledge (that is, outside of any individual's body) that is regarded as useful in interrelating concepts, for example the relationship between assets and liabilities, or between tangible and intangible benefits. Some of this 'knowledge' may be part of our understanding. We may have much of this in common with other people who have been subjected to similar education. But is this the knowledge that we use to make sense of our world? Or do we work with the world that we have 'constructed' in our own minds? As Burr and Butt (1992) note:

> To call something a fact is usually to claim for it an independent status, to claim that meaning belongs to it and is not conferred upon it. In our efforts to apprehend truths we invent theories, generate meaning, create facts. We cannot easily separate the things we perceive from the way we perceive them, the event from the construction of it. This smell is disgusting, that sight terrifying and that music relaxing. But these qualities do not reside in the phenomena, only in our experience of them. It does not, of course, feel as though these meanings are inferred. It feels as though they are the properties of the perceived events. We do not see something and then decide it is terrifying. We see it as terrifying. The construction is in the perception, part of the definition of the fact. (p. 18)

This world of personal constructions can be argued to be what guides us. This world deals with constructions that have our own labels (for example whizz-kid or wanna-be; listener or speaker). A construct is essentially a discrimination which a person can make. There is a complete approach to psychology that has been developed in an attempt to understand the way in which each of us experiences the world, the psychology of personal constructs developed by Kelly (1955). According to personal construct psychology, we can 'do more than point realistically to what has happened in the past; we can actually set the stage for what may happen in the future – something, perhaps in some respects, very different. Thus we transcend the obvious! By construing we reach beyond anything that man has heretofore known – often reach in vain, to be sure, but sometimes with remarkable prescience' (Kelly, 1977, p. 4).

EPISODIC MEMORIES   Some of our decisions may, on the other hand, be based more on personal memories. We may, for example, say that we 'remember how hard it was to get Graham to do the necessary calculations, like the time when . . .'. This second kind of mental material is referred to as 'episodic memories'. It is information that is 'held together' in our mind, as a sequence of events, as occurred in the experience itself. It is a memory of 'episodes' (Tulving, 1972). It retains particulars about the spatial and temporal context of an event. It is not the general principle. Within episodes we can see how some may have a high degree of involvement of the person, and others may refer to the person perhaps more passively encoding and recalling event sequences they have observed or been told about. Higher 'involvement' may mean that additional facets of the situation are registered and additional aspects of 'meaning' of the events invoked.

It is clear that recall can be enhanced where there are additional sensory cues that can be surfaced and utilized, and there is a higher degree of self-referencing potential. Exposure to information that cues you to consider the event in terms of your 'youness' will be easier to recall. If gender is a big part of your identity (and system of construing), perhaps particular events will be encoded in terms of their gender bias in addition to other aspects of the episode. There is still some debate about whether it is the fact that a person is relating episodes to themselves *per se* that is enhancing encoding, or whether it is because material about the self happens to be a particularly rich source of links (Greenwald and Banaji, 1989). Access, ability to verbalize and attributions of vague familiarity depend on the 'richness' of mental material activated in the act of remembering. Richness character-istics include sensory-perceptual features, temporal features, spatial features, affective features, semantic features and records of cognitive operations performed at encoding. Richness varies with the kind of mental material. Each different kind may invoke more or less of these features. Clearly, autobiographical events that have been reflected on will potentially be particularly richly encoded. The more of these characteristics that can be reinstated at recall, the more likely it is that the material will be recalled.

SKILLS   A third kind of mental material may be being brought to bear in our decision, when we may say that 'once we got talking, I knocked together some example cases to see how the applicant got on'. Here we have used our 'skills' to 'come up with' some example tasks that are the 'essence' of the job. We did not feel that we had to do any conscious analysis to 'pick' an appropriate task. We just 'found ourselves' running through a good example. It is non-declarative knowledge (Anderson, 1983).

Skills are the third kind of mental material that we use in decision-making. People go through 'stages' in becoming expert. As a complete novice one is consciously figuring out a plan. 'Are there any other skills that I have that could be cobbled together to achieve the particular goal?' As one is performing the task, it is almost as if one is talking to oneself as actions are consciously deliberated on and guided in their execution. This early stage of skill acquisition is sometimes called the 'verbal stage' (Adams, 1971). Because actions are being directed consciously, the deliberations are more likely to be available to consciousness in a subsequent interview. Once some basic rules are learned during the 'association stage', however, perceptions and reactions are not operating under a system where the person is concentrating on everything that is going on, making decisions and guiding actions. Confirmatory feedback is not needed to guide every decision and action. At its simplest, once one sees the traffic light go to red and amber, one can anticipate what will come next. It won't be necessary to read the diagram on the gear stick to identify the location of first gear. It won't be necessary to talk oneself through the procedure of depressing the clutch and consciously identifying the appropriate point of depression at which to push the gear lever with just that necessary degree of left bias to avoid selecting third gear by mistake. This whole sequence of events will have become 'automatized'. It will be implemented relatively unthinkingly. Unfortunately if one has acquired some bad habits in this way they will be difficult for one to be aware of. They will be difficult to correct.

TACIT FEEL   We may find that the fourth basis for our decisions may be even harder to express. We watched the applicant in action and 'although I can't put it into words, it didn't look right. There was something "unnatural" or "wrong" about the way that he was doing it.' This 'tacit feel' for how tasks are 'normally' done is hard to express, but one can sense when what one is seeing does not fit with this deep sense of the basics of something. Some of the expertise that people have does not appear *ever* to have been verbal knowledge (that is, reflected on during skill acquisition). This kind of mental material is the product of pure experiential learning. It is sometimes referred to as 'inarticulate knowledge' (Polyani, 1958) or 'tacit knowledge' (Berry and Broadbent, 1984). Other terms include implicit learning, latent learning, implicit memory and tacit feel. In this book, the term 'tacit feel' will be used to describe information that is not readily accessible verbally but which can be distinguished from skilled or automatized mental material since it was acquired latently. Tacit feel is 'acquired without going through a conscious, declarative stage' (Hintzman, 1990, p. 129).

How do we know that knowledge of this form exists? Broadbent and his colleagues (Berry and Broadbent, 1984; Hayes and Broadbent, 1988) have shown how people can demonstrate improvement across repeated trials of tasks and yet show no significant difference in their accounts of how they are doing it. Studies of 'intuitive physics' have shown how people make systematic errors in predicting the future motion of physical objects as they exit from curvilinear tubes etc. when they try to verbalize or draw the outcome. They can, however, reliably recognize when trajectories 'look wrong' (Kaiser et al., 1986). As Polyani (1958) observed, tacit feel, or what he called 'inarticulate' knowledge, is the basis of learning and communication in animals. It is based on the imitative process called mimesis and occurs in humans independently of language. It seems clear that our language skills have proved so successful in guiding our behaviour that we rely on them to a very large extent. Indeed, people often feel that *all* of their behaviour should be explainable (and is actually attributable) to verbally mediated processes, that is, our brains have evolved away from more basic animal-like encoding processes. There are clear indications that the parallel brain systems supporting learning and memory tacitly as opposed to declaratively differ in their capacity for affording awareness of what is learned (Reber and Squire, 1994).

UNCONSCIOUS INTERPRETATIONS   Finally, we may find ourselves saying that the applicant's approach was 'too soft and casual. We need someone who thinks cleanly and neatly.' Here we may be sensing our own unconscious preference to handle problems in an organized and logical way, where we break a problem down and do the logical thing. We may be discomforted when we encounter a 'style' that is alien to us. This fifth form of mental material is 'unconscious interpretations'. It is the 'processing' of information at a non-conscious level, about both ourselves and our 'perceptions'. Other observers may notice our whole tone of condemnation of the applicant as excessive. Indeed, our reaction is, in many ways, telling us more about ourselves than it is about the applicant. We can get clues about how well we are managing a balanced approach in our decision-making from the volume and form of 'excesses'.

Some writers have argued that we invent particular entities in our minds as a means to help us understand complex issues. For example, a child may find it hard to understand how a single entity (for example a particular person) can be protector and punisher, that one both loves and hates. Some 'objects' can be invented that can do this, however. We may hear a child talk of the 'bad fox' or the 'silly duck'. These symbols are more adequate for the task of representing the child's concerns and ideas in a way that will promote their own differentiation and thus understanding of the world. Unconscious symbols, in Piagetian terms, have the function of helping us to make sense – 'the symbol itself being the result of a beginning of conscious assimilation, i.e. an attempt at comprehension' (Piaget, 1951, p. 191). In a work context, we may observe how people seek to simplify people and situations where complexity is overwhelming. Perhaps some of their attempts at 'sense-making' still occur in this more simplistic, symbolic fashion.

In the Freudian conception of the unconscious, only 'fragments' of these original iconic representations are used (Freud, 1900, p. 21). For example, parts of an image may be deleted, parts may be replaced by other parts, and parts may lose their original form (Edelson, 1990, pp. 28–9). They are 'a conglomeration of composite structures' (Freud, 1900, p. 324). The unconscious process by which a particular object is created and 'played' is undertaken in order to release some energy which direct behaviour might otherwise have dissipated. Because the conscious routing of such energies has been considered unacceptable by the person concerned, the unconscious play-out is one which, by definition, can get past the 'censor' of the conscious mind, hence its apparent non-sensicality. When a person is attempting to deal with the complexity of emotional information in flow at work (that is, trying to contain conflicting needs and conflicting emotions), they may adopt certain strategies to deal with the situation and achieve stability. Freud identified four major ways in which they may adjust 'normal' thinking: excessive thinking, rigidity/impulsivity, mild transformations and denial. These strategies are discussed in detail in Chapter 6.

Jung also suggested that the unconscious processes can 'check conscious excesses and challenge conscious attitudes of false complacency when either of these tendencies threatens to compromise an individual's capacities to develop his particular potentials to their fullest' (Jones, 1970). If one takes the time and effort required to reflect on one's decision approach, one can see the 'preferences' that one has for dealing with information. As a person places an ever-increasing emphasis on their preferred approach, they impoverish their respective counterparts. When confronted with situations where the 'underdeveloped' approach is invoked, they may manifest 'primitive' reactions in these regards. The 'logician's' relative lack of sophistication in dealing with 'feeling' may result in their projecting emotionality and differences onto the parties concerned in an attempt to 'demonstrate' their 'irreconcilable' differences, and thus 'justify' their own 'best' and 'most logical' solution. In addition, Jung suggested that we may couch issues in certain basic 'archetypal' terms as we attempt to deal with them. Some of the ways in which we do this, and some of the means by which we can 'surface' these tendencies, are discussed in Chapter 6.

Figure 2.1 shows how the classification scheme for alternative kinds of mental material that is being adopted in this book fits in relation to some of the alternative distinctions that psychologists have made between different kinds of mental material.

Forms of thought

It is also clear that mental material can be configured in particular ways to make the processing of it easier. For example, sometimes we may think, as it were, verbally and work something out. Some other times we may picture what happens in particular situations. Putting information together in our minds as propositions and images affects how we go on to use the mental material in our decisions.

32   *Knowledge in organizations*

Consciousness/ awareness (1)	Conscious		Subconscious		
Unconscious (2)					Unconscious
Knowledge type (3)	Declarative		Non-declarative		
Expertise type (4)	Adaptive		Routine		
Memory type (5)	Episodic	Semantic			
Articulate/ inarticulate (6)	Articulate			Inarticulate	
Skilled and tacit (7)			Skilled	Tacit	
Conscious/implicit learning (8)	Initially consciously acquired knowledge			Initially implicitly acquired knowledge	

Framework for book	Episodic memories	Semantic understanding	Skills	Tacit feel	Unconscious interpretations

(1) James (1890)
(2) Freud (1915)
(3) Anderson (1983)
(4) Hatano and Inagaki (1986)
(5) Tulving (1972)
(6) Polyani (1958)
(7) Berry and Broadbent (1984)
(8) Reber (1967)

Figure 2.1 *Interrelationships between classifications of kinds of mental material*

THE PROPOSITIONAL FORM OF THOUGHT   When we seek to establish the 'linkages' that a person has between a particular idea/object/event and any other information in their mind, we are looking for the propositional codes that they have used in the course of experiencing the idea/object/event. In terms of personal construct psychology, we are seeking to establish the way that a person has construed the idea/object/event. This is useful since it can reveal 'those channels through which new experiences, as well as old, may run' (Kelly, 1955, p. 229). Fransella and Bannister (1977, p. 2) cite Kelly (1969) describing a construct as:

a reference axis, a basic dimension of appraisal, often unverbalized, frequently unsymbolized, and occasionally unsignified in any manner except by the elemental processes it governs. Behaviourally it can be regarded as an open channel of movement, and the system of constructs provides each man with his own personal network of action pathways, serving both to limit his movements and to open up to him passages of freedom which otherwise would be psychologically non-existent.

It is possible to 'focus on particular subsystems of construing and to note what is individual and surprising about the structure and content of a person's outlook on the world' (Fransella and Bannister, 1977, p. 4). When we try elicit a person's constructs, we are referring to distinctions that a person draws between elements, how they 'separate' them in their system of construing. In personal construct psychology, constructs are bipolar. We never affirm anything without simultaneously denying something. One thing is in contrast to another. We may refer to a person's dryness of humour, for example. When we use such a term we mean more than humour being 'dry' in contrast to 'not dry'. Our construct will have a second pole. We may separate 'dry' from 'cynical' humour. This bipolar construct is unique and different from our 'dry' in contrast to the 'base' construct of humour. While a person can develop a new construct during the course of discussion, there is 'some lingering degree of permanence in the constructs' (Kelly, 1955, p. 229). A person's basic system of construal is a robust framework.

In this form of thought, mental material is organized in a way that lends itself to a particular type of processing. The material can be worked with in a particular way in order to secure perception and decision-making.

THE IMAGISTIC FORM OF THOUGHT   The collective term 'mental imagery' refers in general to our use of forms of representation that are closely aligned to the physical senses that were used in the initial perception of an event. Image codes are mental representations that have a form that resembles the object they represent. It is not, of course, that the configuration of cells in the brain resembles the object, but the representation behaves as if it had similar properties. This 'second-order isomorphism' (Shepard, 1975) means that it takes longer to rotate a mental image through 90 degrees than through 45 degrees, just as it takes longer to rotate an actual object in space through 90 degrees than through 45 degrees (Shepard and Metzler, 1971). As Fisher and Geiselman (1992) note, the image code of a particular person's face, for example, 'is shaped like the face. Coloring and texture are also represented on the image directly; the mental image has a specific color and texture which can be mentally "seen" and "touched"' (p. 93). Similarly, auditory images exist, and have image codes rather like 'an internalized "tape recording" of the message, where a loud sound is represented as a "loud" image' (p. 94). Betts (1909) classified mental imagery under seven headings. These were visual, auditory, cutaneous (touch), kinaesthetic (body movement), gustatory (taste), olfactory (smell) and organic (moods, states and feelings) imagery. Some people seem to have (or be able to regenerate) images that are rich in detail and feel 'real', while others may feel that they can only utilize vague images that lack richness and detail.

There is a set of trade-offs between propositional and imagistic forms of mental representation. As Fisher and Geiselman (1992) note, in 'translating' the sensory information experienced in the course of a physical encounter into a verbal (propositional) representation, 'as in all psychological trans-formation, errors are introduced. Furthermore, the accuracy of a verbal code depends upon the [participant's] language skills, so that [participants] with poor language skills will have even-less-accurate concept codes' (p. 94). On the other hand, it is 'considerably more difficult to access the image code than the concept code. In addition, it is more difficult to describe verbally the contents of the image code than the concept code' (p. 94).

It can be valuable for people to 'construct' a particular type of representation for certain types of problems. These representations may mediate the decision-making process by lying 'closer' to the form of thoughts required to solve the particular type of problem than the representation that the person initially had in their mind. Larkin and Simon (1987) discuss why a diagram might (sometimes) be worth ten thousand words. They draw a distinction between representations that are informationally equivalent (that is, they have the *potential* to yield the same information) and computationally equivalent (that is, they take the same *effort* to reveal the information). Facilitating the particular form of mental representation that people use for specific instances of decision-making and problem solving affects the analysis that people conduct (Sparrow, 1989). Representations can effectively 'obscure' information if they provide 'computational cues' that set a person thinking in a particular direction. This is why two elements that others may regard as obviously similar may not be seen to be linked. One of the elements may cue a train of thought that is effectively blinding a person to the obvious. The need to understand the role of these 'mediating representations' is clear. The circumstances under which they are spontaneously created in solving problems also need to be clarified. For example, Johnson-Laird's notion of *mental models* suggests that people may construct representations of an imagistic form to help them in reasoning (for example Johnson-Laird and Bara, 1984). Mental models are not 'unitary representations but are the outcomes of using multiple representations' (Bibby, 1992, p. 168). Rogers and Rutherford (1992) highlight how these different 'sub-elements' in a mental model may not in fact be internally consistent. In other words, the 'knowledge' that we have about something as encoded in one representation may logically conflict with the knowledge that we have inherently within another representation. A person's memory of the visual appearance of a particular computer screen may conflict with their memory of the sequence of screens in a particular computer application.

People can think with images as opposed merely to utilizing imagistic thought forms. Clearly, thinking imagistically is the essence of artistic endeavour. H. Daniels et al. (1994), in exploring the imagery–creativity connection, report how Beethoven, Einstein and many others confirm their use of imagery in all sensory modes and often cross-modal imagery. In a counselling context, McMullin (1986) suggests that as 'images do not involve language, clients can shift their perceptions more rapidly and completely using visual images rather than semantics' (p. 273). In occupational contexts, Checkland and Scholes (1990) note how fluent users of soft systems methodology can be observed throughout their work drawing pictures and diagrams as well as taking notes and writing prose, creating what are called 'rich pictures'. These are drawn to 'express relationships and value judgements; finding symbols to convey the correct "feel" of the situation; indicating that the many relevant relationships preclude instant solutions' (p. 45). The authors say that the reason for this is that 'human affairs reveal a rich moving pageant of relationships, and pictures are a better means for recording relationships and connections than is linear prose' (p. 45). Buzan (1993) argues that because pictures 'make use of a massive range of cortical skills: colour, form, line, dimension, texture, visual rhythm and especially imagination – a word taken from the Latin *imaginari*, literally meaning "to picture mentally"' (p. 73), is why they are so valuable a form of thought. Images are therefore more evocative than words, more precise and potent in triggering a wide range of associations, thereby enhancing creative thinking and memory. Morgan (1993) refers to how 'picture power', as he puts it, 'can create opportunities for reshaping the culture and general development of an organization' (p. 215) and how 'modes of visual imaging can break the constraints of an organization's conventional discourse' (p. 234).

We can acquire and refine our skills through imaging *per se*. Annett (1996) has proposed a theory of motor imagery where 'action prototypes' are used in conjunction with 'memories of the perceptual consequences of previous actions of a similar kind' (p. 27). Action prototypes are used in this covert (imaginary) action as well as in actual (overt) action. Memories of perceptual consequences are a substitute for the sensory feedback which would normally arise from overt action. One of the ways in which we store episodic memories is as 'scripts' (Schank, 1982). These are basic 'routines' or 'sequences of events' that we schematized. So, for example, in a supermarket we may have a script concerning the self-selection of items and subsequent check-out. Scripts are not solely linguistic (propositional) sequences. Indeed, we know, for example, that we have quite clear images of the layout of our usual supermarket, and specific procedures for where to go to check out. We can see how we could utilize such imagistic sequences as guidance for our actions in other shopping contexts.

That visual imagery plays an important part in unconscious thought has been asserted for many years. Dreaming and waking reveries primarily have a pictorial form (Nikolinakos, 1992, p. 398). Dreaming, according to Freud, is 'visual thinking'. Such thoughts attract visual scenes from early childhood and bring them to consciousness in the manifest content of dreams (Freud, 1900, p. 546). Freud (1915) outlines two components of conscious representations, the word-presentation and the thing-presentation. He suggests that the thing-presentation, which is of a visual nature, gets drawn into the unconscious. And then, in turn, if thing-presentations rise to consciousness, by means other than words, one forms mental images. As we have seen, much of the wish-fulfilment needed by a person may be carried out through the unconscious dream-thoughts. The play-out takes the form of individual images and interplays (sequences) of visual images. Capturing a visual image that a person may have in a dream, waking reverie or other unconscious thought process is difficult. For as Freud notes, 'once a picture has emerged from the patient's memory, we may hear him say that it becomes fragmentary and obscure in proportion as he proceeds with his description of it. The patient is, as it were, getting rid of it by turning it into words' (Freud and Breuer, 1893 p. 280). Using some means of capturing images more directly (through encouraging people to communicate them in a visual form, for example) may reduce this difficulty. The difficulty may lie in two aspects. It may be that the deflection of thinking into words means that 'access' to the original image is lost at that time. It may be that the process of articulation destroys the image. Indeed, in his theory of hysteria, Freud suggests that symptoms develop because the subject is unable to find verbal expressions to communicate thoughts, and that once these thoughts and the affect associated with them are put into words, the symptoms disappear (Freud and Breuer, 1893, p. 180). In both regards, a more direct 'recording' would be useful.

We can interpret the particular images a person uses symbolically if we 'first assess what is being depicted literally and then use propositional associations that tell us what the image stands for so that the relationship between the objects represented can be assessed' (Nikolinakos, 1992, p. 409). In analysing dream imagery, Freud suggests that we 'entirely disregard the apparent connexions between the elements in the manifest dream and collect the ideas that occur to you in connexion with each separate element of the dream . . . from this material you arrive at the latent dream-thoughts . . . the true meaning of the dream. It has its starting point in experiences of the previous day, and proves to be a fulfilment of unsatisfied wishes' (Freud, 1909, pp. 62–3). We can undertake similar procedures with employees, in considering their visual imagery in drawings. We can identify instances where particular defence mechanisms (for example excessive thinking vs action, rigidity vs impulsivity, mild transformations and denial strategies of splitting and projection) are manifested in the drawings people make. Overall, the contribution that non-propositional thoughts have within organizational life need to be more fully identified and recognized.

It can be argued that procedures that cue imagistic thinking will tend to invoke a different balance of kinds of mental material to those invoked by procedures that cue propositional thinking. In addition, perhaps even the semantic information invoked by the two forms of thoughts will differ. There are organizational contexts where imagistic thoughts predominate.

Different types of thinking

The five different kinds of mental material and two forms of thought can be used by the mind in different ways in the course of decision-making. It is important to recognize therefore that different types of thinking will interact with mental material and thought forms in different ways. If organizations are to understand the perspectives of participants, they need to consider the nature of three major types of thinking process: autistic, reasoning and mood.

AUTISTIC THINKING   First, organizations need to consider the natural, automatic ways that participants intuitively sense their views of people and situations; how, as it were, their non-directed thoughts construe a situation, and use this to guide their actions. This less rigorous, non-tested sort of information processing is what may be involved in daydreaming. It is a form of thinking that is cut off from the outside world. It is 'autistic' thinking. It does not censor itself for not being rational or reasonable. It is free flowing. The issues that are central to a person's thinking can be elicited, and are important knowledge for the organization to have. Asking people questions about this type of thinking by definition stops it occurring. We need to understand its role in people's lives at work and to consider techniques that can give us insights into this type of thinking.

Studies of the process of daydreaming give us some insight into some important issues. Daydreams can be placed along a continuum ranging from planful/anticipatory through to pure daydreaming (Fournier and Guiry, 1993). The content and form of the latter type of daydreaming activity decreases with age. It may be that the radicality of a daydream 'linkage' between two thoughts also decreases with age. Certainly children's imaginations at play seem more unconstrained. It may be that older people find daydreaming 'lapsing' into episodic memory sequences. Quiet, relaxed thought may mean a reduction in the positive mental effort associated with reasoning and working with semantic kinds of mental material. Perhaps in older people the links (even the sequential temporal ones associated with episodic memories) are so strong that completely 'free' thought occurs more rarely. Hence we can see how an 'expert' using 'all their knowledge' may not know how to get round a problem, whereas others can.

There is evidence to suggest that the prevailing tone of particular instances of daydreaming is linked to prior experiences. Valkenburg and Vandervoort (1995) classified daydreams as positive-intense, aggressive-heroic and dysphoric (depressed). They provide evidence that a positive-intense daydreaming style can be stimulated in children by watching non-violent children's programmes, and be inhibited by watching violent dramatic programmes. An aggressive-heroic daydreaming tone is stimulated by watching violent dramatic programmes and inhibited by watching non-violent programmes. We all know that a conflictual day at work may leave us with aggressive musings as we drive home! A person may therefore be operating with a particularly positive mindset. They may be actively seeking to address situations and do what is possible to deal with any problem. This would be in contrast to a person who feels no sense of commitment to the general situation. They may have the same expertise as the other person, but would respond differently across the range of situations because of the overarching mindset.

REASONING   We can get a great deal of insight into a person when we observe them 'figuring out' a situation. In addition to examining the concepts that they use in their thinking, it is also possible to identify what happens when they use some sort of 'logic' to interrelate concepts. In seeking to understand the ways in which knowledge is accessed, created and transacted at work, we need to consider some of the sorts of reasoning that are undertaken in everyday discourse. Thomas (1986) suggests that people look merely for 'internal coherence' where 'certain claims or alleged facts are given as justification or explanations for others' (p. 11). It is important to note that the 'legitimacy' of the justification is 'local', that which is considered acceptable to the interactants, rather than some grand objective rule system. Toulmin et al. (1979) suggest that we view argument as an entire social act where we need to consider 'the whole activity of making claims, challenging them, backing them up by producing reasons, criticizing those reasons, rebutting those criticisms, and so on' (p. 13). The 'acceptability' of a particular argument entails a local process of 'judging by appropriate standards of evidence or appropriate standards of what is possible' (Fisher, 1988, p. 27). This 'argumentation analysis', it is claimed, is used by interactants in the course of discussion. There is a sensible 'flow' to arguments. The local cultural context of the thinking may mean that very different 'rules' may seem to be applying in reasoning episodes taking place in diverse groups.

It may be that the patterns of thinking that particular individuals are engaged in have some degree of commonality across specific situations. It may be possible to glean some insight into patterns at various levels of aggregation. There may well be 'marketing department-speak', 'IBM-speak', 'British argument', and 'Western forms of thought'. How far any of these patterns are part of the internalized thinking of any individual or manifested in the actions of a particular group of interactants will vary. As a minimum, we can see that reasoning involves particular concepts being invoked and combined in some form of relationship. The particular concepts invoked and the specific links described are situated. If we are to understand the sorts of knowledge that are generated at work we need to consider whether there are any particular sorts of thinking that are being practised extensively, and others that are being relatively neglected. If we are to undertake this sort of analysis we need some frameworks to guide us.

Reasoning can be defined as going beyond the information given (Galotti, 1989). We gain different understandings when we undertake different sorts of reasoning. Reason and Rowan (1981) note how different sorts of thinking yield 'explanations' in different terms. For example, causal thinking yields linear sequences; systems thinking yields other patterns of interaction; dipolar thinking takes account of the interdependence of polar opposites; contextual thinking recognizes the cultural and historical context of interpretations; and practical thinking yields knowledge about thinking. It can be particularly fruitful to consider objects and events as consisting of entities, attributes and relationships. In so doing, we can distinguish between three 'levels' of relation (Gentner, 1983). Zero-order relationships are defined as those which obtain between an entity and its attributes. A first-order relationship is defined as that which obtains between entities. Second-order relationships entail relations between relations. The richness of a person's understanding of a domain may, in one sense, be seen as the volume of the zero-order relationships that they have in their mind. This would be a relatively highly fragmented understanding. The higher degree of abstraction involved in establishing first-order relations would mean that we could argue that another person's understanding was fuller, if it included a higher number of first-order relations compared to the first person. Similarly, we could argue that second-order relations are an even more abstract notion, involving as it does notions of analogy or metaphor in considering the nature of relations between the relationships between entities. The more of these the merrier. Our notion of richness of understanding therefore is an understanding that is both, a highly differentiated conception of a domain with a high level of integration, that is, high levels of first-, second- and third-order relations. There is evidence to suggest that it is possible to identify different degrees of the levels of relation in the 'thinking' of experts and novices in particular domains (for example Zeitz, 1994). Experts spot relatively more instances of first- and second-order relations than do novices.

Using this terminology, one can conceive of individuals operating with relatively high levels of first- and second-order relations but relatively low levels of zero-order relations, that is, a deep but narrow conception. One can also imagine a person with an extensive set of episodic schemas associated with particular entities, but perhaps lacking in insight, that is, a broad but shallow conception. One can further imagine the nature of 'exploration' of an issue in a management group. To what extent is the discussion addressing both breadth and depth? Can we identify relative absences of particular relations, and make sure that our management groups address them? Might we find ourselves in decision-making contexts where the social construction of decision-making is such that certain forms of relation are not articulated, entertained or undertaken? It can be useful to have a framework of reasoning in mind when considering the elicitation of a person's or group's conception of issues.

In the course of reasoning, we find ourselves 'pushing' the boundaries of our understanding, by identifying 'new', deeper or broader considerations. We can also sense an increase in understanding as we account for more and more of a phenomenon, through our grasp of how elements interact. We can, therefore, perhaps usefully distinguish between two different thrusts in the course of reasoning. One thrust is for understanding 'separation'. It is a mission to find differences between things. A second thrust is concerned with 'location'. It is a mission to understand interrelation between elements, that is, how they figure in relation to each other. Together these thrusts create different facets to thinking in the course of reasoning.

Separation thinking seeks to define things. It is an approach to thinking where the logical separation of things is the quest. One is seeking to discriminate or differentiate between things. It carries an emphasis on categorization. One is defining one's terms. The whole process might be driven by a basic assertion that 'no two things are exactly equal' and that there is a need to seek a basis for distinguishing between them. One is trying to isolate elements. Using an analogy from physics, one is looking for the equivalent of the Periodic Table's Elements, that is, the basic differentiable elements, the alternatives. One's questions seek to establish what the 'components' are. On this mission, one would be less interested in the processes or links between things. In this focus of thinking, therefore, concern does not lie with chemical interaction. It does not lie with how components fit together to make a whole. The focus is on systematic 'discovery' of the logical alternatives: what are the 'bits'?

Location thinking can have three different facets. All of them concern how the 'bits' fit together. There is an aspect of location thinking that seeks to find 'order' in things. We might call this aspect of the location approach to thinking 'static comparison'. Static comparison includes how one categorizes things. The second way of interrelating things statically is sequencing. A major example of this pursuit is causal thinking. Causal thinking attempts to locate elements in a particular way. It concerns itself with how one element affects another. It seeks to explain how a particular set of elements combine. It seeks to show how the location of an element accounts for its effect on other elements, and/or the effects on it. Causation is only one of the possible 'ordering' systems, however. Elements can be shown to have an ordered relationship in terms of other bases such as temporal sequences, or orders of magnitude. The objective of static comparison, in all instances, is to understand the 'fixed' nature of elements' interrelation to each other.

A second major facet of a location approach to thinking is systems thinking. Systems thinking is about boundaries. It is about defining sets of elements that, at some level, operate in an interacting way. The constituents have something rather interesting in common. It is not a physical property that they share. It is that they can usefully be viewed in combination as they achieve a particular purpose. Systems thinking is about identifying meaningful systems, constituencies of elements that can be construed to be combining to some end. In a like manner, particular subsystems can combine to produce a particular purpose. Systems are about hierarchies of subsystems. There is a further specific feature of a system that is fundamental. It is that the elements within it, can 'adapt' collectively to achieve the goal. As Checkland and Scholes (1990) put it, we can view a system as 'a whole having emergent properties, a layered structure and processes of communication and control which in principle enable it to survive in a changing environment' (p. 22). If we use this image or metaphor to examine what is taking place in a library or a coalmine, we can see how a library operates to achieve its function. We can see what it controls in order to remain in a position to fulfil its function. As Checkland and Scholes (1990) further note, 'To make mental use of that image is to do systems thinking' (p. 19).

Systems thinking highlights a particular facet of interrelationship: interdependency. When engaged in systems thinking one is not merely examining how one element causes another, one is examining the dynamics of an interrelationship where the very nature of an element changes as it interacts with other elements. By way of example, one might use separation thinking to draw a distinction (at some level) between love and marriage. One might use a form of location thinking to see how (sometimes) these two elements can be sequenced so that love can lead to marriage. Note how the nature of the concept 'love' is fixed throughout this process. Similarly, the nature of marriage is a fixed concept. Consider now the interdependency of love and marriage. Perhaps marriage itself affects the very nature of love. Perhaps the nature of an evolving form of love affects the form of a marriage. This systems thinking is about flow and change rather than sequence and fixedness.

A third facet of a location approach to thinking is plurality seeking. Thinking can recognize a wider cultural and historical context of interpretations. Events can be located in a large number of 'histories'. The significance of an event can be located in many cultural frameworks. A quest to consider the multiplicity of meanings is different from seeking the detail of a single explanation. Plurality seeking has an emphasis on multiplicity rather than singularity, therefore. It is about a multiplicity of perspectives and a multiplicity of interpretations. It is a quest for alternative explanations as opposed to 'the' definitive explanation; it is an attempt to locate events in a multiplicity of ways. Going back to our previous example, what do we learn about love and marriage when we say they 'go together like a horse and carriage'? What do we learn when we say 'love is a battlefield'? These are insights that do not stem from the separation thinking that distinguishes between love and marriage. Nor do they stem from static comparison, such as categorizing them as Western socialized behaviours. Nor from sequencing love or marriage. Nor indeed from understanding something of the dynamics between love and marriage. Plurality thinking provides rich insights that are drawn from parallels with other interrelationships among other concepts. As an exercise it is a quite distinct turn of mind.

Figure 2.2 shows how separation thinking and the three forms of location thinking might be applied to analyse a particular object. It shows some of the features of the object that might be highlighted in the course of undertaking the different forms of reasoning.

Reasoning is a type of thinking that is often seen as synonymous with thinking itself. It is clear that it is but one of the types of thinking and needs to be explored fully in its own right.

MOOD   The extent to which people can conjure up particular 'organic states' was considered by Betts (1909) as one of the forms of mental imagery. In that sense of the word, moods are pervasive states that colour the interpretation of and deliberation on events. In Betts's conception, moods are imagistic thoughts that can 'swamp' thinking. Subsequent

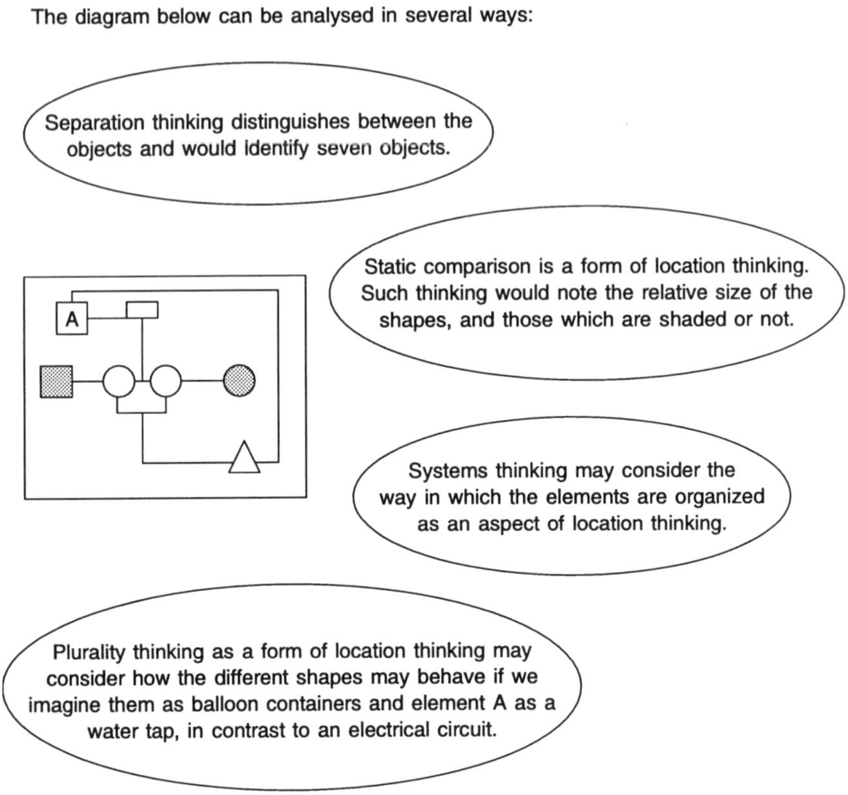

The diagram below can be analysed in several ways:

Separation thinking distinguishes between the objects and would Identify seven objects.

Static comparison is a form of location thinking. Such thinking would note the relative size of the shapes, and those which are shaded or not.

Systems thinking may consider the way in which the elements are organized as an aspect of location thinking.

Plurality thinking as a form of location thinking may consider how the different shapes may behave if we imagine them as balloon containers and element A as a water tap, in contrast to an electrical circuit.

Figure 2.2 *Different forms of reasoning: separation thinking and three forms of location thinking*

research indicates that mood may be a more integrated aspect of cognition in general. Moods are a particular thinking process. They are a type of thinking. The implications of this type of thinking for human beings interacting at work need to be recognized and considered. There are norms at work whereby the 'irrationality' of moods is frowned on and attempts to remove them from decisions promoted. Indeed, a great deal of energy can go into rationalizing decisions that were actually the product of mood. People and organizations can convince themselves that they are sufficiently 'in control' of situations to have no need to consider mood. The realities of the human condition are, however, such that mood does enter organizational life. As a type of thinking it affects how information is accessed and processed. The scale and form of its impact at work can be examined and recognized. Giving people the opportunity to explore their feelings at work is argued to be increasingly important given the increase in the number of people engaged in 'emotional labour' (Hochschild, 1983; Anderson, 1993) The consequences of leaving these emotions to find their own conduit in an individual or group is argued to be one of the major sources of conflict and 'anti-task' behaviours at work (Obholzer and Roberts, 1994).

Two major dimensions account for most of the variation in mood. These are relative levels of feelings of arousal, and relative levels of feelings of pleasure (Watson and Tellegen, 1985). There are classifications of affective well-being that have been developed with occupational behaviour in mind. Measures have been developed that tap what are considered to be two important dimensions of affect, anxious-contented/comfortable and depressed-enthusiastic (Warr, 1990; Sevastos et al., 1992). As a result, the full and subtle gamut of affective states can be embraced. Terms such as surprised, excited, full of energy, delighted, keen, happy, glad and pleased can be sensed around the construct labelled 'enthusiastic'. Bored, fatigued, lacking energy, gloomy, sad, depressed, miserable and dejected are moods that can be sensed around the opposite pole of the construct and labelled 'depressed'. The terms discouraged, dissatisfied, frustrated, anxious, tense, afraid, alarmed and aroused are 'anxious' mood states. Feeling comfortable, satisfied, contented, calm, relaxed, tranquil, drowsy or sluggish can be considered as a construct labelled 'contented' (Warr, 1990) or 'comfortable' (Sevastos et al., 1992). We do have, therefore, the beginnings of a language to describe mood at work.

The feelings that we refer to as 'mood' are particular patterns of thinking. These cognitions 'recycle through the individual's cognitive networks' (Ingram, 1984, p. 443) to maintain the affect. Ellis and Ashbrook (1988) view the impact of emotion in terms of a resource allocation model. They suggest that because 'there is a limited, momentary pool of capacity (attentional resources) which can be allocated to any given task', and mood is effectively the maintenance of particular patterns of thinking, we can account for 'the affects of the generally disruptive mood states on memory' (p. 26). This would account for the poor quality of decisions recorded when people are under stress (Arnold et al., 1991) and other states of heightened or lowered levels of arousal (Palmer and Dryden, 1995). Mood has been shown to affect people's judgements about their own and others' competence (Radenhausen, 1989), goal setting (Hom and Arbuckle, 1988) and willingness to take risks (Deldin and Levin, 1986).

Mood as a type of thinking affects how mental material is processed. There are three relationships to consider. The first relationship is a broad, general, pervasive effect. There is evidence of a 'Pollyanna Principle' (Matlin, 1994), that is, people process pleasant items (words, events etc.) more efficiently and accurately than less pleasant ones. Similarly, the order in which people recall words also tends to be in descending order of pleasantness. It is therefore important to recognize that if a person is in a relatively neutral emotional state their immediately recalled events are not representative of 'typical' events. They are a positively biased set of instances. The second relationship between mood and memory is referred to as the 'mood congruence effect'. This describes the findings that memory is better when the material to be learned is congruent with a person's current mood. Thus, a person in a negative mood (for example, somewhat depressed) might note and reflect on negative words and events more than positive items. The third impact of mood on memory is called 'mood-state dependence'. Here we can observe that people recall items/events where the mood they were in is the same as the mood they are in now. If one is in a positive frame of mind, one will recall positive events more readily. If one is in a negative mood, one will recall negative events more. It is the third effect that is the most relevant in considering knowledge elicitation in organizations. If elicitation is taking place in a negative atmosphere, there will be a preponderance of negative events recalled. We can all perhaps recall meetings where the 'tone' that was set early on coloured the subsequent shape of the discussion. This relationship between mood and memory is particularly important in considering knowledge elicitation because something can be done about it.

It is useful to think of the three basic types of thinking in terms of geometric patterns. Reasoning is thinking in lines. It is going somewhere. In contrast, autistic thinking may be regarded as thinking at tangents. One may picture it as a set of separate elements 'sparking off' in a radial fashion. It is more free. It is not linear. Mood thinking may usefully be considered as thinking in circles. It is constrained. It is a type of thinking that is self-reinforcing. It is necessary to engage people in each of these patterns of thinking if one is to understand their behaviour at work.

In conclusion, understanding how mood affects the processing of mental material and thence decision-making is a major task within organizations. Chapter 5 details some of the ways in which insights into mood processes and effects can be gained.

An overall framework for classifying organizational knowledge

Knowledge is thus the product of particular kinds of mental material, being configured in particular forms and processed in particular ways. Figure 2.3 depicts how the three aspects can be combined. The framework suggests that there are 30 aspects of perceptions that might usefully be considered. It is only through the broad elicitation of all of these aspects that organizations can achieve the comprehensive self-insight in practitioners, and mutuality of insight, that modern and future organizational decision-making requires.

Different frameworks have been proposed by other writers. It is useful to consider any evidence that supports the case for examining organizational knowledge in the way being proposed here. Moody et al. (1996) confirm that most of the popular knowledge-elicitation techniques are designed to elicit rules (that is, procedural knowledge) from the expert, and that there is a need to identify techniques that capture knowledge in the form of cases, 'the unique combination of situational variables and solutions experienced by the expert' (p. 127), episodic memories. Gibson and Salvendy (1992), in seeking

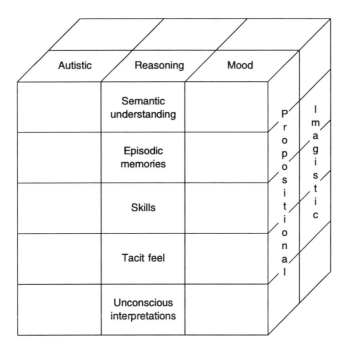

Figure 2.3   *Kinds of mental material, forms of thought and types of thinking*

to determine any common underlying dimensions of human problem-solving for various types of problems and to identify possible contributions to the development of intelligent computer systems, highlight the 'representation involved', the 'level of inductive and deductive reasoning' and the 'level of subconscious vs. conscious processing' as three important dimensions. In terms of the proposed framework, this confirms the value of distinguishing between forms of thought, types of thinking and some of the aspects of different kinds of mental material. Hoffman et al. (1995) place knowledge-elicitation techniques in three categories: 'analysis of the tasks that experts usually perform', 'various types of interviews' and 'contrived tasks which reveal an expert's reasoning processes'. This is in line with the distinctions in the proposed framework between non-declarative knowledge (where knowledge is expressed through performance), propositional (though here, largely, semantic) knowledge, and aspects of reasoning as a type of thinking. Rothe (1994) explores the different efficiency of interviews, questionnaires, group discussions, observations and thinking-aloud techniques for 'declarative' vs 'procedural' knowledge.

While several authors have reviewed knowledge-elicitation techniques, attempted to summarize the strengths and weaknesses of particular techniques and indicated some 'recommended applications' (for example Cooke, 1994; Tomlinson and Johnson, 1994), the proposed framework is considered

to be the most comprehensively premised. The framework raises fundamental issues about the predominant forms of perceptions that are surfaced
in organizations. Much of our knowledge concerning the issues of promoting
mutual understanding within organizations has been based on only a small
subset of these aspects of knowledge.

Capturing knowledge

If we are to understand how organizations operate, then we have to
appreciate the 'stock' of knowledge that organizations possess. Schon (1991)
observes that organizations are 'repositories of cumulatively built-up knowledge: principles and maxims of practice, images of mission and identity,
facts about the task environment, techniques of operation, stories of past
experience which serve as exemplars for future action' (p. 242). He notes
how, through reflection, a manager 'draws on this stock of organizational
knowledge, adapting it to some present instance. And he also functions as an
agent of organizational learning, extending or restructuring, in his present
inquiry, the stock of knowledge which will be available for future inquiry'
(p. 242).

How do organizations create, store and access this stock of knowledge?
To answer this, we need to consider the notion of knowledge more closely.
Sproull (1981) proposes that we consider organizational knowledge as
recipe knowledge or social typifications. Recipe knowledge is the routine
performance programmes and standard operating procedures that provide
people with ways of acting in particular situations. Social typifications are
the shared understandings which are acquired through socialization and
interaction of the people within a collective. A culture's language, environment and history may influence the structure and the content of its typifications. Smircich (1983) depicted organizations as 'systems of knowledge',
where individuals within an organization share subjective meanings to
varying degrees. The coherence of a 'group' within an organization, therefore, requires 'forming a publicly held map that is generally agreed to by its
members' (McCaskey, 1972, p. 22). On entering an organization, a person
may be socialized to acquire the stock of knowledge and orientation that is
required to be a member of the group (Louis, 1980).

It can be useful to distinguish between individual beliefs and collective
beliefs. Many writers have argued that team effectiveness improves as the
volume of collective beliefs increases. Much of this literature refers to this
singular notion of a group's culture. Gagliardi (1986) refers, for example, to
'a group's distinct set of features or traits, which means then, not just its
basic values but also its beliefs and behaviour models, the technology it uses,
its symbols and artefacts, and so on' (p. 126). Finney and Mitroff (1986)
refer to consensual cognitive schemas and scripts embedded in a group's
culture. Langfield-Smith (1992), however, suggests that groups function
acceptably by using '"collective cognitions", more transitory social artefacts

of the group, which are subscribed to in varying degrees by the members of the group at a particular point in time during "collective encounters"' (p. 360). These collective cognitions are a product of negotiation, argument and interaction. They are the use of 'working definitions' of concepts and 'local' logic of argument that people negotiate in social encounters. She argues that shared beliefs and cognitions may arise through successive collective encounters, so that 'in a cohesive group of individuals, there will be a large proportion of shared (common) beliefs and therefore fewer collective cognitions need to be negotiated during an encounter' (p. 362).

Promoting mutual understanding in organizations does not therefore mean homogenizing beliefs and cognitions. Indeed, Weick (1979) argues that groups tend to converge around common means and diverse goals, rather than around common goals, and Bougon (1992) suggests that individuals only need to use common labels (rather than detailed shared concept definitions) if they are to operate with others in a social system. Mutual understanding can thus range from attempting to secure insights into the positions that 'cryptic congregating labels' (Bougon, 1992) play in fellow participants' cognitions, on to more detailed insights into the degree of sharing of meaning of concepts, through to the explicit promotion of shared meaning. Fiol (1994) suggests that the organizational consensus that is needed for organized action can involve consensus around the content of information, and around the way in which communication is framed. It is possible for work teams to develop unified ways of framing their arguments, while at the same time maintaining diversity through differences in the content of team members' interpretations. The suggestion is that diversity in views should be actively encouraged alongside a striving for shared framing of the issues that is broad enough to encompass those differences. In all instances there is a need to understand the terms and ways in which we and our fellow participants think.

The advocacy of an approach to understanding human behaviour through working with people's perceptions is not new. Indeed, some would argue that it is a well-established strategy in organizational research, and others would argue that it is even more than this. It is a paradigm, that is, an entire belief framework with clear implications for the methods through which 'understanding' of human beings can be obtained. The term used to describe this strategy or paradigm is phenomenology. Tesch (1990) notes that phenomenologists 'study the ordinary "life-world": they are interested in the way people experience their world, what it is like for them, how best to understand them' (p. 68). The approach is valued because 'no matter what the circumstances are, or the prevailing official definition, if a person defines a situation in a certain way, that will be the context in which his plans for action are formed' (Woods, 1983, p. 7).

The quest is therefore to gain insight into the thinking that a person is using (or used) at the time of a decision. But there are differences, however slight, between what is felt and thought at a particular time and how those experiences are recounted in the course of a subsequent elicitation (interview etc.) 'Memory for real life events is not a copying process. Rather it is a decision-making process where people see what they want or need to see and actively reconstruct it' (Cortazzi, 1993, p. 80). The way in which a person recollects an event changes over time, depending on the audience and circumstance as well as any reframing in the light of experience.

To embrace other people's 'life-worlds' therefore is not just a matter of asking them what they were thinking or think now about a future situation. It is a recognition that one must make a much more concerted attempt to move one's frame of reference from oneself, and into that other person. It entails a recognition that that 'world' is complex and multifaceted and that it is not a world where decisions are just computed on the basis of clear considerations. It is recognizing that the features of one's own decision-making and thinking, of which one is, in some loose sense, aware in principle (half-thought-out ideas, guesses, feelings, 'automatic' or 'reflex' responses), will need to be 'experienced' if one is to gain insight into another person's thinking in a meaningful way.

The issues raised so far in the discussion of management by perception have highlighted a need to work not only with the conscious aspects of each person's thinking, but also with many of the more subtle, less conscious aspects of their understanding. These latter forms of mental material are important within decision-making for several reasons. First, they may be the most automatic, skilled or habitual aspects of a person's behaviour. They may be the aspects of a person of which they are least aware. It is part of what a person actually does and not just what they think or say that they do. Secondly, less conscious mental material may hold a key to understanding that person's perspective, since it may be where the fundamental assumptions they have internalized, and use as guiding principles in their decisions, reside. As Schon (1991) observed:

> Every competent practitioner can recognize phenomena – families of symptoms associated with a particular disease, peculiarities of a certain kind of building site, irregularities of materials or structures – for which he cannot give a reasonably accurate or complete description. In his day-to-day practice he makes innumerable judgments of quality for which he cannot state adequate criteria, and he displays skills for which he cannot state the rules and procedures. Even when he makes use of research-based theories and techniques, he is dependent on tacit recognitions, judgments, and skilled performances. (pp. 49–50)

We can see that our knowledge of how to ride a bike does not reside in some 'words' or 'principles of physics' that we tell ourselves as we seek to control the bike. Our knowledge is in the actions and reactions we make, just as, 'a tightrope walker's know-how, for example, lies in, and is revealed by, the way he takes his trip across the wire' (Schon, 1991, pp. 50–1). When musicians improvise, they adjust their playing to the 'feel' of the music that they and others in the band are generating.

Any insights gained into thinking and practices within organizations can affect organizational decisions and actions. It is useful to explore the effects of such insights in two ways. First, we can examine how reflection on one's own knowledge and practice can be facilitated, and how it may affect one's actions. Secondly, we can consider how the awareness of other organizational participants' knowledge can be captured, communicated and learned from.

Capturing our own knowledge

The value of capturing and considering our own professional practice has been most effectively expressed by Schon (1991). We have noted how our own knowledge can reside in our conscious thinking and in our actions. We can see that when we use the terms 'skilled' or 'professional', these have connotations of an extensive repertoire of responses and of the speed and certainty of these responses, as well as implying familiarity with the situation in hand. A highly skilled practitioner can diagnose and rectify situations 'as a matter of routine' and 'automatically'. He or she does not have painstakingly to 'start from scratch'. It is in this automation that some of the weaknesses of skilled practice lie. For 'as a practice becomes more repetitive and routine, and as knowing-in-practice becomes increasingly tacit and spontaneous, the practitioner may miss important opportunities to think about what he is doing' (Schon, 1991, p. 61). A practitioner's reflection can serve as a corrective to this overlearning. Through reflection, 'he can surface and criticize the tacit understandings that have grown up around the repetitive experiences of a specialized practice, and can make new sense of the situations of uncertainty or uniqueness which he may allow himself to experience' (p. 61).

We can reflect on our actions after the event (that is, in a post mortem). We can reflect in the course of our actions (that is, in the 'action-present'). Here, we may engage in 'on-the-spot surfacing, criticizing, restructuring, and testing of intuitive understandings of experienced phenomena, often it takes the form of a reflective conversation with the situation' (pp. 241–2). A practitioner's artistry is, however, 'always richer in information than any description of it', and we may need to recognize that the 'internal strategy of representation, embodied in the feel for artistic performance', is different from any 'strategies used to construct external descriptions of it' (p. 276). Schon believes that reflection does not depend on a 'description of intuitive knowing that is complete or faithful to internal representation' (p. 277), but notes that 'certain descriptions are more useful for action than others' (p. 279). There is, however, overwhelming evidence to show, on the contrary, that there is real value in recognizing the different ways in which knowledge is internally represented in our minds, and developing expertise in the specific techniques that can help us access different aspects of our practice. The first major purpose of this book is to present the evidence concerning the value of alternative approaches towards accessing and re-representing our own knowledge representations.

Capturing other people's knowledge

The second major purpose of the book is to present the evidence concerning the value of alternative approaches towards accessing the knowledge of organizational participants. The degree and form of interaction between organizational participants can have implications for knowledge creation in organizations. Nonaka et al. (1996) postulate an 'amplification' and 'crystallization' of individual knowledge into knowledge elsewhere in an organization, through four modes of knowledge conversion. These are: socialization (where 'tacit knowledge' creates 'tacit knowledge'), externalization (where 'tacit knowledge' is made explicit), combination (where aspects of 'explicit knowledge' are combined) and internalization (where 'explicit knowledge' is implicitly acquired).

It would be convenient to assume that people in close and constant proximity and interaction learn all there is to know about each other's perceptions, but it is not the case. A great deal of the research conducted on group processes has explored the developments that take place in informal, naturalistic settings. It is clear that some aspects of group members' views can be elicited as a group matures. More recent research has shown however, that different processes are useful for facilitating the elicitation of different kinds of information. Management by perception requires the intention to maximize mutual understanding to be made explicit. This will affect the functioning of work groups. Specific techniques would be being used deliberately to facilitate the elicitation and sharing of knowledge. The kinds of knowledge created depend on the nature of the encounter. Encounters can vary in terms of the number of participants (that is, individual vs group), the kinds of mental material used, the forms of thought utilized and the types of thinking undertaken. We need, therefore, to explore the 'conversations' that individuals have with their own mental material, in the course of their practice. We need to explore the creation and utilization of knowledge among organizational participants. These issues are the subject matter of this book.

3

The Role of Physical Representations in Knowledge Elicitation

It is not possible to transfer the conception that one person has of an issue directly to another person. There needs to be a communication process. In essence this requires that the information is re-represented in some way, and that this is then decoded by the receiver. As we have seen, everyday discourse entails people putting their perceptions into sequences of words, and co-constructing the notion in the other person's mind with that other person. It is a rapid, dynamic process. Its success depends on the shared language of the parties, and their abilities flexibly to adjust the expression of the message, as 'confusion' is sensed. The immense facility that human beings have for language has perhaps resulted in representations of ideas (in our minds) through words. It has perhaps meant that we tend to communicate sententially, that is, propositionally. We know, however, that this is not the only means of representing and communicating perceptions. This chapter explores what information science and social science have to tell us about the role of representations in communicating meaning.

A physical re-representation is not only a means of communicating one's mental material, form of thought and type of thinking to another person. When we see a physical representation of information we are 'cued' into looking at the material in a particular way. We are primed to undertake particular mental analysis of the image in order to interpret it. Physical images play a key role in knowledge elicitation. They can act as stepping stones in the elicitation process. They can be used collectively to explore different facets of a person's mental material, thought forms and thinking processes. This chapter explores the evidence concerning the impact of physical representations on knowledge elicitation. It considers some alternative ways to classify physical representations, and shows how a systematic endeavour to consider knowledge through different types of physical representation can be valuable.

Information science and social science perspectives

Words are symbols. The word 'tiger' is a symbol for the object. A drawing of a tiger symbolizes a tiger. It is clear that human beings moved from expressing ideas through close physical renditions of objects, through to more shorthand versions and finally on to written words. But are words always the best means of expressing an idea? Try drawing a shape that consists of, say, six lines joined together. See if you can communicate this shape to another person in words alone. It is far harder than communicating the shape through an alternative form of representation, a drawing. The drawing makes the absorption of the information easier for the receiver. Of course alternative representations should contain the same information potential, that is, they should all be capable of giving the receiver all of the data needed to get the idea. In Larkin and Simon's (1987) terms, they are 'informationally equivalent'. The main way in which alternative representations differ is in the computations they require of the receiver to assemble the data in order to get the full information. Alternative representations would be 'computationally equivalent' if they required the same effort to reveal the information (Larkin and Simon, 1987). In fact, there are large differences in the computational requirements of alternative forms of representation. That is why some ways of representing something are felt to be 'good', and others less effective. It is also clear that no particular representation is universally good or universally bad. The effectiveness depends on the specific information for which one is seeking to support the computation.

The physical form of representation of data affects the information that tends to be extracted from it (Duncker, 1945). In some ways it is surprising how little has been established about the appropriate use of different graphical representations for the extraction of information. When one considers the history of mass communication, however, one can see that the printed book evolved a normative level for the use of colour coding, multiple typographical fonts, diagrams, pictures and graphs which had been suppressed through cost considerations. As a result, very few human factors research studies were initially conducted into these potentially cost-bounded issues. There has been virtually no information to guide software designers (and, more recently, desktop publishers) in evaluating the appropriateness of including various options within each of these categories. The users of such systems have had to 'find their way', and very often continue not to take advantage of the representational capabilities of the word-processing or spreadsheet software they are utilizing. Sparrow (1989) conducted a study to examine the information that is gleaned when people are presented with alternative representations (spreadsheet tables, pie charts, bar charts, vertically stacked bar charts, line graphs and multiple line graphs) about some business (sales) data. The study revealed the general strengths and weaknesses of each graphical technique in facilitating the communication of certain facets of data. We need to give particular attention to the alternative graphical means of displaying information when we are seeking to communicate it effectively.

While the study was useful, it sheds light on only a limited part of the considerations involved in the role of physical representations in communication. Three important sets of considerations are omitted by the study. First, it only investigated one particular type of reasoning. When viewed in terms of Reason and Rowan's (1981) types of reasoning, it was a study that focused on causal thinking (as opposed to systems thinking, dipolar thinking, contextual thinking or practical thinking). It restricted its attention to the communication of information that is fundamentally communicable through graphs. There are, of course, many other types of information and many other forms of representation that can be reasoned about. Secondly, the study did not address the appropriateness of alternative representations for autistic thinking or mood thinking. It is likely that different types of thinking are engendered by different representations. Analysis and computation are only subcategories of one type of thinking. The third limitation in the study is that communication is situated. The effectiveness of representations will be dependent on the individuals and the context. This limitation turns our attention away from information science towards the insights into the role of representations in communication from a social science perspective.

The effort required by people to do the necessary mathematical calculations to obtain a particular piece of information may be more onerous for one person than another. Perhaps one person is more familiar and skilled in dealing with particular forms of computations, and as a result prefers a representation that invokes that form of analysis, as opposed to an alternative representation that is more personally demanding. The notion of the objective or theoretical computational effort associated with interpreting alternative representations is an important consideration. It is not the only consideration. Relatedly, there may be varying degrees of interaction between the participants. They may have evolved a 'language' that is very attuned to the specific information they need to transact. Particular representations may symbolize a great deal to them, even though they entail little in the way of construction. Schenk (1991) notes how 'in a very real sense drawing can be seen as part of the language through which designers conduct various aspects of their business' (p. 177). Graphic designers were found to use drawing to communicate ideas during meetings with marketing personnel and account executives, and described themselves as 'interacting with the client through the use of drawing' (p. 177).

Very often we feel that we do not know ourselves what we think about a particular issue until we start to talk about it. Sometimes we surprise ourselves with an insight into something in the course of recounting our own understanding of an issue. In one sense this may be an indication that the knowledge we have is quite volatile. This insight can be viewed as 'new' knowledge. On the other hand, it could be argued that what we are experiencing is not new knowledge, but rather merely high engagement. As Sampson (1991) puts it, thinking itself always involves an internal conversation, with 'one person taking the role of the other person and imaginatively carrying on a conversation' (p. 223). Antaki (1994) has suggested that the social conventions of dialogue *are* the way we think. These 'internal' conversations are an integral part of our knowledge. Just as some people have developed particular competence in words, others have developed a relative strength in visual communication. Imagistic forms of thought may be operating in a similar way when we consider an issue imagistically.

These internal processes place a high burden on our minds. Our 'working memory' can be augmented by additional external sources of 'memorizing'. When we do some mental arithmetic, we may lose track of where we had got to, and have to start again. When we have a pencil and paper to hand, we may be able to jot down some of the outcomes of interim calculations and ease the burden of keeping all of the calculation process in our mind. The process of writing may help us articulate our thoughts more clearly. When reflecting on action, some form of external representation may assist. Walker (1985) notes how writing helps people 'recognize and take account of affective aspects . . . not only helps them appreciate the role of feeling, and clarify the feelings involved, it also helps them name those feelings and own them by expressing them in their own words'. Similarly, Schon (1991) notes how, in the course of reflection in action, a designer has a conversation with his drawing. Several researchers into design have noted how sketching forms part of the thinking of designers. Schenk (1991) confirms the idea of the physical expression of ideas assisting in the conception itself. She cites one designer saying, 'Putting it down makes one realize what one has overlooked' (p. 178). She suggests that designers describe 'methods of producing a combination of written notes and drawn images, thereby maintaining a degree of critical evaluation alongside spontaneous ideation, a kind of dual processing, with words and images working in tandem' (p. 178). Particular attention has been drawn to the role of drawing in the synthesis of new concepts through the juxtaposition and combination of remembered images by visualization (McKim, 1980). Schenk (1991) outlines how what we are terming autistic thinking is deliberately used by designers as they try to foster a climate of relaxed attention and 'appeared to be very casual in their initial uses of drawing in a job and established a reluctance to impose any sort of judgemental criteria on the drawings produced' (p. 178). Goldschmidt (1991) goes further. She suggests that designers deliberately oscillate between two modes of thinking. As she puts it, 'The designer is *seeing as* when he or she is using figural or gestalt argumentation while "sketch-thinking". When *seeing that*, the designer advances nonfigural arguments pertaining to the entity that is being designed. The process of sketching is a systematic dialectic between the "seeing as" and "seeing that" reasoning modalities' (p. 131).

Overall, we need to recognize a self-communication element in knowledge representation. As Wood (1993) puts it, 'cognition is never simply "amplified" or "externalized", but rather cognition is mediated through the external artefacts and collaborators such that the new cognitive system which is formed has a radically different character, structure and functionality than the cognition of the unsupported individual' (p. 2). We can consider the cognition that is taking place in a group context as 'distributed cognition', where we can consider collaborating people together with the artefacts that play a role in their activity as a single 'complex cognitive system' (Hutchins, 1991). Drawing on the work of Vygotsky (Cole et al., 1978), Wood (1993) notes that people's 'relationship with the world, with one another, and with themselves is altered through the use of "mediating artefacts" (products of culture, or "tools" in the widest sense). Things as simple as hammers, as complex as slide-rules, computers and encyclopaedias, or even shared cultural schemas and language itself, condense cultural knowledge and allow us to control our own and other's attention and memory' (p. 2). Wood (1992) explores the notion of 'mediating representations' in this process, more thoroughly.

People may develop 'internal' sequences of representations in order to work their way through a situation. In the context of facilitating the elicitation and communication of perceptions at work, we need to consider if it is possible to construct external (physical) representations of problems that serve as organizing structures that enable subsequent elicitation (or absorption, respectively) to take place more readily.

In essence, what is needed is some guidance on the suitability of alternative forms of physical representations for the dialectical elicitation and communication of different aspects of perception. This is, however, relatively unknown territory. Little research has been conducted on this issue. What we can do, at least, is consider what we know of the possible alternative forms of representation. We will then be in a position to consider the options that we have in endeavouring to promote management by perception. We shall be able to locate existing management practices in terms of the kinds of mental material, forms of thought, and types of thinking they are addressing, alongside the form(s) of representation they are using in transacting (sharing) this information within a group or organization.

Alternative physical representations

We have seen how there is a large range of alternative techniques to depict numerical information graphically. We also noted how there are potentially many other forms of information that we may wish to represent. In seeking to find a convenient classification scheme, a good starting point is an analysis of the alternative approaches that knowledge engineers use in eliciting knowledge from experts in the course of building knowledge-based (expert) systems. This could be appropriate, since these are the people that have had to grapple with coding all of the different forms of reasoning that experts use. Very large, complex, interdependent aspects of knowledge within particular domains have been coded. Turban (1988) identifies three major forms of representation that are used by knowledge engineers, in addition to formal logic (p. 399). These are production rules, semantic networks and frames. Production rules are statements with particular forms. They include 'If premise then conclusion' forms (for example, 'If your income is high then your chance of being audited by the Inland Revenue is

Table 3.1   *Representing knowledge through production rules (after Turban, 1988)*

If *premise* then *conclusion*
  e.g. If your income is high then your chance of being audited by the Inland Revenue is high

Conclusion if *premise*
  e.g. Your chance of being audited is high if your income is high

Inclusion of *else*
  e.g. If your income is high, then your chance of being audited is high, else your chance of being audited is lower

More complex rules
  e.g. If your income is high and your employer does not pay your tax as you earn (PAYE) then your chance of being audited is high

---

high'), 'Conclusion if premise' forms (for example, 'Your chance of being audited is high if your income is high'), 'Inclusion of else' forms (for example, 'If your income is high, then your chance of being audited is high, else your chance for being audited is lower') and more complex rules of each of these forms where 'if' statements are combined with 'and', 'or' and 'not' statements to describe more complex situations (for example, 'If your income is high and your employer does not pay your tax as you earn (PAYE), then your chance of being audited is high').

Turban (1988) notes that production rules have the advantage of simple syntax, are easy to understand and are easy to add to; but that it is hard to follow hierarchies of rules, and they are poor at representing structured descriptive knowledge. Table 3.1 illustrates alternative forms of production rules.

Semantic nets are a graphical means of depicting information. Figure 3.1 illustrates how 'nodes' are connected by 'links'. Each node is named. Each link bears the name of a relation. Turban (1988) notes how semantic networks have the advantage of being easy to follow hierarchically, have easy-to-trace associations and are flexible. Sometimes the meaning attached to nodes can be ambiguous, however.

Frames are data structures that include all the knowledge about a particular object, in a pre-defined manner. The frame is composed of slots (or fields) that contain specific information or statements relevant to that frame. Table 3.2 details an example frame for an object in this case a room. Turban (1988) suggests that frames have expressive power, are easy to set up and add slots to. They are difficult to use in inferences, that is, it can be hard to see how particular objects might affect each other.

It would seem that representations that capture fixed set relationships (for example shared characteristics of dogs, cats and other mammals, as might be expressed in a frame) may fare less well in capturing unique considerations (as might be represented in a semantic net). Neither of these forms is as effective at conveying causal relationships as a production rule representation. In part, however, the preference for particular representations of

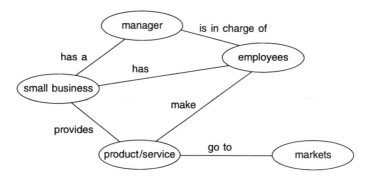

Figure 3.1   *An example of a semantic net representation of knowledge*

Table 3.2   *An example of a 'frame' representation of knowledge*

Object	Room
Slots	**Entries (values)**
Walls	4
Ceiling	1, sloping
Floor	1, level
Doors	2, opening inwards
Windows	3
Lights	4, fluorescent tubes

knowledge that knowledge engineers have is determined by the ease with which each form of representation lends itself to programming. If we pause to think about causal links, we may feel that a decision tree would be a useful representation. And it is, for us humans to follow. It does not provide much of value to a computer (specifically an inference engine), however. While these basic forms of knowledge representation tell us something of the basic nature of different forms of mental material, and demonstrate that large domains of knowledge can be captured and represented, it is to the world of human factors research that we must look for guidance on effectiveness of representations in communication with humans.

Novick and Hmelo (1994) have shown how it is important for a person to have a good mental representation for understanding and solving problems. They examined how different forms of symbolic representations (for example matrices, hierarchical depictions, networks and part-whole depictions) can come to be used by people in the course of 'constructing' information, but note that we have not established 'the structural characteristics of problems that determine the most appropriate type of symbolic representations to use. This in turn will depend on a theory of the interrelations and distinctions among various types of representations' (p. 1315). Bernsen (1994) also notes how 'a principled basis for analysing arbitrary input/

Table 3.3   *Bernsen's (1994) taxonomy of representations*

Category	Well-known atomic type
Language	Hieroglyphs Gestural language Everyday spoken language Written letters, words, numerals and special-purpose notations, e.g. music Touch letters, e.g. Braille
Pictures of something	Pure diagrams, maps, cartoons Photography Pure animated diagrams
Non-visual 'pictures' or analogue representations	Music Touch sequences
Graphs	1D, 2D or 3D graphs Animated (evolving) Sound graphs, e.g. Geiger counter
Representations which need a conventionally assigned meaning in order to represent something	Diagrams consisting of geometrical elements Sound signals Touch signals
Explicitly rendered structurings of information	Frames, table grids, trees

output modality types and combinations as to their capabilities of information representation and exchange is still lacking' (p. 347). In the paper, he goes on to propose a 'common sense classification' which consists of six categories of alternative forms of representation. Table 3.3 is a listing of the categories and the well-known instances within each category.

Bernsen's classification highlights several important dimensions that need to be considered in classifying representations. First, that modalities other than sound and vision have a clear role in communication. Secondly, that we can usefully distinguish between static and dynamic representations. Thirdly, we can distinguish between representations that utilize some form of language system, and those that do not. Fourthly, that there is a dimension of abstraction in representations that are analogues of situations. The classification was developed with human–computer interaction in mind. It therefore does not highlight each of the human physical senses. There are many ways of classifying the senses. For our purposes, we could perhaps usefully distinguish between the isolated reception of visual, auditory, taste and smell information; and a more integrated use of cutaneous, visual and kinaesthetic information in the course of detecting movement.

Given the great emphasis that human beings place on visual communication (and the emphasis in this book on imagistic representation), it is useful to try to develop a finer-grain classification of visual representations. Table 3.4 presents a classification that offers some illumination on the

Table 3.4   *A classification of visual representations*

Basic symbolic and categorization representations
Basic symbolic systems
– text (i.e. prose written report)
– numerical (i.e. raw numerical data and equations (mathematical models))
Categorization systems
– lists (unstructured)
– lists (sequenced on one dimension)
– matrices and other tabular frameworks

Representations that highlight abstract characteristics along specific dimensions
Charts (including pie charts)
Graphs (i.e. scaled consecutive values)
– two-dimensional graphs
– three-dimensional graphs
– radial graphs (e.g. team role)

Graphical abstract representations of complex relationships
Process diagrams
– flowcharts
– critical path diagrams
– soft systems methodology root definitions
Network diagrams
– informal
  • mind maps
  • rich pictures
– formal
  • semantic networks
  • tree charts
  • cognitive maps
Venn diagrams (overlapping circles)

Representations that emphasize wholeness and integrity
Visual analogies/metaphors (e.g. forcefield analysis, fishbone diagrams)
Static images
– geographical maps
– diagrams, imaging, drawings and photographs
– physical models (mock-ups etc.)
Dynamic representations
– animations
– film/video

---

contribution of alternative visual representations in communicating features of data. It will be used to show how some of the apparently subtle distinctions between the examples listed can figure quite strongly when we consider the transaction of different kinds of mental material, forms of thought and types of thinking. It is a useful basis to differentiate between the approaches of those involved in management development and management science. There is an implication of passivity in the term 'description'. It is as if there is a real world out there and the choice of representation is a matter of selecting the means to convey the information. Representation plays a role as a 'construction' of a problem. Each form of representation is a way of framing a problem. Each invokes particular types of thinking. Each highlights different facets of information about an issue, not *the* information.

This whole area seems to be underresearched. Some speculations about the effects of constructing issues in terms of the representations in this framework are outlined below. Finally, the proposed framework can be used to assist in a discussion of the role that re-representation of information (by stepping through several alternative visual representations) implies for types of thinking. While our understanding of the principles that affect the communication and reception of information through intermediate representations is limited, the potential of alternative forms of representation is likely to become more of an issue as we attempt to work with more diverse aspects of perceptions.

The effects of constructing issues from the perspectives of particular physical representations

When we think about the use of physical representations to communicate information at work, we see how much of the process takes place through written memos, reports etc. These documents are written in the classic sequential prose form. Language, of course, has evolved to such a point now that it can communicate extremely subtle distinctions between objects and events. Prose 'takes us with it' along a particular perspective. Using an analogy of a map, however, we may sometimes benefit from seeing 'the big picture', as well as a detailed depiction of each area. In textual accounts, therefore, we may find it useful to have some grasp of the overall structure of the piece, the key arguments, the main instances/variations. We may highlight bullet points.

On closer inspection, the alternative visual representations detailed in Table 3.4 echo the different types of thinking that were highlighted in Chapter 2. Categorization systems emphasize separation, the distinction between elements. Representations that highlight abstract characteristics along specific dimensions emphasize a static comparison type of location thinking. Representations that highlight complex relationships emphasize a systems thinking approach. Representations that highlight wholeness and integrity place more emphasis on plurality seeking. They show how events can be interpreted from alternative frames. Some of the specific ways in which different representations support thinking are detailed below.

Categorization systems

Referring to Table 3.4, we can see how the expressed use of a categorization system, such as an unstructured list (say, of key issues), can help us in getting the big picture. Lists can be abstracted from a piece of text. They tend to focus attention on key concepts and then on any patterns in those concepts, so that we identify concepts of a particular type. We then list the instances of the particular type. For example, if we have been describing telework occupations we might provide an unstructured list to indicate that:

the telework occupations included:

- translation
- design
- planning
- social work
- telephone counselling
- inspection
- legal work
- accountancy
- financial advice
- engineering.

We may go further. We may want to add some additional categorical information. We may structure the list so that the items are sequenced in a particular way. This tells us not just that the items are all instances of a particular type, but something about how they relate to each other. We may therefore go on to list the telework occupations in terms of their relative utilization of numbers of employees, or perhaps in terms of the 'level' of technology they each demand and so on. In both forms of lists, of course, we can repeat the process to reveal subcategories and then 'order' items within each of those.

What we are seeing with categorization is an approach to 'tighten' concepts, to establish 'separation' between them. Categorization is measurement. As Babbie and Halley (1995) put it, it is a 'transition . . . from sometimes ambiguous mental images to precise, empirical measures. Whereas we often speak casually about such concepts as prejudice, social class, and liberalism in everyday conversation, social scientists must be more precise in their use of these terms' (p. 16). Social scientists have distinguished between different degrees (levels) of measurement. Putting concepts into categories is to name them. It is a nominal level of measurement. More sophisticated sequencing of concepts is referred to as using, ordinal, interval and ratio levels of measurement. Each of these levels can be distinguished in terms of the inferences that can be made about the interrelationships between the items. If we are able to claim that a particular sequencing has particular mathematical properties, then we read more into the information from our knowledge of mathematics, for example if we have expressed the numbers of employees in each telework occupational category, we can make statements such as 'twice as many people work in financial advice as in translation'. On the other hand, if we have a less rigorous level of measurement, such as relative 'degree' of technology involved, we may only be able to rank the occupations, but not be able to make assertions about one occupation having twice the level of technology as another. It is clear that tight, rigorous, reliable and valid labelling and sequencing of concepts are the essence of categorization systems.

When we consider the three basic types of thinking we have outlined, we can see how a spontaneous and progressive listing of subcategories of something could be conducted in a brainstorming fashion. The process would benefit from an open, autistic way of thinking. A subsequent closer inspection of the nominal categories might highlight how the basis of a comprehensive listing is there, but that a reasoning type of thinking is needed now to generate comprehensive, valid and reliable categorizations.

Further insights can be gained into particular concepts in categorical lists when we combine two or more alternative bases of categorization. We could put our list of telework occupations into a matrix or table to show both the number of employees and the level of technology for each telework occupation. This of course gives us more information. It tells us about the relationship between numbers of employees and level of technology.

We have focused on the 'translation' of text into categories, but the same issues apply when we are dealing with numerical data. The process of enumeration is, in itself, a categorization. It is a way of thinking. When our reports have numerical information they imply a sense of rigour. They invite attention to the figures, and particular forms of 'interpretation' or 'inferencing'. A lot can be 'buried' in vast displays of raw data. Particular features can be highlighted by showing how particular variables interrelate. An equation or formula is a particular way of expressing such relationships.

Categorization is an important feature of thinking. It is central within personal construct psychology, and hence within our consideration of semantic information. The category systems that people use in their minds are important to us. We need to develop depictions that capture the 'nature' or 'feel' of these conceptions. Inevitably, we will fail in capturing the true uniqueness and subtlety of a person's conception, with all of their personal ways of hierarchically classifying concepts and links with other concepts. We may have to be content with using multiple sets of representations to yield an acceptable approximation of a person's semantic network. In the course of recording people's category systems, we may note interesting patterns across people. We may identify categories ourselves. While these are not the primary data, they will help us in understanding the operation of particular individual category systems. The language of personality preferences (for example Jungian functions such as thinking, feeling, intuition and sensation), outlined earlier provides additional illumination. We often need our classifications to be 'grounded' in the basic information we are working with. We need to see the category systems (construct systems, in personal construct psychology's terms) and then spot any patterns that may provide additional information.

While we may often try to 'read' people, 'on the hoof', we have seen how this degree of real-time reflection on the behaviour of others can be difficult. Much of the potential information passes us by. Management by perception asks managers to take the time to consider the category systems that people are using, carefully, and then identify any meaningful pattern. This process may be undertaken collaboratively with the participants concerned, or independently by one or more of the parties. In both cases there is a useful set of good practice guidelines that have been developed by social science researchers. Dey (1993), for example, provides a very useful presentation of approaches to qualitative data analysis, including content analysis, and gives effective tutoring in the ways that prospective 'categories' of information can be formulated and 'tested out' in ongoing, iterative interaction with the data. We need a means of summarizing large volumes of text (written reports) and language (free conversation) to reveal the category systems of interest. Modern computer software can help in this process. The personal thinking and social process of identifying and considering categories in people's minds have a distinct nature, and benefit from the use of appropriate intermediate representations.

Promoting a more comprehensive analysis of categorizations can make a useful contribution to our understanding and sharing of perceptions. As we noted earlier, however, in discussing the contribution of information science to considering representations, particular representations can highlight particular facets of the data, but in so doing may deflect attention away from other (otherwise apparent) facets. Categorization overall is a way of working with concepts. It can reveal much. But as a way of thinking, by definition, it denudes, denies fuzziness and obscures overlap. We will need to complement categorizing with other forms of representations to support thought processes.

Graphical abstract depictions along specific dimensions

The remaining three forms of visual representations in Table 3.4 (that is, graphical abstract depictions along specific dimensions, graphical abstract representations of complex relationships and visual depictions that emphasize wholeness and integrity) may tend to place more emphasis on imagistic thought. They utilize a language of images to capture and convey properties of data.

Various options for charting and graphing were contrasted by Sparrow (1989). This empirical study compared the effectiveness of spreadsheet tables, pie charts, bar charts, vertically stacked bar charts, line graphs and multiple line graphs in promoting the consideration of particular features of some business sales data. Specifically, the respective sales patterns of four products over a ten-year period were depicted. The materials given to participants were designed to be informationally equivalent. The experiment in effect required the participants to compute several different aspects of information from the data. The aspects of information required were information about specifics (for example, 'How much did Product 1 sell in 1984?'), limits (for example, 'In which year were Product 3's sales at their lowest?'), conjunctions (for example, 'In which year did Product 2 first sell less than Product 3?'), accumulation (for example, 'In which year were overall sales highest?'), trends (for example, 'Which product's sales would you describe as generally rising?') and proportion (for example, 'What proportion of Product 3's sales was made in 1977?').

It was clear from the study that different basic forms of representation influenced the recall of information abstracted from the data. There was no form of display which proved universally to be the most appropriate. The results indicated that a spreadsheet page is very effective in conveying information about specifics, trends and accumulation. It is especially poor at drawing attention to conjunction. A stacked bar chart is inadvisable for the abstraction of specifics, trends or proportions. Furthermore, the perception of accumulation across the dimension that has not been accumulated in the configuration of the representation is very poor. For example, when the diagram represents accumulation across the different products' sales, it is ineffective in conveying overall sales of a particular product. It is, however, a very effective means of conveying accumulation when the diagram has been appropriately configured. A stacked bar chart seems to be a more appropriate means than pie charts and line graphs for conveying the limits of a data set. Bar charts are especially bad at conveying proportion. While they are better at conveying limits than are line graphs, they do not seem to be a more appropriate representation than other forms of display for any aspect of data display.

Pie charts are inappropriate for conveying most features of data, with the exception of proportion. Separate line graphs are a poor means of conveying information concerning limits, conjunctions or accumulation. They fared quite well in the abstraction of proportional information. Representing data on a multiple line graph (where the separate lines for each product are all presented on the same picture) is the most appropriate means of conveying conjunction. It is also an effective means of conveying trends and limits, and the most effective non-tabular means of conveying specifics. It is less appropriate for conveying information about accumulation and proportion.

Overall, the study showed that we need to recognize the strengths and weaknesses of alternative graphical means of displaying information when we are seeking to communicate it effectively. Furthermore, the study confirmed that the promotion of a particular form of interpretation or analysis of data can be at the expense of potential insights. Different representations are promoting different ways of thinking about data. In sharing perceptions, we may want deliberately to consider the facets revealed by each of different graphical representations. 'Cycling through' a comprehensive set of the alternatives will reveal more about the perceptions than will any single representation. There are many detailed texts (for example Tufte, 1983; Bowman, 1991) that can be consulted to find the wide range of graphs and charts that can be used within business communication. Figure 3.2 shows several of the alternative graphical forms of representation that can be used.

	A	B	C	D	E	F
1	Sales figures					
2						
3	Year	Product 1	Product 2	Product 3	Product 4	Total
4						
5	Year 1977	75	130	10	120	335
6	Year 1978	75	120	20	110	325
7	Year 1979	80	110	30	120	340
8	Year 1980	90	105	40	125	360
9	Year 1981	105	97	50	115	367
10	Year 1982	110	95	60	120	385
11	Year 1983	100	90	70	110	370
12	Year 1984	90	80	80	115	365
13	Year 1985	80	70	90	115	355
14	Year 1986	70	60	100	120	350
15						
16	Total	875	957	550	1170	3552

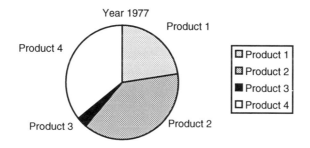

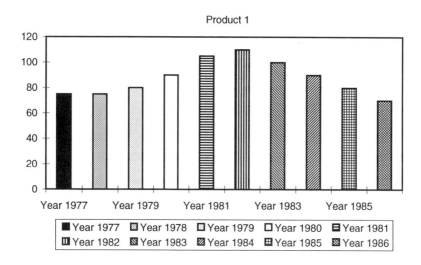

Figure 3.2   *Alternative graphical forms of representation*

Graphical abstract representations of complex relationships

We have seen how concepts can be viewed in their relation to each other along single dimensions. We have seen how separate categorizations of objects can be aligned to reveal more of their properties. Objects can be related to each other in more complex ways. Again, we learn different things about objects (concepts) when we depict their interrelationships in particular ways. There are a set of representations that are used to depict physical processes. Flow charts show the sequence of connection between different elements of a 'system'. Critical path diagrams show the inter-relationship between separate elements and indicate a particular route to an overall goal. Putting things into a process interrelationship gives us new insights. Considering the time or other resources invoked by particular 'objects' and the degree of parallelism that is attainable in their arrangement adds another dimension to our insight.

The activity of searching for a set of systems interrelationships between 'objects' is again a particular thought process. It is the essence of soft systems methodology, for example. There, a set of activities are taken together, 'in such a way that the connected set makes a purposeful whole' (Checkland and Scholes, 1990, p. 24). Elements are marshalled into an interrelationship that constitutes a particular transformation process. A public library, for example, can be seen as a set of transformation processes. Certain 'inputs' are transformed into certain 'outputs'. An entity in one state is transformed into an entity in another state. So, for example, a local library may be viewed as a transformation process whereby a local need for information and entertainment from books, records etc. is transformed to a state where that need is met. Elements can be put into interrelationships that constitute basic systems if they are viewed in terms of there being 'customers' (the victims or beneficiaries of a transformation process), 'actors' (those who do the transformation process), and owners (those who could stop the transformation process), operating in a 'transformation process' ('T', a particular conversion of input to output), within particular 'environmental constraints' (elements outside the system which it takes as given) that is desired, because within a particular *Weltanschauung* (worldview) it is considered meaningful (p. 35).

The consideration of a set of elements operating in this manner as a system could be conducted so that the fundamental purpose of their inter-relationships could be made explicit, that is, the 'root definition' as a '"system to do X to Y in order to achieve Z", where the T will be the means Y, Z is related to the owners' longer term aims, and there must be an arguable connection which makes Y an appropriate means for doing X' (p. 36). We could use soft systems methodology to construct a view of the term 'human resource management', for example, that would highlight its root definition. As Checkland and Scholes (1990) note, the models are 'not models "of" real-world activity, they are models "relevant to" debating it' (p. 309). It is important to note how a particular physical representation would make a particular conception explicit, and how the construction of such a representation *is* the use of a particular thought process. Examples of process diagrams are illustrated in Figure 3.3.

We can also utilize variants of interlinking representations without invoking a coherent purpose, as in informal network diagrams. These 'maps' are loose depictions of some interrelationships between concepts. They can be used spontaneously to support and cue the generation of additional facets. This form of 'radiant thinking', where initial ideas are outlined and further ideas are depicted as 'radiating' from them, is at the heart of mind-mapping (Buzan, 1989; 1993). The simplicity of the means of capturing/recording ideas goes some way to ensuring that autistic thinking is maintained. One can see that as one tries to consider the possible 'location' of a new concept that has struck one's mind, a rapid and intuitive positioning may be better than a prolonged pause to consider the matter explicitly. In the latter instance one would be drawn into a reasoning type of thinking, and might find it hard to return to a more open intuitive mode.

Small pictures, including hand-drawn sketches and icons, can be used within network diagrams. They are a legitimate part of a mind map. They are also advocated by Checkland and Scholes (1990) for the early stages of thinking within soft systems methodology. There, they are referred to as 'rich pictures'. The contribution that the drawn visual images make towards the transaction of perceptions is discussed in the section below on 'visual depictions of real-world characteristics'. The contribution of a network diagram lies primarily in its communication of the spatial relationships between elements. The structure of sets of interrelationships is apparent. The overall complexity of interrelationships is conveyed. The differential degrees of complexity of interrelationships within each of the various 'subareas' is also explicit. 'Core' or 'central' considerations can be perceived in network diagrams.

There are, in a sense, some rules implicit within all forms of network diagram. The initial central positioning of a node, and the efforts at trying to lay out branches in a balanced way, are intuitively sensed. Indeed, Buzan (1989) suggests some 'mind-mapping laws' (p. 95) and gives some important advice on technique (for example, using emphasis, being clear) and layout (for example, using hierarchy, using numerical order) in the 'laws and recommendations' presented in his later work (Buzan, 1993, pp. 93–4).

More formal network diagrams impose additional rules concerning their construction. A semantic network, as we illustrated in Figure 3.1, has a requirement that each link between any pair of nodes has a name. This name conveys *the* nature of the interrelationship. This is useful since it gives a clearer indication of the specifics of interrelationships. There is an assumption that the pair of nodes *only* interrelate in that one way. In fact, of course it is possible for a pair of concepts to have more than one sense of interrelationship. In Figure 3.1, for example, there are many other relationships between 'manager' and 'employees' than 'is in charge of'. We may include link terms such as 'supports', 'respects' or 'understands', for

Flow chart

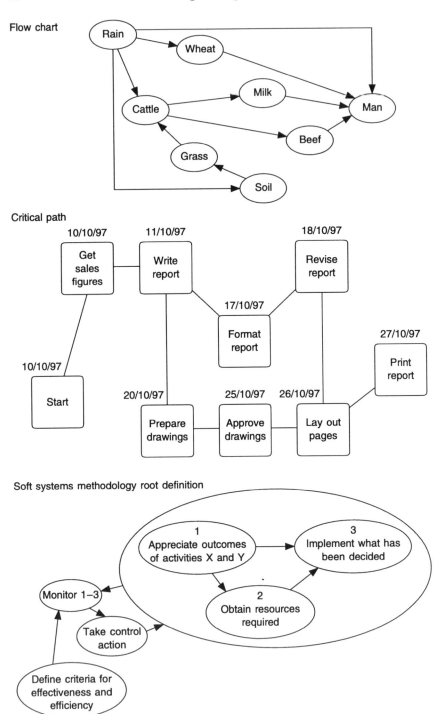

Figure 3.3   *Examples of process diagrams*

example. Indeed, each of those terms highlights a further potential implicit 'rule' in a network diagram. Some diagrams have an implicit 'direction' in the relationship (link) term. All of the examples given concerning the relationship between manager and employees are written as relationships 'from' managers 'to' employees. We can, of course, consider relationships that go in the opposite direction, for example employees 'socially construct a leadership function' for a manager.

It can be useful temporarily to restrict the term used as a link in a network diagram. For example, a map can be drawn of only those nodes that could fulfil the criteria of the link term 'includes'. This would, for example, give us information about the set relationships between a set of concepts. Alternatively, we may restrict our map to nodes with the relationship 'affects'. This would highlight a different perspective. Even more subtle distinctions are revealed if one contrasts the map that uses the term 'varies with' as opposed to the map that uses 'affects' as the link term. Important issues concerning causality would be highlighted. Another powerful link term to focus on is 'precedes'. This can place concepts into a temporal or functional sequence. A more familiar and stylized version of a network diagram is a tree diagram. Here, only simple hierarchical relationships are depicted.

Some of the impacts of the differences in 'rules' associated with various versions of network diagrams are highlighted in Chapter 5. One important variant is noteworthy here. Eden's development of a comprehensive networking approach, 'cognitive mapping' (for example Eden, 1988), means that 'cause maps' can be constructed to highlight how a superordinate node is 'caused' by a particular configuration of subordinate nodes. The approach places a high emphasis on reasoning and causal thinking, and is used extensively in strategic management, where an overall 'aim' can often be articulated, and real value obtained from discussion of the means to achieve the aim. Eden and his colleagues have provided a body of work on means of identifying particular features of causal maps and issues in their transaction (for example Eden et al., 1992). The different forms of network diagram are illustrated in Figure 3.4.

Different considerations in the interrelationships between concepts can be conveyed through Venn diagrams. These are a powerful means of displaying 'overlap' between concepts. Figure 3.5 illustrates a set of relationships using this form of representation.

Representations that emphasize wholeness and integrity

The visual depictions outlined up to this point have all drawn attention to particular facets of the concepts being considered, for example the facet of a manager–employee relationship of 'being in charge of' in Figure 3.1. There is a loss of a sense of holism when one depicts things with some forms of visual representation. As we have seen, this may mean that a more integrated perspective may be missed by those engaged in communication. A

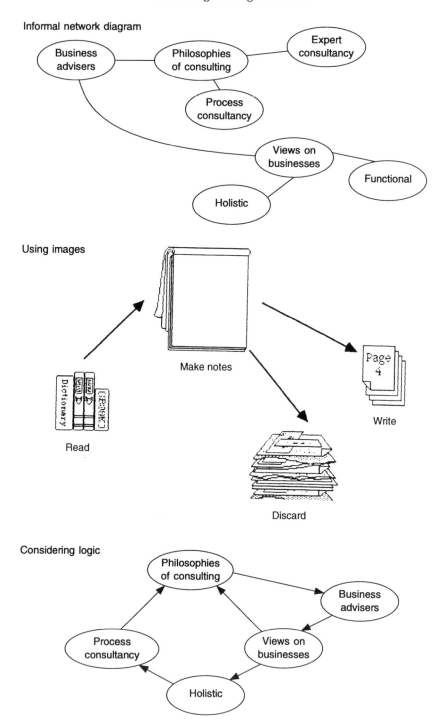

Informal network diagram

Using images

Read

Make notes

Discard

Write

Considering logic

Figure 3.4   *Different forms of network diagram*

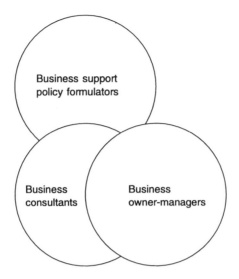

The views held by business consultants about business support
needs have more in common with those held by business owner-
managers than those of business support policy-makers. Business
consultants' views have more in common with business support
policy-makers' views than do business owner-managers'.

Figure 3.5   *An example Venn diagram*

host of graphic conventions have evolved that can be used to convey the
overall sense of a situation or person.

VISUAL ANALOGIES/METAPHORS   A variety of representations can be used
as visual analogies/metaphors. Here certain properties of concepts are highlighted by juxtaposing the concepts in a way that parallels a particular well-
known relationship between concepts from another context. So, for example,
two sets of concepts may be depicted as on either side of a 'balance', or set of
scales. Concepts may be depicted in a circular relationship, to imply a
continuous cycling process. Other commonly used representations include
fishbone diagrams, where contributory factors are positioned along a central
spine, even though they may be abstract considerations and not 'operate' in
any strict sense as a process. Similarly, a 'forcefield analysis' depicts concepts
as 'forces'. Those that are combining to produce movement in one direction
are 'set against' those that are acting in an opposing direction.

There are more creative uses of visual metaphor that can be used in
representations. Particular concepts can be ascribed personalities, physical
forms (such as animals) etc., and placed in arenas where a particular form
of interaction is characteristic (for example circus, race etc.). The subtleties
and multiplicity of interplay of the entities in the parallel setting can
therefore be captured, and can give a very rich set of insights into the issues

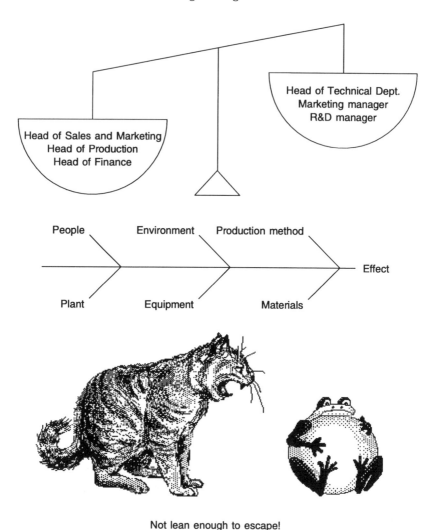

Head of Technical Dept.
Marketing manager
R&D manager

Head of Sales and Marketing
Head of Production
Head of Finance

People   Environment   Production method

Effect

Plant   Equipment   Materials

Not lean enough to escape!

Figure 3.6   *Some example visual metaphors*

in hand. So, for example, fellow team members may be depicted as particular lions, with the team leader as lion-tamer. The 'reactions' of all of the
team members can be considered as a parallel to the reactions in the circus
ring, for example 'Jim is like a "lion", reluctantly going along with the
tamer, but always on the lookout to get him!'. Some example visual metaphors are illustrated in Figure 3.6.

STATIC IMAGES   Ferguson (1977) notes that the developments in graphic
arts over the last 500 years 'have lent system and order to the materials of
non-verbal thought' (p. 197). He outlines the impact of the understanding of

a means for pictorially representing three-dimensional objects (perspective drawings) in the fifteenth century. He goes on to highlight the emergence of subsequent innovations such as an exploded view, an orthographic projection and an isometric view. As a result of these developments we have a sophisticated language of visual communication. A geographical map can capture the overall relative spatial positioning of places far more effectively than a textual account. In narrating an account of an incident, a map of the scene, with the positioning of key players and depictions of movement, is an effective representation. Diagrams, as noted above, have evolved conventions concerning viewing angles and means of depiction that convey a sense of a formal analysis of the object in question. Diagrams tend to use a more restricted and stylized set of techniques to depict something than do drawings. There is often a more linear feel to them.

Modern technologies allow objects and events to be 'imaged' in particular ways. An infra-red image conveys information about objects (heat) that is not otherwise perceptible by human beings. An X-ray slide highlights solidity. Magnification provides particular insights. Imaging depicts information that has been amassed through an extension of the boundaries of our senses. It has an aura of science and fact about it. It requires an education in the language being used.

The extent and means by which a drawing can capture a 'true' likeness of a situation/person can vary (Twyman, 1985). Images can be highly stereotyped and simplified renditions (such as an icon). Consider for example an icon of a telephone, used on a telephone kiosk or on a sign pointing to a kiosk. Alternatively, they can use elaborate drawing techniques to capture shading, texture etc. to create a very accurate impression of an object or scene. In human factors research, the guidelines or rules for the composition of representations focus on the specific use to which the receiver is putting the information. Peripheral or irrelevant details are eliminated. A sense of wholeness is still preserved, however. Drawings, in the main, are used to communicate the essence of something. The term 'elegance' has meaning in visual communication. As Tufte (1983) puts it, 'Graphical elegance is often found in simplicity of design and complexity of data' (p. 9). Drawings can have archetypal qualities. They can 'feel' right, and resonate within us. A particular image may strike us in a vivid way. We may sense a deeper conviction within us when we see certain images. They elicit a feeling of certainty or assuredness that the image is 'it'. We may hear ourselves saying, 'yes, that's it exactly!'. While these may be powerful emotions, we should recognize that such images may not be capturing any deep 'truth'. Nor, indeed, may they necessarily be expressing any archetype from the collective unconscious. They may simply be excellent, succinct and elegant renditions, as they are defined in one's particular culture. As Wetherall (1994) puts it, 'it is often at these points of "natural" recognition of deep truth that we are most gripped by cultural and ideological practice' (p. 508). Drawings are not objective or neutral, however. They highlight particular things and ignore or obscure others.

The notion of realism is highlighted in the use of photographs for communication. Berger (1989) notes that, unlike paintings, drawings and sketches, 'Photographs do not translate from appearances. They quote them' (p. 96). The statement that 'the camera never lies' would afford photography a status that suggests that it is not impressionistic but is objective. Ball and Smith (1992) examine the use of photographs in social science research. Their discussion highlights the key issues concerning photography and realism. They note that aesthetics, posing and ambiguous scenes all undermine this claim.

Overall, it is clear that different forms of static image invoke different thinking. Representations that are powerful and impressionistic may convey different things to those that are colder and more formal, for example. A caricature can be a useful means of communicating the impact of a particular feature of a situation. A discussion of a plan of a proposed new office layout focuses attention on particular features of work life.

The issues that have been discussed concerning two-dimensional representations of objects apply when we consider three-dimensional representations. While they play a much smaller part in the overall volume of visual communication, they too operate to a language. The abstracting of the essence of processes is what seems to be at the heart of the matter. Ferguson (1977) records how models were used in the sixteenth century to consider the order of assembly or logistics of manufacture, as models for machines throughout the seventeenth and eighteenth centuries. A physical mock-up (model) can provide even more information about the holistic nature of something than can a two-dimensional representation. Such representations can reveal a feature of a process that might not otherwise be appreciated from within the context. The 'stepping out from the "real" world' and 'control' over the actions of a model can provide valuable insights. Asking people to create or observe physical models is therefore a means of invoking a particular perspective and form of thinking.

DYNAMIC REPRESENTATIONS   An additional dimension can be introduced into the discussion at this point, the notion of change in state. Static images can capture particular moments in time, or even 'before' and 'after' depictions. The dynamics of a situation are represented more effectively with a visual representation that is dynamic. Details of the nature of the alterations in the change process are revealed. Animated graphs (such as evolving graphs) and animated diagrams can give abstract processes a more tangible form. Animated drawings can appear quite lifelike and yet create reactions in situations, on behalf of people or objects, that have not actually occurred. The dynamics of situations in a time–space continuum are an illuminating perspective. Wilcocks and Saunders (1994), for example, show how the concept of recursion in computer programming can be taught more effectively with the aid of a visual animation. It may be that the use of animation supports implicit learning (and thus tacit feel) differentially. The natural form of these 'graphic' experiences may lead to implicit learning of basic patterns that textual representations may obscure (Rieber, 1996).

The evidence of a film, can be hard to deny. What actually happened is recreated on the screen. While it is possible to mislead through film editing, there is a real potential value in giving people opportunities to reflect on information that is captured on film. As a result it plays an important role in improving the physical nature of things. For example, film may provide security information that indicates prospective security measures. It may highlight certain features of interpersonal dealings that can be addressed. Despite being one of the most comprehensive means of representing events, it is not a sufficient basis, in and of itself. The scene is viewed from a particular vantage point. It may be different from the perspective of particular participants. Inferences about the thinking (including feelings) behind the actions of participants may be flawed. Additional means of representing this form of information may be required.

The relationships between representations and kinds of mental material, forms of thought and types of thinking

The knowledge that somebody has about something can be communicated more effectively when appropriate representations are used. In management, we must learn to see instances where a particular representation can make a useful and timely contribution. We need to remind ourselves that representations can also play a key role in the elicitation process. A person can be helped to gain self-insight by using particular representations to construct their thoughts as they seek to capture them.

Some broad guidelines concerning the relationship between perception and physical representations are apparent. A spirit of active experimentation is likely to yield the true potential, however. Simply trying to find out in practice whether a particular representation cues or conveys a different facet of perception is likely to pay dividends. An indication of some of the prospective general 'strengths' of different representations is provided in Tables 3.5 and 3.6. It is at this stage in our understanding of the issues involved at best a set of educated guesses, at worst an intuitive feel for the 'fit' between techniques, kinds of mental material, forms of thought and types of thinking. Readers may want to consider the tables at length, and explore the implications of various postulations in the entries. Some overall impressions are outlined below.

Each form of representation has been given a score (of one, two or three asterisks) concerning its potential for addressing particular facets of perception. A cursory examination of Tables 3.5 and 3.6 indicates that some representations would have a higher overall score than others. We can see, therefore, that some techniques are more general purpose and others provide more limited (specific) contributions. A comparison of the high-scoring representations indicates that they have different profiles of areas of

Table 3.5 *Some postulated strengths of particular visual representations: representations for different kinds of knowledge*

	Kinds of mental material				
	Semantic	Episodic	Skilled	Tacit	Unconscious
Basic symbolic and categorization representations					
Basic symbolic systems					
– text (i.e. prose written report)	*	***	**	*	*
– numerical (i.e. raw numerical data and equations (mathematical models))	**				
Categorization systems					
– lists (unstructured)	**		*	*	
– lists (sequenced on one dimension)	***		*	*	
– matrices and other tabular frameworks	***		*	*	
Representations that highlight abstract characteristics along specific dimensions					
Charts	*		*	*	
Graphs (i.e. scaled consecutive values)					
– two-dimensional graphs	**		*	*	
– three-dimensional graphs	**		*	*	
– radial graphs	**		*	*	
Graphical abstract representations of complex relationships					
Process diagrams					
– flowcharts	**	**	**	*	
– critical path diagrams	**	**	*	*	
– soft systems methodology root definitions	***	*	**	**	
Network diagrams					
– informal					
• mind maps	*	*	**	**	*
• rich pictures	*	*	**	**	*
– formal					
• semantic networks	**	*	**	*	
• tree charts	**	*			
• cognitive maps	***	**	**	*	
Venn diagrams	**		*	*	
Representations that emphasize wholeness and integrity					
Visual analogies/metaphors	**	**	**	***	**
Static images					
– geographical maps	**	**			
– diagrams, imaging, drawings and photographs	***	***	**	***	***
– physical models (mock-ups etc.)	***	***	*	**	*
Dynamic representations					
– animations	***	**	***	**	*
– film/video	***	**	***	**	

Table 3.6 *Some postulated strengths of particular visual representations: representations for different forms of thought and types of thinking*

	Forms of thought		Types of thinking		
	Propositional	Imagistic	Autistic	Reasoning	Mood
Basic symbolic and categorization representations					
Basic symbolic systems					
– text (i.e. prose written report)	***		*	**	*
– numerical (i.e. raw numerical data and equations (mathematical models))	***			***	
Categorization systems					
– lists (unstructured)	**		*	**	
– lists (sequenced on one dimension)	***		*	***	
– matrices and other tabular frameworks	***		*	***	
Representations that highlight abstract characteristics along specific dimensions					
Charts	*	*	*	*	
Graphs (i.e. scaled consecutive values)					
– two-dimensional graphs	*	**	*	*	
– three-dimensional graphs	*	**	*	*	
– radial graphs	*	**	*	*	
Graphical abstract representations of complex relationships					
Process diagrams					
– flowcharts	*	**	*	*	
– critical path diagrams	**	**	*	**	
– soft systems methodology root definitions	**	**	*	***	*
Network diagrams					
– informal					
• mind maps	**	**	**	**	**
• rich pictures	**	**	**	**	**
– formal					
• semantic networks	***	*	*	***	*
• tree charts	**	**	*	**	
• cognitive maps	***	**	*	***	
Venn diagrams	**	**	*	**	*
Representations that emphasize wholeness and integrity					
Visual analogies/metaphors	**	***	***	**	**
Static images					
– geographical maps	**	**		**	
– diagrams, imaging, drawings and photographs	*	***	**	*	***
– physical models (mock-ups etc.)	*	***	*	**	*
Dynamic representations					
– animations	*	**	*	**	**
– film/video	*	**	*	**	**

strength. The *a priori* distinction between representations that emphasize propositional thinking and those that emphasize imagistic thinking is evident. The relationship between representations that promote imagistic thoughts and those that support autistic thinking is apparent. This is true, in particular, for those representations that permit expressiveness. In general, skilled, tacit and unconscious mental material is accessed better through representations that emphasize imagistic thought.

While reasoning as a type of thinking is supported in some way by all representations, the specific nature of the reasoning process will vary with the use of different representations, as has been outlined above. The specific contribution to semantic understanding will also vary. The potential for insights into episodic memories are evident in the techniques that emphasize wholeness and integrity. Skills are surfaced less by those representations that focus on categorization, that is, propositional categorization systems and their graphical counterparts that represent abstract depictions along specific dimensions. They are revealed through representations that capture dynamics and processes. Everyday actions can be caught accurately in dynamic representations, and will evidence skill and tacit feel. Tacit feel is more elusive. It is captured well with representations that emphasize holism. Further insights can also be obtained from representations that permit expressiveness, particularly of an analogical or metaphorical kind. Unconscious interpretations can most effectively be represented with expressive and symbolic representations. Finally, insights into the impact of mood are considered to be better represented by imagistic representations. Some insights can be obtained from network diagrams that could highlight the prevailing 'mindset' in the constructs a person details. It can be seen in expressive representations. It can be observed in accurate representations of the dynamics of interpersonal behaviour.

It is clear that the processes of eliciting and transacting perceptions can benefit from the explicit support provided by appropriate physical representations. Individuals and groups can prospectively benefit from being guided in their use of comprehensive sets of representations. People may not, in general, be familiar with guiding their self-reflection and communication, with different kinds of mental material, alternative forms of thought and types of thinking, in mind. They can benefit from utilizing alternative physical representations that invoke different ways of eliciting and communicating perceptions.

4
Working with Different Forms of Thought

When an event is perceived, it is represented simultaneously at several different levels of precision. At the most general level of representation an organizational encounter such as a board meeting, for example, may be coded in a participant's mind simply as 'a board meeting'. When the participant uses this very general representation to report what happened, she says only that she attended a board meeting. In one sense this is true and all that needs to be said. The 'meaning' of the concept *board meeting at Unico* is quite well established. The typical membership, location, length, tone etc. are established. The function, process and types of outcomes are established. The event was an instance of this type of organizational encounter. At an intermediate level of precision the event is represented as a set of actions. 'The MD was determined to get some movement on the issue this time. She said she had sensed prevarication at the last meeting.' This type of representation obviously has more specific information than the 'board meeting' statement. At an even more detailed level of representation the board meeting is coded as a string of sensory events containing fine-grained, descriptive information. 'At one point, I could see the production director, shuffling uneasily in his seat. Half way through he was literally clenching his fists, by his side. At the end, he was literally purple in the face, said he would do it, but that he couldn't guarantee success.'

Just because a detailed memory code exists, however, does not guarantee that it will be used, since intermediate and general levels of representation are also available. Memory codes differ (as we have seen in Chapter 2) not only in terms of their precision but also in terms of their format. We have seen in Chapter 2 that it is important to distinguish between propositional and imagistic forms of thought. Information in propositional codes is stored as a listing of meaningful concepts, similar to a definition in a dictionary (Anderson, 1990). For example, the propositional code referring to the production director might include the string of words or phrases *uneasy, angry, purple*, etc. Propositional code is not merely containing the words, it contains the ideas to which these words refer. The person is thinking through language. We can gain insight into a person's view of an issue through identifying the ideas (concepts) that they have linked to the issue.

If we think back to the boardroom scene, we can see how subsequent retellings by the observer may be based on a 'consulting' of the propositional code concerning the gestures and postures of the production director:

the terms 'fists' and 'purple' etc. On the other hand, the observer may consult the image code that she has of the event. Here the specific tightness and movement of the fist may be observed, as well as the details of the facial expression that was being used while the production director was purple. Image code (that is, an imagistic thought) is in the form of an image or mental picture. These thoughts are accessed and handled differently by the mind. They need to be recognized and worked with in organizations.

We can therefore 'configure' mental material propositionally and/or imagistically. This chapter is about how we can enhance the sophistication with which we work with both propositional thought and imagistic thought within organizations. It highlights the ways in which we can specifically consider a person's verbal arguments and ideas, together with exploring their images of events and possibilities.

Securing insights into propositional representations: constructs, categories and maps

How can we gain insight into the way that we or another organizational participant have construed a particular idea/object/event? We can learn quite a lot from listening carefully to people's language and thinking in the course of conversation. People can become remarkably adept at 'reading' other people. There will always be a place for conventional face-to-face conversation in establishing the way that organizational participants are construing situations. Training in interpersonal skills (for example Robbins, 1989) or in interviewing (for example Dillon, 1990; Millar et al., 1992; Kvale, 1996) can go some way to ensuring that relatively less influenced views can be secured from participants than occurs in natural conversation. Indeed, some interview approaches can secure a more comprehensive 'searching' of views than others. Even then, it is hard, as we have seen when discussing the fine line between knowledge elicitation and knowledge creation, to assimilate information in a new form at the same rate that it may be being generated when cued in another form. Interpreting the significance to a participant implied within their account of a particular episode may be difficult to do 'live'. At the very least, we need to recognize that there is a lot of valuable information implicit within what people are saying that we miss in unrecorded encounters. Much of the information that we have acquired through research into organizational behaviour and processes has been derived from detailed qualitative data analysis, after the event. It is possible to record interviews and subsequently conduct more extensive analysis. We can include reflection on our own practices in these analyses. The techniques and skills involved in comprehensive 'qualitative' analysis of data are outlined by writers such as Dey (1993) and Bryman and Burgess (1994).

There are however, more sophisticated means of construct elicitation than 'straight' interviews (or internal conversations). In the main they 'impose' some discipline on the process. Their procedures can secure more comprehensive elicitation. Managers and other organizational participants can benefit from an appreciation of the contribution of these more specific procedures. Several of the procedures are outlined below. They are presented as descriptions of how they can be applied to elicit insights into the views of other organizational participants. They can, however, in all instances be used to enhance one's own reflections.

Eliciting constructs

The best known approach to construct elicitation is the repertory grid procedure. Fransella and Bannister (1977) outline five approaches to elicitation. The first approach uses triads of elements. This is the approach developed by Kelly (1955). He outlined six minor variations within the triad approach, but it is the 'minimum context card form' that is almost invariably used. Here, the elements that are to be used for the exploration are listed on cards. The participant is presented with three of the cards and asked to specify some important way in which two of them are alike and thereby different from the third. The word or phrase that they use to describe the 'similarity' is the first pole of their construct. Many repertory grid practitioners record the process by assigning numbers randomly to the set (say, 1 to 9) of element cards. The triad dealt out is recorded (for example 5, 3, 8). The particular two cards paired are recorded by underlining the appropriate card numbers listed (for example 5, 3, 8). The term used is written alongside the listing of three card numbers, typically on the left-hand side of the page. Having recorded the reply, the participant is asked in what way the third element differs from the other two. The answer to this question concerning the difference is the contrast pole. This word or phrase is written alongside the first pole, on the right-hand side of the page. The participant is asked if there are any other ways in which the highlighted pair differ from the third card, until no additional constructs are voiced. The participant is then asked if the three cards can be grouped in some other way. This grouping is recorded (for example 5, 3, 8) etc. If the participant has identified a second combination and explored the collection of ways in which they distinguish between that pair and the third element, they are asked about the third possible combination of the three cards (that is, 5, 3, 8) and the constructs used. Another deal of the cards is made and the procedure continued until there are no further constructs being articulated.

Practice can vary concerning the choice of triads. Some practitioners prefer to start with one set of three cards, then dispense with two of the cards temporarily, by replacing them with two others. They then replace the original card and one of the others, and so on. Others may rely on random chance in continually re-dealing the cards. The important point is to ensure that the full set of (say, nine) elements is considered, and that each card is considered in several sets of comparisons. The second approach in the repertory grid procedure uses dyads rather than triads. This can be beneficial when one is expressly seeking to compare elements that occur in natural conjunction, for example how particular pairs of people interact with each other. It is also a simpler task, conceptually.

Hinkle (1965) varied the triad procedure to 'ladder' up and down from each construct they articulate. For example, if the construct 'dry in contrast to cynical' humour has been articulated, a participant may be asked whether they feel it is preferable to have or be the first pole or the contrast pole. The participant is then asked to articulate 'why' this is the preference, that is, the 'advantages of this side in contrast to the disadvantages of that side as you see it' (Hinkle, 1965, pp. 32–3). A response might be, for example, that 'dry humour is less hurtful than cynical humour'. Each of the new constructs articulated can then, in turn, be laddered up from. Similarly, it is possible to ladder down from a construct. Here, participants are asked to express some example ways in which one can distinguish between the two poles of the construct, that is, the different evidence or characteristics of the contrast. Dry humour may be regarded, for example, as 'where one makes quite insightful and pointed comment about the state of affairs' in contrast to 'tending only to make more negative observations'. Landfield (1971) pictures this progressive laddering process as a pyramid. Each pole of a construct is further explored. The one construct at level one is extended to a pair of constructs at level two; a construct to further differentiate the left-hand pole, and a construct to further differentiate the right-hand pole. In this way a pyramid is developed with one construct at level one, two constructs at level two, four constructs at level three, eight constructs at level four, and so on.

The final procedure outlined by Fransella and Bannister (1977) is referred to as self-characterization. Here, participants are invited to write a character sketch of themselves as it might be written by someone who knew them intimately. The terms that are used in the description can be used as left-hand constructs, and the participant invited to articulate their contrast pole.

There are many examples of the repertory grid procedure being used to elicit the construct systems of people within organizational settings. Stephens and Gammack (1994), for example, outline their use of the approach in a systems analysis context. The approach can easily be used in one's own reflections on practice. Imposing the discipline of systematically contrasting elements on oneself is a powerful procedure that enhances casual recollection and introspection.

The 'laddering' development to the repertory grid procedure that Hinkle (1965) developed (outlined above) has gone on to become a knowledge-elicitation procedure in its own right. It is particularly well suited to promoting the verbalization of propositional thought. The potential of laddering as a technique in eliciting knowledge for expert systems is reviewed by Rugg and McGeorge (1995). A computerized version of the approach is outlined by Corbridge et al. (1994).

Burr and Butt (1992, p. 80) refer to an approach called 'McFall's Mystical Monitor'. Here, participants are asked to speak (in private, into a tape recorder) for 75 minutes on the selected topic. They then listen to the tape, erase it, and record a 30-minute session. The scaling down, in a sense, invokes separation thinking, such that the main points are distinguished. The key issues are articulated. The procedure is advocated as a self-exploration journey. One can imagine briefer and briefer versions helping a person to clarify what they construe to be the 'nub' of a matter.

In seeking to promote this type of thinking, one is attempting to establish how differentiated our (or another person's) understanding of a domain is. As noted in Chapter 2, one is placing an emphasis on zero-order relations (Gentner, 1983), to surface the 'entities' that the person conceives, and the attributes the person considers the entities to have. It is clear that in inducing a person to consider sets of elements, one is going to cue thinking about the relationships between them. Repertory grid procedure seeks explicitly to do this.

Categorizing

We can therefore identify the terms in which we or others construe a particular issue/object/event. We can also examine the ways in which entire systems of construal are organized. Construct systems are hierarchical, with constructs standing to each other in subordinate and superordinate relationships. As Fransella and Bannister (1977) put it:

> This is something that is recognized in formal logic in that *modes of transport* subsume *boats* which subsume *sailing boats* which subsume *dinghys* which subsume *Mirror dinghys* and so forth. It is recognized in common argument when we talk of important ideas, central ideas, the main features of this or that as contrasted with detail, trivia and so forth. (p. 8)

In invoking separation thinking in the course of using the repertory grid, for example, we may find that a person distinguishes between three facets of management influence, for example telling – co-creating, controlling – servicing and task-focused – person-focused.

In addition to focusing on the richness and diversity of construals, we can examine their interrelationships. The 'laddering' process in the elicitation of constructs can shed some light on the hierarchical organization of constructs that a participant has. It is also very useful to engage ourselves and other participants in a subsequent stage of grouping and interrelating the constructs that have been generated in the elicitation interview. Some form of visual representation is appropriate. Semantic nets are a particularly useful means of depicting interrelationships between constructs. The pooling of constructs into certain headings can highlight particular 'fundamental' dimensions of a situation/person/event. These dimensions can become the basis of a framework which is, in turn, used to highlight additional aspects of a participant's personal construct system.

Categorization is a technique that people use for framing, structuring, and making sense of their surroundings (Neisser, 1987). Promoting categorization has been shown to be useful in the course of problem-solving, for example. Rickards (1990) suggests that one of the most flexible forms of structuring technique is 'morphological analysis' (p. 121), where the basic structure or shape of something is studied. Various graphical means (two- or three-dimensional grids etc.) can be used to depict the location of various example entities in a larger framework. The main point to be made here is that deriving and using a framework is a specific type of thinking. It might not automatically be invoked in asking a person to consider the 'set of things' that concern them. It can be valuable to facilitate one's own or others' articulation of constructs through the explicit development/ refinement of a framework. There is clear value in using this dialectical strategy.

The Q-sort procedure (for example Nutt, 1984, pp. 123–7) induces location thinking. It asks participants to sort different 'elements' (the labels for which are printed on cards) into piles. As a process this generates groupings and thus helps locate different elements in relation to each other. In so doing, it highlights a term which can be used to further differentiate between elements, and thus implicitly serves as an aid to separation thinking. K. Daniels et al. (1994) utilized a visual card sort mapping procedure to elicit differences in managerial cognitions of competition. They asked participants to write the names of competitor organizations on cards. The procedure 'required participants to arrange the cards such that those firms in close competition were placed most closely together' (p. S23). The maps are recorded 'by simply photographing the arrangement' (p. S23). Bougon (1983) utilizes a sort procedure, the 'Self-Q technique', as an element in the elicitation of cognitive maps. Barrett (1995), in seeking to assess person–environment congruence in terms of the fit between a subordinate's perceptions of the requirements of the job and those perceived by the supervisor, used the Q-sort procedure. Both sets of respondents rated the relative importance of a set of work behaviours by assigning them into categories. The degree of agreement between subordinate and supervisor assessments was then correlated. Active categorization is a useful way of gaining insight into people's propositional codes.

Mechitov et al. (1994) explore the relative merits of two basic approaches to identifying the underlying decision rules used by experts. The first approach is the direct elicitation of decision rules in terms of productions (see Chapter 3 for examples of this physical form of knowledge representation). The second approach involves classification of multiattribute objects by the expert. It was found that it is easier for experts to perform the classification and then consider decision rules than it is to formulate production rules directly. Again, therefore, we can see that invoking a particular form of thinking assists the introspective process.

The ways that managers categorize their own firms in relation to competitors has been studied by Porac et al. (1987). The general categories and subcategories can be represented in a hierarchical tree diagram. The researchers show how two restaurants serving pizza, for example, may define themselves in very different ways. One may see itself located in a framework that classifies it as 'a family restaurant'. The other restaurant may regard itself as a 'fast food outlet'. The bases of classification and the position in which one places things can be revealing. Hierarchical representations feel reductionist, however. If we sit down with a person and ask them to map out various elements into a hierarchy, we may, in effect, force participants to generate what they deem to be the 'logical' classification rather than their own basis. The very nature of tree diagrams suggests a complete and singular way of locating elements. People may have some aspects of location established in their minds, and be able to categorize and classify them. There may be other aspects of one's views that are not fully thought out. 'Forcing' an allocation may give a misleading impression of the way that the person is considering the various elements generally in other contexts.

Mapping

Relationships between constructs or categories can also be considered. Here, we are concerned with how such relationships can be mapped. There are three major forms of maps that are used in organizational research. These are perceptual maps, mind maps and cognitive (cause) maps. They are discussed more fully below.

PERCEPTUAL MAPS The term 'perceptual mapping' refers to a process where statistical techniques are used to identify mathematical interrelationships between elements, and any specific element (person or product etc.) can be depicted in relation other 'members'. Sinclair (1990) reports how a statistical technique called multiple discriminant analysis was used to locate seven different products that can be used for siding residential properties (brick, plywood, cedar, aluminium etc.) in terms of 11 attributes (price, fade resistance, dimensional/shape stability, status/quality image etc.). The position of each product is mapped onto sets of two-dimensional charts. In the example given, brick is seen as a high-status and good weathering siding in relation to others. Different siding products can also be mapped onto other pairs of attributes (for example dent resistance and application economy). As the term 'multidimensional scaling' implies, it is possible to locate specific elements on a large number of dimensions, in a wide conceptual space. Other multiple dimensional scaling (MDS) examples from the marketing literature include Hartman and Lindgren's (1993) analysis of consumer evaluations of goods and services.

In addition to the sets of two-dimensional representations that are generated by MDS, it is possible to use cluster analysis techniques to depict the progressive 'similarities' between elements. Dendograms can be drawn which show how elements can be classified. The root of a dendogram may, for example, be 'animal'. This may then divide into two branches. One perhaps called 'four legged' and one called 'two legged'. The 'two legged' branch may divide into 'two legged with wings' and 'two legged without wings' etc. Within the 'two legged with wings' category we might find 'hens' and 'geese'. Under the 'two legged without wings' category we might find 'humans'.

It can be useful to depict the category membership scheme that people are seeming to use. This may of course contrast with any formal logical classification scheme. The above classification 'worked' for the pigs in George Orwell's *Animal Farm* but may not figure in zoological texts. As one might expect, there are debates concerning the implications of making alternative sets of mathematical assumptions associated with the use of different grouping techniques. Alternative statistical techniques to aid the process of mapping consumer cognitive structures are examined by Hodgkinson et al. (1991). The authors note that MDS and conventional (hierarchical) cluster analysis (HCA) carry mathematical assumptions that 'force' a structure onto data in a way that the additive similarity tree (AST) (Sattath and Tversky, 1977) and extended similarity tree (EST) (Corter and Tversky, 1986) approaches do not. MDS and hierarchical cluster analysis identify abstract groupings. They are the mathematical 'essence' of what a human rater's (for example consumer) judgements seem to be based on. They are not *the* bases of judgements themselves.

Mappings of elements using AST and EST reveal differences in terms of the extent to which particular elements classified together are representative of the category in question. Particular exemplars of a given category are not all equally representative of the class to which they belong in the mind of raters. In a sense, therefore, AST and EST approaches generate classes that are more akin to the notion of a psychological prototype (Rosch, 1973). It will be recalled from Chapter 2 that a psychological prototype is a concrete image of an average category member. Rosch (1975) notes that prototypes act as 'cognitive reference points' against which other exemplars of a category are compared. Hodgkinson et al. (1991) suggest that 'advertisers who stress the similarities and differences of their products in relation to empirically identified prototypes yield more effective results than those who do not' (p. 57). While the groups (classes) are still only mathematical concepts, they are argued to be more similar in assumptions to those which human beings make than are categories derived from MDS and HCA procedures. Perceptual maps may approximate the 'membership' categories that people use in their judgements. For example, Hodgkinson et al.'s (1991) AST analysis of breakfast cereals indicated consumers making separations into 'low fibre' as opposed to 'high fibre' groups; high fibre cereals being categorized as 'wheat based' as opposed to 'health' products; and health cereals that are muesli-like being distinguished from those that are 'bran'. It is important to note that this categorization does not juxtapose logical alternatives, for example 'wheat based' is not the opposite of 'health'. It is a mapping in terms of perceptual rather than logical categories. It can be a useful aspect for discussion of issues with participants. Sparrow and Bushell (1996), for example, utilized cluster analysis in addition to their qualitative analysis of the issues which personal business advisers (PBAs) take into account in supporting small and medium-sized local businesses. The dendograms were discussed at a feedback session with the PBAs, and used as part of the process for guiding further work with the group in exploring their disparate perceptions of appropriate approaches to support enterprise development. The introduction of such depictions requires careful management. Their interpretation necessitates some preliminary introduction to the notion of statistical similarity.

MIND MAPS   As we saw in Chapter 3, 'mind maps' (Buzan 1989; 1993) can serve as a useful means of locating different elements in relation to each other. Although in one sense they are a graphical means of representing information, and might be regarded as restricted to working with imagistic forms of thought, they can support propositional thought, and specifically categorization. Within mind maps, 'basic ordering ideas' are used to cluster elements. Buzan (1989) argues (pp. 93–4) that the depiction has a number of advantages over the linear form of text. He suggests that:

(a) The 'centre' and the 'main idea' are more clearly defined.
(b) The relative importance of each idea is more clearly indicated since more important ideas are drawn nearer the centre.
(c) The links between the key concepts are more readily recognized because of their proximity and connection.
(d) As a result of the above points, recall and review will be more rapid and effective.
(e) The nature of the structure allows for the easy addition of new information.
(f) Each map can be made to look different from other maps. This can aid recall.
(g) The open-ended nature of a mind map will enable the brain to make new connections more readily.

Seeing the ways in which a person chooses to relate ideas is a useful point of departure for a discussion. Two important considerations are raised in considering the role of mind-mapping as a process. First, it is useful to consider the generations of maps that may be produced. When used in an autistic type of thinking, a map is generated in an essentially cumulative unrevised manner. In this section of the chapter, we are considering how mind-mapping can be conducted in a more analytical way. In this mode, revisions can be made to the map. It is progressively redrawn until it best captures the person's way of ordering things. The type of thinking involved in considering a map's appropriateness is different from autistic thought. Elements are ordered through analysis of the meaning of elements in relation to each other.

The second consideration that is raised in mind-mapping in this more analytical context concerns the use of maps in group settings. Maps can be used as a basis for discussion. They can be pooled. They can be modified in the course of discussion. Buzan (1993) outlines seven major stages for the group mind-mapping process (pp. 168–70). The process involves:

1 Defining the subject.
2 Individual brainstorming.
3 Small group discussion in groups of between three and five members where individuals exchange ideas and add them to their own mind maps.
4 Creation of the multiple mind map.
5 Incubation: a period for the group map to 'sink in'.
6 Reconstruction and revision. The group needs to repeat stages 2,3 and 4 in order to capture the results of the newly considered and integrated thoughts.
7 Analysis and decision-making. The group map is used to make critical decisions, set objectives and devise plans.

It is interesting to note how Buzan feels that the iterative process benefits from a repeat individual mapping, as opposed to leaving the reconstruction and revision to free-form group processes. Brant (1993) outlines how mind maps can be used in all forms of training sessions. She suggests, in particular, that they can 'provide trainees with a unique at-a-glance "picture" of the training session content plus a record of all the ideas generated. My trainees thereby see the whole evolution of the session. Crucially, the map uses their own ideas' (p. 21).

STRUCTURED MAPS, CONSENSUS MAPS AND COGNITIVE (CAUSE) MAPS   The term most frequently used to describe elaborate depictions of the inter-relationships that a person holds between things is 'mapping'. There is some confusion therefore between the recording (mapping) of the generative (autistic) thinking of people engaged in mind-mapping, and the more formal, and essentially descriptive mapping of a person's conception of a matter. Several major forms of formal maps and mapping processes have been developed. Most methods follow a mapping method developed by Axelrod (1976) for use in political science. The basis for the approach was that when a map is 'pictured in graph form it is then relatively easy to see how each of the concepts and causal relationships relate to each other, and to see the overall structure of the whole set of portrayed assertions' (Axelrod, 1976, p. 5). Further work in the political science arena ensued. Individual decision-makers' maps have been examined by Klein and Cooper (1982) and Stubbart and Ramaprasad (1988). 'Average' causal maps were considered by Bougon et al. (1977).

Structured maps Hammer and Janes (1990) use the term 'interactive management' to refer to the use of 'an integrated set of techniques to generate ideas and insights and to analyse and structure them, while at the same time increasing and clarifying the group's knowledge of the problem and its immediate environment' (p. 11). The process produces what the authors refer to as a 'structured' map. They quote a case study manufacturing company using, in our terms, separation thinking (specifically, the nominal group technique) to generate 29 key observations on the state of the company. These were then structured into a map by the use of the relationship 'strongly contributes to' being used in interpretive structural modelling. The map depicts, for example, how the narrow engineering-based company culture, together with limited access to bank funding, strongly contributed to the poor promotion of products which is one of the factors in the company's inability to sell products in markets. The structured map goes beyond a simple mapping of 'causal' relationships. It allows elements to be grouped along other dimensions simultaneously. In the information given above, for instance, the elements listed are all coded in the structured map as 'marketing'. The map acts as both a sequencing and clustering representation of order.

Consensus maps   Hart et al. (1985) use the term 'consensus mapping' to refer to a process where participants can be aided 'to visualize, to review critically, and to organize what clearly were interrelated and sequence-dependent ideas' (p. 589). The approach produces a graphic map of the interrelationships among the individual ideas generated in earlier stages and enables group participants to adapt, rearrange or supplement the structure as the ongoing group discussion requires. It provides 'a vehicle through which a group may engage an issue with many sides and to develop results that reflect necessary levels of interdependency' (p. 589). The technique is applied in the context of the group's dialogue and, as such, stimulates the generation of consensus recommendations.

The authors see consensus mapping as a five-stage process. The first step is a 'search for structure'. The facilitator encourages individual participants to search for clusters and categories of listed items, then co-ordinates consideration of different approaches to organizing the ideas and helps group members work to reach agreement on a single, unified classification scheme. Having agreed the basic elements, the full set of participants can then be split into smaller groups for more detailed work on interrelating elements. The second stage is the development of a 'strawman map'. This first map is intended as a springboard for discussion, assumption surfacing and revision within the subgroups. It is an inclusive first approximation. The third stage is 'map reconfiguration'. Here, each subgroup works to fashion a mutually acceptable solution structure. The fourth stage is 'presentation in plenary'. A representative from each subgroup presents their subgroup's revised map to the representatives from the other sub-groups. The fifth stage is 'map consolidation'. Representatives from each of the subgroups work to produce a single consolidated map.

Cognitive (cause) maps   The most referenced approach towards mapping interrelationships between elements in management settings is the 'cause map' (also known as 'cognitive map'), pioneered by Eden and his colleagues from Strathclyde University. Eden and his colleagues have developed an

action research approach to support senior managers in combining perceptions of strategic options (for example Eden, 1989). As Langfield-Smith
(1992) puts it, it is a means 'to describe an individual's conscious perception
of reality, with sufficient detail to capture the individual's idiosyncratic
world view, while filtering out the myriad details which relate to specific
situations or detailed instances of the individual's experience' (p. 350).

Cognitive maps can be seen as a picture or visual aid in comprehending
the mapper's understanding of particular, and selective, elements of the
thoughts (rather than thinking) of an individual, group or organization.
These maps are 'captured in the form of a means/ends network leading from
detailed actions to broadly-defined individual or corporate goals'
(Ackermann, 1992, p. 24). It can be useful to consider separately issues
concerning the basic knowledge-elicitation process, the mapping process
and the group processes involved in map utilization (Ackermann and
Belton, 1994). Issues concerning elicitation and utilization will be outlined
later.

The most fundamental point about cognitive maps concerns the means by
which separate statements can be structured into a map of this basic form.
Ackermann et al. (1990) provide detailed guidelines to direct map construction. The guidelines advocate working with relatively clear words or
phrases that capture the essence of each particular concept. A further
guideline advocates looking for opposite poles for each concept (node) of
the map. In this way the left-hand expression of a node can be read as an
outcome/action which stands 'rather than' or 'as opposed to' its opposite. It
can be useful to try to make phrases used at nodes have an imperative form,
that is, have an action perspective. The phrase (expression) at each node
should be the 'words' from the participant. It can be useful to make the left-
hand expression of a concept the alternative that the participant 'prefers'.
Overall, these phrases can be placed as 'nodes' on a map. They can be
structured in a hierarchical way. Hierarchy is argued to be best built up by
provisionally locating 'goals' (typically ideals) towards the top of the map.
In order to do this, it will be necessary to have a constant eye out for
concepts that are goals as opposed to strategic directions or actions
(options). Actions that are more significant in terms of requiring changes in
culture, having long-term implications, cost, irreversibility, and have
relatively extensive breadth and complexity of subordinate actions are likely
to be 'strategic directions'. These should be located as nodes below goals,
but above potential options nodes. The apparent superordinate goal should
be written about two-thirds of the way up the page.

More specific hierarchization can be achieved by viewing concepts as
means leading to desired ends, that is, superordinate concepts. Arrows can
be drawn from one concept to another. A plus sign on the arrow can
indicate that the left-hand pole of one node is a contributor to the left-hand
(rather than right-hand) superordinate node outcome. A minus sign would
indicate that the left-hand node of a subordinate node would contribute to
the right-hand node of its superordinate node. Concepts can also be

hierarchized in terms of some nodes being more generic than others. Generic concepts are those for which there may be more than one specific item for achieving it.

A final guideline concerns looking out for 'isolated' concepts (those not linked to the 'main' part of the map). 'Isolation is an important clue to the problem owner's thinking about issues involved' (Ackermann et al., 1990, p. 8).

A computer program called COPE (Cropper et al., 1990) has been developed which aids mapping, the subsequent navigation of maps and interpretation. A number of colour-coded categories can be produced allowing concepts to be sorted into goals, key issues and possible options. This aids navigation of a map. Eden et al. (1992) provide some additional practical guidance. They advocate the removal of any loops that may have arisen because of 'coding accidents', circularities in argument as opposed to the possible existence of dynamic considerations such as growth, decline or feedback control. Secondly, they suggest that attempting to 'read' any further structural insights into a map of only a small number of nodes (between six and ten) may not yield any added value. Any emerging characteristics may be better described through words. Indeed, graphically mapping such 'small' arguments may be of more value for communication than for facilitating analytical thought. Given a reasonable number of nodes (more than ten), they note that the need to locate nodes that are linked close to one another and the need to keep the number of crossing links to a minimum determine layout. One finds that one knows the subareas of a map that will be 'big', and positions them accordingly.

In addition to these broad design principles, Eden et al. (1992) demonstrate some of the analyses that can be performed on cause maps. These advocated analyses give further insight into the 'logic' that Eden and his colleagues are seeking to force/intensify into interrelating concepts. The analyses provide indications of features of the map and enable emerging features to be detected. A large number of nodes may be an indicator of the complexity (or at least comprehensiveness) of the grasp of the issue in hand. The ratio of links to constructs can indicate the 'density' of a map. In addition to global density, 'local density' can also be considered. It is possible to calculate the total number of in-arrows and out-arrows from each node, that is, its immediate domain. Some nodes' immediate domains are more complex. These may be considered to be nodes which are 'cognitively central', 'core' or 'cryptic' concepts. Bearing in mind that a 'head' in a map is a node for which there is no superordinate node, and a 'tail' is a node for which there is no further subordinate node, it is possible to calculate the ratio of the number of heads to the total number of nodes, or the ratio of the number of tails to the total number of nodes. Identifying 'a relatively large number of heads in relation to total nodes', may indicate 'a concern for meeting multiple and possibly conflicting objectives' (p. 364). A 'large number of tails in relation to the total number of nodes' may indicate that 'causal arguments are not well elaborated and use short chains of argument'

(p. 364). It is also possible to identify areas of a map that are 'islands'. In many complex hierarchic systems, intracomponent linkages are stronger than intercomponent linkages and discovery of where the weakest linkages lie can be a useful indicator of a lack of cognitive complexity. Another interesting notion is that of 'potent' nodes (p. 367). Potent nodes are ones that reach many heads. They may, for example, indicate particularly valuable options to pursue, in a strategic options development and analysis (SODA) context (Ackermann, 1992). High numbers of potent nodes may indicate that one is operating in a domain where one needs to 'define situations in ways that consider multiple ramifications' (Eden et al., 1992, p. 368).

The shape of a map can be informative. A 'flat' map, with a lot of short paths between tails and heads, may indicate little depth of thinking, but can also suggest a high range of choice of options. A thin tall shape, with a small number of long paths between tails and heads, may 'indicate detailed argument without a consideration for alternative definitions of the situation' (p. 368). Loops can imply dynamics. Loops involving a small number of nodes are generally already realized by the participant. A loop with a large number of nodes may be one that a participant has not previously realized. The map depiction may facilitate detecting counter-intuitive dynamics (Forrester, 1971). Loops with an odd number of negative links depict a 'self-controlling' dynamic. Alternatively, an even number of negative links (or all positive links) suggests that 'perturbation can lead to exponential growth or decline' (p. 369).

Taken together, the guidelines and indicative analyses tell us much about the form of thinking involved in causal 'sequencing'. It is important to recognize the high emphasis on logicality in some applications of causal mapping. Loops in thinking can, in one sense, be regarded as inconveniences, and felt to be beneficially 'driven out'. Eden suggests that we 'break' them by deciding which of them is the primary or higher goal. This can certainly be useful in attempting to decide between alternative higher-order strategic options. It is not necessarily, however, a process that people spontaneously go through in the course of their decisions and actions. People do not hierarchize systematically, and 'compute' implications and options. People do not act solely in terms of the semantic logic of a map. Loops in thinking can be problematic for people. They may not resolve them through hierarchizing. Eden, of course, recognizes this, but feels that the benefits of structuring arguments with ends in mind necessitates such simplifications. The nodes in such maps are 'concepts', that is, they are objectified terms that are seen to operate in their logical world.

In contrast, Bougon (1992) suggests that it can be particularly valuable to focus on the intersections of loops at particular nodes between different participants. He argues that it can be advantageous to regard nodes as labels, not concepts. They are the points at which different participants converge or interact and share terminology. They 'provide the glue of social systems. This cryptic glue makes possible the loose coupling of social systems (Weick, 1976) through the indeterminate meanings and loose understandings it produces' (p. 376). To suggest that such nodes are concepts is to claim that they have the same meaning for all participants, or that there is some deeper underlying reality to be discovered. In Bougon's (1992) terms, the 'socially constructed reality of a system of cognitive maps congregated by cryptic labels *is* the social reality' (p. 377). A congregate cognitive map is not an aggregate map. Eden refers to processes of comparing maps and establishing group maps through 'merging' or 'overlaying' the node labels of individual maps presumed to denote similar concepts, regarding the same labels from different people's maps as equating with similarity of meaning, and linking any nodes that ought to be linked. These procedures help groups to identify their shared reasoning and meaning. The argument behind a congregate map is that participants congregate into a social system by minimal connection through a few but crucial (and strategic) congregating labels. It is more appropriate, according to Bougon (1992), to 'describe organizations as created by shared labels rather than by shared meaning or by shared concepts' (p. 372). Seeking to identify congregating labels requires different forms of interviewing and workshops from mapping with aggregation in mind. In congregate mapping, nodes are codes (Weick and Bougon, 1986). Only labels previously uttered by the interviewee can be utilized to probe for further causes or consequences. Secondly, the principle that congregating labels are crypts means that an important objective for interviewers is to identify congregating labels early, since they provide 'with almost certainty, potent entry points into an individual's cognitive map' (p. 382). These are the points of interaction with others where labels are shared. They provide solid ground from which to build.

One can gain a sense of this process by considering how a person's account of their world lurches from a congregating label that they share in one social context to one that they share in another social context. The 'bridging' terms that they use in their thinking feel less certain. Identifying congregate labels early is primarily important since they constitute the glue of the social system carrying out the strategy. Once one has identified congregating labels, they can be reused in interviews with other participants as their cryptic character is explored with each additional participant. Bougon (1992) suggests that it can be useful to identify the people one expects to be the most useful in these regards. An interviewer might first:

> seek people one may characterize as the idea man or woman, the saboteur, the creative person, the person with the power to act, the champion for an idea or product, and perhaps the satisfied customer or the angry customer. The issues these people raise are likely to be congregating labels because it is most likely that these issues affect them deeply, hence connect to their own cognitive map. (p. 383)

There are important differences in the workshop where group explorations of cognitive maps occur between aggregate mapping and congregate mapping. A cryptic congregating label that a facilitator has identified from the initial individual interviews can be used at the outset to attract the interest of most if not all of a workshop team. The process in aggregating maps may be different. For example, Ackermann and Belton (1994) report how the individual maps 'were then entered into the computer and merged together to form a single model reflecting all the individual views', in order for the group 'to work together adding and amending where necessary' (p. 167). This 'backroom' stage produces the equivalent of Hart et al.'s (1985) 'strawman map'. It is the evolving depiction of shared reasoning and meaning.

This raises the importance of the agenda and context for any workgroup exploring cognitive maps. In terms of strategy formulation, Donnellon et al. (1986) suggest that teams may agree on a specific action merely because the proposed action leads to the same outcome as the alternative actions, which they might individually elect. It is not necessary for them to agree on what these actions mean, and it is not necessary for their reasons to be the same. The people only need to want these actions taken. In forums where mutual insight is a key objective, then explorations may be more searching. Bowman and Johnson (1991) contend that 'surfacing what is taken for granted in the process of strategy formulation' (p. 3), reveals considerable variance among managers, and can lead to healthy debate 'not just about alternative strategies, but about schisms between various subgroups of the management team, and between managers and directors' (Fiol and Huff, 1992, p. 269).

Langfield-Smith (1992), in seeking to identify a shared cognitive map within a team of six fire protection officers, outlines an individual cognitive mapping procedure. She used a short (30-minute) interview with individual officers to extract the themes or elements to be mapped. This was followed by a sorting procedure where each individual sorted their terms into a '"logical order" and described how each element related to each other element in terms of cause and effect relationships' (p. 354). This information was then represented as a visual cognitive map (by the author) and then fed back to the individual concerned to 'amend or add elements and relationships that were not included in the map' (p. 354). She hoped then to be able to let the participants meet as a group, with the list of all of the elements generated in the individual sessions to 'reach agreement on the elements that should be included in the collective map, and to investigate the causal relationships between those elements' (p. 354). She elected not to use the individual maps 'as it was felt that the process of integrating several maps would be too complex, and individuals recognizing their own map might bias their responses' (p. 355). In the event, the group sessions were not successful. The group did not function well as a whole, and there were very protracted discussions about the different meanings that individuals attached to some of the elements, and the problems of identifying the dimensions or boundaries that constituted an element. She reports her speculations about the relative maturity and diversity of the group, the format of the group session, and the existence in general of collective beliefs. She suggests that there was not an extensive collective belief system (some form of relatively enduring phenomena that was part of their culture and that is activated in the course of group discussions) that could be mapped. The group functioned, in the main, through transitory 'collective cognitions' that they negotiated in any particular collective encounter.

It seems clear that it is possible to get management groups to use a relatively abstract 'model' of causes and outcomes, to help them consider alternative strategic options, as Eden's extensive work confirms. This may, however, be because the group is prepared to negotiate and work with 'loose' labels for concepts, as means to its ends. Cognitive mapping has the hall-marks of rationality with which management teams may feel comfortable. They may find the processes of considering causes and effects, means and ends, natural and appropriate in the work context. Indeed, Jenkins (1993) reports how he used the COPE package to explore the thinking about business growth of two managing directors. One was the managing director of a retail business with two outlets. The other was the managing director of a larger chain of 12 outlets. Jenkins concludes that the approach could 'be used in an interactive mode to intervene in the strategy development process', at the 'start-up phase', or 'as a mechanism for achieving the transition between the various phases of the business life cycle' (p. 10). Invoking this reasoning type of thinking helps individuals to see gaps in their articulation of elements and planks of argument in their views of a domain. There are many additional complications involved, however, in attempting to use this type of thinking in explicitly seeking to promote mutual insight.

In conclusion, we have seen how different approaches can be used to elicit propositional forms of thought. In Chapter 3, we saw that the process of physical representation in itself affects thinking. A framework of representations was presented in Table 3.5. Different insights into one's thinking can be obtained by pursuing the different thinking processes that are invoked by each of the representations in Table 3.4.

Overall, we can see that the ways that organizational participants use to make sense of their experiences are mentally represented, in part, by constructs (that is, propositional code). The next section of the chapter explores the additional insights that we can secure into their experiences and perceptions by focusing on an alternative form of thought, imagistic thought.

Inducing and working with imagistic thought

Providing some form of pictorial support can aid the comprehension of ideas/objects/events (for example Newton, 1994). There is evidence that problem-solving performance can be enhanced with training in imagery. Important relationships between kinds of mental material and forms of thought need to be considered. Much of the work conducted by Eden and his colleagues on cognitive mapping is utilizing a visual representation to work with semantic information. He has demonstrated that this visual technique is useful to elicit causal relationships between constructs, and that it is becoming increasingly possible for models and analysis to be conducted 'on the hoof'. As a result, individuals and client groups undertake more effective and faster problem construction and modelling (Eden, 1993). In particular, the approach seeks to recognize the significance of multiple perspectives and can capture them in a visual interactive modelling process (Eden, 1994).

Dobson and Markham (1993) report how self-reported vividness of visual imagery relates to a person's ability to recall the source of episodic memory. It has been noted how semantic memory stores information in the abstract. The original source of information becomes separated from the information itself. In episodic information, the material is retained essentially in terms of its context and sequence. The ability of a person to recapture images vividly, as we have seen, varies. Respondents with greater imagery ability can more reliably associate the original source with the information than can their less able counterparts. Oliver et al. (1993) report how inducing imagistic thinking as opposed to more verbal semantic 'analysis' in considering advertisements affects the tacit impression of the 'perceived novelty' of the product depicted. Nikolinakos (1992) attempts to show how mental imagery relates to Freud's theory of dreams and the activity of dream interpretation. The impact of undertaking this type of analysis in organizations has not been established.

Pause to recall, if you can, when you last had a picture of something in your head. When you telephoned somebody perhaps, did you recall the room where the other person was? Could you see her in her office in your mind's eye? Or maybe you can recall when you thought about your next meeting with your boss. Did you experience it as a scene? Could you see and hear her interacting with you? How did the meeting go? What happened? Or perhaps you can recall the last difficult customer that you had dealings with. Have you got a vivid recollection? Are there parts of the episode that make you feel uncomfortable? What is that feeling? Does that feeling remind you of another occasion when you felt that way? Perhaps when you were excruciatingly embarrassed, or frustrated.

All of these experiences are happening because you are thinking with and through images. These are not reasoned arguments where decisions are 'computed'. These are more like cinema projections on a screen. But the processes and outcomes of these episodes in your imagination may affect how you actually go about your activities in the future. You may act in accordance with the 'play' that you construct. In your play the characters seem to act in particular ways, and entire scenes are enacted in your mind. The play may involve the various people behaving very 'true to style'. Sometimes entire sections of the play are 're-runs' of a previous episode. Often, an episode typifies this particular person–context combination. Sometimes your construction of the scene involves your imagination of how events may proceed.

The power of imagination lies in its ability to account for the actions of people or objects as they react *in toto*, as coherent total integrated entities.

This means that the outcomes are not reasoned towards, on first principles. In projecting a person into a scene, the theoretical possibilities of all their alternative possible motives and preferences are not computed and resolved. The image of the person has sufficient substance to operate. It is as if the person is alive in your mind, and behaves as they would in reality. This tells us a great deal about the potential of imagistic thought as an aspect of organizational perceptions. Many of the expected reactions of participants that a particular employee has in their mind are the product of key episodes or 'views' held in mind as complete 'objects' or 'sequences'. Many of the ideas about what might be possible in the future may be arrived at through imagination. Listening to a person's account of what they might be doing in five years' time, or of what might be happening in the organization in five years' time, is an insight into the person themselves.

The play that a person constructs may operate with images. The specific behaviour or 'interplays' may be the product of several kinds of mental material. We have suggested that episodic mental material may make a significant contribution to the projected events. Perhaps certain aspects of the play will be 'tripped out' with things operating in their usual manner. The highly skilled, automatic ways of linking or sequencing things play their part in the construction of the scenes. Perhaps the basic tone of the play is an indication of the tacit feel that the person has of the people or organization. Tone may be defined by dominant themes (crises, accidents, jokes etc.), attributions to the main characters (for example, all 'victims'), the underlying emotional qualities (pride, sadness, anxiety etc.) and the dominant narrative forms (tragic, comic, suspense, epic etc.). Some of the plays that people construct may be of an archetypal form, that is, they appear to have essentially singular, deep messages. The 'moral of the story' may give us some insights into the role of the unconscious in the construction of the play. We may find, for example, the playwright as hero, survivor, victim etc.

Imagistic thoughts can be utilized in each of the three types of thinking. The form that we have been outlining to date is perhaps one that is operating in the course of autistic thinking, the free-flowing, musing type of thinking. The behaviour of people and objects in this form of play is perhaps their most 'natural'. In contrast, the behaviour of people and objects in a play constructed in something other than a 'neutral' mood may differ. Here we may find actions and reactions that confirm the legitimacy of our mood. In some plays we may find that people may be expecting certain things of us, that we feel we cannot do (anxiety), for example characters may assume threatening extremes of behaviour. Alternatively, we may observe that the people may contribute to the highly positive tone of a specific play and play particular sides of themselves, for example Jill will be humorous, Joan will be kind. They will 'be' their most positive features. The positive mood state would thus be maintained. In a depressed mood, in contrast, the characters may 'conspire' to legitimize that mood. They will highlight the futility of actions. Most things will demonstrate pointlessness.

The tide of events may suggest a world in which there is not much that can be done by the playwright. The characters will 'be' the things that 'give you a hard time', they may be fellow victims whose efforts failed. We can see, therefore, how the induction of different moods could draw attention to the positive, threatening, depressing or other emotional tone-related aspects of people and organizations that operate in their mind's eye.

Imagistic thoughts can also be the vehicle for a reasoning type of thinking. Indeed, this is where the term 'imagination' is often used. People may be asked to picture how things might be: to 'imagine it'. They may be told to break out of their current way of thinking and 'use your imagination'. Here the 'shackles' of working with cohesive integrated entities operating in the routines of the organization can be shed. We can create images in our minds where things are done differently. We can see where we have been 'blind' and have been doing things inappropriately. A person who is both Jill and Joan, or part of each (as drawn to our specification), will enact the scene for us. It is here that the power of imagination lies. The gap between the things which we are currently capable of dealing with, controlling or handling, and the things that our minds can at least reach will be considered. As the poet Robert Browning put it, in *Andrea del Sarto*, 'Ah, but a man's reach should exceed his grasp. Or what's a heaven for?' In imagination we can bring the entities that we can reach in our mind's eye into our grasp and consider them more closely. Some of the wonder in this process lies in the fact that, as we grasp what was once a more remote prospect, a new world of possibilities vaguely dawns, tantalizingly within our reach.

The thinking that operates in envisioning a future can benefit from being of an imagistic nature. While reasoning on some of the basic propositions that emerge from a visioning process will be reasoned with in terms of further propositions, many of the clues and implications can be manifested in the operation of images. Heron (1985) and Harri-Augstein and Thomas (1991) describe how mime can be used to promote learning. Focus groups can be used in a way that lets participants respond to hypothetical situations that are put to them (Morgan, 1988). Role-playing can be used to reveal key features of particular issues (Mannix et al., 1995). Hypothetical situations can also be simulated. Participants can enact the way that they imagine they would respond to a possible scenario. Chatman and Barsade (1995) utilized computer gaming, for example, with simulated organizations, to highlight relationships between individual personality, organizational culture and forms/extents of co-operation.

Imagery therefore uses a particular form of schema, i.e. mental template that organizes information. As we outlined in Chapter 2, particular people, objects and events may be schemas in a person's mind. Each schema, in a sense, carries with it a set of expectations. These are the expectations based on experiences, that have been integrated as a coherent 'set'. Schemas include prototypes of particular objects and specific assemblies for 'real' people/objects. These collections of expectations operate in our 'plays' as vivid, explicit people/objects. The second form of schema that is involved in the construction of our 'plays' is a script, a specialized schema for action. A script is a schematic retention of context-specific mental material about events and event sequences. When faced with a familiar situation we activate an appropriate script. Schemas can operate imagistically. People can experience the enactment of 'plays' based on their schematic characters and scripts.

It seems clear that imagistic thought plays a tangible role in organizational thinking. It would be useful to be able to consider the images that we and other organizational participants have of people, events and the organization. Asking people to give verbal summaries of these images and sequences is not sufficient. We need to use techniques that can help people 'enter' their world of images, access and express their images. We need to use techniques and processes that can help groups consider the images expressed by others and collaboratively work with images in their thinking.

Guided imagery

We have noted how there can be different frequencies with which people may switch between primarily propositional thought and primarily imagistic thought. At the conscious level there is some degree of awareness of the material one is processing in one's mind. Designers may recognize the rapid oscillation between the two forms of thoughts. Managers may not have developed the metaknowledge of their own thinking practices. While they will undoubtedly know when they have been daydreaming and imagining, they may not have reflected on any 'switches' in forms of thought that are occurring in their everyday decisions. Perhaps designers' self-insights into the switching process also provide them with implicit training in managing specific switches. There is evidence to suggest that people can be explicitly trained to manage the thought form that they are using, and that self-induced imagery can reduce fear in phobic people or perceptions of pain (Worthing, 1978), for example. Managers and many other employee groups may need some guidance on the skills of recognizing imagistic thought and explicitly undertaking it.

Rainer (1978) suggests that 'imagery is an intuitive process that depends upon relaxing and trying to clear your mind of daily concerns and conscious controls. But in guided imagery you choose to visualize self-nurturing images' (p. 88). She advocates an initial restful projection into a particular 'spot' and then populating the place with the appropriate characters. Vaughan (1979) advocates an initial focusing of attention, possibly on one's own body, and then a progressive movement into a relaxed state. The initial 'bringing to mind' of the imaginary scene is brought about, in most writers' guidelines, through a vivid set of visual images being reinforced by the sounds and smells etc. as appropriate. Very often, therefore, some initial preparatory visualization work is advocated. People may find it easiest to conjure up images of restful places with tranquil sounds and pleasant smells.

They may be able to 'feel' themselves lying on grass on a hillside. Having conjured up an initial scene, and begun to feel comfortable with this form of thought, people may move on to less archetypal settings. They may develop an ability to create any scenario at will. Gawain (1982) advocates frequent practising of bringing images to mind (p. 16). People can be aided in developing imagery skills through basic familiarization exercizes or more extensive training. Anthony et al. (1993) advocate an imagery process where some initial self-induced relaxation or prompted relaxation is undertaken for three to five minutes because 'relaxation has been shown to promote the emergence of more graphic imagery' (p. 50). The ultimate vividness with which one can depict scenes may also depend on basic imagery 'ability'. Betts (1909) suggests that people differ in their 'ability to summon before the mind images of the various types, and the degree of clearness and vividness of the images' (p. 10). A more refined measure of mental imagery vividness has been developed by Sheehan (1967) which has been used in subsequent studies of imagery (for example Wheatley et al., 1989).

Anthony and his colleagues (for example Wheatley et al., 1989; Anthony et al., 1993; Zmud et al., 1993) have investigated the value of guiding participants in their imagery. This is a process that 'combines an individual's private experience and imagination with specific stimuli during periods of relaxation . . . The specific stimuli consist of external guidance, script, or suggestion . . . that facilitates a sharp focusing of attention and a bridging of the gap between rational and emotional awareness' (Wheatley et al., 1989, p. 37). Like the scripts in prompted relaxation, the scene to be imagined is read out slowly to participants. The example script given by Anthony et al. (1993, p. 48) addresses 'all of the appropriate senses', and uses 'clear, vivid, unambiguous language' (p. 47). Scripts should be read in a way that fosters immersion, that is, slowly, with pauses for the imagery to be conjured. The authors suggest that time should be given for the participants to 'translate script imagery into personally meaningful experiences and expectancies' (p. 51). In a sense, they have to apply the 'missing' imagery to put the general scripted outline into the context that they know, and enter into the imagined scene themselves. Once participants are as it were 'living' the scene, then they can be given additional 'information' or 'developments'. The argument behind guided imagery is that this later information will be processed imagistically. The participant then notes the reactions of themselves or imagined others in the scene.

Wheatley et al. (1989) used guided imagery to enhance the creativity and imagination of strategic planners. They found that it was an effective method for getting individuals to entertain unique, diverse and radical alternative scenarios for organizations, and (at least for those with higher imagery ability) also useful in promoting individual goal-setting productivity, that is, capacity to define and articulate concrete objectives to be accomplished in a future state. It is interesting to note the apparent distinction between imagery being able to promote the consideration of basically 'new' (though 'looser') general conceptions, and the sustained working with imagery to translate states into 'concrete' implications. The latter task requires a more sophisticated degree of imagery. Of course, it may be possible to operate strategic planning in much the same dialectic way that designers operate. The visions can be analysed in terms of their implications (and, in particular, implementation considerations) propositionally.

Guided introspection

Just as people can benefit from some external cueing to help them enter and explore imaginary worlds, they can also be guided in their self-reflection. Managers may not be experienced in extensive introspection. Betts (1909) advocated the use of a 'guide to introspection' (p. 52). He suggested that in learning how to introspect, it can be useful to know some of the things one may expect to find as parts of one's mental content. He asked people to search for and consider sensory elements, feelings of relation, images, feelings of effort and personal feelings. Specifically, people can consider sensory elements of their introspection when they ask of themselves which of the senses is in play in their minds, for example 'Are you smelling anything?', 'What can you hear?'. They can ask themselves about how they 'relate' to the thought, for example 'Are you experiencing feelings of recognition?', 'Do you have a feeling that your thoughts are meaningful?'. People can be asked to consider the particular images themselves, for example 'How bright is the light?', 'How heavy does the object feel?'. They can be asked to consider whether particular forms of effort are evident, for example 'Do you have a feeling of compulsion, strain, intention, expectation etc.?'. In addition, personal feelings can be considered, for example 'Do you have a feeling of pleasure or displeasure, interest, cheerfulness, sadness etc.?'. People are urged 'to mention all the elements discernible, explain their nature as far as possible, and tell the order in which they appeared. Be careful not to refer . . . to any element which may arise in your mind NOW, but was not in your mind THEN' (p. 52).

Several comments on these guidelines are relevant. First, it is interesting that Betts recognized that different degrees of 'effort' can be put into thought processes, and that this is in itself noteworthy. In some ways this seems similar to our distinction between autistic (effort-free) and other types of thinking. Secondly, Betts felt it useful to consider the prevailing emotion of a thought process. This is in line with our suggestion to consider mood thinking. Thirdly, Betts notes that engagement in introspection can 'add' thoughts to those in operation at the time. Reasoning (sense-making) affects thought processes in specific ways.

It seems clear that people should learn how to introspect. The meta-knowledge concerning their own thinking processes is an important element in management by perception.

Inducing and supporting visual thinking

It was noted in Chapter 2 that the major form of imagistic thinking that people undertake is visual imagery. While the general issues outlined above concerning the support of induction and reflection on imagistic thinking apply, it seems appropriate to offer some guidance on additional specific recommendations for inducing and supporting visual imagery.

INDUCING VISUAL IMAGERY   The sophistication of people's artistic appreciation clearly varies. There is evidence to suggest that there is a developmental process involved, that there is a maturation in people's depth and form of grasp of different 'languages' of art. From a business/ organizational point of view, it is visual information that is most relevant.

Parsons (1987) provides a cognitive developmental account of aesthetic experience of visual art. He identifies five stages of aesthetic development. These reflect a progression from intuitive 'favouritism', to a bias for 'beauty and realism', to an appreciation of 'expressiveness' of forms and emotions beyond beauty and realism, to an acceptance of the legitimacy of an artist operating within a particular tradition of 'style and form', to a final stage that he calls 'autonomy' where people can appreciate instances where an artist has moved out from certain languages and frameworks to operate in their own right. The progression through stages one to three is largely attributable to age (and implicitly the 'standard' levels of exposure and reflection on visual art). As such one can distinguish between a child's and an adult's sophistication of appreciation. The progression through stages four and five is what will distinguish in the main between different adults' appreciation of art. A relationship between stage (and possibly within-stage level) of aesthetic appreciation and use of visual imagery in everyday problem-solving seems plausible.

Perhaps a distinction needs to be made between an 'academic' appreciation of art (where a person knows why something is or is not being done) and an experientially based appreciation (where a person knows how something is being done). It may be that a person who is artistically literate in the former sense does not necessarily attend to visual information more than others. It is difficult not to argue that a person that is visually attuned in the latter sense is so sensitized to visual material that they attend to it ahead of other media. There is evidence that people with a higher level of spatial reasoning are more able to *integrate* two different kinds of visual representation of the same event in their minds than are less spatially adept people (Barsam and Simutis, 1984).

People may need to overcome two widespread and damaging beliefs that Buzan (1993) feels have led to the modern rejection of our visualizing skills. These are that 'images and colours are somehow primitive, childish, immature and irrelevant' and 'that the power to create and reproduce images is a god-given talent dispensed to a tiny minority' (p. 74). Buzan (1993, pp. 74–7) outlines an image exercise which aims to utilize the visual cortex, enhance the memory's storing and recalling capabilities through the use of images for emphasis and association, increase aesthetic pleasure by enjoying the images themselves, break down resistance to the use of images in learning, aid mental relaxation and begin to develop the powers of visualization and perception. He uses a mind-mapping approach, where a central image is used as a basis to initiate ten radiating branches, each having a different visual image on it. He suggests that a good starting point may be a central image of 'home' because it provides plenty of opportunities for easy associative image development. The essence of his argument is that people can build up their abilities to undertake imagistic thinking. Townsend and Favier (1991) outline a warm-up procedure where very basic 'found' images (for example sketches of a tortoise, pen, guitar) are used to get people into the swing of relaxing and making connections.

Similar developmental stages could be used in the construction of rich pictures as they are used in soft systems methodology. Pictures may usefully limit themselves to a smaller vocabulary, initially. Simple icons such as crossed swords, handshake, light bulb may have to be used. In time, some of the more subtle variants on these themes may come to be used.

Most of the guidelines concerning visual imagery have been derived from studies that have induced autistic thinking, often with the objective of enhancing creativity. As a result, a high emphasis appears to be placed on the 'flow' of ideas. Propositional thought is minimized through attempting to enforce a continuous, rapid and spontaneous thought process that is operating with visual images. It is possible, of course, to use visual representations in the other types of thinking, such as mood thinking and reasoning. In mood thinking, for example, one may not be placing so much emphasis on the 'product' of drawing. The drawing process itself may assist in capturing and maintaining a mood. Rapid random scribbling may be a legitimate process, in this context. It does produce an image that reflects a concept in itself. 'Getting into' visual thinking in a mood setting can be secured through the general guided imagery procedures outlined above and mood induction procedures detailed in Chapter 5.

In using images in the course of reasoning, we have seen how attention can be drawn to particular interrelationships that might not otherwise be apparent in sequential text or tables of numbers. We have seen how particular features of data are addressed in the course of using different graphical forms. The use of images in a reasoning context is related more perhaps to visual and abstract reasoning abilities than artistic or aesthetic appreciation. Accordingly, inducing and supporting the use of graphical representations may be more a matter of education in the range of alternative forms and conventions of graphs than of inducing a form of thought. Visual representations can contribute to reasoning with semantic mental material. In particular, cognitive maps can be constructed to highlight important principles of semantic understanding. This particular application of visual techniques will be discussed more fully in the section on techniques for working with semantic information in Chapter 6.

SUPPORTING VISUAL IMAGERY   Certain occupational groups need to work with visual images. They feel completely at ease with them, and may not consciously control their switching of thinking from a propositional mode into an imagistic one. The 'dialogue' with the image is part of their reflection in action. They may switch between seeing something 'as' an object (imagistically) and 'seeing that' (propositionally) it has particular properties. There is a dialectical relationship between these two modes of operating. When we try to use imagistic thinking, we are doing so with a view to a subsequent propositional mode. We may deliberately design in a large 'gap' between the two forms of thought. In that case, we may try to get into the feel of using images. We may want to do this in an essentially uninterrupted manner. We may want to capture as much of the imagery as possible. We may want to resist efforts at thinking about the images too much. It is at a later time (perhaps even another day) that we invoke some propositional thinking to interpret what we were imaging. We may be using the images as a 'springboard' for our propositional thinking. This separation between imagistic and propositional thinking can be useful. In a brainstorming session, for example, we may want ideas to come, and continue to come. We may feel that *any* more rational reaction would act as a censoring device on our own thinking. We may wish to keep imagistic thinking as a distinct phase in the process.

It can be useful to consider the external support of visual thinking under two headings. There are those issues that concern facilitating the generation, composition and capturing of visual images when people are physically creating their own graphical images. The main issues here concern support for the execution of drawing, sculpting etc. There are also issues concerning the promotion and exploration of visual thinking when people are working with pre-prepared (found) images. The main issues here concern guidance for the selection and analysis of images.

Supporting Graphical Image Generation   It is possible to record the relatively pure graphic image-creation process as it occurs. Video recording would be an obvious possibility. It can be useful to capture the sequence and dynamics of image generation. It can also be useful to appreciate the 'language' that is used alongside the production of images. Very brief self-explanations (often virtually 'mutterings') can be illuminating. Researchers who have studied the work of designers have found that it can be useful to have such a rich record. Current research is trying to see how the dynamics of sketching when 'drawing on screen' (or any computer-linked drawing surface) can be captured (Clark and Scrivener, 1993). Nancy Flint, a multimedia designer, has been investigating the potential of records that include video, 'en route' sketches, interim computer screens and 'talking aloud', to serve as means of capturing the design process (Flint and Sparrow, 1995).

Such records can serve as useful representations for subsequent reflection and interpretation. In general, participants will need to have a medium to express their ideas rapidly and spontaneously. Wood (1993) notes how the medium should support six major dimensions of 'interaction'. Minimizing 'delayed gratification' is important. People need to feel that their representation 'device' does not get in the way of expressing their ideas. Using computer graphics software, for example, can mean that it can take too long to achieve the desired result. Paper and pencil can be transparent, in that one can make the desired mark without wasting cognitive resources on interacting with the interface. A second important consideration is 'diffuseness' (that is, a comprehensive facility for participants to communicate overviews of ideas and their relationships). 'Perceptual cueing' is important, so that typographical conventions (such as case, size, underlining, bulleting) and means of positioning elements (for example use of proximity and lines to associate ideas) can be used. 'Accessibility' of ideas is also important: people need to be able to put images down and pick them up again. Surfaces that allow seeing where all of the images are will help. Laying things out across a table can be helpful, but we can soon lose what we want in a pile of papers. This reduction in accessibility may impede the flow of imagistic thinking. 'Premature commitment' refers to instances where an image promotes too much fixation. People need to be able to express ideas as natural, ill-formed, scruffy images. The use of pencils, crayons, felt-tips and dry markers may engender different textures and grains of images. Computer drawing packages have a formality and finality of image that computer paint packages can escape. Fish and Scrivener (1990) show that artists' sketches are incomplete and ambiguous and point out that Leonardo Da Vinci believed that untidy indeterminancies in the sketch allow the artist to imagine different options. The final element of interaction that is important is 'viscosity', a power of resisting the arrangement of things. Free-flowing thought needs media that have low viscosity. For example, a 'complete re-draw' may often be felt to be required. An 'intelligent' piece of software that understood the links between elements could reconfigure a diagram far more quickly that it could be redrawn on paper and thus be, in fact, less disruptive to thought. Overall, we can see that an environment where the natural flow and development of ideas can be supported is an important aspect of supporting imagistic thought.

Drawings by participants can be used as a method of data collection (for example Denham, 1993). I first began exploring managers' attitudes and approaches towards using drawing in the course of self-insight several years ago. Over the years, a particular scenario has been refined. In one variation, participants are given the following instructions:

> You work in production/operations in a medium-sized manufacturing company. Your company has recently acquired a small manufacturing operation which used to operate as one of your major suppliers of part-finished goods. The managing director wishes you to take the post of Logistics Manager. He has asked you to manage the entire re-equipping and synchronization of operations across the two plants. What images come to mind?

Participants are provided with A3-sized sheets of paper and some pencils. The drawings that are produced can be interpreted to give some insights

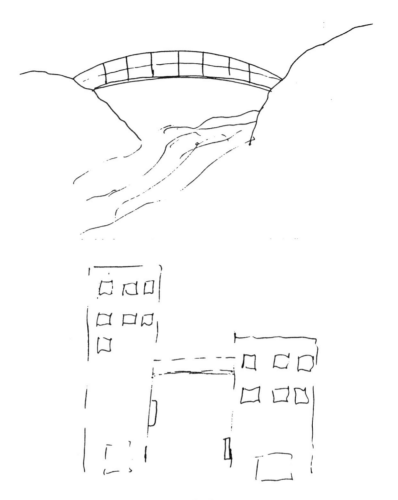

Figure 4.1 *Images drawn by iNtuitive-Thinking types*

into both tacit feel and unconscious interpretations. Figures 4.1 to 4.5 are examples of the drawings produced. Some example interpretations in terms of tacit feel for organizational processes and unconscious interpretations are given in the respective sections of Chapter 6.

Our interest at this stage concerns some of the characteristics of the drawings themselves as images. Over the years, drawings have been generated by many managers. In order to gain some insight into the 'nature' of the drawings produced by managers, an example set of drawings was given to two graphic designers, Les Arthur and Nancy Flint, in a repertory grid procedure. Each designer was asked to contrast any pair of drawings with a third, and to state the construct that captured the differences between drawings. The procedure was continued until no further constructs were readily forthcoming. Table 4.1 lists some of the constructs elicited by the

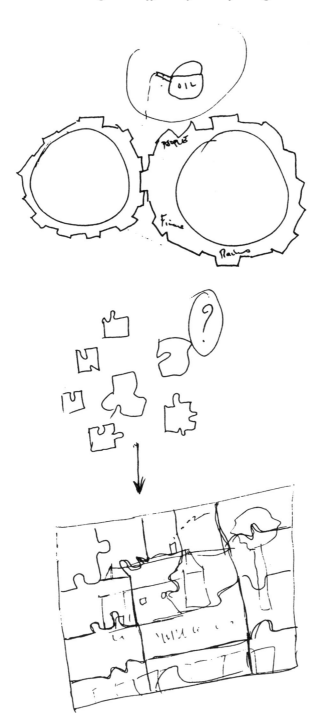

Figure 4.2 *Images drawn by Sensing-Thinking types*

Figure 4.3   *Images drawn by iNtuitive-Feeling types*

procedure. We can see that drawing may be bounded by several limitations in the abilities of individuals to express themselves physically on paper. There can be a clumsiness in drawing that could be argued to impede expression of 'felt' impressions. There can be some limitations in the insights that people get, in the course of executing a drawing, that is, they may not benefit from the 'dialectics of sketching' (Goldschmidt, 1991), in the way that professional designers evidence. Nevertheless, the overwhelming majority of participants report that they knew what they wished to

Figure 4.4   *Images drawn by Sensing-Feeling types*

convey, and while the image they drew was known to lack sophistication, they were happy that they had communicated the gist of their view. The 'interpretation' of a participant's images is a joint exploration, and not a set of pronouncements. Most participants find the subsequent review process revealing and valid.

An extension to the drawing approach towards the creation of images involves participants in making physical artefacts that express their views. Annie Rubienska, a colleague at the University of Central England, worked with a group of students to explore their images of organizational cultures using sculpture. The approach tended to generate 'coherent' metaphors. One group used 'weather' as a parallel. They had 'whirlwind' figures and 'clashes of thunder and lightning'. It was notable that detailed knowledge of meteorology was not evidenced. There were no references to thermals, precipitation etc. This may be due to at least two factors. First, the approach is meant to capture the powerful and immediate aspects of an issue, rather than a neat, perhaps contrived or even forced metaphor. Maybe only the basics get expressed in such approaches. Alternatively, the education of the participants may be lacking. They may not be able to sense deep and powerful metaphors that offer multifaceted insights. It is always notable that classical scholars such as Jung could sense parallels because of their exceptionally rich set of prospective metaphors.

There is inevitably less spontaneity in the sculpting/modelling of an artefact than in a freehand drawing. The group approach towards creation

Figure 4.5 *Examples of 'splitting' and 'anima' in drawings*

means that much of the benefit of the imagistic form of thinking takes place in the design debates. The time and energy involved in the actual creation of the artefact may not be justified. There can be occasions when it is apparent that too much time has been spent on a high-fidelity model or feature, at the expense of metaphorical thinking. Many of the most revealing artefacts are not coherent, unified entities. In contrast, they are odd 'assemblies' of features that combine to offer a much larger set of insights.

In the ideal situation, the design process is continued, in the imagistic mode, with features and developments being added to the artefact intuitively. The interpretation, presentation and discussion of the artefact can be deferred. One example of such a complex assembly consisted of a pink box, with straws of varying lengths protruding from it denoting the connections and distances between different 'players' in a situation. Each 'player' had their own 'form', sculpted to attach to the protruding part of the straw. One was a ball, another a streamer of coloured crêpe paper, and another a tinsel star. Examples of the effects that different players experienced when they went into their own particular motions were dramatically enacted.

The separation between the pure 'imaging' phase and a propositional phase need not therefore be abrupt. Just as designers freely roam between the forms of thoughts and use them dialectically, so could our participants. We need to support both forms of thought. In addition to the issues

Table 4.1 *Some of the constructs used by two graphic designers to contrast different drawings made by managers*

organized	less organized
dyadic structure	more considerations
limited vocabulary of artistic concepts	richer vocabulary
convergent	divergent
diverse	narrow
verbal only	uses some numerical symbols
attempts visualization	no concept structure
rationalist	less constrained
punchy	less lively
shows drive	restrained
very literal translation	sees ambiguity
demonstrates engagement	an 'exercise'
keeps feet on the ground	flies
having a go at exploring	constrained
gets a lot of information down	does not get complete issue
fertile	*laissez-faire*
shows issues as isolated elements	shows connections between issues
predictable imagery	less predictable
uses standard basic shapes	uses own observation/design
conveys an atmosphere	does not
indecisive	more decisive
rambling (elements with no purpose)	less rambling
fragmented	coherent
sees all the pieces in isolation	sees pattern
diagrammatic images	more creative images
flamboyant (moved around)	stays within confines of areas on page
raises questions (question marks)	does not
uses variety of shapes	more restrictive range of shapes
shows understanding of space	does not
shows understanding of perspective	does not
has humour	does not
angular	softer/circular
rooted in school-book art	has advanced
formal	less formal
stylized images	personal interpretations
more pictorial	very textual
uses standard images (icons)	more realistic
diagrammatic	trying to draw
graphical (interpreting quantity visually)	numbers
emotive	less emotive
conceptual/human	quantities/amounts
simple	complex
uses different perspective	uses single perspective
adds sense	does not
creative	uncreative
uses concept to hold an idea	no deeper concept
tells a story	does not
lines/schematic	abstract
dry	expressive
more mental involvement	less mental involvement
pleasing to the eye	not pleasing
confusing	clear

outlined above concerning image expression and capture, we need to consider the issues in supporting parallel propositional activities. For example,
we may need there to be separate places for notes to be made. We need
means of organizing notes in a more logical and structured way. There are
paper and pencil options here. There are also computer software packages
that specifically support idea structuring.

Supporting the use of 'found images' in imagistic thinking   We can provide
participants with a directory of images, and allow them the opportunity to
wander through the collection of images and work on any ideas that strike
them. Interacting with a 'found image' in this way takes a little practice. We
can make some suggestions for participants, however. An important consideration is giving people a basic orienting frame of reference. They may,
for example, be asked to think about 'considerations in implementing a new
system of dealing with customers'. They may want to look at the images
from a client's point of view. They may want to try to see things in the
pictures that they (as a client) may spot because they parallel the client's
new experience.

A wide variety of visual images can serve as a basis to provoke some
imagistic thinking. It is possible to locate images along a dimension that
ranges from perhaps a single overwhelming 'message' to more complex
images that lend themselves to multiple interpretations. It can be useful,
therefore, to select images that involve several people/objects in various sets
of relationships to each other. Figure 4.6 is a reproduction of a collage
produced by the New York poet/artist Sandy McIntosh that is used by
Patton (1987) in his work with professional auditors. It is a good example of
an image that lends itself to multiple interpretations. You may, for example,
like to try to focus on the relationships between senior management in your
organization and other organizational participants, and then look at the
image. What strikes you about the image now? This is a particularly rich
image that I have found of value in working with participants in many
contexts.

The same principles can be applied to particular images that have been
specifically designed with promoting subsequent imagistic thinking in mind.
These techniques often have their roots in psychoanalytic theory, and are
referred to as projective techniques. They will be discussed in those terms
when we outline techniques specifically attempting to elicit unconscious
mental material. There are two famous examples of projective approaches.
The term projective is used because the stimulus is vague, often so vague
that there is no 'real' meaning to the image. In other approaches the image
is unclear or obscured in some way. In both instances, it is argued that,
since there is little or no 'story' in the image itself, any description given by
a participant must come from the participant himself. They have projected
something of themselves on to the image.

Perhaps the most famous of these approaches is the set of ten symmetri-
cal ink blots developed by Rorschach (1921). There are over 5000 reported

Figure 4.6 *An example 'found' image that can be used to promote imagistic thinking.* [A reproduction of a collage by Sandy McIntosh, printed in Patton, M.Q. (1987) *Creative Evaluation* 2nd edn. Newbury Park, California, Sage, p. 158.]

studies that have used the 'test'. The ink blots are, in fact, so abstract that people can move away from the images in their 'excursions'. They may begin to operate on propositional thinking when making associations and elaborating on them. This is not necessarily a critical issue in the clinical use of the test. In discussing the role of the unconscious, it may be appropriate. For our purposes in this section, however, we can see that the technique has great potential but requires very skilful management of the process, if imagistic thinking is to be retained throughout.

Perhaps the second most famous approach that uses ambiguous images is the thematic apperception test, developed by Murray (1938). This is a series of ambiguous pictures, mainly of human beings, which people can consider and describe. An immense number of variants have been developed. The essence of the approach can be conveyed if one imagines a scene with a man at a desk. He is at work. He is looking down, out of the window. We cannot see anything below the window. We could ask people to tell us what has happened. Who is this man? What is he thinking? What has led up to this situation? What is likely to happen? By encouraging the participant to enter into the scene, and play out (in their minds) the events, they can be encouraged to continue to think imagistically. It is possible to create one's own sets of images that are sufficiently obscured, through a repeated process of successive photocopying.

Oppenheim (1992) outlines the use of picture interpretation in social and consumer research. He notes how, for example, when a particular set of images asks people in effect to guess what the person in the picture's mother might be like, that people will quite willingly do so. Very often we find that the impressions are quite pressing. There can be a clear sense of conviction about the matter. People can see or at least sense something in images that cues other strong images. The flow of thought can be quite different from that associated with propositional thoughts. An example may help here. If we ask people to consider the numbers 2, 3, 5 and 6, and ask them which digit might also be included in this list, we can observe their thinking. What do you think the missing digit might be? How are you thinking about the issue? Are looking at the gap between 2 and 3, then between 3 and 5? Or have you seen that these are the digits that have curves in their shape, unlike 1, 4 and 7? So you would suggest we include 8 or 9 in the list of numbers? Graphic designers may see that link more readily than accountants. It is a different form of thinking. We can promote it. We can take advantage of it.

Photo elicitation was first described by Collier (1967) as a very simple variation on the theme of open-ended interviewing. The nature of the roles of interviewer and interviewee is discussed by Harper (1994). In a photo elicitation interview, discussion is stimulated and guided by images. Typically these are photographs that the interviewer has taken of the participant's world. Alternatively, they can be drawn from a historical archive, or be images from the participant's home collection. As the participant interprets the image a dialogue begins. It is likely to go in particular directions because of the participant's links with the image. An obvious use is in considering people's reactions to their physical environment. Alternative sets of scenes can be used to tap into the intuitive appreciation of certain visual features of settings. In considering issues of a less visual nature, the photographs serve merely as a starting point for discussion, and the interview moves away from images quite early. The strengths of the approach can lie in cueing participants to notice aspects of their cultural setting that they may otherwise not consider. A possible variation therefore, might be to use many images to elicit the initial perceptions associated with them. They could be administered in a 'flash-card' manner. Thoughts may then remain in a more imagistic mode.

Supporting access to images in memory

One of the main instances of how imagistic information can be of value in organizations concerns the images people have stored in their minds of particular organizational episodes. These are part of the impressions that a person will 'consult' when considering alternative future actions. As we have noted, not all of the meaning of an event will have been abstracted and encoded propositionally. It is possible to help participants access and articulate their memories of episodes, so that insight can be gained into those key events that have been stored, and the ways in which they are then interpreted. As we have seen with all instances of supporting imagistic thinking, there is a need to help participants attune their thinking. Imagistic thinking is less 'controllable' than propositional thinking. It can take some discipline to bring an image to mind and to keep it there.

Perhaps some of the exercises that are more attuned to promoting a free-floating exploration of links and associations that a person makes between concepts are not optimal for this form of access. Research in the facilitation of eyewitness accounts of incidents has advanced our understanding of some of the key issues and approaches in promoting this form of access to images in memory. Fisher and Geiselman (1992) highlight some important considerations in probing people's image codes. Most emphasis is placed on the visual images of particular episodes, but the guidelines can be used to elicit the full set of sensory information associated with a memory. Preliminary verbal discussion with participants can secure some of the basic aspects of a situation. These cues can be used in any subsequent attempt to help guide the person back to the situation that is being considered. They confirm that visual imagery can be susceptible to influence from any other visual stimuli present and so it can be useful to ask participants to close their eyes and concentrate on the particular mental image. It is useful to tell the participant to take 'several seconds to concentrate exclusively on developing the image before describing it' (p. 134). Let us suppose that we are interested in the image that a participant has of a recent meeting with her boss. We could encourage her to develop the image of the meeting. Fisher and Geiselman's (1992) guidelines advocate that questions are asked 'slowly, deliberately, and softly, so that [the participant] can maintain the image without being distracted' (p. 135). They suggest that questions are explicit but open-ended so that the participant can supply an extensive answer.

It is also often necessary to follow up on incomplete narrations. Participants can be encouraged to refocus on the image, and then consider some particular part of it more closely. Participants are likely to 'interpret' events once they have begun to recount them. They may well enter a quite extensive phase of reasoning about the causes or outcomes of the issue at hand. This will lead to the loss of the image temporarily. They will have to be supported in retuning to the image. Some of the statements from the last 'visit' to the image can be used to help the participant regain it. It can take several 'visits' to a particular episode to cull its full set of significant features.

Imagistic thought contributes to organizational knowledge. This section has focused on key issues in inducing and supporting this form of thought. The first step in electing to undertake imagistic thought explicitly, probably comes from an appreciation of its relative neglect in organizational interactions. In Chapter 3, a framework of physical representations was developed. Organizations may wish to analyse their interpersonal interactions in terms of the framework of representations presented in Table 3.4. Simply stepping through the classification, line by line, and asking oneself, 'What additional considerations might I have recognized if I had attempted to use this representation?', can expose the potential.

Self-managing one's use of imagistic thinking offers great potential. It is clear that the explicit use of non-propositional thought will be new in some quarters. This may mean that any unease concerning the use of such techniques will need to be managed. It is unusual for people at work deliberately to undertake induction procedures to try to cue different ways of thinking. There may be difficulties in initiating such a procedure. There may be a degradation in the rigour of implementation of such procedures if they are used by a work group over a considerable period of time. They may not undertake the process as conscientiously as they did at some of the earlier instances of induction.

Overall, however, it seems clear that individuals and workgroups can develop the skills of working with imagistic thought. The benefits may be considered so valuable that (as with those who work in design environments) they become second nature, an automatic part of the thinking approach.

5

Invoking Different Types of Thinking

We have seen throughout the book that everyday organizational encounters are a particular form of discourse. The world of work socially constructs organizational encounters in ways that promote particular thinking processes. We have noted in Chapter 4 how different forms of thought are used to 'configure' mental material. We shall see in Chapter 6 how this can have implications for the particular kinds of mental material accessed and created. In this chapter, we explore more fully, the classification of alternative types of thinking that was outlined in Chapter 2: how the particular configurations of mental material are 'processed' by the mind. These thinking processes were defined as autistic thinking, reasoning and mood. Each of these alternative types of thinking influences the nature of organizational encounters, the forms of thought used, and the kinds of mental material accessed and knowledge created.

Promoting an autistic type of thinking

The distinction between thinking where there is a 'sense of effort' and a feeling that one is the agent of certain perceptual changes, and thinking where one is virtually the passive recipient of new information, was referred to by James (1892). When we hallucinate we experience a complete lack of effort. Disciplined effort occurs when we are concentrating or deliberating on an issue.

The relative degrees of relaxation of mental effort can be detected in the brain's electroencephalograph (EEG) activity. A number of distinct waveforms or rhythms have now been isolated from the general electrical mosaic. The most common rhythms observed in waking adults are alpha and beta waves. Alpha waves (8–13 Hz) are observed most commonly in relaxed individuals at rest with their eyes closed. Beta waves (14–30 Hz) accompany states of relative alertness. In addition, delta waves (<4 Hz) occur during sleep, but are rare after waking up. Theta waves (4–7 Hz) are a normal component in EEGs of children, but are rare in adulthood, except in episodes of emotional distress. At any given moment the adult EEG is unlikely to comprise waves of only one sort. Rather, one wave-form will be predominant. Physiological self-regulation can be used to control EEG activity voluntarily (Kamiya, 1968). It is possible to control the degree of relaxation in the mind by self-inducing alpha waves. The accompanying awareness of thought contents and patterns suggests that relaxed thought is of a less rigorous (controlled) nature.

There are many physiological measures that can be fed back to a person to enhance their self-regulation. Voluntary control has been 'reliably demonstrated over heart rate, blood pressure, skin temperature, brain waves, muscle tension, vasomotor tone, salivation and the electrical conductivity of the skin' (Carroll, 1984). As we have noted, imagery can play an important role in movement control. A degree of physiological self-regulation can therefore be achieved through appropriate thinking processes. There is a general consensus that there is a greater volume of uncontrolled thought activity in 'non-normal' levels of activity. It is possible during hyper levels of activity for a stream of consciousness to be unleashed that might not otherwise occur. This can be observed in situations where mass hysteria is induced through revelry. This is still a part of life in countries with voodoo cultures, such as Haiti (Hall, 1994). It is unlikely, however, that approaches that rely on 'excesses' will be practised in organizations. We may find efforts that seek to reduce conscious control through minimizing physiological activity more appropriate.

A state of relaxation can be induced through imagery. Typically, a script where different parts of the body are referred to is used, and participants are asked to concentrate their minds on the part of the body in question and relax muscle tension. The procedure works up from the feet through to the neck and face, until the whole body is in a state of relaxation. This is a different form of imagery to that associated with 'projecting' oneself into an imaginary scene (for example Vaughan, 1979). Here the focus is on physiological arousal *per se* and not on the connotations of a particular setting. In this relaxed state, one can then muse. Many writers suggest that sitting (or lying) with one's eye's closed can reduce the invasions of thought that seeing particular objects may invoke. Darkening the room can also help in this regard. The daydream can be allowed to continue for some time. Subsequently, the contents and patterns of thoughts can be analysed. This can be done in an explicit process where the thoughts are recorded and then examined systematically. Often, however, there appears to be an intuitive recognition that something in the thought process is relevant and significant to an issue in hand. Insights into what one may have been feeling or doing in particular situations are arrived at, in parallel with the autistic thinking, or certainly immediately afterwards without systematic analysis. There are a large number of alternative techniques that have been developed in the East and West to promote relaxation (see, for example, Hewitt, 1982).

There is evidence to suggest that daydreaming invokes a different kind of mental material than dreaming. Metz (1994) compares and contrasts the total dream state (that is, night dreams and daydreams) in relation to the state that people are in while watching fictional films. The author contends that night dreams belong to children and night, while the film state and daydreams are more adult and belong to the day. There is a qualitative distinction between the imagery used in dreams and daydreams. Autistic thinking is more likely to reveal the associations of the conscious and subconscious mind rather than the unconscious mind. Dreaming may reveal more about the unconscious than the subconscious or conscious mind. I would suggest that the imagery is less radical and altogether more coherent in autistic thinking than it is in dreams.

Fournier and Guiry (1993) suggest that it is also possible to distinguish between planful (anticipatory) daydreaming and 'pure' daydreaming. Anticipatory daydreaming is a kind of fantasizing, where one projects oneself into a particular future or scene. It is largely an exercise of imagination. One is 'establishing' how the world might be if the fantasy was real. As such, we may have a feeling that we are dealing with real people and 'figuring out' how a situation and people's reactions may progress. There is perhaps, therefore, a higher degree of 'order' to the thought process than may occur in 'pure' daydreaming. Autistic thought can therefore, usefully be considered along a dimension of reality adjustment. This might range from planful fantasizing through to pure daydreaming and on to dreams. One might expect to find relatively higher emphases on conscious, subconscious and unconscious mental material at the three points along this reality–adjustment continuum. The cueing of thought that goes with guided imagery is likely to begin with a more planful form of daydreaming. The person is being cued to fantasize within particular parameters. Perhaps watching fictional films or television could also induce daydreams. It may be that more varied (or even random) images induce a less planful daydreaming episode. It also feels intuitively correct that a longer period of time spent in a daydreaming mode may mean that there is some drift between planful and pure daydreaming. It is unlikely to be a simple single drift from planful to pure daydreaming. It is more likely that there will be longer periods of planful daydreaming interspersed with occasional forays into pure daydreaming. Recent work on thought-sampling methods (Singer, 1993) may enable people to reflect systematically on different forms of daydreaming episodes. It may be useful to use some form of time-sampling approach, where participants can be encouraged to note and reflect on their daydreams at various time intervals. Of course, the very process of disrupting the flow of thoughts in this way could conspire to distort the patterns of thought. It can take time to get back into a daydreaming mode of thinking. One has the feeling on some occasions of wanting and being able to get back to the point where one left a daydreaming episode. One has the feeling of wishing to get back to the 'warmth' of the experience. One is also aware of how one is going about reconstructing the scene and experience. It may be possible to help people gain some skills of more rapid relaxation and re-entry into daydreams.

Autistic thinking may be operating largely on imagistic thoughts. Most of the techniques referred to in the literature utilize visual or other forms of imagery. One technique that does not restrict itself to imagistic thought is free association. The original form of free association was developed by Freud. Patients were 'asked to relax on a couch and say whatever came into their minds, however absurd, unpleasant, or obscene it might appear by everyday standards' (Brown, 1961, p. 17). Taylor (1961) distinguishes between this pure, unstructured form of free association where the stream of consciousness is uninterrupted, and a mixed or structured form. In the latter form, shorter sequences of associations are promoted. A 'section' is then revisited and used to initiate further associations. Taylor was writing from an idea-generation context, and advocated selecting items from free association lists that seemed to have special implications for the problem. For example, in coming up with a name for a soap, one might initiate associations with the word 'clean'. These may include terms such as 'sunny' or 'bright'. The term 'sunny' might then be selected, and used for further elaboration. A product name, such as 'Sunny Suds', may be conjured up. If one was unhappy with the results of the elaborations on 'sunny', one might go back to the term 'bright' and undertake free associations from that point. It may be that unstructured free association is able to capitalize more on imagistic thought. Approaches that use a mixture of unstructured and structured phases may remain more rooted in linguistic (propositional) thought. In a work context, it may be useful to examine some of the associations that people have with 'actual' situations. Perhaps some of the more immediate associations can more usefully be systematically pursued, rather than reflecting on a stream of consciousness that may range some way from the original term or concept. On the other hand, it may be that the latter gives a fuller and truer picture of the 'position' of the issue in the mind of the participant, even if several sessions are required to allow totally free rein.

An even more controlled set of concepts or words can be used in free association approaches. In creativity exercises, people may be encouraged to 'fish' for ideas, by consulting a dictionary or other database of ideas, in a random (or at least less rigidly sequenced flow) than they might undertake unaided. The associations with particular terms can be captured and considered. The distance of a term from a matter in hand may mean, however, that the technique is better viewed as a mechanism to cue metaphorical or analogical thought. Here, parallels between some of the 'properties' (including implications) of the dictionary term can be considered and related to the matter in hand. As can be seen, however, the focus would be on a reasoning mode of thinking for much of the process. The use of metaphor will be discussed later in the chapter. At this stage we might reserve the use of 'listings' in cueing thought to their role in promoting free, immediate, spontaneous associations.

Imagistically oriented forms of free association can be cued. With regard to visual images, Miller (1987) suggests that creative drawing can be a useful process, because 'our intuitive consciousness communicates more easily in impressions and symbols than in words' (p. 91). Drawing may produce intuitive, sometimes archetypal symbols. Drawing can be restricted to particular icons that epitomize what a situation feels like. It may be, however, that without a relaxation or other imagistic induction procedure the images will remain more 'literal'. It may be more useful to 'try letting the images flow without conscious direction, as if the items on the paper were telling you how they wanted to be' (Miller, 1987, p. 92). Like its more linguistic counterpart, imagistic free association can be allowed to operate in an unstructured way, so that thoughts are, as it were, grown organically, and an uninterrupted flow of images is encouraged. A more structured approach can be adopted when using techniques such as mind-mapping, discussed in Chapter 4. Buzan (1993) suggests that 'one can start with a central image that expresses the concept' (p. 85). The term (or perhaps an image) is drawn on to a page of paper. Typically, one then proceeds with a branch from this central image. This association is referred to as a 'basic ordering idea' (p. 84). The branch and word (image) are then drawn. A quick spray of associations may radiate from a basic ordering idea, which are drawn in turn. In the course of this process, perhaps another basic ordering idea (BOI) strikes the person. This is drawn like the first BOI, as a branch off the central image, and so on. The process encourages rapid execution of ideas, but supports the process by having a physical representation (map) that helps participants locate their ideas, and cues them into further thought. One has the feeling, as one moves through the branches to those that are branches off branches, that one is imposing some sort of logic on the set of terms one is using. In general, one feels tempted to check whether the set is complete (exhaustive) and mutually exclusive. It is, however, often when one is part way through a lower-order set of associations that an entirely new set of thoughts (BOI) is elicited. The skill, in so far as capturing yourself in a map is concerned, is to place as little emphasis as possible on the logic of the entries.

Non-visual forms of imagery can also be used as a vehicle for autistic thinking. Projecting oneself into a particular imaginary world can enable one's associations with that context to be manifested. We have seen how guided imagery can be used in a strategic management scenario-building context. Some of the basic prejudices that one has about certain facets of the world of work can be revealed in this process. For example, one may picture a process-control world of clean, professional tranquillity with what seem to be equals operating harmoniously. On the other hand, one may imagine a hierarchical world of peripheral employees, struggling within a chaotic environment. What is the role of technology in your particular vision of the future? In a similar way, a future search conference (Weisbord, 1992) can enable participants to extrapolate key dimensions of an organization's development, from its past to its present state, into possible futures. The flow of ideas and consequences stemming from such possibilities can be captured through an autistic thinking mode.

It is also possible to gain insights into the associations you make with particular individuals or situations by enacting an imaginary scene where you play the role of another person experiencing the context. If you attempt to role-play another 'real' person from the actual context, then you may find that your skills in tactfulness limit the value of potential insights. It may be more fruitful to invite somebody from outside the context to experience it. Garfinkel (1967) used this approach when he played a 'guest in his own home', to gain insight into how one treats 'close' as opposed to 'outside' people in the home context. This 'guest' was a generalized concept of guest in Mead's (1934) sense of a generalized other. It is possible to gain insights through imagining an actual person (though not one who would expect to encounter the situation) operating in the particular context. It may be that a balance has to be struck between the clarity and ease of playing a highly stereotyped figure (such as Gandhi or Salvador Dali) and the narrowness of insight that one gains by placing such figures in the scene. Figures that are too powerful will cue thoughts concerning that facet of personality *per se*, rather than associations of the context itself.

In all instances of using such imagery in an autistic mode of thinking, it is important that one mentally 'experiences' the scene, and does not just 'figure out' what might happen. This latter form of analysis has value, but is more in tune with a reasoning mode of thinking and the insights that it can bring. Within the autistic mode one needs to consider the degree of 'immersion' in a character or scene. We can sense this when we reflect on the language that we sometimes use in everyday discussion, when we consider positions other than our own. One can sense an increasing immersion as one progresses from gaining insights from 'wearing a different hat', through to 'looking at it from their point of view', through to trying to 'imagine if you were in their shoes', on to 'putting their shoes on and walking around a bit'. This latter form of imagination involves a genuine absorption of characteristics, and a more rounded and spontaneous experience of the context.

Finally, it should be noted that group processes can play a role in cueing and maintaining autistic thought. The findings concerning thinking rule systems such as brainstorming and other structured techniques (VanGundy, 1988) have shown that it is possible for groups to help individuals break out of the confines of their own patterns of self-censorship in thinking. The focus of such exercises lies outside an individual, on ideas, names and so on. Accordingly, we may not gain much insight into the thinking of particular individuals from such processes. It may be, however, that the hallmarks of particular groups' autistic thinking can be discerned.

Overall, the essence of the contribution of an autistic mode of thinking lies in its ability to establish the location of particular ideas or events in an individual's or group's mind. As we shall see, some of the automatic links that are made in free-flowing thought can give particular insight into tacit feel and unconscious interpretations.

Promoting reasoning as a type of thinking

Imagine if we ask somebody who has just come out of a meeting what they thought had been going on. We could listen to their account in a non-directive way. We might note the aspects of the episode which they report after they have consciously considered it. We could ask a more searching question, such as 'Who didn't say anything?'. We might hear our respondent exclaim: 'Yes! I noticed that Bill didn't say anything.' We have aided the respondent's recollection. On the other hand, the reaction may be: 'Mmm. I hadn't thought about it that way. But I suppose Bill said the least.' We have structured their reflections. It is not the respondent's initial mental material that has been accessed. Similarly, if we ask the respondent to rank order the participants in the meeting, to indicate the extent to which each of them spoke, we have used a systematic means of amplifying the initial information. Specifically, we have made sure that the respondent goes through each of the people present, considers their behaviour and comments on it in relation to each of the others. We have invoked a particular form of reasoning process, in order to gain the particular form of insight.

Taking the argument one step further, we may notice that the respondent has obtained many insights into the subtleties of the distinctions between the views of the people involved in the meeting. We may ask the respondent to map out the basic arguments that each participant appeared to have. The response may come easily. In contrast, there may be lots of 'gaps' in our respondent's understanding that we 'hear' being filled as they recount the positions of the various participants on the issue in hand. Our structured approach to establishing the cause-and-effect arguments with which the respondent explains the other participants' arguments may help with highlighting these facets of the respondent's mental material, or may guide their thinking and 'force' a kind of thinking and associated set of insights that are not really part of the respondent's initial mental material.

We can see, therefore, that there is a negotiated verbal model of events. We can see that some aspects of mental material may get 'lost' in an account. We can see that there may be various structured means of securing more searching interpretations of accounts. We can see that promoting different kinds of thinking about situations in itself highlights different features of the situation. Invoking reasoning means that we are asking ourselves or our respondents to undertake a definable form (or set) of thinking steps. This can be useful to the extent that it can serve as an aid to recall, by virtue of the fact that we or the respondent may have engaged in this form of reasoning at the time, and the re-engagement now has assisted. It can also be useful as an indication of the sort of information that we or the respondent may include if we or they were to embark on the particular form of thinking at a future date.

If we could identify some basic forms of reasoning, we could examine how we and other participants in organizations construe people and situations in the particular ways highlighted by the spectrum of different forms of reasoning. Chapter 3 presented a framework of visual representations (Table 3.4) and showed that different representations invoke and sustain particular forms of reasoning. Individual reflective practitioners and organizations may need to consider the limitations they may have in their mental material because they fail to utilize a comprehensive cross-section of representations to elicit knowledge. Chapter 2 identified a distinction between the form of reasoning that places an emphasis on distinguishing between things (that is, separating them out in some way, to try to find the variation in form) and reasoning that tries to locate the separate things in a wider sphere of things. So, for example, we might attempt to establish the different forms of chairs of which you are aware. We could aid you in thinking about the basic ways in which chairs differ. We could induce what we have referred to as separation thinking. In contrast, we could ask you to consider chairs in terms of particular shared characteristics. We could ask you to interrelate them with other concepts, such as comfort, office furniture etc. We would be inducing location thinking. This section explores some ways in which different forms of reasoning can be invoked and the facets of organizational knowledge that they highlight.

Promoting separation thinking

Promoting separation thinking means supporting people in the articulation of the terms they use when they construe objects and situations. It seeks to elicit and promote the linking of one particular idea/object/event with other concepts. To the extent that two ideas/objects/events can be found to have 'differences', they can be separated in the person's knowledge framework. Often, of course, an event which is indistinguishable from any other instance of the 'same' type of event, by one person, may be distinguished (separated) by another person. One particular board meeting may be seen to be like any other by one participant, and distinctly problematic by another. It is not just whether distinctions (separations) are made or not that is at issue (although it seems clear that 'experts' are able to make more subtle dissections than novices).

The terms in which distinctions are drawn between events varies between people. We have seen in Chapter 2 that there is a close relationship between semantic mental material and propositional reasoning. In Chapter 4 we discussed many of the issues and the specific techniques involved in the elicitation of the propositional codes that a person is using to construe an idea/object/event (that is, an entity). Invoking separation thinking is therefore to draw a person's attention to the characteristics of a particular entity, its attributes. Chapter 6 will focus on the issues involved in elicitation of different kinds of mental material *per se*. In this chapter we need to consider the extent to which a situation is cueing a 'searching' breakdown or analysis of an idea/object/event. It is possible to create an environment where it is legitimate to be pedantic. It is possible to adopt systematic procedures that invoke and maintain this particular emphasis in thinking.

The reader is referred to Chapter 4 for more detailed presentations of procedures that have been found to be particularly effective in this regard with propositional forms of semantic mental material, that is, repertory grid procedure, laddering, McFall's Mystical Monitor, the Q-sort procedure, perceptual mapping and mind-mapping. Of particular note here, however, are the instances where the compelling logic of challenging a person's conceptualization is the main force within a knowledge-elicitation technique. While all of the techniques listed above are appropriate for eliciting semantic understanding, and are all systematic procedures, in the main they are techniques where the respondent is guided or encouraged to think differently and to consider the distinctions that they make between ideas/objects/events. There are some instances where the elicitation approach is more challenging and 'checks' on the consistency of the respondent. Any instances of inconsistency are then drawn to their attention. The tone of the approach becomes one where, in a sense, it is the logic of the categorization that is being pursued rather than the system of construal itself. These techniques invoke this particular form of analytical thinking as a key component. Examples of such approaches are the computerized laddering approach outlined by Corbridge et al. (1994) and the computerized guessing tool outlined by Mussi (1995). Mussi's tool tries to guess an interpretation of the knowledge entered by the expert. The tool self-customizes its guessing capability, remembers 'failures' in guessing, and when they occur elicits their explanations. The overall resulting effect is that 'the tool digs up tenaciously, causal knowledge from the expert's mind' (p. 725).

Overall, separation thinking can be brought to bear to shed light on the sophistication and bases of differentiation that participants use in considering issues in a particular domain. The more systematic and rigorous a procedure, the more likely it is to be able to 'surface' the constructs that a person uses. Slavish pursuit of information through systematic procedures can promote thinking to such a depth that 'new' insights are distorting the impression of a person's construct system that one obtains.

Promoting location thinking

Location thinking differs from separation thinking in that the quest is to identify how different elements that we might perceive may relate to each other, that is, how one element can be located in terms of its interrelationships with other elements. In decision-making, for example, *implementation* can be construed as what one does with solutions that have been selected. That *option selection* and *implementation* are separate facets of decision-making is arrived at through separation thinking. That they can be categorized as subprocesses of decision-making is an example of separation thinking. Option selection and implementation can also be expressly compared with each other along particular dimensions. This comparative type of thinking has been referred to in Chapter 2 as static comparison.

How implementation relates to option choice in an overall system of decision-making is another example of how they can both be located. It is a different form of location thinking from static comparison. It is specifically highlighting interdependency rather than contrast. It is systems thinking.

Considering the ways in which option selection and implementation resemble political processes is a third form of location. Here the terms are being located more broadly through more abstract interrelationships with other spheres of knowledge, that is, they are contextualized. The more flexibly and comprehensively that one relates option selection and implementation to knowledge of other processes, the more insight one might gain into the two elements. This is a drive for plurality. Plurality thinking is the third form of location thinking.

These, then, are the three basic forms of location thinking that were outlined in Chapter 2: static comparison, systems thinking and plurality-seeking. They each invoke a different set of characteristics of the reasoning process. In the course of natural discussion, people may stray into periods of different basic forms of analysis when they are considering a matter. The issue here is whether a more explicit and systematic attempt to engage in each of the three forms of location thinking will help us gain insight into our perceptual world or that of participants. By enabling the expression of insights in these different forms, we can learn more than we could through some more limited account which we might more typically undertake. There is the ever-present danger of embarking on a process of elicitation that is, in itself, so demanding that it is less an indication of a person's current conception and more an education. If we promote extensive reasoning, we will generate new insights. If we spend a long time in such a process, we will be bringing about new knowledge quite extensively. This is, of course, not in itself wrong. At whatever point we leave the elicitation process we have secured an insight into mental material at that point in time. If it is appropriate to engage in some more challenging self-reflection, then we have not left the situation with less valid information. Perhaps we have, however, had more influence over the mental material itself than we might with less searching elicitation and/or less volatile aspects of mental material.

Where our agenda is to secure insights into current organizational knowledge, we may choose to use techniques that invoke reasoning quite sparingly, and very much in the mode of a facilitatory means of representing the person's knowledge. Where our agenda is more concerned with extensive self-development or promoting the sharing of organizational knowledge *in situ*, we may explore whether we and others wish to use reasoning processes more extensively to explore issues. There is an education agenda in that context. An overemphasis on reasoning approaches to knowledge elicitation and sharing can produce an atmosphere where participants are cued to find the *right* steps to take in the light of what they find; in other words, an abstracting process where individual views are subjugated to compelling logic. Here, the very purpose of seeking to establish the various perceptions of an issue is undermined.

Overall, the use of reasoning approaches requires careful management. There is clear value in using alternative reasoning processes to highlight different features of one's understanding of a matter. Slavish adherence to the dictates of the process may have to be guarded against. The three forms of location thinking (static comparison, systems thinking and plurality-seeking) are outlined below.

STATIC COMPARISON One way in which order can be sought regarding entities is in terms of their relative standing. For example, chairs may be considered in terms of their flame retardation. We can understand more about a particular set of chairs if we can locate them with each other along that particular dimension. We start with making a nominal distinction between the chairs. We can establish that they differ in terms of flame retardation. In a sense, we can say that Chair A has Chair A's worth of retardation, and Chair B has Chair B's worth of retardation and so on. We may be able to go further. We might be able to put the chairs in some form of order concerning fire retardation. This is relating them in terms of retardation using an ordinal level of measurement, for example Chair C first, Chair A second and Chair B third. We know more about the chairs by virtue of knowing how they stand in relation to each other on this scale than we would if we only knew that they differed. Similarly, we may also be able to grade fire retardation, for example on a five-point scale (where 1 is a low level of retardation and 5 is high). If we could relate the chairs to each other on this scale we would know yet more about them, such as that Chair C has a fire retardation of 4, Chair A has a retardation of 2 and Chair C has a retardation of 1. We know that the 'gap' between C and A is bigger than the 'gap' between A and B. With only ordinal-level information, we could merely put the chairs in a rank order. With this interval level of information, we can more clearly see how they interrelate.

If we are able to use an even higher level of measurement to interrelate the chairs we can know even more about them. If our scale of fire retardation was a measure of time that a lighted cigarette can rest on the chair before it catches alight, we may now know that Chair C's rating of 4 means that it can last for ten minutes before catching alight. A rating of 2 means that the chair can last for five minutes, and a rating of 1 means one minute. This ratio level of measurement means that we can make statements such as retardation lasting two, five or ten times as long, in relation to the set of chairs. Sophisticated categorization, using various levels of measurement (Babbie and Halley, 1995) can be a valuable process. Order-seeking in its most basic form provides useful location information.

People may find it hard to put things into an order. There are techniques that can be used to help individuals and groups do this. Bryson et al. (1994) highlight four common difficulties that groups face in dealing with complex qualitative information. There may be a vagueness in participants articulating preferences. It may be hard to put qualitative information into numbers. It can be difficult to combine the participant's preferences into a meaningful group preference. There can be difficulties in attempting to deal with a large number of alternatives. They propose a Group Support System (GSS) where a computer can assist the group in scoring and ranking alternatives. The imposition of a systematic procedure can be of value to groups. Thinking in terms of relative scales/positions can reveal key considerations in participants' thinking.

A complete group approach for handling prioritizing decisions is Interpretive Structural Modelling (Moore et al., 1987). The process begins with an element set and a subordinate relation. So, for example, a local council may be faced with a need to make budget cuts. It may have an element set of community programmes that it runs. The subordinate relation may be 'should be cut before'. By systematically making paired contrasts between each of the programmes, it is possible to tease out a listing of programmes that should be cut before others. Moore et al. (1987) note that subordinate phrases can 'be taken from at least one of six types of relations: impact, influence, definitive, spatial, temporal, mathematical' (pp. 82–3). Relation could include 'is subordinate to', 'reports to', 'should be eliminated befo 'is caused by', 'helps to achieve' etc. As the title suggests, Interpre Structural Modelling permits individuals and groups to interpret struc and model. 'The method is interpretive in that the group's judgment decides whether and how items are related. It is structural in that, on the basis of the relationships, an overall structure is extracted from the complex set of items. And it is modeling in that the specific relationships and overall structure are portrayed in a graphic form' (p. 78).

It can be very useful to have insights into the ways that we and other participants locate particular sets of elements along a particular dimension. There are many different forms of relationship between elements, however. Kahney (1993) notes the range of different relations commonly found in tests of intelligence. Some researchers have attempted to catalogue and classify different relations between elements. Pellegrino and Glaser (1982) identify seven major types of relation. Elements can be in class membership, part–whole, order, property, functional, conversion or location relationships. With regard to class membership, for example, biology is a science and sculpture is an art; dog is a domesticated form and wolf an undomesticated form of canine. In both instances, terms are instances of more general classes. An example part–whole relationship is a word being part of a sentence, and a sentence is part of a paragraph. In an order relationship, one term always follows the other, for example acorn to oaks. Elements are in a property relationship where one term has the property or quality defined by the other, for example emeralds have the colour green. A functional relationship is where one term performs some function for, or action on, another, for example man eats bread. A conversion relationship is where one term is made from or is a product of the other, for example sails are made from cloth. A location relationship means that the terms can be located in, on or about each other, for example a train travels on rails; butter goes on bread.

Systematic analysis of a cause–effect process may help us capture our own or another person's current location of concepts. For example, the causal chain of sales revenue being dependent on sales volume, which is dependent on the volume of goods available for sale, may be the view of sales revenue generation. Decisions may be based on that basic model. If sales revenue needs to increase, increase the volume of goods for sale. We (or Person A) may be blind to the argument that production depends on capacity and utilization of capacity, that production and stock constitute the amount that is available for sale, that the volume of sales also depends on demand, and that sales revenue also depends on unit price. It can be useful to undertake systematic cause–effect analysis if one is to see the particular elements and relationships that are being brought to bear in a decision. Even then, the use of one form of relationship thinking can blind us to other information. It can be useful to consider more systematically the various forms of relationship between elements. We may find that Person B and Person C share the same basic cause-and-effect model of sales revenue, and yet propose different courses of action for increasing sales revenue. If we restrict our attention to that single form of reasoning we may not account for their differences. But if we explore some of the other aspects of relationships between the elements, we may understand. For example, in terms of a conversion relationship, Person B may feel that altering unit price is an easier thing to do than altering sales volume. So Person B advocates the raising of price in order to increase sales revenue. In terms of a class membership relationship, Person C may note that production and stock fall under the production manager, whereas matters concerning sales demand involve one manager and matters involving pricing involve yet another. Armed with this information, and some insights into the politics of getting changes through the organization, Person C figures that arranging for minimizing stock levels is the best course of action to increase sales revenue. We can see how we might be able to gain some insight into the knowledge that guides participants' thinking if we explore the different forms of static comparison that they are using.

There are many techniques that we can use to depict relationships. As was noted in Chapter 3, different physical representations often carry with them different informational and computational characteristics. It is useful to examine some of the major forms of representation used in business decision-making, and consider the facets of problems that they emphasize. Scatter diagrams are a quick and simple method of identifying whether there seems to be a connection between two sets of data. Cooke and Slack (1991) give an example of how plotting the co-occurrence of pairs of variables on a graph can capture relationships. They show how an unusual relationship (for example indicating that the more visits made by a maintenance department to customers, the more they were satisfied) can be revealed with a scatter diagram. Closer inspection of the data revealed that the number of preventive maintenance visits made had a clear effect on satisfaction. The number of emergency service calls made had a slight but negative relationship with satisfaction. People often have basic beliefs about the strength and direction of correlations between sets of events. It can be useful to encourage participants to estimate relationships between things.

Consider the nature of the estimated relationships that Persons A, B and C might have reported between their efforts in addressing each of the causal elements of sales and sales revenue. A refinement of estimating correlation between effort and outcome is Pareto analysis. Pareto charts help prioritize data sets. They are particularly useful for ranking problems and helping focus improvement efforts where potential gains are greatest. Pareto's principle is that in any data set, a few important elements (empirically 20 per cent) describe most (empirically 80 per cent) of the situation, for example 20 per cent of the causes account for 80 per cent of the variation. It is a relatively straightforward technique which involves arranging information on the types of problems or causes of problems into their order of importance. In the example we have been using, perhaps 80 per cent of sales revenue comes from 20 per cent of the customers. Might this knowledge affect the positions that Persons A, B and C hold on the issue of increasing sales revenue?

We have noted how a casual enquiry about what creates sales revenue, and what might therefore be done to increase it, in itself invokes a particular form of static comparison. It is possible to depict the interrelationships between variables in a highly stylized way with a fishbone diagram (also known as a cause–effect or Ishikawa diagram). The procedure is straightforward and involves stating the end result in an effect box as the head of the fish. Identifying the main categories for possible causes of the effect is the next step. There are five categories that are frequently used in the continuous improvement (quality) literature for the main branches (bones) that stem from the spine of the fish. These are machinery, manpower, materials, methods and procedures, and money. Systematic fact-finding and group discussion can be used to generate possible causes. Anything which may result in the effect which is being considered is put down as a potential cause. These can be listed under the most typical five headings, or categorized into whatever number of major groupings seems appropriate for the issue in hand. An examination of the group of issues under each particular heading is then considered to see if any further examples can be generated. It is the process of considering the interrelationships between factors that lies at the heart of the success of the technique. The process can be undertaken more or less rigorously. A genuine endeavour to consider the logic of a situation is the invocation of a particular form of thinking. The analysis can be extended to a point where there are bones off bones, and then bones off bones off bones etc. As an iterative process, it is useful as a device to generate separate elements (separation thinking) as well as to locate them. The conventions concerning the physical depiction of causes as hierarchies of branches means that the approach does not address interrelationships between causes themselves that may 'cross' major bone branches.

We have seen in Chapter 4 how it is possible to consider propositional constructs, categories and their interrelationships. A large body of literature was reviewed which showed how management can use insights into the ways that participants see things 'going together'. A particular emphasis was placed on how events interrelate causally. A variety of mapping approaches were outlined. Seeing how constructs 'chain together' is an analysis process. It is a thinking process in its own right. In its basic form it invokes a linear way of thinking. Beyond sequencing there comes a more advanced set of relationships where the dynamics of interrelationships are considered. Here we need to consider ideas such as growth and reciprocity. Investing in broad-based training, for example, can lead to greater scope and skill variety at work. This, in turn, can develop deeper and broader skills in a workgroup. Looking for links is to regard the world as sets of interrelated elements. Looking for dynamics is a further type of thinking: systems thinking.

SYSTEMS THINKING: FOCUSING ON INTERDEPENDENCY   Senge (1990, p. 75) argues that the 'key to seeing reality systemically is seeing circles of influence rather than straight lines. This is the first step to breaking out of the reactive mindset that comes inevitably from "linear" thinking. Every circle tells a story.' The word 'system' descends from a Greek verb that means 'to cause to stand together'. Analysis, in contrast, originally meant 'understanding the parts'. As Balle (1994) puts it, 'the classical thinker tends to use linear causality: this is a flow chart mentality; we will try to draw chains of events and consequences under the assumption that a cause can be distinguished from its effects' (p. 30). He notes that this is 'a static view of the world. In a dynamic view of the world, causality is no longer one way. Cause creates effect that becomes cause, and so on' (p. 31). The argument we are making here is that it can be useful to try to see the world 'as' systems. Checkland (1988) suggests that we use the term 'holon' to refer to the systemic models that we construct to help us in our enquiry, and leave the term 'system' for its lay use, where particular configurations of elements are held to 'be' systems. Checkland uses the term soft systems methodology to refer to a process of enquiry where 'accounts' of wholes are used to learn about the world. Checkland and Scholes (1990) propose that:

> we engage in the world by making use of concepts whose source is our experience of the world; this process of engagement, usually unconscious as we live everyday life, can be made explicit; one way of doing so is embodied in so-called 'systems-thinking', based on the idea of making use of the concept of 'a whole'. In systems thinking, accounts of wholes are formulated as holons, and these can be set against the perceived world, in order to learn about it. (p. 23)

Many writers have suggested that managers should use systems thinking because organizations and society are systems, and there is a language of systems dynamics that helps us understand what is happening in our world. Richmond (1993) argues that 'while the web of interdependencies tightens, our capacity for thinking in terms of dynamic interdependencies has not kept pace' (p. 113) and that a core body of systems dynamics concepts should be an integral part of the education process. Waelchli (1992) attempts to distil frequently mentioned and significant ideas encountered in the literature of general systems theory into 11 theses. Senge et al. (1994) outline methods, tools and principles to look at the interdependencies of forces as part of a common system. Kim (1993) suggests that certain patterns of structure recur again and again, and that these generic structures or 'systems archetypes' are common themes and recurring plot lines that are recast with different characters and settings. Senge et al. (1994) outline 11 such 'key archetypes'. In this book, however, our concern is not with the possible value that can be obtained from identifying or even construing specific subforms of systems. We are concerned with the value of facilitating systemic thinking to gain insights into our mental models or those of other participants. Once again, therefore, we are seeking to establish the 'theories-in-use', as opposed to the 'espoused theories' (Argyris, 1990).

We can undertake an elicitation process that taps into this type of thinking if we provide people with some minimum set of concepts that capture the idea of systemic thinking, and record their thinking processes and 'resultant' models. Of course, the process of construing systemically will lead people into fresh insights. We can use this approach as a methodology to promote self-reflection, refinement/development of models and organizational analysis. Much of the literature on soft systems methodology is focused on the benefits of the insights into, and subsequent enhancement of, organizational processes that can flow from a holonic enquiry process. Our interest lies perhaps more in the value of 'surfacing' holonic theories in use, and using such information as part of a broader transaction and mutual understanding process.

Checkland and Scholes (1990) suggest that only four concepts are fundamental to systems thinking. These are the notions of emergent property, hierarchy, survival and communication/control. A complex whole has 'emergent properties' that are meaningless in terms of the parts which make up the whole. Only when the parts of a bicycle are put together in a particular way does 'vehicular potential' become an emergent property. Furthermore, the process through which power applied to pedals is translated into movement of the wheels can be seen to be part of an overall holonic conception of a bicycle, that is, there is an emergent property of 'movement potential' in a pedal–chain–wheel configuration. This is a definable layer within the more complex whole. It is the ability to name emergent properties which defines the existence of a layer in hierarchy theory: the second concept of systems thinking. A hierarchically organized whole, having emergent properties, may in principle be able to survive in a changing environment if it has processes of communication and control which would enable it to adapt to shocks from the environment. Soft systems methodology entails considering human activity systems in these terms. In essence, what is the transformation process that promotes a particular emergent property? How does it operate and how is it monitored and controlled?

Asking ourselves or other organizational participants to outline 'What is going on in this organization?' could highlight accounts of 'the way that the business as a whole functions'. It could also educe accounts of 'how morale is maintained', or 'how career planning is managed' etc. or any other of the theories-in-use concerning work-related processes. Senge et al. (1994) regard systems thinking and process mapping as a 'natural combination' (p. 184). Although superficially (diagramatically) similar, a process map shows sequence and chronology, while a causal loop diagram looks at the dynamics of relationships. As tools to aid thought, they both invoke imagistic forms of thought. Literally thinking 'circles' helps one move into this type of thinking and to see patterns. People can be encouraged to use diagrams to convey and capture their holons.

Levin (1994) suggests that if we wish to know how professionals interact with real-world problems and clarify their underlying values for professional practice, we need to understand their meaning-construction processes. This, he argues, highlights the common concerns of action research and critical systems thinking. The integration of systems thinking in movements such as TQM is increasingly apparent (for example Mulej and Rebernik, 1994). Indeed, many systems thinkers argue that the limits of understanding associated with linear cause-and-effect types of location thinking impede organizational learning. Kim and Senge (1994) suggest that, in particular, large organizations face a class of systemic decision-making situations in which learning is extremely unlikely. The facts that cause and effect are often not that close in space and time, that obvious interventions do not always produce obvious outcomes, and that long time delays and systemic effects of actions can make it almost impossible to judge the effectiveness of actions, may mislead managers. Engaging in systems thinking is not just good management theory. It is the management process. Checkland and Haynes (1994) suggest that soft systems methodology aids organizational understanding of real-world complexity because its very process of enquiry is systemic. It is a participative approach, premised on the notion that learning is axiomatically good. Tsouvalis and Checkland (1996) suggest that the initial distinction between the 'real world of the problem situation ("above-the-line") and the consciously organized systems thinking world ("below the line") . . . can be taken to indicate a false dualism' (p. 35). Systems thinking is, in itself, an integral part of human activity systems.

Brocklesby (1995) suggests that the guidance embodied in SSM's technology and its concepts of hierarchy and holism are real benefits in this regard. The approach can be used in a group setting and participatively. Brocklesby (1995) suggests that the conceptual models create learning and insight in a distinctive way, and uses the approach to develop competence profiles that are not 'meaningless because they are abstracted from the broader social context from which they emerged' (p. 70). Tonges and Madden (1993) also argue that systems thinking can operate as 'a conceptual framework for making the full pattern of conceptual complex interrelated actions clearer and helping people see how to change them' (p. 39). They show how Senge's (1990) systems thinking-based problem-solving ideas, such as running a vicious circle backwards, can contribute in a nursing context. Akkermans (1995) defines 'participative business model-ling' (PBM) as a management consulting method based on a mix of systems dynamics modelling, group knowledge-elicitation techniques, and a process consultation attitude. It is argued that the method is well suited to strategic management decision-making because it provides support for both the technical and organizational complexities. Vennix (1995) outlines a case where a qualitative systems dynamics model was built to support strategic decision-making in a Dutch government agency. Risch et al. (1995) used interviews, archival data and observation to build a model of a company's management's model of the dynamics of their market. They show how the systems dynamics approach revealed an underestimation of a particular effect, in the management's thinking. Endeavours to reconfigure entire 'production' processes through business process re-engineering (for example Buchanan and Wilson, 1996) utilize systems thinking in their analysis and design. This 'designing from scratch' can re-confirm the fundamental pur-pose of particular processes. Gregory (1995) argues that the logic implicit within systems thinking means that it can make a big contribution to knowledge elicitation and representation. Gregory (1995) states: 'the struc-tured approach to knowledge elicitation by logico-linguistic modelling is much more powerful . . . It clearly brings out what the stakeholders know and do not know and, more importantly, what they need to find out' (p. 568). At Royal Dutch/Shell, 'the relatively simple dynamic modeling software STELLA (which they still use), had a major impact on the organization's understanding of the long-term implications of complex resource policy decisions' (Tenaglia and Noonan, 1992, p. 16).

While systems thinking has a number of epistemological advantages over positivist science and the mechanical paradigm, it has its own limitations. Berman (1996) notes how systems theory tends to ignore crucial social and historical contexts, individual differences and aspirations and is still a basic search for 'order out of chaos', and that there is a danger of it being promoted uncritically as a world view. This is cautioned against, in part because of the 'authoritarian outlook' that can be a part of systems thinking. Terms such as 'de-memorizing' (Rebernik, 1994) may carry impli-cations that go beyond education or participative enquiry. Grey and Mitev (1995) also caution against the overemphasis on 'technological rationality', and the blind simplicity of the business process re-engineering approach towards analysis of production processes. Systems thinking can be too pure. While it has a clear role to play in the deliberations of people at work (and hence in the knowledge-elicitation process), it is only one form of location thinking, which is one form of reasoning, which is itself only one type of thinking.

PLURALITY-SEEKING: FOCUSING ON CONTEXTUALIZING   The third form of reasoning has been referred to in Chapter 2 as plurality-seeking. It is a desire to see things from additional perspectives. It is a quest for second-order relations, in Gentner's (1983) terms, that is, a quest to understand the relations between relations. There is a range of techniques that can be used to help people see a situation from many different perspectives. The 'ladder of inference' helps people understand and admit that their conclusions, logic, claims and behaviours are based on subjective processes. As Weiss (1996) puts it, 'By learning to admit and see one's reasoning as a process, a person can then feel free to change these conclusions and adopt another's ideas. Climbing down the ladder involves acknowledging and owning one's reasoning as just that – reasoning, not an eternal truth' (p. 175). The ladder of inference enables a person to understand and admit their statements, behaviour and positions. It involves highlighting and experiencing 'reasoning' by passing through a series of self-reflective steps. These draw attention to how one takes action based on beliefs; adopts beliefs about the world; draws conclusions; makes assumptions; adds cultural and personal meanings; selects data from what one observes; and observes data and experiences. Dialogue begins when participants learn to perceive their conclusions as beliefs or assumptions instead of non-negotiable truths. Teams trained in these methods can help each other question meaning and strive for open problem-solving and joint solutions. They encourage plurality thinking by opening up opportunities to share information, experiences and ideas from different perspectives.

Plurality thinking can be supported through a systematic analysis of an issue from a multiplicity of relevant perspectives. The meaning of a proposed change for the various interested parties can be considered. The stakeholder approach (Freeman, 1984) can help identify and map internal and external organizational relationships to identify who is affected by a presenting issue, problem, opportunity and planned outcome. It can help in the management of political, economic, social and business relationships with a range of groups who have an interest, claim or stake in the business's survival and/or success. More recently, the approach has been adapted to help organizations manage their social responsibility and ethics in complex contemporary environments (Weiss, 1994). In essence, the approach entails clarifying the issue, the stakeholders and the alternative perspectives. The 'map' of stakeholders in such approaches is often little more than an image depicting the particular viewpoint as a central node with the various other stakeholders radiating out from that central point. Bryant (1989) suggests that:

> every individual is a nexus linking a set of subjective worlds: the varied stages on which he plays parts. Each of these segments of a person's life is peopled by others whom he perceives as being significant, self-determining actors in the relevant ongoing social processes. These others can be enumerated as 'cast lists' for a particular individual and scene (situational segment). A number of conventions can be used to portray the set of persons or groups whom an individual sees as caught up with him in a specific problem field. (p. 227)

He describes Bowen's (1983) mapping approach where the relationships between participants can be structured into a hierarchy of collective terms. For example, Lecturer A can be depicted as part of the small group of operations research lecturers, who are part of a team of staff teaching a particular degree, who are part of a business school, which is part of a business faculty of a particular university, which is part of . . . etc.

Bryant (1987) advocates a more flexible means of depicting embeddedness. His notation is based on the Venn convention. Set membership is denoted by inclusion within a topographical region. The advantage is that the extent of overlap of the various areas can be indicated in addition to the strict hierarchical information. It is possible to see the size of the team of operations research lecturers of which Lecturer A is a part. One can see the proportion of the particular degree's teaching staff that the OR team constitutes, the scale of the course in the overall activities of the business school, and the size of the business school in relation to the business faculty etc. It is also possible to capture some of the issues involved in a scene with a particular cast list. It is not just the view of the world from Lecturer A's point of perspective that is of relevance. We need to see that Lecturer A sees that Lecturers B and C are involved. He also has a model of how B and C see things (which may or may not tally with the way in which B and C actually see what is going on). Indeed, part of A's model of B includes how A thinks B views A's view! Likewise, there are sets of embedded views held by Lecturer B of Lecturer A and Lecturer C. Bryant (1983) uses the term 'hypermap' to label this form of multiple perspective map. Bryant (1989) suggests that using these various depictions of cast lists and hypermaps can help one to appreciate or understand any conflicts of opinion around an issue.

Being willing to put oneself in a group situation where different perspectives may surface is not enough. Plurality thinking is not about social skills. Seeing a problem in different ways does not just mean from different individual points of view. It includes seeing an issue from a diverse set of frames of reference. A decision to move an organization in a new strategic direction can benefit from having embraced some of the symbolic meanings of the re-orientation, not just a stakeholder analysis. Consider a major thrust towards computerization. What is the change manifesting in terms of feminism? What does it mean in a Marxist sense? In what ways does the process resemble unpicking some knitting? We are talking here about how a problem is framed and reframed. Goffman (1974) contends that in making sense of events, we employ one or more schemata of interpretation (or frameworks). As Rorty (1989) puts it, 'most things in space and time are the effects of causes which do not include human mental states' (p. 5); the 'world is out there, but descriptions of the world are not' (p. 5). There is no account that categorically fits reality better than any other. There are, however, alternative ways of framing. The postmodernist movement argues that the search for universal, authoritative, true explanations of reality is always problematic and incomplete because it ends up elevating the priority of a particular perspective while downplaying others. Heisenberg (1958) and Bohr (1958) showed how the observations in even the most scientifically controlled experiments are not independent from the perceiving (measuring)

system. If one studied light as a particle it revealed its particle-like properties. If one studied it as a wave it revealed itself as a wave. The mindset or,
as Kuhn (1970) referred to it, paradigm, plays a major role in shaping
knowledge. As Morgan (1993) puts it, 'For any given situation, it's always
possible to generate multiple authentic readings and story lines, because
readings are just orderings of reality and are always shaped by the horizon
of the reader and the interest to be served' (p. 285).

Readings can be made from a frame of reference in two ways. The first is
an interpretive framework which *embraces* the issue in hand. The second is
an interpretation from a framework that *parallels* the issue at hand. Love
between a man and woman may be sociologically viewed as 'socially
prescribed in a society', for example. It is an instance of socialization. The
analytical framework embraces the concept in question. Love being a
physical force, a journey, a sickness, a madness, a form of art, war, wealth
and nourishment (Lakoff and Johnson, 1983) are metaphorical frames of
reference. They apply to the extent that love can be construed to have
relationships akin to the terms listed. Plurality thinking is about the
acceptance and exploration of multiple frames. Black (1979) writes of
human beings *constructing* 'implication-complexes'. As du Preez (1991) puts
it, 'in considering love as divine frenzy and a work of art' we are seeing it
both in terms of attributes that 'are so rapidly generated as to seem ready-
made' and in terms of attributes that 'are reached only by turning over
images, uses, contents, implications and structures' (p. 75). There is effort
involved in the construction of a perspective.

While, in one sense, there is equal value in seeing love as an instance of
socialization, or as war or as a volcano, perhaps some frames of reference
make more of a contribution to our insights because they are more 'theory
constitutive' (Boyd, 1979, p. 358), that is, they locate the concept more
comprehensively in a more elaborate web of implications and generate more
hypotheses about the concept. Plurality thinking is not merely an arbitrary
juxtaposition of concepts and a cursory examination of implications. It is a
more rigorous search for powerful insights. In poetry, for example, an
effective metaphor is 'the union of unlike things (pictures to ideas, ideas to
feelings, feelings to objects, objects to pictures, and so on) such that the
mind discovers unexpected relationships and comes upon new insight'
(Briggs and Monaco, 1990, p. 3).

Morgan (1993) refers to the value in using metaphor in working with
workgroups to explore their own functioning or handling of an issue. He
argues that the approach 'can provide powerful tools for helping people
look at themselves and their situations in new ways and, as a result, see and
act in the world somewhat differently. The process operates by creating a
tension between existing and potential understandings, creating space for
the new to emerge' (p. 291). He feels that several aspects of the process are
important. First, because metaphors involve the generation of a 'constructive falsehood' (for example, My manager is a fox), the bounds of normal
discourse can be broken. Secondly, metaphors require people to find and

create meaning. In our terms, it is valuable for plurality to be found, and related to other knowledge. Thirdly, there has to be resonance and authenticity in a metaphor to create energy and involvement in a group. A mechanistic search for insights will not sustain interest. Fourthly, groups seem to be able to generate (with support) more powerful metaphors (for them) than they can consider if brought in from outside. Fifthly, if a metaphor is brought in from the outside then the parallels at least should be established by the group. Finally, the tentative nature of metaphors help to create open modes of understanding that have a capacity to self-organize and evolve. Embrasive interpretive frameworks (for example sociological concepts such as socialization) may also require careful management in a group setting. They may have more of an air of legitimacy than metaphor. They may therefore divide rather than unify a group. They may be less readily shared, because they require more detailed explanation. They may engender a spirit of reading and searching outside of the problem, 'to get a fuller understanding', as opposed to metaphor's relative emphasis on exploring within the group/context.

In examining issues from stakeholder perspectives, and with both forms of framing, there is a need for us and other participants to accept the value of plurality. There is a need to live with ambiguity.

Conclusions concerning the promotion of reasoning as a type of thinking

Separation thinking and the various forms of location thinking are distinct forms of reasoning. It is important for those engaged in the processes of eliciting their own or sharing other people's understanding to recognize that the organizational knowledge utilized in the course of these particular turns of mind is different from that involved in contexts where other types of thinking (such as mood and autistic thinking) are practised. 'Reminding' somebody of some of the distinctions that they draw and the links that they make can be facilitated through the use of techniques geared explicitly with different forms of reasoning in mind. Managers should consider the extent to which their everyday practices span the alternative forms of reasoning and provide the insights needed. A comprehensive adoption of techniques aimed specifically at separation thinking will pay dividends. Similarly, exploring the assumptions that we or other participants operate under, by unearthing the sequences, dynamics and parallels of mental models, makes an important contribution to mutual understanding. The recognition that these forms of thinking are an integral part of human (and specifically organizational) experience means that the process of mutual enquiry (e.g. action research) can benefit from associated use of these forms of thinking in the learning process itself.

Overholser (1993) draws attention to how, in a psychotherapeutic context, the explicit use of different forms of reasoning can promote self-learning. Three aspects of using inductive reasoning in psychotherapy are presented. 'Enumerative generalizations' use pattern identification to support a conclusion about an entire group of events. This, in our terms, is an example of categorizing as a form of location thinking. 'Analogical comparisons' are argued to help clients transfer knowledge from familiar to novel situations. This is an example of plurality thinking. 'Eliminative causal reasoning' involves manipulating environmental conditions to examine possible causes of specific problematic events. This action learning approach helps people develop models of situations in a static comparison cause-and-effect sense, and possibly in a systems thinking interdependency sense. A mutual enquiry process may therefore benefit in general from the use of different modes of reasoning, in the course of accommodating the views of others.

The term 'mapping' can be used in a generic sense. It can be taken to include any graphical recording of cognitions. Working with different forms of graphical mapping involves different thinking processes. Reading the work of the many authors who have developed particular techniques to map cognitions reveals that there is an emerging 'technology' of thinking tools. This technology recognizes both the individual and social aspects of exploring cognitions. Mappings of all forms are considered valuable because 'they provide a way to structure and simplify thoughts and beliefs, to make sense of them, and to communicate information about them' (Fiol and Huff, 1992, pp. 271–2). Furthermore, 'the graphic representation of a mental map is in itself a useful form for helping managers to make sense of complexity. Graphic representations can both simplify ideas and facilitate the transmission of complex ideas from individual to individual and unit to unit' (p. 273).

A range of alternative graphical means of depicting the relationship between individual maps can be used. In the main, researchers whose work uses particular elicitation techniques, or attempts to locate information in particular ways, tend to restrict their graphical representations to particular forms. For example, Bowman and Johnson (1991) use statistical techniques to identify the key factors within a team's conceptions, and map each individual's position on a graph showing the key vectors. In terms of the classification presented in Chapter 3 (Table 3.4), they are utilizing a 'representation that highlights abstract characteristics', by using a 'graphical abstract depiction along specific dimensions', with a graph that uses 'scaled consecutive values' in a 'radial' presentation. The very nature of the depiction draws attention to the concept of 'overlap'. The specifics of arguments are not highlighted, rather the basic pattern. In contrast, means–ends network diagrams, highlight the logic that individuals are using. Perceiving overlap is more problematic. In terms of the classification presented in Table 3.4, a 'formal' network diagram is being used in a 'graphical abstract representation of complex relationships'.

Researchers tend to find the most appropriate means to depict the information they are addressing. When viewed in terms of a classification of visual representations, however, the nature (focus and form) of the thinking inculcated in the analysis process is more clearly revealed. The potential of other variants in reasoning processes and representations can then be explored. Simply asking oneself how numbers might be attached to a series of elements, how they might be listed and categorized, how they may be assessed in proportion to each other, how they might be graphed, how they might be depicted in a process diagram or a network diagram, how they might overlap, how they could be considered metaphorically to interrelate, how they might be conveyed in totality, and how they might be made to alter to depict the nature of change processes or dynamics invokes different forms of reasoning.

As Fiol and Huff (1992) note, 'not only do cognitive maps have the potential to play a more important role today than ever before, there is a growing need to specify and manage the intersections of different kinds of cognitive maps' (p. 272). They offer a further framework for considering the appropriateness of alternative forms of maps. They note that different forms of maps will 'focus attention'. By definition, maps 'highlight some information and fail to include other information' (p. 267). Secondly, referring to the work of Alba and Hasher (1983), they note that different maps 'trigger memory' differently. Different memories may be cued. Taken together, the particular focusing and triggering implications of particular mappings will have implications for the general decision-making process in terms of the way that 'issues will be structured' (p. 275). Thirdly, as suggested by Abelson (1981), they note that different forms of maps 'supply missing information' of different natures. A causal map, for example, invites questions about whether the listed factors account adequately for some outcome. A tree diagram, as noted earlier, raises questions about categorization and classification. In the social context, mapping can lead to analysis paralysis or it can 'promote closure' (p. 276). Different maps in different contexts may add different value to the closure process. Too little exploration may mean premature closure. Too protracted and comprehensive an exploration can impede closure.

Mapping can be conducted to a depth that reveals agreement. At some level group members may think alike. If the mapping is not very searching, then the challenge to thinking may be limited and groupthink may persist, a blinkered unchallenged form of thinking. On the other hand, a searching exploration can always reveal differences. There may be periods where opinion is too fragmented. Crossan (1991) showed that high levels of cognitive complexity and diversity can be dysfunctional. Some maps by their nature highlight consensus, others highlight difference. Judicious use of different maps at different times in group discussions can help the overall decision-making process.

A technology of using different mappings as thinking tools is not very well developed. As we have seen, different combinations and sequences of maps can lead to different decision processes. In the absence of definitive guidelines, workgroups can be encouraged to 'review' their processes in a meeting at various junctures to consider the potential value of alternative mappings from that point on. Restricting attention to a single map may not yield the best results. Eden et al. (1981) showed that collective mapping following individual mapping allows groups to manage disagreements by cross-level absorption. Group maps absorbed some of the issues of individual maps and vice versa. Fiol (1991) found that members developed overlapping maps of the context of negotiations, while maintaining separate and non-overlapping maps of the content of their argument. There are no reports of crossing over between map types, however.

Fiol and Huff (1992) categorize maps of managerial cognitions into three subgroups. Identity submaps reveal the terms of self-identity in organizations, and 'provide the point of self-reference' (p. 278) needed to utilize other forms of maps. The essence of such mappings is the identification of the key dimensions along which identity is defined in relation to others (for example Bowman and Johnson, 1991). Categorization maps reveal the 'means by which managers sort events and situations on the basis of their differences and similarities' (p. 279) (for example Porac et al., 1987). Causal and argument maps provide 'understanding about how individuals link events occurring at a particular time to other events occurring at other times. The relational links that these submaps convey capture judgements about the link between actions and outcomes' (p. 279). Fiol and Huff (1992) feel that managers should utilize all of these different types of maps because 'if only one map is used other submaps will be implicitly assumed and remain unquestioned' and 'they are not equally interdependent' (p. 280). They feel that there is a need to have some form of identity submap to ground the information from other mappings. Managers need to know what they currently consider they are doing if specific action is to be taken.

Switching between alternative means of representation (and associated forms of reasoning) can be done in an *ad hoc* way. As our understanding of the contribution of different ways of reasoning increases, however, we may be able to derive additional benefit from the appropriate sequencing of approaches. Different approaches yield different insights, but they also involve different actions and reactions. Brown (1992) suggested that there may be some general differences between alternative approaches to knowledge elicitation (when used in isolation). She contrasted cognitive mapping, opinion surveys, structured interviews, clinical interviews, systems mapping, systems diagramming, repertory grids, comparisons matrices and soft systems methodology in terms of a variety of considerations. She highlighted truthfulness, value-tapping capacity, richness, reliability, data quality, amenability to analysis, large sample suitability, training requirement, ease of use, tedium inducement, esteem threat, ethical acceptability, client usefulness and dependence on investigator skills as important considerations. She did not consider any issues concerning the sequencing of different techniques.

There are likely to be several important principles in sequencing reasoning activities. Wood and Ford (1993), for example, suggest that it can be useful to go through four phases in interviewing experts to elicit knowledge for expert systems. First, the descriptive elicitation phase reveals the important entities and concepts in the domain, as reflected in the terms and specialized language used by the expert. The structured expansion phase is designed to probe the relationships between the domain concepts and the organization of the expert's knowledge. The scripting phase relies on the declarative knowledge found through the previous stages, to discover procedural knowledge. The fourth and final stage is a validation, which is used to ensure that the knowledge is correct and adequate. This, in effect, invokes a reasoning mode of thinking.

From my own work, I would also suggest that it can be useful to progress through different modes of reasoning (for example separation thinking, a categorization mode of location thinking, and a sequencing mode of location thinking) in some order. An initial elicitation of elements can be derived from individual knowledge-elicitation sessions that focus on a *separation* mode of reasoning. This step essentially only yields semantic information. The repertory grid procedure can be used in the first stage of knowledge elicitation and transaction. An example is given below. Other examples are detailed in Chapter 6, under the heading 'Semantic under-standing'. It is also possible to use group techniques in this first stage. An example use of a focus group at this stage is also given later in the same section. Sparrow and Wood (1994) outline a study in the hospitality (food service) industry where the 'realities' of a food server's job were being sought. In many cases procedures and training are designed for specific problems. How all of the information is put together by food servers is not understood. Their 'models' of service situations could surface important issues or problems in the team/restaurant. The restaurants in question were interested in continuous quality improvement. If we want to understand what helps us in continuous quality improvement we need to understand what is guiding people when they are doing their jobs. What are they taking into account? What makes them do what they do? If we can see what a person considers in dealing with a customer who needs service to be speeded up, we can see how policy and standards fit in, but we can also see where constraints may lie. Maybe a food server handles the situation differently depending on the time of day, the type of customer, the state of the team at the time, the chef(s) on shift and so on? Only if we get to know what these considerations are can we improve the situation. This is not so that we can 'eliminate' variation and have a rigorous standard or manual – there lies robotics – but so that we can see the instances where a system needs to flex, where a food server should prioritize in the way she describes. She also needs to see where that approach may conflict with other staff's require-ments and be causing difficulties in operations. So of course we need to establish how all the staff are seeing various situations. And then, most crucially, they all need to see how the others are seeing things and why they are doing them that way. The team can then develop improvements to the way they operate.

The authors used situational interviewing and repertory grid procedures in combination to gain insights into a wide range of service situations. We wanted each food server to take us through nine different service situations and to explore the differences between them. We wanted to be sure that the sample of situations in which the food servers were put did not unduly restrict their thoughts. An earlier study by Sparrow et al. (1992) had revealed that food servers respond differently to the size of customer group. Situations which involved individual diners, couples, table groups (four to six people) and large parties were explored. Food servers had also been seen to be sensitive to the nature of the occasion. Situations which involved business, quiet informal and celebration contexts were explored. Service and manufacturing operations practitioners use frameworks such as Money, Machinery, Manpower, Material and Method to guide them in considering flexible scheduling. Situations which involved negotiation of price change, something excluded from a standard dish, service in a hurry, different table configuration, change of order after the start of preparation, something cooked in a special way, something added to a standard dish, a late announcement of the necessity for separate itemized bills and a need for service to be slowed down were explored. In a similar way, the context of the situation (similar to a 'Range' statement in an NVQ competence) was varied. Situations were explored which involved many business lunches, quiet periods, breakdowns of major items of equipment, another very large party going on, a lot of single diners occupying tables, busy period and virtually full, being very short-handed, shortage of equipment (such as cutlery), running out of a major foodstuff occurring right on closing time and where only less skilled staff were on duty. This framework provided $4 * 3 * 9 * 11 = 1188$ theoretically possible situations (complications). A computer program was developed which would randomly generate unique combinations of 'circumstances' ('complications' which might arise). Each food server was given a separate listing of nine 'complications'. My own preference is to restrict 'backroom analysis' at this stage to a mapping that merely clusters elements. Figure 5.1 gives a broad overview of the way in which elements combine to yield the impact of a particular 'complication'. It would seem that operational procedures are the result of policies, facilities, processes, people and customer (image) requirements. These procedures mean that complications have the potential to create areas of friction. However, the particular policies, facilities, processes, people and customer (image) requirements also combine to create an 'inherent self-correcting potential'. This is the ability to 'flex' so that disruption can be contained/eliminated. It is these two potentials which combine to produce an impact.

It would be possible to move on at this stage with individuals/workgroups to consider alternative ways to *locate* service situations. First, *categorization* could be used. The nature of complications is further clarified through explicit consideration of the meaning or implications of several alternative ways of grouping situations.

Figure 5.2 shows some of the issues raised in a particular subgroup of situations, attempting to respond to requests to provide 'service in a hurry'.

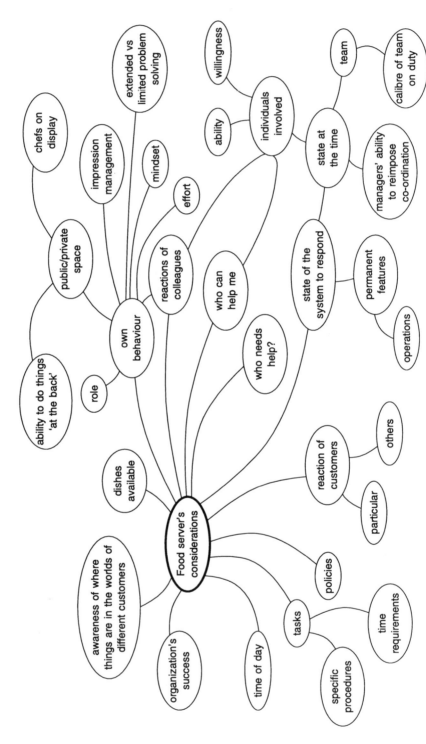

Figure 5.1 *The food server's considerations*

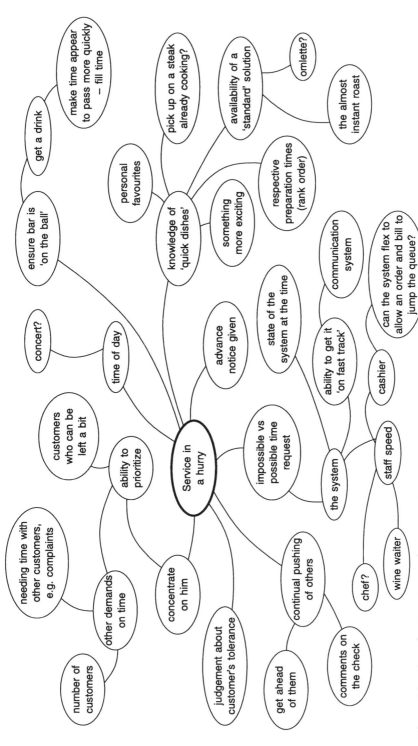

Figure 5.2 *Considerations in speeding up service*

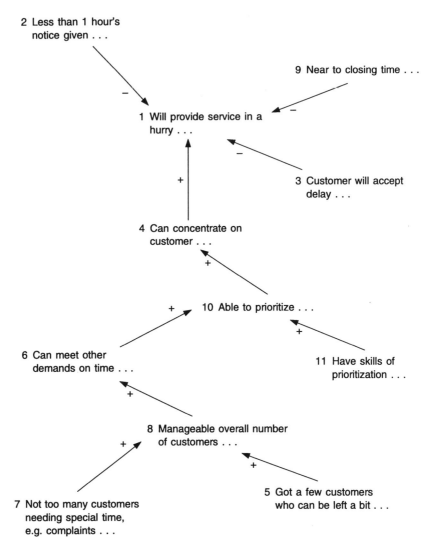

Figure 5.3   *Cognitive (cause) map of responses to service in a hurry*

It shows the wide range of considerations which determine the food server's decisions about a reaction. This is an example of a model which contains a high degree of procedure. This map has been used with workgroups to explore some of insights that can stem from *sequencing* information. It would be possible to re-represent much of this map in another way (for example as a decision tree or as a cognitive map). Figure 5.3 presents a brief extract from a cognitive mapping of the considerations outlined in Figure 5.2. There are unique thought processes involved in this, as opposed to other forms of sequencing this information. There is considerable value added through cognitive mapping. Readers may wish to consider any additional insights that are highlighted if the information in Figure 5.3 is re-represented as a decision tree. Here, the elements are being sequenced in terms of priority and temporal considerations.

It can therefore be useful deliberately to step through different ways of looking at (reasoning with) such information. In fact, there can be some sequences that are effective in moving from semantic mental material to episodic, skilled, tacit and unconscious insights; and from propositional to imagistic forms of thought. I have tended to build from propositional semantic insights as outlined above towards other kinds of mental material. People see a value in imagistic thought when they have felt a need to identify subconscious and, in particular, unconscious considerations. Mood insights may need to be the final stage of insight. They may require more mature groups and appreciation of what is 'missing' from the insights to date. There is a need for extensive research into individual and group process issues surrounding sequencing in knowledge elicitation in general.

In the absence of a mature technology of thinking tools in organizations, one can perhaps take some comfort from the argument that individuals/ organizations going through a process of comprehensive mapping 'must' have learned. If we put processes into play, we can be somewhat assured that certain learning is taking place. Rather than assessing where we (or an organization) 'are', what we/it know and how we/it have developed as particular 'steps' are taken, we can be reassured if we see that we/it are at least undertaking a comprehensive portfolio of knowledge-elicitation and transaction procedures. Seeing the contribution of reasoning as a type of thinking stems in part from appreciating the unique contributions of different modes of reasoning, alongside insights into the different insights that come from exploring kinds of mental material other than semantic understanding, types of thinking other than reasoning, and forms of thought other than propositional.

Promoting mood thinking

Chapter 2 outlined how mood is a type of thinking. We are all aware that we can find ourselves in different moods. When we reflect on our behaviour afterwards, we often notice how we weren't 'thinking straight', or can't explain why we 'saw it that way'. When we see others in atypical moods, we often feel surprised by the insights that we get into their personality and, more specifically, their behaviour under those conditions. It can be useful to reflect on emotion generally and develop our emotional intelligence (Goleman, 1995). We have also suggested that the images we have of ourselves and others at work may have studiously avoided information about which work factors lead to particular mood states, and how we actually feel and react to events at work. Three approaches can be adopted towards surfacing and incorporating mood information in our perceptions of ourselves and others. The first approach involves encouraging expression and reflection on mood thinking as it occurs naturally at work. The second approach involves recollecting episodes where mood thinking figured quite strongly in a work situation. The third approach involves inducing a mood state so that mood-congruent memories can be elicited.

The first approach towards learning about the impact of mood thinking on perceptions, decisions and actions involves not turning a blind eye to emotional episodes. It involves not urging people always to 'calm down' or 'take a more balanced view' when they report negative reactions. It involves an acceptance that emotion is legitimate. Legitimized emotion can be analysed. The issues involved can be addressed. People may not have the willingness or skills to encounter and analyse emotion at work, however. Just telling people that it is now OK to cry or be angry at work will not be enough. From an early stage, research on enhancing sensitivity in work-groups has found value in explicit training. T-groups, encounter groups and other experiential approaches to sensitivity training are reviewed by Smith (1980c).

Lundgren and Knight (1978) studied the stages through which groups appear to progress when participants are allowed to encounter each other in an essentially unstructured (though explicitly constituted) experiential process. They identified three periods that they labelled 'initial encounter', 'interpersonal confrontation' and 'mutual acceptance'. In the first stage, members tend to avoid personal issues, present themselves in a positive light and provide each other with positive feedback. Overall the period is characterized by restraint and the development of psychological safety. In the second stage, there is a more intense focus on individuals and increased negative feedback among members. The period is characterized by an emphasis on the task at hand and frustration that people are not 'doing it right'. In the third stage, there is less emphasis on the task. Time is spent on managing or resolving what were earlier regarded as conflicts and confrontations. The atmosphere is more relaxed.

Farrell (1976) suggests that groups need to find their way through five debates. They have to resolve their positions on authority (restoration vs revolution), on intimacy (in relation to authority and in terms of degree of closeness), on individuation (the recognition and legitimacy of individuality), on expression (the arbitrariness of 'rules' of discourse) and on work (task and group process agendas). He suggests that groups in general tend to address these issues in the sequence in which they have been presented above.

It can be seen that 'natural' confined exposure to others can surface and promote the exploration of emotional expression. Some degree of control over the circumstances of encounter seems to help members develop the willingness and skills to explore emotion in interpersonal dealings. Campbell and Dunnette (1968), Smith (1980c), Golembiewski et al. (1982), Nicholas (1982), Guzzo et al. (1985) and Neuman et al. (1989) have reviewed organizational development interventions and found some changes in behaviour after explicit experiential sensitivity training. In addition to naturalistic encounters, group encounters can be structured to highlight particular features. Schutz (1967), for instance, developed a whole range of non-verbal activities designed to encourage the more direct interchange of feelings between group members. Indeed, Reddy and Lippert (1980) note that the 'evidence on structure and design is counter to experiential training lore, namely that structure is anathema to effective learning. Structured groups seem more satisfying to some participants and contribute to positive change' (p. 66).

There is a huge range of means by which people can be helped to encounter and consider each other. The overall objective in both unstructured and structured approaches towards developing sensitivity is to enable workgroups to acknowledge and work with interpersonal diversity, including emotion. Organizations can benefit from such generic development. It may mean that they would then be able to consider the facets of mood that figure at work. For this to happen, however, may require that the issues are dealt with at the time that they arise. Only those issues that occur naturally can be dealt with. The evidence outlined in Chapter 2 would suggest that, even with the skills of interpretation, people may not be able to conjure up sufficiently rich pictures of a previous mood experience for any additional insights to be gained subsequently. Our interest here, lies in the notion of 'accelerating' the learning about mood impacts at work. The suggestion is that it would be useful to encourage reflection on prior mood thinking, or induce mood thinking in ourselves and other participants, so that we/they could learn to order about the causes and effects of that type of thinking in our/their decisions and actions at work.

The second approach towards mood consideration reveals that it is possible to get at mood information to a limited extent in the absence of immersion in the mood. Several studies attest to the affective quality of autobiographical memories (for example Baumgartner et al., 1992). Furthermore, Menon (1992) argues that 'cold' experiences are not well remembered as separate instances because they become schematized as semantic understanding. Sujan et al. (1993) therefore suggest that 'with the passage of time, the bulk of our autobiographical memories that remain "intact" involve emotion' (p. 423). More distant memories, that can be accessed as relatively complete episodes, can thus provide some insights into mood effects prevailing at that time. It may be possible for participants to reflect on such memories. The difficulty lies with the arbitrariness of the memories that 'come to mind' when asked. Using a technique such as the critical incident procedure (Flanagan, 1954) can perhaps restrict the episodes that are recounted to 'important' ones in the work context. Here, participants are asked to recount incidents where there was a significant deterioration or improvement in work procedures or outcomes. It may be possible to pursue those episodes generated in this way which appear to be stored relatively completely in episodic memory, and which have a clear emotional overtone. Participants can be helped to consider characteristics of their own behaviour in the course of mood thinking. Overall, while the approach provides some insights, it may most usefully fulfil a supplementary role to 'live' experience and mood induction, rather than be a sufficient basis in itself.

The third approach towards reflection on mood thinking involves mood induction. We have seen in Chapter 2 that it is possible to induce mood in people, and that the effects on thinking that ensue are similar to those involved in less-managed mood thinking. The focus here is therefore on the alternative ways in which mood can be induced in occupational settings. In general, the procedures emphasize imagination. Participants are instructed to try to feel the mood in question. The first person to report an experimental induction of mood was Velten (1968). His approach involved the participants reading silently, then aloud, sets of statements about a particular mood. Other approaches towards mood induction include hypnosis; musical induction; watching particular films/stories; 'trick' scenarios where participants are led to believe they have received a particular gift or have succeeded or failed in an important task; pure (free-choice) imagination; and facial expressions. All of the techniques encourage participants to engage in their own efforts to get into the mood in question. Clark (1983) summarizes findings when participants are asked to describe the strategies they use in order to change their mood. A wide range of different strategies are used and several people report using more than one strategy. Depression strategies include concentrating hard on the music, sighing, recalling past unhappy experiences, imagining possible future unhappy experiences, indulging in wild horrific fantasies about death, curling up into a ball, and trying hard to stay absolutely still. Elation strategies include humming to the music, dancing, tapping feet, recalling past happy experiences, indulging in pleasant fantasies and thinking about future pleasant events. Gerrardhesse et al. (1994) review findings for many of the alternative induction procedures in laboratory and research settings. In a practical setting, the skills needed tend to rule out hypnosis. The need to use the procedures many times rules out the gift and success/failure procedures. The Velten, musical, facial expression and story procedures may fare better than the untutored imagination approach outlined by Riskind and Rholes (1985). Each of these procedures encourages participants to 'imagine' the mood. In addition, they provide supporting cues/context.

As mentioned previously, the Velten Induction Procedure (Velten, 1968) consists of asking participants to read silently, and then aloud, sets of 60 self-referent mood statements, and to 'try to feel the mood suggested' by the statement. The statements gradually progress from relative mood neutrality to greater degrees of the mood in question. Each of the different sets of induction statements has items that fall into two categories: statements associated with behaviour (things that a person can do, or is doing, and which are associated with the target mood) and statements describing the body and mental feelings of the moods. A depression example of the first category is: 'Every now and then I feel so tired and gloomy that I'd rather just sit than do anything.' An elation example of a somatic statement is: 'This is great – I really do feel good – I am elated about things'. A Musical Induction Procedure was devized by Sutherland et al. (1982). This procedure involves playing participants mood-suggestive music and asking them to use the music as a background to their own efforts to induce mood. It is stressed that music by itself will not automatically induce the desired mood state and that they should try really hard to get into the mood, using whatever means they find most effective. By way of example, Bower and Mayer (1991) report using *Coppélia* by Delibes and portions of the *Brandenburg Concerto No. 2* by Bach as 'happy' music. The 'sad' selections were 'Russia under the Mongolian Yoke' from the opera *Alexander Nevsky* by Prokofiev and *Nocturne No. 15 in F minor, Opus 55 No. 1* by Chopin. Typically, two ten-minute selections are used in the induction procedure. Any music selection of less than ten minutes can be repeated in a tape loop so as to fill up the necessary time.

Schneider et al. (1994) used sets of 40 slides depicting happy or sad facial expressions varying in intensity. Participants look at each slide (in a self-paced format) and try to feel the mood expressed by the set of pictures. It is possible to inform participants that they can mimic the expressions they see, among any other strategies they may wish to pursue. The story procedure outlined by Robins (1988) asks participants to use imagery procedures when they are given stories of cases with which they try to empathize. Typically, the overwhelming majority of participants respond to the induction. The moods can quite readily be maintained for 20 to 30 minutes. Participants can be encouraged actively to reinstate the mood throughout any interviewing that is taking place. In the organizational knowledge context, therefore, facilitators may want to ask participants (or you may want to ask yourself) to begin to consider work experiences which have resulted in feeling a particular mood. Record, as fully as possible, the antecedent conditions and how you/they reacted at the time. Alternatively, people can be asked to consider how they would react to a particular change if they were in their current mood. It is probably best to avoid analysis and interpretation of any of the information generated, in the period when the participant is in the induced mood. The time is better used for elicitation. On a subsequent occasion, it may be possible to explore with participants how they might deal with the situation outlined in the mood session, in a more neutral mood. They may consider what might be done to change the situation so that the effect on their mood is reduced. They may want to consider how they can react to the situation differently. It is possible to undertake these procedures oneself, and note the appropriate responses, for consideration later.

Two observations about the range of moods that can be induced are noteworthy. Nearly all of the research evidence has focused on 'fundamental' moods such as depression and elation. Referring back to Warr's (1990) classification of well-being, outlined in Chapter 2, one can see that more subtle positions along displeased–pleased, anxious–contented and depressed–enthusiastic dimensions, such as 'tense', 'discouraged', 'bored' or 'cheerful', might also be worth exploring. There is no *a priori* reason why any particular mood cannot be induced using the standard set of procedures, so long as it can be defined reasonably clearly. Some of the more subtle distinctions may provide a challenge to one's musical knowledge, however, if musical mood induction is to be used! The second issue concerning the range of moods that can be induced concerns the induction of moods as they are uniquely defined and labelled in a participant's mind. The effective standard induction procedures involve using some appropriate language, posture or music to reinforce any efforts that participants might make to self-induce the mood in question. The pre-prepared procedures constitute a positivist approach to studying mood and, in fairness, there is quite a high degree of consensus about the meaning of mood terms and the associated psychological and physiological correlates. If a particular unique 'category' of mood is voiced by a participant, however, and it is felt that some induction procedure could assist, then the participant will need to be urged to undertake self-managed induction through imagination and any postural mimicry they consider appropriate. It will not be possible to establish statement listings or selections of music that reinforce the mood as it is uniquely defined. One possible exception might be a person who is particularly self-perceptive and 'knows' the music that uniquely captures the mood they have in mind.

Overall, the value of mood-reflection approaches lies in the insights that they can provide into the impact of alternative mood states at work. Beyond the experiencing of and reflecting on mood thinking at work, it is possible to raise one's emotional competence/intelligence. Anderson (1993) notes that training in the service industries used to attempt to develop a false face for dealing with the public. He suggests that, for example, 'flight attendants today, are encouraged to be more natural and sincere than in the earlier years of commercial aviation when acting a role and projecting a favourable image of the airline' (p. 13). Recognizing one's own perceptions is seen as a key to emotional coping, and 'trainees need to reflect critically on their own motives, values and goals. The use of a learning journal, or small group discussions, can greatly assist in this regard. No amount of training, supervision or blandishments from others can substitute for an honest assessment of one's guiding principles' (p. 14).

Goleman (1995) details two programmes that have been developed to assist in raising emotional intelligence. The first programme that he cites (pp. 301–2) was developed by the WT Grant Consortium (1992). It distinguishes between emotional skills, cognitive skills and behavioural skills. It seeks to help participants develop emotional skills in identifying and labelling feelings, expressing feelings, assessing the intensity of feelings, managing feelings, delaying gratification, controlling impulses, reducing stress and knowing the difference between feelings and actions. It highlights the cognitive skills of self-talk (that is, an inner dialogue to help cope with a topic or challenge or reinforce one's own behaviour), reading and interpreting social cues, and using steps for problem-solving (in contrast to a relatively unconsidered approach), understanding the perspective of others, understanding behavioural norms, self-awareness and positive attitude. Finally, in terms of behavioural skills, the programme seeks to develop non-verbal and verbal communication skills. The second programme that Goleman (1995) cites (pp. 303–4), was developed by Stone and Dillehunt (1978). Its main components are self-awareness, personal decision-making, managing feelings, handling stress, empathy, communications, self-disclosure, insight, self-acceptance, personal responsibility, assertiveness, group dynamics and conflict resolution. Overall, it seems clear that mood plays a significant part in organizational experience. Mood thinking can be invoked and reflected on. The skills of working with mood thinking can be developed.

There is very little evidence concerning the effects of mood thinking on organizational decision-making *per se*. The whole area of mood at work is likely to become a research agenda in its own right. What sort of task might organizations consider when they seek to assess the impact of mood thinking at work? Given the ethical issues surrounding direct mood induction, it may be possible in larger-scale studies to ask participants to complete mood inventories, such as the Multiple Affect Adjective Checklist (see Ellis and Ashbrook, 1991) or a more basic procedure such as the self-reported indication of mood, developed by Teasdale and Russell (1983), whenever they complete other questionnaires or surveys in the organization. In the latter procedure, participants are merely shown cards headed 'At this moment', with 0–100 line scales, on which 0 is labelled 'I do not feel at all X' and 100 is labelled 'I feel extremely X'. For different cards, X can be 'depressed', 'anxious' and 'happy' etc. Over time, significant relationships may be established between the detailed responses on the questionnaires and mood states.

More direct relationships may be observed if open or projective techniques are used to obtain the views of organizational participants. Convoy and Laird (1984), for example, report on the projection of feelings and story content. 'Imaginary' stories about how events, careers etc. may progress in an organization could be considered in relation to mood. More direct experimentation can be undertaken if assessments of performance are taken at the time that mood has been induced. While there are ethical concerns with prospective mood induction at work, it is important to note that the 'changes in mood induced by experimental studies are not extreme and well within the natural range of fluctuation experienced by most people . . . (high workload, stressors, conflict etc.) which commonly occur in professional and personal decisions . . . often produce more extreme states than those induced within the experimental studies' (Maule and Hockey, 1996, p. 465). If participants are willing, they could complete questionnaires, work 'simulations', computer gaming etc. while in a particular induced mood. Again, the effects may, in general, be more readily discerned in open, projective techniques, but it would seem to be possible to examine the impacts of mood on access to semantic, episodic, tacit and unconscious mental material. Skills may be less susceptible to mood effects. It may be possible to examine the effects of mood thinking in subsequent debriefings after participants have been encouraged to use imagistic thinking in the drawing or interpretation of graphical information. While I am not aware of any evidence of this, I suspect that it would be more difficult to sustain any induced mood effect in a group interactive situation, where other factors are likely to 'break' the form of thinking induced.

Important insights can be gained into aspects of work life that we and other participants can less readily articulate in more neutral moods. This neglected area of organizational thinking should be researched further.

6

Focusing on Specific Kinds of Mental Material

In this chapter, some of the unique insights that can be gained into a person's perceptions of a situation will be explored by focusing on each of the different kinds of mental material that people have. There are two sets of advantages in using the framework of the five kinds of mental material (semantic, episodic, skilled, tacit and unconscious) outlined in Chapter 2. First, the framework highlights the breadth of insights that we can get into a person's views. The framework cues us to consider aspects of perception that are represented in the person's mind in the form of different kinds of mental material. Everyday discourse, as we have seen, tends to cue only a limited set of mental material representations. The second advantage in using the framework stems from the potential of particular 'tailored' approaches to elicit more of each kind of mental material than general endeavours may achieve. The specific 'tools' that can be used to gain particularly significant insight into one kind of mental material will not be optimal for gaining insight into the other kinds of mental material.

Gaskell et al. (1993) report how the mental processes that people go through in answering even a simple question systematically vary. In certain situations people undertake quite extensive exploration of the meaning of the issue being considered. They search their mind for what the term means and then make assessments about its frequency on the basis of some reasoning processes. In other instances they may rely on a scan of the episodes they can recall to formulate their view. If the question asked of a person implies it being a low-frequency event they will spend time formulating their definition of the event and then try to calculate their own estimate of its frequency. So, being asked how frequently one gets annoyed when the scale includes response categories such as 'every few months' and 'once a year' puts people into a different way of thinking compared with instances where the frequency is implied to be higher. When the scale includes categories such as 'every day' and 'most days' people use virtually a completely episodic approach to search their memories. They search for recent days and calculate their response accordingly. The rapid pace of a survey questionnaire is not optimal for demanding cognitive tasks (Krosnick, 1991) such as trying to estimate when events occurred (Friedman, 1993). If people take up the cues from the method they will not access all of their memories.

This chapter will highlight the range of ways in which different kinds of mental material can be elicited within organizations. The relative strengths of different physical representations in the elicitation process were outlined in Chapter 3. Readers are referred to Table 3.4 to consider the role of physical representation *per se* in the elicitation process.

The chapter sheds further light on the nature of each of the different kinds of mental material by reviewing studies that have worked with each separate kind. It therefore reveals the implications of particular kinds of mental material for organizational behaviour. The chapter also provides guidelines on how to use the tools most appropriate for the elicitation of each kind of mental material. It includes references to studies where the impact on organizational participants or organizational processes of using tailored approaches to elicit mental material has been evaluated. Each of the five kinds of mental material is discussed in turn.

Semantic understanding

Semantic memory, it will be recalled, refers to our understanding of ideas/objects/events. The particular construction that a person has of a situation has been shown to be determined, in part, by their personal experiences, including education and training (Walker et al., 1995). To the extent that life experiences are structured, there may be discernible differences between genders, races and ages (Wohlers et al., 1993). Each of these different groups may see situations differently. Their understanding of different facets of a situation will vary. There may be some 'gravitation' into particular jobs, which appear to demand certain knowledge (and implicitly other basic elements of understanding). There may be some 'reinforcement' of particular perspectives once like-minded people work together in particular settings. The model held by an employee may depend, therefore, on the functional specialism or department (Dearborn and Simon, 1958) or the management level (Ireland et al., 1987). The nature of an understanding may also depend on features of particular organizations (Ansoff and McDonnell, 1990; Glaister and Thwaites, 1993), industries (Gordon, 1991) or national cultures (Brewster and Tyson, 1991; Kriger and Solomon, 1992). Are we aware of the constructs we use in the course of our interpretation of events? We may 'hear ourselves' voicing certain arguments and 'see' what constructions we are making while we are involved in discussion. But all of this would have to be in the heat of the moment. If constructions are what guide us, perhaps it would be useful explicitly to seek to identify them, and consider what they may mean for our interpretation of events. To what extent, therefore, is such mental material consciously accessible?

If we are actively engaged in looking at the world in a certain way, there is a degree of momentum in the process that curtails any potentially unfettered access to our knowledge/memory. This 'model dependence' in our thinking means that the same event can be construed completely differently by separate people. Indeed, once we begin to search and access information, this, in itself, inhibits the pathways we go on to search. As a result, we may easily miss certain obvious or major aspects in our recounting of an episode simply because of the way we started the account, and the 'predictable' subsequent train of thought. We have become so skilled at managing access and following logical paths that our thinking is referred to as being reality adjusted as opposed to autistic. As we have seen, autistic thinking is that which operates in its own world and perhaps in a more random way. It goes where it will rather than where the learned conventions of searching direct it. Often, the pattern of thinking that we follow when we start to consider an issue is predictable and logical. It is, however, by no means complete. There is no questioning of the adequacy of the approach. There is a confusion between the feelings of comfort that go with memories of events that proceeded easily with a justification for them to remain the same. There is no analysis. Reflection is not just passive recollection. The result of this strategy will be a repetition of the same behaviours, even in situations where a little thought could reveal their inappropriateness in the new setting. This *Einstellung* effect stems from not testing the applicability of what we do, not seeking negative information.

Even when we can gain conscious access to our semantic understanding, how much reliability can we place on the information that we retrieve? Is it a *good* cross-section? Does it give us the *main* points? If we ask somebody to tell us the most frequent form of accident, they may start to search their memories for examples. They will assume that the pattern of accidents that they manage to conjure up is representative of the 'true' (overall) pattern. Unfortunately, they will be confusing retrievability with representativeness. The distribution of accidents that they can think of is determined by how easily the different types can be brought to mind, and not the actual statistics. The ease with which something comes to mind is determined more by factors such as the recency and/or the trauma of the event etc. It would be convenient to be able to rely on the information we get from a person when we ask them to tell us their favourite breakfast cereal. What they tell us may not be their favourite at all. It may just be the favourite of the ones they could recall at the time. This may be due to many other factors. They may not buy their favourite often. When asked the question they may simply trawl their memory of their recent supermarket trolleys of foodstuffs and decide which of those cereals they think they feel most enthused about. Indeed, it may be that if they have just eaten something rather stodgy for dinner, they will review the cereals and conclude that they like the one that they think they feel like eating when they 'consult' their stomach. We cannot rely on the spontaneous recollection or recounting of issues.

Overall, people need help to access their own conceptions and constructions. A great deal of the work that has been done on managers' understanding of their organization and industry has utilized the cognitive mapping approach developed by Eden and his colleagues and discussed in Chapter 4 (for example Eden, 1988). This approach elicits the constructs that managers have concerning an issue (for example the dynamics of their industry) and places this mental material in a network diagram. The diagram allows participants to design a 'hierarchy of means and ends' (Ackermann et al., 1990, p. 1). This 'cognitive map' is a representation of the way in which they understand the dynamics of the issue in question. It can capture what the individual considers to be the links between particular actions and the achievement of goals. The map can reveal the propositions that the individual seems to be using in their decision. Eden argues that as a visual interactive modelling method, it is particularly suitable for exploring system dynamics (see, for example, Bennett, 1994; Eden, 1994; Williams et al., 1995). In many ways, the approach can be considered to focus on the linkages between issues rather than on the issues themselves (Eden and Ackermann, 1993).

It is this exposing of the 'logic' that people are using in their decision-making that is the key strength of approaches that focus on semantic mental material. Many other researchers have gleaned semantic mental material from participants, and examined its impact on their decision-making. Courtney and Paradice (1993) report developments in an alternative graphics software system to support managerial problem formulation. Hukkinen (1995) analysed the structure, substance and institutional context of the mental models with which key policy-makers in Finnish waste management rationalize their long-term decisions. Other research has examined people's logics in domains other than strategic management. Anthony et al. (1994) identified the network of causal assertions offered during a major US political debate. Koukouris (1994) examined the causal relationships among factors that athletes maintain in their decisions to disengage from organized competitive sport. Bitonti (1992; 1993) reports the underlying cognitive self-schemata that women used in evaluating their perceptions of themselves in the course of major life transitions. Insights into the personal logic that people are using in their decisions at work is clearly an important part of management by perception. It is only one of the elements of semantic understanding that we need to address. The particular techniques that tend to be used in examining managers' semantic understanding place an emphasis on the reasoning and decisions that are being made, that is, causal models. Because much of the work also concerns strategic planning, there is a separation of personal experiences, feelings etc. from the analytical components. When working with a broader set of organizational participants, however, we can see that there is a need to include many more facets of semantic understanding. The next section outlines some of the approaches that can be used.

Eliciting semantic understanding of issues

We can get to know the terms in which a person 'sees' issues in the course of interacting with them. Felcher (1995) for example, used participant observation and interviews to gain some insight into the ways that car sales people view customers and the sales encounter. The terms that sales staff used to categorized customers (moochers, professors etc.) were evidenced in their everyday discourse. We have seen, however, that we can move beyond the conventions of everyday discourse to gain additional insights. A general term that can be used to describe attempts to get at semantic understanding is depth interview. This involves supporting the participant to explore and articulate their thinking through a more thorough searching of their understanding.

We have seen how there can be a lack of emphasis on the affective side of understanding. Open questions concerning how that issue/event makes the participant feel can play a valuable role in eliciting semantic understanding. We have noted how there may not be a singular set of views concerning any issue. We may behave differently according to different prevailing emotional mindsets. The aspects of a situation that strike a person in one mood may be completely absent in another. Depth interviewing involves techniques that can assist the participants to project themselves into particular situations in order to shed light on particular aspects of their understanding. We have also seen how imagistic forms of thought can be used in addition to propositional thoughts. Practitioners are advised to utilize aids to imagistic thinking in the course of eliciting semantic understanding. Encouraging people to draw things, showing people pictures, videos etc. can help in securing insight.

We have further seen how attempts to foster a 'systematic' reasoning type of thinking can help in securing more comprehensive insights into the zero-order, first-order and second-order relations (Gentner, 1983) that the participant is using in considering issues. We have argued that it can be useful to induce reasoning types of thinking that focus on: (a) separation (the differentiations that a person makes between entities), and (b) location (the relationships that a person construes between entities). Given the essentially propositional and reflective nature of semantic understanding, it seems appropriate to structure the outline of semantic understanding techniques in terms of these different types of emphasis in reasoning. The emphasis here is on the content of the thinking used by participants. Given that the contribution that invoking different types of thinking can make to knowledge elicitation has already been considered, this section will examine the nature of semantic mental material that can be elicited in organizational settings, and how it can be used.

INSIGHTS GAINED BY INVOKING SEPARATION THINKING   The 'sense' that a person makes out of a situation may not relate to the prevailing intentions of organizational players. The actions that people take in the course of their work are based in large part on their conscious understanding of the issues and consequences associated with alternative actions. Most of the techniques operate by placing entities in juxtaposition and exploring what is raised by the participant in the course of this process.

Firlej and Hellens (1991) distinguish between listing and concept sorting in knowledge elicitation. Listing the constructs that a person uses in a 'naturalistic' context can be a useful starting point. The participant can then be presented with the first provisional list, to check for completeness or accuracy. As Firlej and Hellens (1991) note, lists can provide quick and easy feedback, but care should be taken to avoid reading too much into the frequencies of particular constructs used. Frequency of reference does not mean importance or centrality. It will be necessary to record any limitations of generality or scope of a term. A concept without such information may later suggest, erroneously, that its scope is universal. Some words and concepts can be too general to be meaningful without contextual information. More than a list of words may be required to contextualize and qualify terms. Lists alone may fail to elicit missing, unusual or complex information or connections. Listing ideas, considerations, options etc. is nevertheless a useful process. It can help people to 'see' what they have so far failed to mention. It is a basic form of information that can be valuable in a comparative way. The words listed by one group of participants can be seen to overlap or differ markedly from those used by another group. This can be a good starting point for building mutual understanding.

Firlej and Hellens (1991) use the term 'concept sorting' to refer to any of the elicitation processes where terms are explicitly contrasted. Typically, constructs are written on cards. The participant can be asked to say why, or in what way, two or more cards are alike, or to outline the way in which a grouping alters if a particular card is taken out of the grouping. Additional cards can be added as further terms strike the participant. The 'language' of the participant is established in the course of these processes. The 'minimum context card form' of the repertory grid procedure outlined earlier 'requires' that pairs of elements are identified and contrasted with the third element. This systematization can be particularly helpful when one is seeking to explore issues where participants' understanding may not have had a great deal of opportunity to be articulated. As we have seen, the process of exploration tightens up one's representations of issues. This can make subsequent access easier.

There can be instances where participants' understanding may be less rehearsed and clear, however. For example, in the UK, community and mental health service providers were required to provide their services for purchasers within the National Health Service. The doctors who serve the general public (general practitioners) were able to purchase services. The bases that they might use to guide their purchasing decisions were inevitably unclear. Sparrow et al. (1993) undertook a study using the repertory grid procedure to elicit the constructs which GPs use in contrasting different community and mental health services. Interviews were arranged with a number of GPs in a case study area to obtain the terms (constructs) used by GPs to assess quality. The sample of GPs was selected to ensure representativeness in three main respects. Practices were selected to cover the full range of GP practice sizes, various levels of social deprivation in their area and potential attitudinal issues associated with being fundholding or not. Eight repertory grid interviews were held using the set of community and mental health services (district nursing, health visiting, palliative care, continence, evening nursing, physiotherapy, foot health, speech and language therapy, adult and acute mental health, and drug and alcohol service) as elements for the grid procedure. Over 200 aspects of quality were obtained in the repertory grid interviews. The initial group of GPs was then asked to indicate which of these issues were the most important. Quality aspects were also grouped into major categories and 24 major aspects of quality were identified. These were the aspects of quality which GPs considered to be the most important in using community and mental health services. The 'performance' of the services was then assessed by a wider set of GPs in the case study area. Responses were obtained from 91 per cent of practices in the area, from a total of 68 GPs. Factor analysis of the responses identified three major clusters of quality aspects. These were patient service aspects (integration between services, information sharing, information to patients, meeting patient expectations, communication with patients, patient skills, client-centredness, sensitivity, demographic planning, internal co-ordination, flexibility, being a neighbourhood service, geographical accessibility, and initial waiting time), constitutional/technical aspects (division of responsibilities, promotion of services, information systems, GP involvement and communication with GPs) and management and structural aspects (operational style, overall organization, staff professionalism, comprehensiveness and overall management). The framework was considered to be valuable to the various service providers and was used to guide their future service-provision decisions. The study highlights how 'customer' views can be elicited even in quite complex purchasing areas. The structure of the technique promotes the articulation of a very comprehensive set of separate constructs.

Another application of an in-depth approach to surface patterns in perceptions for organizational decision-makers to consider was conducted by Ward (1994), while working with the author. Kevin Ward had been working for Rank Xerox (UK) Ltd, and had become aware of the many programmes that large organizations initiate to secure improvements in effectiveness. In Xerox's case these included initiatives to address employee communication through noticeboards and the internal magazine; employee knowledge and skills through programmes of induction and training; feedback/control through programmes of recognition, appraisal and employee satisfaction; as well as quality initiatives, through programmes of leadership and benchmarking. His concern lay in how well the initiatives had been marketed internally. He wanted to know what the 'language' was that 'recipients' of these initiatives used in considering them. A repertory grid procedure was used with junior and middle managers to contrast the different initiatives. The managers generated 25 different constructs that they used to differentiate between the initiatives. There were three clear groupings of constructs. One set concerned the extent to which programmes aided specific and individual personal development (for example 'rewarding', 'motivational', 'developmental'). Another set of constructs concerned the level of impact that initiatives had had (for example 'valuable', 'positive', 'meaningful', 'well communicated', 'constructive'). A third set concerned the extent to which the initiatives constituted practical tools that could be used by managers themselves (for example 'measurable', 'two-way'). Furthermore, when the 'profiles' of initiatives were examined in these terms, they were grouped in participants' minds in ways that did not correspond to their designed function (communication, knowledge/skills, feedback/control, quality). The benchmarking initiative, for example, was seen as more akin to a communication initiative (and thereby, perhaps, more supportive in tone) than to another quality initiative, that was seen far more as a controlling, appraisal-like approach. Overall, the information was considered to be valuable for future decisions concerning internal marketing.

An example application of a knowledge-elicitation technique to surface semantic and other aspects of mutual perception is provided by Sparrow and Rigg (1993). They undertook an analysis of a particular public-sector management job. The management job selected had the title district housing manager (DHM) and provided incumbents with quite a high degree of autonomy in the way that they managed their district's housing services. There is a lot of research evidence for differences between men and women in their styles of management. In the main, studies have shown women managers to be more open and intuitive, less independent and 'tough' and to have greater anxiety. There appears to be a greater emphasis on a 'transformational' approach to leadership (which involves participation and motivation through inclusion and power through charisma) rather than a 'transactional' approach (which involves motivation through exchange of rewards and power through position) among women. Women managers tend to have wider goals, and more commonly want to succeed at the same time as wanting to make the work environment more fulfilling for everybody involved in the business. The study wished to examine the perceptions of all of the DHMs about each other's 'style', and to consider whether there was any evidence of differences in style between the male and female DHMs.

It is, of course, possible to ask people directly to comment on whether they feel there are differences between men's and women's management styles, and to state any terms they use to distinguish between the styles. There would be clear limitations to such an approach, concerning the ways in which desire to be seen to be politically correct may affect responses. Furthermore, such an approach would be premised on the notion that people have reflected on such issues and have established a gender 'framework' that they use in their conscious thinking. An alternative approach was to examine how participants see each DHM differing from every other DHM, with the aid of the repertory grid procedure. The approach in essence consisted of using the DHMs as 'elements' which were then systematically contrasted in threes, by each participant, to identify the qualities which are associated with job performance. The local authority had 16 DHMs (12 men, 4 women) split into three area teams. The frequency of contact of DHMs within teams was considered sufficient for them to be able to make assessments of the differences between the trios of DHMs with whom they worked. The director for housing was informed about the purposes of the study. The DHMs were only told that the study was seeking to identify the real demands of the job. Incidentally, all of the DHMs felt this to be worthwhile, since the existing job specification did not in their view capture the needs for the job. Extensive interviews were held with all DHMs. In total 374 constructs concerning approaches to the job were elicited.

The initial content analysis of all constructs revealed five major headings under which job requirements could be classified. If it were assumed that the job had only male incumbents, a profile could be produced derived from the constructs which male incumbents used in describing male incumbents. Similarly, a profile could be produced from the constructs used by women incumbents in describing women incumbents. Table 6.1 shows the qualities indicated for the two 'jobs'. It seems clear that the two profiles differ substantially. The requirements for each version of the job are in line with previous studies of stylistic differences between men and women managers. The findings concerning the apparent alternative ways in which to conduct the job were fed back to the participants. It was an insight they had not hitherto had.

Mostyn (1994), while working with the author, used the repertory grid procedure within a small group of professionals in a recruitment agency, to promote their exploration of the ways in which they each distinguished between different employing organizations. As a recruitment agency, they had developed a shared language concerning the attributes of job seekers. This was partly derived from their use of standardized assessment procedures. When the team asked themselves which characteristics of prospective employing organizations they drew to the attention of applicants, they realized that they each outlined the firm in their own way, and that the terms that they used may not necessarily be the most useful for distinguishing between the demands (atmosphere etc.) of different client organizations. Nine companies that each of the six consultants knew well were agreed as an appropriate cross-section of their client companies. Each consultant contrasted the companies using the minimum context card form of repertory grid administration. The language of the participants included a rich set of constructs that the team found very useful as they explored patterns in their thinking. Some feel for the richness of insight can be gleaned from a consideration of some of the constructs elicited. Examples include 'metamorphosis – static', 'crisp – unprofessional', 'growing – burned-out case', 'pride – indifference', 'autocratic – flair', and 'old boys – meritocracy'. The team went on to consider group similarities. They used some of the statistical patterns between the 'scores' that they gave to each of the nine companies in each of their regards, to see whether there may be some underlying common features that characterized any individual's perceptions and the group's views in general. They examined the ways that they each tended to cluster the nine client organizations into particular

Table 6.1 *The different 'jobs' of district housing manager seen by different participants (from Sparrow and Rigg, 1993)*

Aspect	'Job' A The female job	'Job' B The male job
The priorities they see for the job	Team management central Effective service delivery	Vision Entrepreneurship (i.e. not confined to administering) Ability to package ideas for funding
Working style	People-oriented Works through people Moderate and measured	Political Forceful High profile Flamboyant Confident Aware of external events Paternalistic
Decision-making approach	Not snap decisions Familiarizes self with key aspects	Quick Action-oriented Detached Analytic Systematic
Interpersonal relationships with own team	Understanding of people Care for individual feelings and development Sensitivity Rich perception of human beings	Supports own team Looks after their interests Defend them to the hilt
Interpersonal relationships with clients	Empathy Understanding of different needs	Can use pressure groups

groupings. As a group, they were involved in an industry where softer information is commonplace. They understood the importance of mutual understanding. They were comfortable with using statistical procedures to shed additional light on 'raw scores'. Even so, they hinted at the over-complexity of analysis that Coshall (1991) had observed, in saying that repertory grids of all types have increasingly come to be analysed by over-sophisticated techniques involving a positivistic or hard science approach, as opposed to what Kelly probably envisaged as a more humanistic framework. Despite this, 'the team seemed fairly happy with undertaking the interview and were surprised at the level of detail from the analysis' and 'would be happy to use the technique again' (Mostyn, 1994, p. 57).

Sparrow and Bushell (1996) utilized the repertory grid procedure, some qualitative data-analysis software and concept-mapping techniques in an action research project with a small team of personal business advisers

(PBAs). The elements they contrasted were different 'stages' in a business life cycle. The nine elements were pre-start, existence, survival, control of planning, expansion, slow down, stability, supergrowth and decline. PBAs were asked to consider 'businesses in general' at these various stages, and to indicate the ways in which businesses at any pair of stages (selected from the set of three stages drawn randomly from the full set of cards) may face similar issues, that differed from those being faced by businesses at the stage indicated by the third card. In particular the PBAs were asked to indicate what they, as a PBA, felt the businesses 'might need to be supported in, and how'.

Each PBA was interviewed for about one hour. The interviews produced very rich accounts of the ways in which businesses were considered to differ, the things they may need to be doing, and the ways in which they could be supported. Each interview was transcribed. Systematic qualitative data analysis was conducted with the aid of computer software (HyperResearch, 1995). Used in conjunction with graphical concept-mapping software (Mind Maps Plus, 1995), the qualitative data analysis suggested a structure that could be used to contrast the constructs used by the various members of the team. PBAs were felt to offer accounts that differed from each other in 73 major terms. The frequencies with which each PBA referred to each of the 73 terms were computed. The software also allowed various patterns in the use of particular subsets of concepts to be discerned. In addition, statistical software was used to compute a hierarchical cluster analysis to shed further light on patterns in referring to particular terms across the set of PBAs. Different subgroupings of PBAs (defined in terms of similar patterns of reference to concepts) were also explored.

The analysis highlighted seven fundamental tensions that seemed to characterize differences in approaches to supporting businesses. The apparent basic pattern of Business Link Sandwell's PBA thinking about business support and differences in the group were fed back to the group in a workshop session. A colleague from the University of Central England Business School Department of Management acted as observer for the session. He sensed a 'lot of suspicion' in the early stages of the workshop, and suspected that some 'had never previously engaged in this kind of reflective exercise'. There was a general defensiveness. Reactions included denial (claims that the observations were not valid, or that things had moved on), and a general assertion that what they were doing already was the 'right' thing to be doing. As the session progressed there was awareness that 'differences' within the team that had been sensed tacitly were now being discussed explicitly, and that this was a helpful process. The team felt that they would like to consider these issues and their team functioning further. This was an action research project and further work with the team subsequently took place.

The key points to note here concern the value of the repertory grid procedure (and allied tools to aid interpretation/analysis) in eliciting insights into one's own semantic mental material, and that of other organizational participants, in a way that can be used to consider implications. The elicitation process itself is generally seen to be comprehensive and in-depth. The retention of the language of the participant is valued. The ability to discern pattern in the mass of data produced through other systematic (usually computer-supported) procedures is valuable, but can become too elaborate for the taste of particular individuals/organizations. The author used some of the printed output from the statistics package (dendograms) to show participants how the issues they referred to clustered, and how there were degrees of similarity between the perception of different clusters of personal business advisers. Some difficulties were apparent in the group. Their lack of understanding of hierarchical cluster analysis procedures meant that the potential immediate value of the physical representation was not obtained. This should not be taken to suggest that alternative physical representations of statistical relationships are inappropriate in general. Other studies have shown clear value in enabling clients/stakeholders to 'picture' the results of complex statistical analysis (for example McLinden and Jinkerson, 1994). The overall time required to make a comprehensive interpretation of this form and volume of data is quite considerable. Participants tend to feel that the effort is justified. This calculation depends in part on how the information goes on to be used by the individual or workteam. The value added by the detailed knowledge-elicitation process *per se* seems to be adequate. There is a clear impact on the nature of the interaction between team members in discussing mutual perceptions, when compared to interactions based on everyday self-reflections and discussion. The quality of self-insights is also improved.

The repertory grid procedure is probably the most widely advocated technique for enhancing this type of thinking and generating semantic mental material. Its general utility has been reviewed by Brook (1986) and its uses in business summarized by Stewart and Stewart (1981). Its strengths and weaknesses in relation to other techniques of knowledge elicitation are considered by Brown (1992).

The goal in using separation thinking in eliciting semantic understanding is to try to generate as many of the entities and attributes that are used in the participant's decision-making in a particular domain. It is rare to restrict attention to the terms themselves and not the information that is generated concerning their interrelationship, however, and so techniques that also assist in location thinking tend to be used in elicitation. One often has the feeling that the choice of elements may not be adequate in manifesting the thinking of participants, and it is certainly useful to keep an eye on the volume and exhaustiveness of terms used in understanding a person's mental models of an issue. One may secure high-quality but inadequate understanding unless one keeps asking oneself if there are any terms that need to be explored.

INSIGHTS GAINED BY INVOKING LOCATION THINKING   Location thinking refers to the ways that a person uses to consider the interrelationships between ideas/objects/events. In Chapter 2 and Chapter 5, we distinguished between different forms of location thinking; specifically, static comparison, systems thinking and plurality-seeking. The reader is referred to those chapters for a more general outline of using reasoning-enhancing techniques. The focus in this section will be on the nature of insights into semantic mental material that can come from using location thinking.

Card-sorting approaches can be used to gain insights into the categorizations that people use. Participants can be asked to explain the basis of their thinking by grouping terms in particular ways. Being able to see a set of terms and move them about seems to help people in assigning concepts in the flexible and multiple ways that we know they often do. People often feel that the elicitor is interested in the their main way of grouping things. It is important to encourage the participant to play with the cards without feeling conscious of the need to have generated another complete category. It is the mental freedom to spot the vast array of familiar interrelationships that needs to be cherished at this stage. This informal process allows the participant to 'arrange the cards in hierarchies, trees, in a decision-making ladder or in order of importance. The elicitor then questions [the participant] about the relationships, why one concept is placed higher than another or why it is grouped with another, and so on' (Firlej and Hellens, 1991, p. 149). As we have seen, particular conventions can be used as 'rules' for interrelating concepts. These additional elements of formality can generate a great deal of insight into the semantic understanding which the participant has of the domain in question. Some of the alternative conventions that can be used to guide elicitation are discussed below.

Going back to the approach proposed by Socrates in the fifth century BC is still argued by some to be a useful general discipline (Overholser, 1993). Socratic method involves obtaining knowledge in two stages. The first stage is to collect instances of a term or issue under discussion. These examples are examined to discover in them some common quality by virtue of which they bear that name. This common quality is thus abstracted from the 'accidental properties of time and circumstance which belong to each of the [instances] individually . . . Thus the inductive argument is, as its Greek name signifies, a "leading-on" of the mind from individual instances, assembled and regarded collectively, to a comprehension of their common definition' (Guthrie, 1967, p. 77). As Aristotle put it, 'Socrates posed questions without answering them' (Ferguson, 1970) and the 'essence of the Socratic method is to convince the interlocutor that whereas he thought he knew something, in fact he does not' (Guthrie, 1967, p. 74). We can see our 'muddled' thinking in the course of such a process of questioning. Of course, the purpose of the approach is to resolve any loose thinking and get to the essence of a matter. In this sense it can be a disruptive (knowledge-generating rather than knowledge-eliciting) approach. Many of the 'arguments' that one uses in the defence of one's position are, however, part of one's thinking already, and the process is a useful device for cueing these additional elements of understanding. In a social context, it is the heart of debate, where the statements of others are subjected to rigorous questioning to 'tighten them up'. Subjecting one's ideas to the rigours of Socratic questioning is one of the formal (disciplined) ways in which one's ideas can be located. 'Devil's advocacy' can assist in eliciting one's own views. It is possible to self-manage this activity. Some sort of a checklist of searching questions may be of value to maintain rigour in one's own thinking.

Specific interviewing strategies can be adopted in order to secure a more comprehensive searching of a person's understanding. Reynolds (1988), for example, reviews laddering theory and method in in-depth interviews. Particular probing techniques or interview devices can be used to invoke search around a particular issue. Some of the specific issues involved were discussed earlier when repertory grid procedure was outlined. Kvale (1996, pp. 133–5) categorizes interview questions, and urges that the different types are used appropriately. 'Introducing' questions are opening questions designed to elicit spontaneous rich descriptions. 'Follow-up' questions promote the extension of the participant's answers through a 'curious, persistent and critical attitude', which are cued by '"red lights" in the answers – such as unusual terms, strong intonations, and the like – which may signal a whole complex of topics important to the subject' (p. 133). 'Probing' questions pursue answers without stating what dimensions are to be taken into account. 'Specifying' questions attempt to get more precise descriptions from general statements. 'Structuring' questions indicate when a particular theme has been exhausted and the participant is to be guided into another area. 'Interpreting' questions may involve merely rephrasing an answer or more inference on the part of the interviewer. They are put back to the participant for further comment. Kvale (1996) also refers to the importance of silence in the interview and the judicious use of direct and indirect questions. Overall, one is seeking to achieve a firm and conscientious effort to surface the participant's understanding.

There are many more specific disciplined forms of categorical thinking that can be used to guide the elicitation of knowledge. The Delphi technique (for example Linstone and Turoff, 1975; Delbecq et al., 1975) can be used as a developmental process in organizations. Anonymized statements on an issue can be circulated among organizational participants. Each statement acts as a spur to thinking. It often represents a position diametrically opposed to the view that a particular participant has. They are cued to edit statements and offer their own particular statement of position. There is a danger, however, that the set of initial statements will fail to cue additional considerations and merely focus attention on subscribing to or refuting initial statements. After several 'rounds', the consensus position has been clarified and expressed to general satisfaction.

Floyd and Wooldridge (1992) in a sense modify the approach when they propose a three-stage process to obtain 'consensus maps'. The process begins with interviewing participants to 'provide a list of strategic priorities in the "language" of the firm. We ask about the business conditions facing the firm, its major goals, the strategies chosen to pursue goals, and activities currently receiving special attention' (p. 30). The second stage involves the distillation of the interview material into 'a list of descriptors in each area of consensus content (environment, goals and strategies)' (p. 30) to create a questionnaire. The questionnaire items are listed as statements, and the fuller set of respondents indicate their agreement with each statement, as a matter of fact (whether that is what the firm is doing/experiencing), and as a matter of opinion (whether they feel the firm 'ought' to be doing/ experiencing these things). The third stage involves summarizing the information into maps of broad issues. For example, two-dimensional maps can depict the relative extents to which different levels or groups of participants understand the firm's strategy to be cost based vs differentiation based. Another map can depict the position in terms of commitment to the strategic position. Consensus maps can help to 'surface the varying viewpoints as to what priorities . . . ought to be . . . and commitment to a series of trials and pilot projects . . . [can form] the basis for alternative strategies' (p. 34). As a process, it can assist participants in expressing their views. Its focus is on creating consensus and mutual recognition of differences is not pursued.

Stating the essence of one's views is thus an instance of using a reasoning mode of thinking (specifically categorization) to elicit semantic understanding. Insights into the understanding that organizational participants have can also be enhanced by using the second form of static comparison, 'sequencing', as a mode of thinking. Drummond (1992) maintains that 'it is vital that decision-makers are able to distinguish fact from assumption. A simple but effective means of doing so is to classify information as follows; knowns, unclear, assumed' (p. 10). Significant insight into cause and effect can be obtained if one subjects unclear or assumption information to rigour, tries to be 'ruthless in exposing doubt' (p. 12) and asks 'what if?'. '"What if", basically means confronting the possibility that assumptions may be wrong. It often involves thinking the awful and the unthinkable, refusing to be hypnotized by propaganda or paralysed by the existence of sacred cows' (p. 12).

Using these simple analytical tools can assist in surfacing semantic understanding of ideas and their interrelationship. Interpretive structural modelling (Moore et al., 1987) can be used to describe relational properties such as causality, severity, importance or priority, and precedence (order) to make an implicit structure explicit. Backoff and Nutt (1988) show how issues facing a mental health centre planning group could be prioritized. As noted in discussing the technique earlier, Hammer and Janes (1990) show how the 'narrow engineering-based company culture', together with 'limited access to bank funding', strongly contributed to the 'poor promotion of products' which was one of the factors in a case study company's 'inability to sell products in markets'. In this technique, particular forms of relationship are used to 'view' the entire set of elements. The elements are then structured in terms of this particular view. Much can be learned about a person's semantic understanding in observing them putting elements into particular orders. The technique is more frequently used in a group setting, however. Here, it has been shown to have value in promoting groups to reach consensus on issues. Any insight into the views of particular individuals is really only an incidental by-product of the approach. By 'forcing' consensus, one loses some of the insights into each other and other options.

A technique which restricts itself to hierarchical relationships is Hierarchical Task Analysis (Annett et al., 1971). This approach seeks to establish a 'superordinate objective' (what the person is trying to achieve) and then breaks this down into operations (behaviours required to achieve that objective) and then suboperations (behaviours required to achieve that objective) and so on. The technique is usually used in a way that generates a language that describes 'the' operations needed to achieve a task. As such the operations can be carried out by 'any' human or even machine (Patrick et al., 1981). It is, however, also possible to use the technique deliberately to elicit the idiosyncratic ways that individual job incumbents define and approach their job. We can see how it would be interesting to hear what different individuals think is the superordinate operation for their job. Perhaps different people are seeking different things. In attempting any suboperation, different people may feel that it invokes different issues. In applying the technique in this way, one is using it merely as a systematic procedure. In examining each operation, one asks what are all the (next level) suboperations that are necessary to achieve it. Having ensured that that level of operations is a complete set, one then breaks down each of those suboperations. In the original format, one is aided by the 'logic' that certain operations 'have' to be performed in order to achieve the higher-order objective. Indeed, one of the intuitive tests that one performs is to test whether each particular operation could be performed if the full set of suboperations were to be executed. In a more individualized application, the technique will operate as a 'backbone' to guide introspection. Its contribution lies in the particular rules that it carries. It reveals what we can learn if we look at tasks hierarchically.

We can see how we obtain different insights if we attempt to consider our work operating within opposing forces. We can consider aspects that are moving collectively in one broad direction, and contrast them with any factors that are opposing that direction. Forcefield analysis is a technique used for identifying and analysing the various forces that act positively and negatively on a situation. It is a visually effective way of recording the forces. The technique is often used in continuous improvement initiatives, to assess ease or difficulty in changing a situation, determine how successful a solution might be and to plan to overcome barriers to change. The process involves listing driving and restraining forces, considering (for each driver and each restrainer) how significant the consequences are of changing it, and how far it is possible to change it. A simple addition of the two scores for each force gives an indication of the major and minor considerations. Scores can be computed to assess the impact of alternative solutions. A solution with a better relative balance between the driving and restraining forces should be preferred. Majaro (1988) suggests that the technique is best

used in a group setting. Group members can list and discuss their perceptions of the forces. The group leader can draw a diagram showing the
forces and their respective directions. Some writers suggest upwards vs
downwards directions; some refer to right-moving vs left-moving directions.
In both instances the former term refers to the positive direction (that is,
drivers). Once provisionally depicted, the diagram can aid the team in its
determination of the relative impact of each factor. Again, the consensus
position can be represented diagrammatically by adjusting the relative
lengths of the arrows, such that the longest arrows are the most powerful
forces. The mental search that is made in looking for opposing forces and
assessing their strength is different from that involved in considering
hierarchical relationships. The discipline of attempting to list a comprehensive (exhaustive?) set of factors is the essence of the contribution of the
technique.

Episodic memories

Using Abercrombie's (1960) definition of schemas as 'experience organized
in fairly well-defined patterns' (p. 54), we can see how many of our experiences are held in memory as particular episodes, or sequences of events.
They are episodic schemas. When we confront new situations we may be
reminded of previous experiences, and cue recall of a previous episode. In
the course of discussions with other people we may make reference to our
own experiences in this way. Episodic schemas are a major part of how we
store, access and use experience in our decisions and actions. Many of the
specific experiences that we have are not stored intact in memory for very
long, because they are not 'significant' or 'distinguishable' from routine
experiences. Many specific experiences get encoded as particular 'types' of
problem, or causal accounts, and the knowledge is not retained as a distinct
sequence (episodic schema), but as 'meaningful' information (a semantic
schema). But there are some experiences that are stored episodically.

It would be useful if we could identify some of the major areas in work
life where events are stored as episodic schemas. While we may find that
previous episodes can colour our judgement in a subsequent decision,
episodes cannot always be brought to mind to order. If we as individuals,
and organizations generally, are to consider experiences that are regarded
as key episodes, some of the features of episodic schemas will need to
recognized.

Gaining access to one's personal memories is a difficult thing to do. We
have often experienced situations in which we feel that we remember
something but seem to be unable to access the information we know is 'in
there somewhere'. A slight alteration in the 'cues' can help us. There is
evidence to suggest that if there is a degree of similarity between the cues
that were available at the time of learning and those available at the time of
retrieval, then recall is easier (Tulving and Thomson, 1971). Bourne et al.

(1986) refer to the fascination throughout history with the idea of things that spur recollection. They note how courts have tried to formulate definitions of retrieval cues, since they play such an important role in aiding witnesses to recall events. In legal theory, anything that actually refreshes a witness's memory may be used. It could be 'a song, or a face, or a newspaper item' or ' the creaking of a hinge, the whistling of a tune, the smell of seaweed, the sight of an old photograph, the taste of nutmeg, the touch of a piece of canvas' (p. 163). This 'encoding specificity principle' (Tulving, 1983) means that recall can be enhanced if the context that occurred at encoding can be reinstated. Smith (1988) showed it is possible for people to 'spontaneously reinstate their own imaginary versions' of events to get back at memories. Korminouri (1995) demonstrates that action events can be recalled more effectively when they have been encoded both episodically and semantically. Indeed, there is evidence to suggest that episodes are concurrently encoded across multiple representations, that include, in part, propositional codes (Sirigu and Grafman, 1996). The contribution of episodic mental material *per se* is increasingly being recognized. Hofbauer et al. (1994) argue that because organizational problem-solvers rely quite extensively on episodic mental material, and employees co-operate and seek each other's experiences (particularly in complex domains where semantic understanding becomes more sparse), computer-based decision-support systems should assist in working with episodic mental material *per se*. They propose a decision-support architecture that uses case-based reasoning and analogical reasoning, and facilitates the exchange of experiences. Moody et al. (1996) highlight how knowledge-elicitation approaches that capture episodic mental material are particularly important for case-based expert systems.

  To what extent are specific 'episodes' an identifiable part of people's current actions? Iyengar (1996) suggests that contexts that emphasize episodic encoding (to the detriment of semantic encoding) may lead people to attribute issues to individuals rather than deeper or broader underlying causes. The suggestion is that because a person has stored information in a non-semantic way, the event cannot be interpreted within a 'rich' setting where understanding of causes and implications are associated with the memory. The memory is of a sequence of events, and so any subsequent 'explanation' of events will be restricted to the episode and the actions of the key agents, as opposed to any broader (semantic) explanation. To what extent are experiences stored as episodes, as opposed to the interpretations we have placed on them? When might experiences tend to be stored episodically? Bedard and Graham (1994), in exploring the organization of experienced auditors' knowledge, found that the auditors frequently framed their knowledge in a 'client-centred' way, that is, within specific cases, rather than as generalized cross-case rules. There is some evidence to suggest that the direction of movement of any developments in the ways that ideas/objects/events are encoded may not merely be a progression from episodic encoding towards a 'richer' semantic encoding. It is often assumed that episodic encoding is a shallower analysis of ideas/objects/events and that reflection can assist in locating experiences more fully. Studies of consumer behaviour suggest that people may come to code experiences in case-based ways, as their expertise concerning a brand increases. It may be that people initially locate the world of product brands in a complex multidimensional way. All brands can be considered in terms of this 'universal' semantic framework. If, however, a person becomes loyal to a particular brand, then their evaluations of other brands may become based on simple comparisons with their preferred brand (Finlay, 1996), that is, the particular case becomes the focus of the way that their mental material is organized. All things are thus seen in terms of the focal case(s). Case-based knowledge organization and reasoning are becoming major research issues in general.

It is often easy to see the effects of particular traumatic events within organizations. People may recount a specific episode many times over a series of meetings. It is possible to see how this episodic mental material is colouring their judgement quite markedly, and yet for the person not to recognize that tendency in their thinking. Personal and organizational events may be reflected on (and re-represented as semantic declarative knowledge). This 'sense-making' version of mental material is not the only mental material that then contributes to future decision-making. Episodes may not be reflected on at all, or not very comprehensively, and continue to contribute to the inferences used in interpreting current events. Reflective practitioners and organizations need actively to elicit episodic information in its 'rawer' form and explore its relationship with the conclusions drawn from it and subsequent impact on decisions.

Reflective practitioners need to consider the extent to which their own practices are rooted in schemas that are essentially complete episodes. The transferability of such episodes is often questionable, and reflection frequently exposes such episodic mental material to subsequent schematization that abstracts key principles rather than entire 'chains' of argument which may not hold in other situations. Practices that have been adopted previously, by oneself or others, can be somewhat blindly applied as general principles. It is important for individuals and organizations to consider the extent to which their practices are so informed. It is interesting to speculate what some of the consequences of a greater level of episodic mental material within an organization might be. It is possible that one might shift references from general principles towards more individual perspectives. It may be that one achieves greater empathy. In terms of the 'learning' implications, one can see that reflecting on fuller accounts of experiences may lead to more insights from a semantic mental material point of view when one interprets events. At the organizational level, one may also encounter more learning as the situations where practices that were previously informed by individual episodic schemas become more influenced by shared semantic understanding. It is important to recognize the contribution of episodic mental material *per se* in our own and others' actions. Some of the techniques that can be used to elicit it are discussed below.

Eliciting episodic memories of issues

Once one is aware of the distinction between semantic and episodic mental material, it is possible to discern the elements in a person's conversation that are derived from the two respective sources. We can observe the movements that people make in their discourse between semantic mental material and episodic mental material. When one considers the likely impact of the two different kinds of mental material, one begins to see how the person's mental material may affect their decisions and actions in the future. It will be recalled that mental material that is 'strung together' as an episode may well 'direct' subsequent related behaviour, either as a complete re-run of the action or a complete avoidance/negation of the action. The 'meaning' of any in-between course of action is, by definition, semantic mental material. In contrast, when we hear knowledge that is held together in a coherent analytical way, we might expect to find that subsequent behaviour is informed by the knowledge, but not necessarily in line with the specific example given. The specific material we are hearing merely exemplifies the concept that the person has in mind. The person's subsequent decision/action incorporated the broad concept.

In an ideal world one would seek complete perceptions of issues from participants and establish those aspects that appear to be schematized within semantic understanding, and those that are held episodically. As we have seen, however, the discourse situation itself affects the relative emphasis that a participant places on abstract and personal concepts/ideas. Nolan (1994), for example, highlights the syntactic, semantic and pragmatic 'rules' that guide the construction and understanding of different discourse genres. A scientific report genre entails the application of its particular 'discourse operator' (p. 146). The discourse may operate a syntactic rule, such as 'construct the discourse in accordance with the laws of classical logic'; a semantic rule, such as 'use words in accordance with the practices of the relevant scientific community'; and a pragmatic rule, such as 'make no references to individuals except by way of citation' (Nolan, 1994, pp. 148–9). Any 'reading' of a discourse in a natural language 'requires its subsumption under at least one discourse operator' (p. 146). In considering any material that we feel may carry the thinking of a participant, we must recognize the discourse operator(s) that the individual may have been operationalizing. The discourse operator may have inherently reduced or enhanced the proportion of episodic mental material referred to.

One may glean little of the relative influence of episodic mental material in a particular scientist's thinking were one only to consider their 'scientific' writings. It is possible, however, deliberately to select material that is likely to carry more elements of episodic mental material, and consider the specific information that is encapsulated in episodic as opposed to semantic codes. Consider the following extract from Jerome K. Jerome's *Three Men in a Boat* (Jerome, 1889). In considering a scene that involved Maidenhead, he writes:

Maidenhead itself is too snobby to be pleasant. It is the haunt of the river swell and his overdressed female companion. It is the town of showy hotels, patronized chiefly by dudes and ballet girls . . . We went through Maidenhead quickly, and then eased up, and took leisurely that grand reach beyond Boulter's and Cookham locks. (p. 117)

One can recognize that the material is constructed with effect in mind and operates within a humorous exaggeration genre. Nevertheless, we can see that the references to types of people that frequent Maidenhead are categories that are *typified* by the terms he uses, whereas the pattern of behaviour concerning the navigation of the river is an episode. One can only speculate, of course, about how these two 'pieces' of mental material might affect the author's actions on encountering another river town. Might he make 'assessments' of the hotels and some inferences about the types of patrons, and the town in general? He may use his semantic understanding of river towns in this way. In contrast, should he find himself floating along a pretty section of river, might we hear him say that he elects to take the stretch 'leisurely', 'like I did on that grand reach beyond Boulter's and Cookham locks, outside Maidenhead'? One can perhaps sense that the perception of the new river scene might cue some individuals more than others to retrieve a related episode.

Lapadat and Martin (1994) suggest that people with a preference for imaginal processing might retain more episodic detail from experiences. Markowitsch (1995) conducted neurophysiological research that suggests that the right hemisphere might subserve episodic memory retrieval, and the left hemisphere be involved in the retrieval of mental material from semantic memory. It is possible, therefore, that those individuals most competent with imagistic forms of thought may find access to episodic mental material easier (Huffman and Weaver, 1996).

Participants can be helped to explore their own memories for events by using particular devices in the course of an interview. In addition to the general desirability of open questions and a non-evaluative stance, particular 'prompts' and 'probes' can be used to direct the interview away from semantic mental material, and more towards episodic mental material. For example, if we ask a participant to 'Tell me in your own words what happened this morning' (Memon et al., 1994, p. 647) we might cue a 'free recall' of memory. If we imagine a person responding to us we might see how they may be looking for cues from us to guide their decisions about how much 'pedantic' or 'pedestrian' detail to give. We have all been trained to 'get to the point'. Left unprompted, we may find that the account we receive moves quite rapidly from a description of a scene towards some principles and thence towards some basic values or beliefs. Such a progression may be apparent in the account of a person who 'understands' such situations quite fully. In contrast, we may get an account of the morning's events that remains largely in the descriptive mode. This may occur in discussions with individuals who do not encode events so fully in the semantic sense. Can we read into unprompted accounts? Does a relative emphasis on semantic information (as opposed to episodic) give us any insights into how the participant might behave in the future? Or is the record merely an arbitrary product of the process, reflecting the spontaneous and insignificant meandering of the interaction? Certainly, any 'response' from the interviewer can affect the kind of mental material articulated. Questions such as 'Why?' or 'What did you think?' or 'How did you feel?' will direct the participant's account away from episodic mental material. Keeping the participant's focus on 'what happened' and 'how' something was done can secure more insights into episodic mental material. The objective here is to identify those aspects of a person's mental material that are structured (organized) around particular cases or events rather than principles or categorizations.

Specific suites of techniques have been developed by various professionals to secure more effective elicitations of episodic mental material. These approaches will be discussed under four headings. These are critical incident technique, the cognitive interview, storytelling, and focus groups and role playing.

CRITICAL INCIDENT TECHNIQUE Flanagan (1954) wrote, 'People have been making observations on other people for centuries . . . Some may have even made a series of relatively systematic observations on many instances of a specific behavior. Perhaps what is most conspicuously needed to supplement these activities is a set of procedures for analysing and synthesising such observations' (p. 327). The first large-scale systematic effort to gather specific incidents of behaviour in a designated activity was conducted by Wickert (1947). The study concerned incidents. It concerned actions. It did not seek opinions, or personal theories. It sought recollection of episodes. It specifically requested participants to 'Describe the officer's actions. What did he do?'.

Subsequent research revealed that instructions to recall one's own or other people's actions yielded different episodes, depending on the time frame that the participant was being asked to consider. Requests to consider events over a period including several months previously demonstrated the selective recall of dramatic or other special types of incidents, whereas requests to outline recent incidents were a more balanced set (Nagay, 1949). Flanagan et al. (1953) showed that groups of 24 people reporting incidents daily reported 315 incidents, groups reporting weekly reported 155 incidents, whereas the group that reported only once at the end of the two-week period reported only 63 incidents. Differences in wording in the instruction can produce minor differences in the nature and number of episodes defined as incidents. Instructions to think of a time when a foreman has 'in your opinion, shown definitely good foremanship – the type of action that points out the superior foreman', or 'done something that you felt should be encouraged because it seemed to be in your opinion an example of good foremanship', produce different profiles of episodes (Flanagan, 1954, p. 332). Flanagan (1954) sought to bring together 'a flexible set of principles' that would support the cueing of episodic memories that participants felt were different from the norm. He recommended that a clear 'delimitation of the situations' needs to be made (p. 338), and that an episode should be reported 'if it makes a "significant" contribution either positively or negatively' to the general aim (p. 338). An emphasis should be placed on accounts of behaviours. An example question might be, 'Tell just what this employee did which caused a noticeable decrease in production' (p. 341). He suggests that the selection of incidents to be reported should be tied down in some way, 'to prevent the giving of only the most dramatic or vivid incidents' (p. 341). The interviewer should 'avoid asking leading questions'; make 'neutral and permissive' remarks to show understanding; and ensure that he does not only receive part of the story, only by 'restating the essence' of the participant's remarks, in order to 'encourage him to continue' (p. 342). The approach seeks to allow the participants to give their own accounts, in their own words, without implying or questioning any implicit theory that may lie behind the participants' accounts.

The critical incident technique has been used most extensively in job analysis and personnel selection contexts. It has also been found useful to support self-reflection, assumption-surfacing etc. O'Driscoll and Cooper (1996), for example, use the approach to identify the specific behaviours that individuals engage in when coping with stress, rather than focusing on global styles of coping. Weisinger and Salipante (1995) used the approach with 35 technical professionals to expose assumptions that lead to multi-cultural conflict. They were able to use the incidents in a process that helped participants to deal with such situations. Parker et al. (1995) advocate the use of the approach in supporting the development of reflective ability in nursing/midwifery students. The approach has been used by Shaughnessy and Kivlighan (1995) to show the different incidents that participants consider to be most important to their experience of a group. Securing the views of particular stakeholders has also been undertaken with the critical incident technique. Feinberg et al. (1995) revealed differences between the service quality expectations of customers of an organization in three different countries. Johnston (1995) elicited 579 anecdotes from customers of a UK bank to identify determinants of service quality. Keaveney (1995) elicited 800 critical episodes from customers of service firms that had switched firms/services, to define eight major categories of causes.

Adopting a focus on one's own or other participants' schemas of significant episodes can provide valuable information.

THE COGNITIVE INTERVIEW   Episodic elicitation approaches such as the critical incident technique operate on the assumption that participants will, unsupported, be able to retrieve episodes in a reasonably comprehensive manner, regardless of context. Some difficulties in bringing memories of episodes back to one's mind have been identified, however. An interview approach that has been expressly designed to enhance the recall of episodic mental material is the 'cognitive interview' (Geiselman et al., 1986). Fisher and Geiselman (1992) note that the early version of the approach:

> consisted of only four basic instructions that were given to the eyewitness at the start of the interview: (1) Try to recreate the psychological (e.g. thoughts) and environmental (e.g. lighting) conditions of the original event, (2) Do not edit anything from the report; say whatever comes to your mind when you think of it, even if it seems trivial or out of place, (3) Describe the event both from your (E/W's) perspective and that of another prominent person at the crime, and (4) Change the order of reporting; after describing the sequence in the natural, chronological order, try to describe the events in reverse order. (p. 195)

Nevertheless, using these instructions elicited 41 pieces of information per eyewitness, compared to 29 pieces of information per eyewitness with the standard interview. Approximately the same percentage of pieces of information (15 per cent) were incorrect (Geiselman et al., 1986). A meta-analysis of 37 studies on the cognitive interview found that significant improvements in correct recall over the standard interview generally occur, although there is a small increase in the number of incorrect details expressed as well (Koehnken et al., 1994). The technique has been refined over the years, and Fisher and Geiselman (1992) present guidelines under the headings of: recreating the context of the original event, focused concentration, multiple retrieval attempts, varied retrieval, recalling specific information, witness compatible questioning, and probing image and concept memory codes. While the guidelines are drafted with assisting eyewitnesses to recall experiences, they are valuable for supporting reflective practitioners themselves and interviewers in work contexts. It is important to recognize that many of the 'ingrained' reflection and interviewing practices that one has developed may limit the effective implementation and thus effectiveness of the cognitive interview (Memon et al., 1994).

In the course of the cognitive interview, one should try to create a calm atmosphere. This can be done individually with some relaxation. An interviewer can use the principle of synchrony, by 'speaking in a calm, even-heeled voice and behaving in a relaxed manner' (p. 29). The context of the original experience can be recreated by encouraging thinking about the original context, or by asking questions that require thinking about it. A form of words suggested is, 'Try to put yourself back into the same situation . . . Think about where you were standing at the time, what you were thinking about, what you were feeling, and what the room looked like' (p. 100). It may typically take between five and ten seconds for a person to recreate a context. Sometimes one has deliberately tried to store an event in its sequential (episodic) form. One can assist one's retrieval of the memory if one can 'recreate the thought processes of how [one] tried to memorize the event' (p. 102).

Retrieving a detailed memory requires intense concentration. It may be tempting to resort to a simpler task of describing an event at a more general level. A suggestion can be made to encourage focused concentration. An example is, 'I realize that this is a difficult task, to remember the details of the [event]. All of the details are stored in your mind, but you will have to concentrate very hard to recall them. You have all the information, so I'm going to expect you to do most of the work here. I understand that this might be difficult, but try to concentrate as hard as you can' (p. 103). Having secured concentration, it is important to take steps to minimize factors that might disrupt it. Minimize other distractions, including one's own movements. When interviewing, although initial direct eye contact is useful to show interest, while a person is trying to concentrate on a recalled memory it can be distracting. Rather than look away, the interviewer may look at the lower part of the participant's face (p. 104). The single most important skill is not to interrupt the participant 'in the middle of a narrative response' (p. 105). If a person loses concentration, they can be guided back to the point where they left off, if one tries 'to repeat her words verbatim, or as closely as possible' (p. 107).

Recall may require multiple retrieval attempts. Very often we know that we know something, and have the patience to keep trying to recall the information. Indeed, if something is 'on the tip of the tongue' it will very probably be recalled later (Brown and McNeill, 1966). It is also sometimes the case that we can recall information that we do not feel that we have. Multiple retrieval attempts are worth making, regardless.

The approaches towards retrieval can also be varied. Changing the order of events being considered, changing the perspective one is using and changing the sensory modalities one is focusing on can all enhance recall. There is a degree of forward momentum in recalling events in the original sequence. One may omit elements that do not seem to be part of the logical flow of events. Recalling events in reverse order may help here (p. 110). Fisher and Geiselman (1992) also suggest altering the perspective on an event. For example, the view that another participant who was present at the time might possess could be considered and articulated. Boon and Noon (1994), however, were unable significantly to increase recall of accurate information with this approach. Shifting focus from considering, say, the visual features of a scene, towards the auditory features, and thence other sensory modalities, is likely to enhance recall.

The recall of specific features of previous experiences can be aided if one uses general ('event-free'), contextual and subjective attributes. In trying to recall a name, for example, Fisher and Geiselman (1992) suggest thinking about event-free properties such as its commonality, length, syllables etc.; contextual characteristics such as the speaker's voice when they said the name; and subjective characteristics such as whether it reminded you of another name, sounded pleasant etc.

It can be useful to develop a strategy for the overall attempt to aid recall that is compatible with what one gleans to be the person's memory and individuality. Having established the basic images that a person has of an event (from a general narration), it can be useful to develop a global questioning strategy that outlines: 'Which images should be evoked? Which details should be extracted from each image? In what order should the

Knowledge in organizations

images be probed?' (p. 128). This is because different images that are all part of a memory of an event may each have different detail and be more or less appropriate for securing fuller recall of particular information. It is also because 'every act of drawing up an image into consciousness increases the difficulty of the task and causes recollection to suffer' (p. 125). One should use the most detailed image to answer any question, and exhaust an image before moving on. Because it can be fatiguing to recall detailed information, it may be useful to 'first activate and probe the image with the most relevant information, then progress to the less important images' (p. 130).

In probing any impressions that a participant may have formed of an event (propositional codes), it can be useful to recognize their individuality. For example, an accountant may recall more about properties of the numbers in a situation than might others. Some of the specific issues associated with probing imagistic thought forms have been discussed in Chapter 4. A general principle in considering a detailed image is to work across and down it slowly rather than jump to different parts of it.

Taken together, these cognitive interviewing guidelines can significantly enhance recall of episodic information. It is interesting to note that enhancing recall of a participant in an interview situation leads, in turn, to better recall by the interviewer in subsequent recounting of the information (Kohnken et al., 1994). One can see how more detailed episodic information might cascade through an organization.

STORYTELLING   There is an emerging literature on the role of storytelling in human interaction. Stevenson and Bartunek (1996) observed that differences in formal power, informal influence and organizational position were associated with differences in the stories that organizational participants told about their organization. Different cultural viewpoints were discernible within the distinct 'networks' of participants. Bowles (1995) notes how storytelling has been used for centuries as a powerful vehicle for communication, education, recreation and the preservation of cultural identity, and is an accessible and powerful tool for contextualizing and humanizing knowledge. The stories that circulate organizations do not have to be reconcilable. Indeed, they demonstrate what Boje (1995) refers to as a 'plurivocal' theory of organizational discourses. Gabriel (1995) regards stories as part of the 'organizational dreamworld' in which desires, anxieties and emotions find expression in highly irrational constructions. He argues that stories contribute, alongside myths, jokes, nicknames, graffiti and cartoons, to fantasy as a force in organizations. This fantasizing is 'a symbolic refashioning of official organizational practices in the interests of pleasure, allowing a temporary supremacy of emotion over rationality and of uncontrol over control' (p. 479). As such, stories form part of the 'unmanaged organization', which is created in the process of seeking to manage.

It is interesting how some of the 'rules' of discourse can suggest that there must be a purpose or message in a story. At the individual level, there can be a discouragement of stories and a preference for the 'lessons' (Strickland, 1994). We often condemn people who 'launch' into stories that 'don't go anywhere' and seem 'pointless'. At the organizational level there is an approach to analysis that seeks meaning *in* the stories, as opposed to the meaning *of* the storytelling.

Stories are, of course, constructions of events. Those that circulate, and have therefore in a sense survived, reflect aspects of understanding that have a place in organizational life. Gabriel is suggesting that stories fulfil a psychological role as part of the unconscious coping strategies used by employees. There is evidence from non-organizational contexts that stories may have a role in contexts where little 'theory' has been developed. Fiese et al. (1995) demonstrate a high emphasis on family stories between partners in the early stages of parenthood. Flint and Sparrow (1995) report a high degree of reference to basic episodic experience in design when operating within multimedia design (where there was little in the way of a body of knowledge to guide design decisions). Attention to the episodic mental material recounted by others may guide us in our own decisions. It may be particularly valuable where there is a relative absence of clear, 'reasoned' predictions. Patients, for example, may develop coping strategies from the recounting of the approaches used by others.

It may also be that storytelling is a major form of sense-making within organizational contexts with high degrees of uncertainty, such as during the course of organizational change. Here, stories may not have any 'meaning' beyond their simple sequencing (chaining) of actions and consequences. In general, however, it may be that episodic mental material in organizations exists in contexts that parallel its existence in individuals' memories. Recent events may be 'coded' that way. While they may go on to be interpreted more semantically, their initial construction may guide current action. Significant (and, especially, traumatic) events may be retained as episodes. These 'messages' may become basic axioms that people use in their reasoning. Episodic information may guide us more in situations where the time or energy cannot be afforded for 'deliberation'. As such, episodes may guide us in complex or stressful situations. They may also guide us in situations where we are not prepared to engage in deep analysis, for example 'It worked for him, it will be the same for me.' Episodes may, in part, be a construction of meaning developed from the unconscious. Events may have been construed with some unconscious process in play.

In the organizational context, stories can tell us a lot about 'sense-making' and, indeed, 'coping' within organizations. Organizational stories have been used to study some of the unstated (and perhaps unconscious) codes for resolving conflicts, approaching decision-making, determining perceptions of positive and negative organizational forces, and the guiding of role behaviour (Hansen and Kahnweiler, 1993). Covin et al. (1994) have examined their potential in the diagnostic phase of planned organizational change. Feldman (1990) refers to what anthropologists call a 'liminal' condition, a situation 'betwixt and between more stable and predictable social-structural arrangements' (p. 813), and notes how, within organizations, stories abound and contribute to the creation of subsequent meaning in such situations.

Some of the ways in which episodic schemas can influence business practices are evident in a study that the author conducted with Patrick Bentley at the University of Central England Business School (Bentley and Sparrow, 1997). The study concerned the ways that small businesses managed risk. If owners had been asked to explain why their business is structured in a particular way, they might have given logical and sensible accounts of risk assessments and legal liabilities. But when they are asked to talk about their actual business practices, there is often evidence of how episodic schemas (such as their own experience or a story of business practice from others) are part of their 'logic'. The logic of deciding not to focus on a few major customers, in one business, was based on the following 'principles':

> Well we had a customer try to back out of a contract 12 months ago, and it was very serious, and at the end of the day I had to talk to the fellow fairly seriously, and let it be known that even though he had not signed the contract that he had had in his possession for many months, I considered that the contract was sealed because he and I had been working in conjunction in accordance with the provisions of that contract and I had to say that I would take him to Court if he insisted on backing out, anyway he backed down. Oh yes, that would have been a major disaster.

The logic of why a company is structured in a way that it can retain its capital if it ever needed to, in one business, was based on the following 'reasoning':

> They actually overpaid us by £24,000, which was quite nice. It took them 14 months to get it back and they were threatening all sorts of High Court this and High Court that, sort of thing, but they got away with it to be honest, the company had too much cash. If the company had been like most computer dealers and running on a nice little overdraft, I would have said 'OK put it into liquidation' and then they would have been quite happy, and they actually said they would have been quite happy to write it off . . . So, the position now is . . . So if I was in a position where someone, a customer say, went down still owing a lot of money to me and I thought that there is no way on earth I am going to get that back, I would basically just go to the bank, pull all the money out, stick it into another company, I have got three companies.

An as yet unpublished study by the author, Clare Holden and Graham Wright from the University of Central England, and Fay Goodman from the UK Federation of Small Businesses, tried to find out how much stories of crime played a part in the thinking of business owners about running their businesses from inner-city locations. Owner managers were asked 'what it was like running a business' in their part of town. They were asked to recount 'any stories they had heard from others about business and work in the area' and to talk 'about anything that anybody's told you in recent times about working in this part of town'. As an example of whether the part of town was considered to be risky, one participant reported:

> One story that springs to mind was a colleague of mine who works on this estate, we were talking about security of the cars and it is very bad in this immediate area. The cars, we're having cars broken into even on this car park or the car park opposite. Well the particular incident that he related jumped to mind as soon as you said about a story, was, he was thinking about buying an RS Cosworth car. The guy delivered it down to him from the garage to test drive and he test drove it and he said, 'This is really fabulous, I really want this car' and the guy said 'Are you going to come to work in it and park it here?', and he said 'Oh yes, I have to use it for work.' And this garage advisor said, 'I won't sell you the car because it will go from here. What they'll do', he said, 'even if you have the most expensive alarm system with immobilizers etc., it will go from here. They'll just come and put it at the back of a tow truck and take it away.' He said 'There's no way I'm going to sell you that car', well I thought it was a terrible situation.

That the personal experiences and stories influence one's thinking as well as facts is evidenced in another participant's comments:

> I mean you can look at statistics and you can see that maybe a fraction of half of one percent of people going to work are ever assaulted, attacked, abused in any way, shape or form, and so therefore, you would look at those statistics and you would say 'this guy does not know what he is on about, the guy is living in a false world', and you may well be right, but you have to be aware. If you are not aware, I was going to say, you are dead.

Personal experiences and received stories are major forms of episodic schemas.

That these episodic schemas inform even some of the most important of decisions is confirmed by Rees (1992). He quotes one of Ronald Reagan's aides' (Michael Deaver) account of Reagan's decision to run for the presidency. The aide reports Reagan saying, 'I remember in the movie *Sante Fe Trail*, I played George Custer as a young lieutenant. The Captain said, "You have got to take over" and my line was, "I can't". And the captain said, "But it's your duty". And that's the way I feel about this – I'm going to run' (p. 41).

FOCUS GROUPS   Focus groups can be used to encourage a particular form of discussion that can surface key patterns in thinking (Krueger, 1988). D.L. Morgan (1988; 1993) reviewed developments in the approach as a general social science method. The abilities of focus groups to allow participants to recount episodes and consider their own reactions to possible developments is a clear advantage in the technique. O'Connor (1996), for example, used 40 focus groups, involving 162 employees, to gain insights into the gendered nature of organizational culture in two Irish Health Boards. Packer et al. (1994) report how focus groups were used in a participative evaluation and redesign of vocational training and rehabilitation services. The public setting may lead to participants wishing to appear rational in their reports and reactions, and so care needs to be taken to secure more open co-operation and to avoid too much emphasis on drawing 'lessons' from the experiences. It can often be useful in a focus group to summarize with some general principles that have emerged. This semantic emphasis could detract from a 'purer' use of the technique in eliciting episodic mental material, however.

An example of the use of the focus group approach to explore episodes that participants may consider important is provided in an unpublished study that the author undertook with Annie Rubienska at the University of Central England Business School. The study concerned the behaviours of lecturers, and in particular the examples that they used to elucidate principles in their lectures. A focus group of an appropriate subset of students was convened. The students were urged to consider any episodes they could recall where they had found a particular example that a lecturer had used to be 'particularly valuable'. Once initiated, most of the participants, were able to recall one like that. Many of the episodes were stored with 'morals of the tale'. There were examples of how to be 'funny', how to be 'sexist', how to 'name drop', how to be 'practical', how to be 'out of touch' etc. It was also possible to explore the participants' views about the implications of some possible changes in the form of examples that staff may go on to use in the future. They were asked to consider how they, as students, might react to particular changes. This cued a set of personal experiences from the students, where they had felt uncomfortable because of an inappropriate fit between examples used and the person using them, or examples and the context etc. What was clear overall was that lecture experiences are not stored solely semantically, in terms of things such as 'good', 'bad', 'effective' etc. They are stored episodically, and these episodes affect the students' judgements about the quality of the educational experience.

ROLE PLAYING   Mannix et al. (1995) report the use of role-playing to gain insights into organizational knowledge and practice. Participants role-played the negotiation of resource allocations across three divisions of a company. The basic distribution principle (equity, equality or need) that was used was in line with the prevailing organizational culture (for example economically oriented, relationship oriented or personal development oriented). Role-playing can engage participants in the dynamics of situations to such an extent that they place less emphasis on the consistency of their actions with fundamental principles (semantic understanding) and evidence practice. This may give some insights into the episodic mental material that participants have (particularly if they are encouraged to 'recall' the way that they previously performed this scene). In general, however, the approach can give more insight into the skills and tacit feel that are embedded in the actions themselves, and may not even be a part of the participants' conscious thinking. It will be discussed more fully (in conjunction with the role of simulations) in the section on eliciting skills.

Skills

In Chapter 2 we saw that there are aspects of our capability that are evidenced in our practices and are not consciously directed. These subconscious aspects of performance have been categorized as skills and tacit feel. In considering the ways in which these two forms of subconscious forms of mental material can be elicited, we need to recognize that the primary distinction that can be drawn between them is in the initial learning process. It will be recalled that skills are acquired consciously but proceduralized to a point where the information is no longer represented declaratively, and is thus difficult to articulate. Tacit feel is defined as mental material that is represented non-declaratively, but that has never been conscious. It was acquired implicitly.

Some of the limitations to this non-conscious learning process (which we are only now beginning to appreciate) may give us some clues as to whether subconscious mental material that is evidenced in practice is skill as opposed to tacit feel. The whole issue is confused by wide variations in the terms used to describe subconscious mental material. According to the distinctions we have drawn, skills can be acquired 'on the job'. They are not restricted to knowledge that has been 'formally trained'. Some writers use the term tacit knowledge to refer to any knowledge that has not been formally trained. Others regard any knowledge that is not conscious as tacit knowledge. Many of the studies of the impact of skills on performance are labelled as studies of tacit knowledge. In addition to the confusion added by different uses of the terms, there are real difficulties in distinguishing empirically between 'pure' skills and 'pure' tacit feel. This is because both are aspects of mental material that are implicit in expert performance and are not readily accessed as conscious rules (semantic understanding) or conscious cases (episodic memories). It is not possible to determine the source of the learning of such mental material at the time of its subsequent elicitation.

In the main, therefore, the techniques of elicitation that have been derived for subconscious mental material will be discussed under the heading of skill elicitation. Those techniques that appear to elicit subconscious material above and beyond the typical conscious learning processes that a person undertakes will be discussed in the section on tacit feel elicitation. It is likely, therefore, that some of the techniques discussed in this section are, in addition to picking up on skills, tapping some aspects of tacit feel.

It is clear that expertise has many assets. It also has some liabilities. Personal or organizational procedures that are (to any reasonable outsider) unnecessarily complex may not be 'seen' as such by those executing them. Even if they are asked to have a 'root and branch' review of the procedures, so much of what is done will be considered to be 'unquestionably appropriate' that the automatic approaches will continue. Reflective practitioners, and organizations generally, need to consider the forums and techniques they use and their ability to surface less conscious aspects of their performance.

Skill and expertise

As has been noted, much of the public record of what is happening in organizational decisions is based on interactants apparently sharing and using declarative mental material. Closer inspection (for example, in watching production engineers fault-finding) reveals, however, that they interact through media other than words, and incorporate their skills in the process. The steps they take and the links they make are not coming from any process that resembles looking things up in a textbook (that is, consulting their declarative mental material base). It is not enough to know the 'procedures' that the organization (and they) know to do the job. If we are to understand how people carry out their work, we need to recognize and incorporate non-declarative aspects of their mental material.

As Squire et al. (1993) note, 'by virtue of the nonconscious status of these (non-declarative) forms of memory, they create much of the mystery of human experience. Here arise the dispositions, habits and preferences that are inaccessible to conscious recollection but that nevertheless are shaped by past events, influence our behaviour, and are a part of who we are' (p. 486). Anderson (1983) uses an analogy with computer software. There are computer hardware and software configurations that can operate through a language/program that reads and interprets each statement (instruction) as it were 'line by line'. There are also systems that can 'compile' a set of instructions so that they can be processed more rapidly (without the need for interpretation each time). Overall speed can be improved if more and more of the computer instructions can be compiled. The interpretive language, however, has the flexibility required to create new sets of instructions. He suggests that a process like 'compilation' takes place with information that is repeatedly linked together in human minds. It moves from being information that can be declared in statements (propositions) to information that can be rapidly executed unthinkingly.

Holyoak and Spellman (1993) point out how declarative information plays a particular role in explicit thinking. They note how 'explicit representations of knowledge allow us to imagine what is not the case, but might be, and how we might make it so' (p. 290). They refer to recent research that shows how 'procedures initially represented implicitly, such that they can achieve routine tasks must be re-represented at a more explicit level before they can be manipulated to accomplish novel tasks' (p. 289). Knowledge compilation does not seem, therefore, to be a simple, constant subconscious progression. The evidence suggests that people become skilled through alternating processes of reflection and automatization. Again, it would seem that indications of how a person achieves a particular task may require the use of elicitation techniques that can 'surface' both of these elements.

Holyoak and Spellman (1993) outline the related distinction made by Hatano and Inagaki (1986) between two forms of expertise: adaptive and routine expertise. Adaptive expertise entails 'flexible transfer of knowledge to novel types of problems and the ability to invent new procedures derived from expert knowledge'. It is 'a much more subtle notion' than automatic skills such as typing. It must be 'evaluated by the capacity to handle novel situations, to reconsider and explain the validity of rules, and to reason about the domain from first principles'. It entails 'the recognition of relevance relations across contexts' and a much 'deeper understanding of the target domain' (p. 302). Routine expertise refers to 'rapid and accurate solution of well-practised types of problems', where compilation accounts for 'stable superior performance on representative tasks for which reproductive methods and specific knowledge are central' (p. 297), that is, skill acquisition. It would seem that the types of 'tests' that one might need to deploy to determine the form and extent of expertise need to pick up on the distinction between adaptive and routine expertise.

The value of skills at work

The value of skills within organizations has been recognized by psychologists for a long time. Bryan and Harter (1899) studied the learning curve of telegraphists and noted very significant improvements in productivity. Hull (1928) noted that the best spoon polishers produced five times as much as the worst, but that a ratio of about 2 to 1 in productivity between the best and worst workers was more typical. As Cook (1988) notes, most of the early studies analysed 'output in repetitive production work, where it is (relatively) easy to measure' (p. 2). Schmidt and Hunter (1983) conducted a more comprehensive review and found that the top 5 per cent do twice as much as the bottom 5 per cent.

There have been a number of studies of skilled performance extending over long periods of practice. One of the longest is documented by Crossman (1959). He reports the speed of performance of women operating cigar-making machines. Even after making ten million cigars over a period of about seven years, the women were still showing continued improvements in skill. Of course, the rate of improvement slows down as skill increases. In some tasks there may be a practical limit to the advances in speed. There may be a cycle time of a machine, that ultimately places a ceiling on the level of skill. The shape of learning curves (the timing and distribution of periods of most rapid gain) will vary from job to job. In a study of taxi drivers, Ghiselli and Brown (1955), for example, noted that driving performance improved by a factor of 50 per cent in seven weeks, but then remained constant for twelve weeks. Over the following ten weeks additional training brought about another 50 per cent improvement in performance. There may be many learning curves in most jobs. Some tasks are mastered more quickly than others. Multi-skilled jobs will have multiple learning curves, and potentially multiple aspects of potential productivity gain. As discretion increases, the latitude for potential gains may increase. There is no theoretical limit to the increases in expertise that can be acquired in the course of knowledge-based jobs.

Treating skill as synonymous with speed is to do the concept a grave injustice. Skill is the depth and breadth of the performance elements that can be executed with limited cognitive demands. The 'freedom' that is afforded to think and plan, to deal with novelty, is the true value of skill. A comprehensive skill base enables a person to acquire related new skills more rapidly. It enables a person to deal with complexity and unpredictability far more competently. The skills that a person has are one of the most useful indicators of their 'potential' to deal with new developments on the immediate horizon, that is, transfer potential (Sparrow, 1984).

Attempting to recognize and assess skills is a valuable goal. It is also a difficult task. In some ways, management abandoned the goal when it began to consider the notion of competence as a performance management approach. Competence concerns performance of specified ranges of tasks to specified standards in specified ranges of contexts. It is an inference to claim that a particular competence implies a future potential. Where competencies are developed with transfer in mind, employees are exposed to a comprehensive set of tasks and contexts. As a result, it is likely that they have developed a skill base that enables subsequent transfer to proceed smoothly. The mere ability to perform one of the tasks in a particular context is less likely to have large transfer implications. The performance itself may not be 'skilled' in the psychological sense, and the 'hierarchies of skills' needed for transfer may not have all been developed. A competence assessment is a convenient shorthand. It is not necessarily a good indicator of skill.

Of course, organizations need to know whether people can do the particular tasks they require in their context to the standards they seek. As such, a competence approach may meet their immediate needs. As Torrington and Blandamer (1992) note, competency-based profiles of employees 'set a performance standard representing a level of performance that would ensure the job was being performed effectively' (p. 141). As the competencies required become 'softer' and include concepts such as 'initiative' and 'creativity', the need for comprehensive competence-development approaches increases.

The general lack of recognition of human skills is evidenced in the alternative approaches towards management control that have been developed over the years. Child (1984) highlighted four particularly significant strategies of control in organizations: personal (centralized), bureaucratic, output and cultural. Personal control means that decision-making and leadership are centralized around a leadership figure. The tasks of others are simple and minimal. The 'hands' that are employed are there to undertake essentially simple tasks, that have been simplified to an extent that their demands are such that virtually all members of the labour market are capable of executing them. They are, in so far as it is possible, skill-less tasks. The value in such organizations lies in the knowledge and skills of the owner-manager. A second way in which management control systems have served to minimize the need to 'record' or 'understand' skills is evidenced in bureaucratic control. Here, detailed specifications of how tasks should be carried out have been developed. The tasks themselves contain little discretion. The value in such organizations lies in their detailed understanding of the environment and the prescriptions they have in place. The value lies in the sophistication of the manual, not in the skills of the employees. Output control evades the need to understand the skills of employees by placing an emphasis on what they produce and less on how they produce it. Value lies in procedures that can co-ordinate the efforts of employees, rather than in their personal skills. Finally, cultural control neglects skills, by placing an emphasis on commitment, motivation and effort, rather than skill. Employees will be empowered to develop their skills as they see fit (though in what ways is of little concern), through managing the broad backcloth and tone of the enterprise.

Organizations can no longer afford to neglect skills. Chapter 1 outlined how the nature of work is changing, in such ways that mutual understanding is paramount. Understanding the skills invoked in the decisions and behaviour of employees is an essential element of management by perception.

It is ironic, therefore, that the formal approaches towards job analysis that have been developed have, in the main, shed little light on the aspects of work performance that are acquired informally and yet which may account for much of the efficiency and effectiveness of employees. Many of the approaches, in fact, restrict their attention to the verbalizable aspects of performance. The problem may stem from what appeared to psychologists to be 'unscientific' ways of training and learning, where operators learned by 'sitting by Nellie'. It was felt that 'bad habits' may get transferred, and that the 'appropriate' knowledge could be more systematically established, documented and trained into employees. By definition this denuded the conception of task performance, by ignoring its context and the value of individuality. In the extreme case, the 'requirements' of jobs were identified through a 'logical' analysis of the operations that would need to be performed in order to achieve the overall objective. As a process, it was argued to be 'psychologically celibate', and to reveal how 'the' job needed to be done rather than the various ways in which it was actually being done. As Myers and Davids (1993) put it, most analyses of skilled behaviour tended to be 'founded on a rather narrow conceptualization of human performance, emphasising formally prescribed procedures at the expense of the contingent knowledge base' (p. 118). It may be that computer scientists' realization that the 'logical' way to do tasks was not efficient in computational terms led to a greater recognition that the heuristics and particular way that experts had got their knowledge organized were important considerations in problem-solving. If one is to understand people's behaviour at work, one needs to recognize their expertise regardless of the degree of formality in its development. One needs to recognize its multiplicity, rather than seek the single set of rules that best characterizes it.

Eliciting skills

If we wanted an expert to train a novice, we might pause to wonder whether or not they will be able to articulate their expertise. It might be tempting to say: 'But they are experts so they will be good at that, surely!' The designers of computer expert systems soon realized, however, that experts need help to get at and verbalize their thinking (Blanning, 1984). They developed methodologies that surfaced the assumptions that experts may be making. Systems analysts had long realized that it was necessary to get a complete picture of why users needed a computer system to do certain things. Often they found key elements that the user had not realized in their first outlining of the desirable features of the system. In a similar way, knowledge engineers found that by being ignorant of the particular domain about which they were seeking to elicit knowledge meant that they asked pertinent questions.

When one considers the alternative approaches that can be used to gain insight into skilled performance, there is one word that characterizes the approaches. They focus on how the tasks are 'practised'. Attempts to get at the ways that people perform will suffer if they attempt to separate knowledge elicitation too far from actual performance on the task. It will be difficult to gain insights into the skills that a participant has by asking them to consider their performance in abstract. One may require a participant mentally to reinstate a task and reflect on the apparent decisions and actions. The 'flow' of skilled actions (the ways in which elements are chained together) by definition means that 'steps' in the middle of a sequence may not be being consciously considered. If one does not 'see' the procedure, one may not appreciate the inherent steps.

There are three main ways in which one can gain insight into skilled performance. One can 'review' detailed (for example video) records of actual job performance and consider any implicit decisions. One can seek to glean insights into the skills from an analysis of structured samples of actual performance (for example work samples, simulation or role-playing, situational interviews). One can seek to obtain some account of knowledge/skills concurrently with task performance.

ANALYSING JOB PERFORMANCE Actual task/job performance can be observed. A great deal can be learned about skilled behaviour through observation. Methods can 'vary from note taking, use of a checklist, field diary or log, use of an observation schedule or other fairly structured recording device, tape recording, photography, audio-visual recording etc., or may involve a combination of these methods' (Mullings, 1984, p. 6). Recording may be done on a time-sampling or event-sampling basis, or as a combination of the two. Observation is used wherever 'actual behaviour is of primary interest instead of statements of behaviour, attitudes, opinions, feelings etc.' (Kunz et al., 1977, p. 28). Mullings (1984, p. 11) lists several advantages of observation as a method of gathering information.

Observation allows one to capture what actually happens rather than a respondent's version of what happens. It is independent of a subject's willingness to report accurately. It can include the behaviour of people who may be unable to answer questions or explain their behaviour (such as children). It can capture the things that are taken for granted by the participant, but that may be noticed by a trained observer. It is relatively inexpensive. She also lists several limitations of observation. These include the fact that observation is not suitable for collecting data on people's attitudes and opinions. It is not suitable for recording events that may occur either very rarely or at very unpredictable times. It can be time consuming. Observation has been used quite extensively as an approach towards job analysis. It will not, however, reveal 'the importance of any task, nor its level of difficulty' (Pearn and Kandola, 1993, p. 15).

Observations should be of behaviours that are learned, meaningful to the participants, reliably observable, separate and distinct from each other, and related to job performance (Rackham and Morgan, 1977). Systematic enquiry using observation requires disciplined training and rigorous preparation. Most applications of the approach include a subsequent 'observation interview' where the participant is questioned further on the behaviours. Monnickendam et al. (1994) used observation to reveal nine distinct patterns of usage of 'case records' by social workers. The fact that such usage was, in the main, 'automatized' meant that the manual case record had several inherent limitations that the social workers had not recognized. Thomas (1994) used observation (supported with a computerized event recorder) of nurses in primary, team and functional nursing wards to reveal subtle differences in interpersonal behaviour with patients in the three contexts.

A person's practices can be recorded and played back. A 'rich' and 'faithful' record can be valuable for highlighting aspects of behaviour that have become skilled, and which a participant might not note in being asked to describe retrospectively what they did. There is a wide variety of approaches that can be used to 'capture' practice. One is seeking to minimize the intrusiveness of the recording process and yet, at the same time, capture what may be quite subtle aspects of behaviour. Aspects of work that are executed in definable contexts (for example work areas, times of day, particular 'episodes'), may lend themselves to audio and video recording. Other, more spontaneous or sporadic aspects of behaviour may require less obtrusive observation than a roving camera permits.

In situations where a participant interacts with a particular piece of technology, it may be possible to undertake some form of 'system logging'. The term here is being confined to situations where 'a record of what the user has done . . . has been taken automatically by the system itself' (Clegg et al., 1988, p. 167). Such logs lend themselves to analyses of patterns in throughput, and records of what a user typed (or clicked), together with the system's response. The approach has been used to capture automatically and support groups in idea consolidation (Aiken and Carlisle, 1992), capture drawing/design activity (Clark and Scrivener, 1993) and contrast user behaviour with different computer interfaces (Schar, 1996). The record needs to capture aspects of the skilled behaviour that subsequent conscious recording by the participants themselves might miss. Diaries can be used to good effect to capture details of what participants realized that they did. They would not capture some of the skilled subconscious aspects of performance. In all instances, the strength of the approach lies in its ability to 'replay' and 'pause' performance. A further feature is that it can reveal patterns in behaviour over time periods that might otherwise escape attention. Fast-forwarding a video recording can reveal features of the 'dance' between participants, or sequences in movements. Armed with a comprehensive record of behaviour, participants can 'explain' how particular considerations guided them in their skilful action.

ANALYSING STRUCTURED SAMPLES OF ACTUAL AND PLANNED PERFORM-ANCE   Insights into certain aspects of practice can be obtained through standardized work samples, role-playing and simulation exercises. Behaviour in particular 'scenarios' can be cued and observed, if participants feel able to recreate a context sufficiently well to 'perform' in the 'usual' way. Work samples have primarily been constituted with personnel selection in mind. Originally, they focused on 'physical' activities (psychomotor behaviour), but in later years were extended to include 'individual, situational decision-making', 'job-related information' and 'group discussions/decision-making' (Robertson and Kandola, 1982). It can be more appropriate to focus on meaningful samples of behaviour rather than signs of predisposition as predictors of later performance. In the personnel selection context, this is referred to as 'point-to-point correspondence' between a predictor and a measure of job performance. In that context, 'too close' a relationship may mean that one might be able to predict 'immediate' job performance, but that subsequent differences in learning rates may mean that applicants who appear best now may be 'overtaken' by other, less competent performers in due course. In the present context, this designing of structured work samples is the key process. Selecting tasks that 'typify' job performance is difficult. In psychomotor contexts, this can be achieved by using some form of time or event sampling of job performance, and subsequent assessments on this set of tasks. In other (less constrained) contexts, the approach may yield 'situations' rather than tasks. Here, some form of recreation of events may be necessary. Some of the major ways in which this can be achieved are detailed below.

Typically, role-playing focuses on one-to-one interpersonal dealings and involves fairly low levels of fidelity in terms of other 'props'. Woodruffe (1990) describes how role-plays might be with customers, subordinates, colleagues, bosses, outside contractors, government agencies etc. Such role-plays might typically highlight approaches towards fact-finding, decisions and negotiation. More elaborate exercises involving groups can also be designed. Insights into problem-solving and negotiation are well supported by such role-plays, for example (Cascio, 1982). Here, each participant might represent a different department and be involved in negotiating for office space, or problem-solving to a particular brief.

Simulations attempt to provide additional temporal and situational cues that enhance the fidelity of the scenario with that of the real situation. Chatman and Barsade (1995), for example, utilized computer gaming with 'simulated' organizations to explore issues concerning individual personality, organizational culture and co-operation. In a management context, the most familiar simulation is the 'in-tray'. This simulates the 'typical pile of papers that might confront a job holder, for example, on return from a business trip or holiday' (Woodruffe, 1990, p. 68). The ability to set priorities can be measured via the in-tray by collecting the participants' out-tray every 15 to 30 minutes, and time-stamping each collection. In-trays can also reveal interpersonal competencies, if participants are required for example 'to write memos showing self-confidence and a letter requiring sensitivity' (p. 68).

A simulation exercise that uses no other participants or props and has been found to be particularly valuable in revealing skilled aspects of behaviour is the situational interview. Here, participants project themselves into a hypothetical situation, and report how they would respond. In essence they reveal how they would act in a future situation. Latham et al. (1980) developed the situational interview as a refinement of Maas's (1965) interview procedure. Maas (1965) developed a procedure that involved having interviewers who were familiar with a job brainstorm traits that should be exhibited by effective job incumbents. They then wrote examples of behaviours that illustrated high, average and low degrees of each trait. A second set of raters rated the legitimacy of particular responses representing the particular level of ability. The items with high levels of agreement among raters were used to 'score' an interviewee's performance in the subsequent job interview.

Latham et al. (1980) found significant correlations between the rated 'performance' of interviewees in the situational interview and assessments of their job performance on the job 12 months later. Unlike the Maas (1965) procedure, the responses are 'scored' in terms of the skills (behaviours) used, rather than traits. Robertson et al. (1990) showed that performance in interviews that drew ten situations from a bank of 50 developed for administrative jobs in a financial services organization correlated significantly with job performance a year later. McDaniel et al. (1994) showed that situational interviews were more predictive of subsequent job performance in general than were more traditional job-related interviews or psychologically based interviews. Durivage et al. (1995) found that situational interview performance did not correlate with IQ, and may thus be more a measure of 'practical intelligence' than reasoning.

An idea of the level of detail provided in scenarios can be gleaned from three examples that different authors outline. Latham (1989) writes:

> You are in charge of truck drivers in Philadelphia. Your colleague is in charge of truck drivers 800 miles away in Atlanta. Both of you report to the same person. Your salary and bonus are affected 100% by your costs. Your buddy is in

desperate need of one of your trucks. If you say no, your costs will remain low and your group will probably win the Golden Flyer award for the quarter. If you say yes, the Atlanta group will probably win this prestigious award because they will make a significant profit for the company. Your boss is preaching costs, costs, costs as well as co-operation with one's peers. Your boss has no control over accounting who are the score keepers. Your boss is highly competitive, he or she rewards winners. (p. 172)

A second example scenario for consideration here is one presented by Weekley and Gier (1987). They detail: 'A customer comes into the store to pick up a watch he has left for repair. The repair was supposed to have been completed a week ago, but the watch is not back yet from the repair shop. The customer becomes very angry. How would you handle the situation?' (p. 485). A third example scenario is illustrated by Motowildo et al. (1990). They detail: 'You and someone from another department are jointly responsible for co-ordinating a project involving both departments. This other person is not carrying out his share of the responsibilities. You would . . .?' (p. 642).

In all instances, participants are asked to explain what they would do. The things that they would consider and decide are compared to the responses that experienced job incumbents regard as most appropriate. Our interest here is not in the predictive validity of such a procedure for job applicants, but in the ability of the approach to act as an indicator of the skills that a respondent may have, and utilize, in work situations. Peters and Sparrow (1994), for example, show how a situational interview could be used as a general approach to identify the knowledge of middle and junior managers in hotels. The interview detailed a brief case study, asking the respondent to consider 'the management actions required to increase levels of employee productivity'.

Schuler et al. (1993) show how the behaviours that respondents detail need not even be their own. They can, they note, observe 'filmscenes' and make assessments of the 'appropriateness' of particular behaviours. These assessments highlight the respondents' social competence and cognitive performance. There is good evidence to suggest that the specific behaviours that people detail in responding to situational interview scenarios are more reliably assessed by different raters than are the responses that are generated by more conventional interviewing (Maurer and Fay, 1988). One of the major potential drawbacks of using a verbal approach towards eliciting skills is the danger that participants may give the 'socially desirable' answer rather than their 'automatic' answer. In personnel selection contexts, some degree of stress or urgency is evident. In more general contexts, it may be necessary to impose some sense of urgency, to restrict the opportunity for participants to consider and 'screen' their answers with impression management in mind.

The situational interviewing approach was used in an organizational development context in some work that the author conducted with Roy Bimson from British Telecom. The study aimed to surface differences between a team of 12 senior managers. Two forms of task were felt to capture the work that they undertook. One aspect of their work is working as the manager of a team of their own. A second aspect is working within a team of managers themselves. The following scenarios were presented to each participant. The first:

> You have been told that you have to introduce a new personal development process into your team in exactly three weeks' time. You suspect that this will not be well received by your people, but you understand that this implementation is viewed as important by your boss's boss. The instruction that you have been given on exactly what is required, what outcomes are expected, and how to complete the task are very clear. You have already attended a seminar at which questions were encouraged and your colleagues who also attended will be required to roll out the program in the same timescale. Describe what your main priorities will be, what you would now do, in what order, and who would be involved, and why.

The second scenario read:

> Your boss has asked you to help improve the professionalism of his team. Describe what your main priorities will be, what you would now do, in what order, and who would be involved, and why.

Detailed analysis of the transcripts of the 12 managers' responses indicated some interesting patterns in the 'automatic' approaches that managers took. There was evidence of differences in the emphasis on human involvement as opposed to systems. Managers whose strategies were about human involvement were using language such as 'involve', 'encourage', 'question', 'explain', 'support' etc. An emphasis on systems was evidenced through terms such as 'implement', 'test', 'sample', 'break down', 'control', 'arrange' etc. There was evidence of differences in the assumptions that the managers made about people. Some managers viewed leadership in management and control terms. Others viewed leadership as an empathic supporting process. Management/control language included 'pre-empt', 'appoint', 'demonstrate', 'run', 'political', 'control' etc. Empathic language included 'listen', 'consult', 'reticence', 'uncertainty', 'relate', 'counsel' etc. Directive, as opposed to responsive, approaches were distinguishable. Directive approaches emphasized 'inform', 'speak', 'present'. Responsive approaches emphasized 'listen', 'agree', 'consider' etc. Finally, differences were also noted in the comprehensiveness of references to task management ('plan', 'decide' 'produce' etc.), self management ('reserve time', 'think', 'diary' etc.), and the mechanics of the process ('check', 'record', 'book' etc.). Time was taken to work with the team to allow them to consider the automatic approaches that different managers can take, and some of the assumptions within their skilled performance. Unlike the personnel selection context, alternative approaches were not screened as 'effective' or 'less effective'. Rather, the process was used to enable participants to secure insights into their own skills and practices. The situational interview is thus a useful approach towards eliciting skills.

ANALYSING ACCOUNTS OF THINKING IN ACTION   Verbal accounts of what is going on when one performs a task have long been gathered. In the early years of psychology, the direct observation of mind in operation was taken as the primary method for obtaining information about the mind and its contents. James (1890) states, 'Introspective Observation is what we have to rely on first and foremost and always' (p. 185). Titchener (1909) notes how 'attention must be held at the highest possible degree of concentration' in order to secure a record that is 'photographically accurate' (p. 24). The early approaches towards introspection were, however, subjected to quite extensive criticism. Attempts were being made to reveal what were conceived to be 'elementary units of thinking' and the 'sensory components'. It is not possible to gain insight into the way in which the brain processes sensory information through introspection.

Nisbett and Wilson (1977) reviewed literature on verbal reports, and concluded that people may be '(a) unaware of the existence of a stimulus that importantly influenced a response, (b) unaware of the existence of the response, and (c) unaware that the stimulus has affected the response', and that reports are 'based on a priori, implicit causal theories, judgments about the extent to which a particular stimulus is a plausible cause of a given response' (p. 231). Bainbridge (1979) considered the information that might be elicitable from operators. She felt that verbal protocols could be useful for eliciting information on some aspects of cognition more than on others. She considered them useful for information on decision sequences and general types of cognitive processes; possibly useful for general information on which variable affects which, general information on control strategy, numerical information on control strategy, and technical aspects of process; but unable to obtain information on a full range of behaviours (p. 366). Bainbridge (1979) also considered the extent to which an account may be compromised because of various mental processes that particular techniques cue. She considered verbal protocols in terms of six constraints on the data that can be obtained using knowledge-elicitation techniques. She felt that verbal protocols are valuable when they can be elicited in ways that avoid the operator having to imagine, where limitations in vocabulary are made less relevant, that can pick up on real time pressures, that require insights into the effects of particular contexts. They may, however, encourage rationalization and impose sequences on behaviour.

A model of the way in which human beings process information was used by Ericsson and Simon (1980) to identify specific forms of verbal account that may have validity. They suggest that it is possible to (a) elicit verbal accounts of the verbal concepts that one is actively using in the course of decision-making, (b) try to express verbally (label) information that is held in a non-propositional form, (c) consider what a person thinks at the time of executing a task is their rationale for undertaking decision-making in a particular way. These concurrent accounts are considered to be useful. One form of concurrent account is questioned, however. Accounts that are elicited by other people in the course of one's task performance may promote deviations from the usual behaviour, and hence be misleading. Accounts of thinking processes can also be obtained retrospectively. These accounts of what one thinks one was thinking may be flawed and inadequate. Retrospective accounts of one's rationale may be open to other information-processing, and thus bias.

Other than in situations where accounts are sought immediately after task performance, or where the approach is considered to be so highly skilled that one can assume the same retrieval processes would be used in the recounting as in the actual task performance, retrospective accounts may be misleading. Ericsson and Simon (1993) suggest that 'probes' into retrospective accounts that cue 'a general rather than specific interpretation of how the subjects were performing the tasks' may be even more problematic. Questions of the form: 'How did you do these tasks?' may only elicit 'the general procedures, or "programs", they are using . . . without reference to the specific behavior they produced', or 'general knowledge on how one ought to do these tasks' (p. 23). Ericsson and Simon (1980) referred to the three valid forms of concurrent account as Levels 1, 2 and 3 verbalization respectively. They present a model of how information is processed in the mind that shows how each of the three levels of verbalization 'externalizes' information that is in short-term memory. The Level 1 verbalization process is considered to be valid and non-disruptive, since it 'allows information to be vocalized by automatic verbal translation without making additional demands' (p. 225). Level 2 verbalization's naming or labelling of non-verbally coded information (imagery) makes only 'modest demands on processing capacity and processing time' (p. 226). This means that 'some heeded information may not be vocalized when other task-directed processes take priority' (p. 226). Level 3 verbalization concerns the self-explanations that one may undertake in the course of monitoring one's own thinking. They are not considered to change the approach to the task 'in the way that requested explanations would' (p. 226). There is some evidence to suggest that Level 2 verbalization may affect task performance, however. Toms (1992) found evidence in an empirical study that 'verbalising may have encouraged subjects to rely on oral representation of the information', and that for a task that was 'normally visuo-spatial in nature, it seems likely that a verbal representation of this type was simply inappropriate' (p. 321).

As an approach towards providing insights into 'live', skilled performance, verbal protocols carry six core assumptions (Ericsson and Simon, 1993). These are that what is said is 'information that is in the focus of attention' (p. 221), 'a verbal encoding of the information in short term memory' (p. 221), 'initiated as a thought is heeded' (p. 222), 'a direct encoding of the heeded thought and reflects its structure' (p. 222), corresponds as a unit of articulation 'to integrated cognitive structures' (p. 225) and provides 'good predictors of shifts in processing' through pauses and hesitations (p. 225).

Verbal protocols have been used successfully to gain insights into many aspects of skilled performance, including the cognitive processes involved in learning a programming language (Anderson et al., 1984), the skills of experts in solving political science problems (Voss et al., 1983), the skills involved in selecting applicants for an educational programme (Davey et al., 1994) and the skills that efficient teams of operators use mutually to adjust their representations of events (Samurcay and Delsart, 1994). Akin (1984) used the approach to make explicit the intuitive problem-solving behaviour of a single architect engaged in a complex design problem. Lloyd and Scott (1992) used protocol analysis to capture some of the features of the creative process in engineering design. Verbal protocols may, in general, be more useful for revealing 'what subjects are thinking about', but provide less information about 'how they are thinking' (Rouse and Morris, 1986, p. 352). Their value depends on an appropriate overall process (Green, 1995). This includes careful instructions to participants (Ericsson and Simon, 1993) and appropriate analysis (Crutcher et al., 1994; Eckersley, 1988). Green (1995) details the process as involving task specification, data collection, data transcription, exploration, construction of a theoretical framework for the analysis of verbal data, segmenting (parsing), encoding and analysis.

In terms of the data-collection approach itself, specific procedures have been advocated. Participants should be given opportunities to practise giving verbal protocols with tasks such as multiplying 24 by 34. Performance on the actual selected task can be examined with different procedures. A 'talk-aloud' procedure can be cued by asking participants to 'talk aloud as you work on the problems. What I mean by talk aloud is that I want you to say out loud *everything* that you say to yourself silently. Just act as if you are alone in the room speaking to yourself. If you are silent for any length of time I will remind you to keep talking aloud' (Ericsson and Simon, 1993, p. 376). A different procedure is involved in a 'think aloud' process. Here the subject is instructed:

> think aloud as you work on the problems given. What I mean by think aloud is that I want you to tell me everything you are thinking from the time you first see the question until you give an answer. I would like you to talk aloud constantly from the time I present each problem until you have given your final answer to the question. I don't want you to try to plan out what you say or try to explain to me what you are saying. Just act as if you are alone in the room speaking to yourself. It is most important that you keep talking. If you are silent for any long period of time I will ask you to talk. (p. 378)

This second instruction (the think-aloud procedure) gives insights into any of the thoughts that come into the mind in the course of executing a task. The first instruction (the talk-aloud procedure) restricts attention to the propositional knowledge content involved in the performance of the task. The instructions concerning talking to oneself rather than talking to the 'elicitor' are important, since it has been established that the additional requirements of constructing meaningful and appropriate expressions to other people affects the overall process. External speech is more explicit, consists of more words per description, and employs conventional references to size, shape etc. as opposed to analogies (for example 'looking like a talking penguin'). Indeed, Bonnardel (1993) has shown how experts provide different accounts when they are working with novices as opposed to fellow experts, when attempting to transfer their knowledge. In terms of analysis, some steps have been made towards computer-supporting the encoding process, with systems such as the Multiple Protocol Analysis System (MPAS) that presents individual protocol segments in a randomized order to one or more coders and then stores the entered codes for later output (Crutcher et al., 1994). The differences in insight that can be gained from parsing protocols at different levels has been examined by Eckersley (1988). If one is to understand the expertise that one has, then the 'characteristics' of the way that one is approaching a task have to be gleaned from the transcript. This is often usefully done by examining the 'logic' of the approach. One can quite readily become aware of the readings and assumptions that one is making in the course of skilled task performance.

Two example applications will be outlined briefly. The first concerns the personal reflections on the design process that Nancy Flint has undertaken (Flint and Sparrow, 1994; 1995). She trained herself to express Level 1, Level 2 and Level 3 verbalizations in the course of designing a multimedia product. Her study took place over many months and, unlike more laboratory-style implementations of verbal protocols, she allowed her verbalizations to be, on some occasions, Level 1, and on others to be Level 2 or Level 3. The situations where Level 1 verbalization was maintained were 'complex' decisions, where careful conscious deliberations on alternative design elements were being made. Given that multimedia design includes visual and auditory design elements, she undertook Level 2 verbalization quite extensively. Her interest in 'learning' about design through 'reflection in action' meant that she pursued Level 3 verbalization in less familiar design deliberations. As a result of her work, she identified how the technology itself combined with her design skills to affect the creativity process (Flint and Sparrow, 1994). She was also able to identify a comprehensive insight into the range of considerations that a multimedia designer addresses in the course of design (Flint and Sparrow, 1995).

The second application of the verbal protocol approach was undertaken by Tim Hancock who worked within transport and logistics operations at British Telecom. He was involved with major capital purchase decisions for computer equipment. The process used a particular proforma to elicit key information for the decision-making panel to consider. The procedure had been in place for some time and, in considering redesigning the process, some insights into the ways in which the skilled decision-makers used the form and its information were needed. Hancock elected to elicit verbal protocols from decision-makers as they 'worked through' the form. The approach elicited Level 1 and Level 3 verbalizations. The protocols revealed how the sequential layout of the form was not the sequence that the decision-makers used in considering the overall information. It revealed how they 'processed' the information, and what additional 'computations' they made.

Capturing skilled performance in its practice is, as has been seen from information-processing theories such as Ericsson and Simon's (1993) model, necessary if one is to secure valid insights. Verbal accounts can provide valuable information for personal and organizational reflection.

Tacit feel

Tacit feel can arise from work experiences. Jemison (1987) feels that much of the 'learning by doing' in organizations produces tacit feel. It is the cumulative learning that is deeply embedded within the organization's dynamic routines and operating systems. In discussing skill acquisition in the previous section of this chapter, it was noted how it is possible for even the most procedurally informal activities, colloquially known as 'tricks of the trade', to have been acquired in a 'self-taught' manner. While these behaviours might become automatic and subconscious, they are nevertheless skills. Tacit feel, for our purposes, is defined as those aspects of performance that are executed subconsciously, but that have also been acquired subconsciously. Because this mental material has never been consciously considered, it may be even less articulable than skills. Much of the research that has referred to tacit feel has been referring to mental material that is subconscious and automatic, and that is 'procedurally informal' and/or 'inarticulable' (Leplat, 1990). The research that is discussed in this section is that which can be considered to refer to tacit feel in the more focused sense.

The kind of mental material that people acquire (including tacit feel) is determined in part by the 'knowledge management' that is practised by the organization (organizational characteristics such as employment systems, career patterns and organizational structure). Most organizations and managers probably do not recognize that this is happening. They are certainly not explicitly managing tacit mental material. These 'disorganized and informal aspects of work and organizational life' (Wagner and Sternberg, 1985) do not get transferred consciously within and between organizations (Argote, 1993). As such, tacit feel may not appear to form much of organizational life or learning. There may be three sets of reasons for this. It may be partly because such mental material tends in any case to be rather 'simplistic' (Seger, 1992). It may, for example, be the sort of information that is so general that people feel 'uncomfortable' in expressing it. It is the 'basic impression' that employees may have. When pushed, people may express these basic impressions but elaborate them with further conscious mental material (language) to present arguments that appear more rational and reasoned. Secondly, it is, by definition, mental material that is difficult to articulate. Information that has never been verbally mediated requires very tentative initial expression, and a willingness to get at and cast the mental material from a number of angles. It is a 'fuzzy' notion. People may experience frustration because they cannot 'find the words' and say that they know what they mean but cannot say it. People may be reluctant to put in the private (let alone public) effort to establish a verbal expression of tacit feel. The third reason may be that it is information that the 'receiver' finds difficult to implement, when received in an explicit (verbal) manner (Holyoak and Spellman, 1993).

The implicit learning capability

The accumulation of tacit feel may, of necessity, be a slow experiential process. It appears that the use (transfer) of such information can only extend to very similar tasks. More distant transfer is not readily obtained (Berry and Broadbent, 1988). This suggests that implicit learning proceeds in a very incremental way, and that it is difficult to accelerate the acquisition process. It may be that conscious learning manages to encode 'attentively selected contingencies' but tacit learning stores all contingencies (Hintzman, 1990). Limitations in capacity may force a constant process of simplification to occur, so that the most 'economical' account is preserved. This would be of the pattern of events that is the most generally 'true'. The fact that this pattern-seeking learning is independent of any conscious direction or subconscious biases may make it a good capturer of the general. Unfortunately, it may (in line with its evolutionary origins) have very pronounced limits in the 'rules' of event co-occurrence that it can discern. It may discern aspects of situations that appear to be relatively invariant. There may be an identification of simple associations between events (for example conjunctions) but an inability to discern more complex interrelationships between events. As such, the learning may have the hallmarks of 'overgeneralizing' and 'oversimplifying'. The degree of 'rule difficulty' in the co-occurrence of events that can be discerned was studied by Haygood and Bourne (1965). Their research concerned conscious verbalized learning, however.

Many of the limits of implicit learning processes in these and other terms remain to be established. There is evidence to suggest that only self-evident features of situations can be acquired implicitly. Chmiel and Wall (1994) suggested that the salience of features in experiences has three dimensions. These are delay (the time lag between cause and effect), meaningfulness (the extent to which cause and effect conform to expectation) and complexity (the number of interacting causes). As with its explicit counterpart, therefore, there appears to need to be contiguity between events for implicit learning to occur. Events that are separated too widely either spatially or temporally are not learned from (Cleeremans and McClelland, 1991). Gardner et al. (1996) conducted an experiment that manipulated the level of meaningfulness of relationship between a fault and a symptom. They showed that the difference between the learning evidenced in the fault-finding task performance and questionnaire test of performance was greater in non-meaningful fault-symptom situations. In other words, implicit learning appears to acquire patterns in juxtapositions of events that may not be meaningful. The authors also showed that implicit learning outstrips conscious learning to a greater extent in more complex situations than in simple ones. That there is some limit to the number of interacting variables (that is, complexity) within which pattern can be discerned was established, however, by Proffitt et al. (1990). Some of the limits or constraints on which covariations can be learned implicitly have also been examined by Seger (1992).

Overall, therefore, it would seem that implicit learning appears to flourish in situations where explicit thinking is not cued (Reber et al., 1980). Conditions may be so salient that they enter consciousness and become encoded as conscious mental material. Subsequent attempts to see whether the information was simultaneously represented in a tacit form are not possible in such situations. The fact that the insight is conscious means that, by definition, the 'test' for tacit feel of its being non-conscious is ruled out. One is left in such situations with attempting to use neurophysiological evidence to establish if simultaneous encoding as subconscious mental material has occurred. It is possible to argue that the implicit learning mechanism is not invoked if pattern has already been consciously discerned. It is also clear that there are limits to the material that can be learned tacitly. Features have to be discernible, they have to co-occur within a reasonable time lag, and there cannot be highly complex interactions among the different variables involved.

Tacit feel may capture the essence of situations in terms of their basic sequences. A routine procedure may be gleaned from a set of experiences of different procedures. In a sense, a set of basic 'scripts' (Schank, 1982) may be learned that are sufficient to cover the ground in which the individual normally operates. The number of scripts may be a product of the variations in the situation. If one routine basically holds up, then this may be all that is stored. If there are consequences of the 'failure' of a single script, then perhaps a small number of variants evolve. The key argument here is that there are only the number of scripts that are required to typify usual experience. In a similar way to the evolution of a minimum number of variants of scripts, one might postulate a minimum number of categories that a person uses to interpret their world. Implicit learning may be so basic that tacit feel is, in part, a store of 'prototypes'. A prototype (Rosch, 1973) refers to a proposal that humans might not store concepts such as 'bird', for example, as a list of defining characteristics, but instead develop single conceptions that best represent examples of a category, a representative instance. In a sense this would be the epitome of a 'bird'. As a further example, we may develop a prototype concept such as *game* in our mind. This prototype is based on lots of examples of 'games' that have some loose sort of family resemblance to each other. The examples do not each have any single characteristic in common, however. Nor is there a 'definition' that works for all examples that we would readily categorize as 'games'. Instead, we have a prototype of 'game' and we categorize certain things as games if they are close (in their features) to our prototype. The result of implicit learning may be tacit feel in the form of abstract (but instantiated) prototypical representations. Our task is to identify the nature of the basic scripts and prototypes that we or other organizational participants are using. What evidence is there of implicit learning occurring in non-laboratory situations? What evidence is there for basic scripts and prototypes at work?

Tacit feel at work

Subconscious mental material certainly plays a role in organizational life. It has long been recognized that the skills that employees have developed are a major asset in organizations. There is increasing recognition that some of the practical intelligence that employees have developed may also have implications for the organization's competitive advantage. At the loosest level, 'common sense' may be regarded as the aspects of knowledge that have largely been acquired informally and perhaps implicitly. Measures of the traditional conception of 'intelligence' can usefully be augmented with measures of common sense (Sternberg et al., 1995). It may be implicit learning that managers are most able to acquire, on some occasions. In situations of higher anxiety, it may be that implicit learning/performance is less affected than explicit learning/performance (Rathus et al., 1994). Managers operating in a high-stress environment may struggle to reflect and spot patterns explicitly. Their tacit recognition may be less affected.

The contribution of tacit feel has been assessed at the task, job and organizational level. Several studies have explored the contribution of tacit feel to task performance. Broadbent et al. (1986) examined performance in a simulated complex control task. Stanley et al. (1989) studied the tacit mental material associated with a process-control task. Gardner et al. (1996) examined tacit feel in a simulated fault-diagnosis task.

At the job level, Kusterer (1978) recognized that the real efficiencies with machines came from operators learning the 'idiosyncrasies of their individual machines' (p. 51). This learning was, so far as can be ascertained, implicit. Wagner and Sternberg (1987), for example, have shown that tacit feel for business management is related to business experience and performance. Kerr (1995) demonstrated how an overall measure of business management tacit feel related to performance in an assessment centre set of management role-playing exercises. Scribner (1986) found substantial differences in the way that novices and experts operated in a milk-processing plant. In working with numbers, for example, she showed that experts had departed from the 'formal algorithms' used to make calculations, and developed simpler and more efficient approaches in, so far as could be seen, an implicitly learned manner. There was no evidence of such approaches being taught or discussed. Myers and Davids (1993) highlight several studies of learning in jobs where the nature of the performance improvements are consistent with an implicit learning process. They conclude that 'direct experience may support more formal perceptual-motor behaviour in a number of ways. These include the development of less formally recognized, and often inarticulable, procedures in attaining performance goals' (p. 132).

At the organizational level, Bruton et al. (1994) suggest that acquisitions of firms that are not financially distressed can, in general, proceed quite smoothly, even in the absence of previous acquisition experience or related business experience. In acquisitions of financially distressed firms, related business combinations in which the acquirers had prior acquisition experience performed best. The authors suggest that the results imply that subconscious mental material about the acquisition process and about how to integrate and manage the assets of distressed firms may be key to their successful acquisition. In general, decisions concerning transferring of capability to manufacture products or provide services need to recognize the importance of tacit feel. The less codifiable and harder to teach a technology, the more likely it is that difficulties will emerge in attempting to move from the base of skills and tacit feel (Kogut and Zander, 1993). Hu (1995) suggests that the international transferability of a firm's advantages is influenced by, in part, the relative non-transferability of its tacit mental material. Perhaps even highly skilled personnel cannot recreate all of the necessary elements for all of their subconscious mental material (including tacit feel) to be evidenced and capitalized on. Sobol and Lei (1994) suggest that competitive advantage in the acquisition and utilization of new technologies cannot be obtained as readily from explicit knowledge as it can from tacit mental material. Explicit knowledge is 'transparent' in the sense that any firm with comparable skills can understand it and apply it. The effective learning that can come from the 'insight, practice and cumulative learning that is deeply embedded within the organization's dynamic routines and operating systems' is an influential factor in securing competitive advantage. Taken together, these studies provide a potentially useful additional insight into the concept of decision overreach outlined by Wilson et al. (1995).

The loss or relative lack of tacit feel opportunities can have important consequences. Mackenzie and Spinardi (1995) suggest that the historical record of the development of nuclear weapons indicates that tacit feel is crucial to nuclear weapons development. If design activity ceases, then in an important (though qualified) sense they will have been 'uninvented'. Their renewed development would have the characteristics of reinvention rather than recommencement. Ceasing production in businesses in general, therefore, may jeopardize any subsequent recommencement. The loss of a skill base in a recession is well documented. The loss of tacit feel is less recognized. Skills can be re-trained. The deep basis of 'common sense' that operated in a particular context, and was responsible for some of the effectiveness of the production or service, may be difficult to reinstate. 'Impoverishing' the work experience may reduce the contribution that implicit learning can bring towards securing effective job performance. Raghuram (1996), for example, suggests that telework decreases the ability to socialize, and may deny workers the opportunity to acquire knowledge through socialization, mentoring and observation. This can have implications for overall knowledge creation in organizations, when one considers the role that tacit feel plays in the knowledge 'conversion' processes highlighted by Nonaka et al. (1996) and discussed in Chapter 1.

Tacit feel is increasingly being recognized as an important component in training/educational contexts. There is evidence that physical depictions, such as animation (Rieber, 1996) physical presence (Raghuram, 1996), and direct manipulation (as opposed to conversational) human-computer interfaces (Schar, 1996) can all be used, with good effect, to create implicit learning. When learning is structured to permit increasing levels of complexity, then individuals may attend to the incremental features and learn in an explicit way (Reber et al., 1980). Where experiences are less neatly incremental, only implicit learning may occur.

In conclusion, it would seem that the procedures that one adopts in the course of problem-solving or other work activities may utilize basic concepts that one has acquired. As we have seen, at the tacit level, these may be the basic prototypes that one has developed. Any particular work scene may be perceived as 'in tune with' or 'at odds with' the expectations inherent within the appropriate prototype. 'Problems' perhaps become labelled as such when situations that depart from these subconscious expectations cue conscious effort (because of the felt need for exploration and understanding) and out-of-specification situations are confirmed by conscious analysis.

Eliciting tacit feel

In the light of the unique nature of tacit feel, one can see that it is difficult to deploy techniques that elicit such mental material in an unequivocal way. In particular, it is easier to identify tacit mental material in the course of its acquisition than it is in its embeddedness in expertise. We may be able to observe employees in the course of their development, and record those aspects of their performance improvement that are, at no stage, consciously considered. This may be a relatively pure sample of tacit mental material. Even then, the sample may include aspects of performance that have become skilled through conscious deliberations that we failed to capture (such as imagistic thinking). Nevertheless, much can be learned from an 'immersion' in the world of others. Many of the aspects of that world that may be learned implicitly can be revealed. Beyond this, we can gain some insights through examining established expertise in particular terms. Approaches towards identifying tacit mental material that rely on established expertise can be divided into two broad groups: one that focuses on the tacit prototypes that participants may use, the second that explores the tacit scripts that they may use.

PARTICIPANT OBSERVATION   In discussing skilled behaviour, reference was made to the role that observation can play in revealing 'automatic' aspects of behaviour that participants may fail to appreciate. These behaviours are apparent to somebody who is not 'in the know' and can bring a 'fresh eye' to proceedings. A particular form of observation, called participant observation, can provide insights into tacit mental material. This perspective can provide insights that external observation may fail to capture. The approach focuses on the meanings of human existence as seen from the standpoint of insiders. Insiders 'manage, manipulate, and negotiate meanings in particular situations, intentionally and unintentionally obscuring, hiding or concealing these meanings' (Jorgensen, 1989, p. 14). Participant observation seeks to 'uncover, make accessible, and reveal the meanings (realities) people use to make sense out of their daily lives' (p. 15). The insiders' conception of reality is 'not directly accessible to aliens, outsiders or nonmembers, all of whom necessarily experience it initially as a stranger' (p. 14). Through participation, one is able to 'observe and experience the meanings and interactions of people from the role of the insider' (p. 21). Participant roles may be assumed nominally, or one may become more completely and intensely involved. At one extreme, therefore, one may not experience the world of fellow participants, because one is not really 'in it'. At the other extreme, one 'becomes the phenomenon' (Wax, 1971) and loses sight of the role of reflection and study. A different realm of insights is therefore provided by participant observation.

Many studies have revealed subtle aspects of particular workgroups' worlds, as a 'researcher' immerses themselves into their world. Studies have revealed the 'struggle' between car sales people and their customers in the sales encounter (Felcher, 1995), the 'coercive' nature of organizational politics (Voyer, 1994) and the ways in which 'professionalism' can become institutionalized in an organization through a combination of micro and macro level forces (Prasad and Prasad, 1994), for example. The ways in which people at work subconsciously come to adopt particular practices have been studied. Watson (1996) outlines how managers come to shape their self-identities and learn to handle the shifting demands of their work, on the basis of participant observation. Persson (1996) notes how the product-oriented rather than person-oriented role of a musical maestro allows students to reconstrue harsh and insensitive criticism as something positive and 'necessary'. The tacit readings that participants make of situations can be observed and experienced. The skills of reflective practice are required to bring them under conscious scrutiny. Being able to enter and participate in other people's worlds involves an attunement to the others' stock of knowledge, emotional and motivational attunement to the group's concerns, an assumption that one can contribute appropriately, and being able to assume that one's identity is not under threat (Ashworth, 1995).

PROTOTYPICAL RESPONSES   Some approaches towards eliciting tacit feel from established expertise seek to highlight basic prototypes that have been acquired implicitly. While any evidence for such basic knowledge will inevitably include acquired perceptual skills, the approaches may give a greater feel for tacit mental material than the procedural accounts used for accessing skills that were outlined in the earlier section on skill elicitation (concurrent verbal protocols etc.). The essence of such approaches is captured in, what might be called a rapid shot-calling exercise. The procedure is based on the studies of 'intuitive physics' (for example Kaiser et al., 1986), that showed how people (while making systematic errors in seeking to verbalize or draw the 'future' motion of physical objects as they exit from curvilinear tubes) can reliably recognize when trajectories that are shown to them 'look wrong'. It may be possible, for example, to outline a situation to participants, and then list some of the actions of key players. Some of the hypothetical actions will 'ring true', while others may be felt to be 'unlikely'. If sufficient pace can be maintained throughout the exercise, then one may get quite close to the intuitive feel that participants have for particular individuals. The procedure could be varied to explore the perceptions that participants have of particular groups' or departments' likely actions. Other 'entities' could also be used. For example, one may ask if the depicted 'output' from a particular process looked right and so on.

Wagner (1987) adopts a looser definition of tacit feel than that used in this book. He regards it as 'practical know-how' that has been acquired through experience, usually without direct instruction, and often by observing others. This definition may include 'skills' that have been acquired informally, in the course of experience. It may be a definition of subconscious mental material generally, rather than tacit feel alone. Wagner (1985) developed a measure of business management tacit feel, the Business Management Tacit Knowledge Measure. Scores on this measure have been shown to relate to the amount of business experience that respondents have had, and to be unrelated to measures of ability (Wagner and Sternberg, 1987). The measure attempts to assess participants' feel for business situations by asking them to indicate their intuitive reactions concerning the effectiveness of some indicated strategies for particular business situations. Because tacit feel is largely inarticulable, participants are not asked to outline their own knowledge/appreciation concerning particular situations. They are merely asked to indicate their assessment of the effectiveness of some given strategies. In fact, the approach has some additional arguments concerning tacit feel. Distinctions are drawn between responses to situations, given the realities of the actual business world as they understand it (scores on the 'actual' scale); and indicated strategies for situations, in an ideal business setting (scores on the 'ideal' scale). The questionnaire has 120 items, with questions about each of 12 'situations'. Situations are structured to concern 'local' (short-term) and 'global' (long-term) issues. Situations concern managing self, managing tasks and managing others. Scores are calculated on the basis of the overall differences between the responses of a participant and the mean scores from a set of ratings obtained from experienced senior managers in major companies.

Subsequent studies by Kerr (1995) suggest, however, that these different forms of tacit mental material (actual, ideal, local, global, managing self, managing tasks and managing others) are not confirmed by detailed statistical analysis of the scores. In fact, it seems that the tacit feel measured by the questionnaire may be one general factor. Assessments of the effectiveness of strategies in terms of 'how effective you think they would be in a business setting' can be compared to the responses of the experts to give a single assessment of tacit business feel. This assessment may give an indication of the 'core' of tacit feel that might be broadly applicable across managerial situations. Tacit feel that is specific to a particular industry, organization, department etc. would not be being assessed.

It may be possible to develop 'tailored' sets of assessments of tacit feel for one's particular work situation, along the lines indicated earlier. In order to minimize the inclusion of semantic understanding, episodic memories and skills within the responses of participants, 'basic' and 'rapid' situations and responses should be utilized. There is a high degree of overlap between the approach within the Business Management Tacit Knowledge Measure (Wagner, 1985) and that within other 'situational inventories'. Motowildo and Tippins (1993), for example, describe a 'marketing situational inventory', consisting of 59 situational problems, where respondents have to indicate 'the action they would most likely take'. The approach is, in their view, tapping into the overall set of knowledge and skills needed for effective job performance, and not specifically tacit skills. Structuring questions in ways that minimize the contribution of semantic and episodic mental material is required if an assessment is to provide insights into tacit mental material *per se*. This is a difficult task.

ANALYSING SCRIPTS Some approaches towards eliciting tacit mental material through analysing established expertise focus on deeper, characteristic patterns in events that may have been gleaned by participants in the course of their organizational experiences, that is, scripts. Two imagistic and two propositional approaches towards identifying scripts will be outlined here. It will be recalled from Chapter 4 that participants can be encouraged to draw their sensing of a particular situation. Figures 4.1 to 4.5 depicted different participants' reactions to a situation of a company acquisition, and their role as logistics manager attempting to synchronize the two plants. Interpretations of the images can be made from a number of unconscious perspectives. These are considered in the section on eliciting unconscious interpretations below. Here, we can consider whether insights can be gained into any basic tacit categorizations and processes that the participant utilizes. A framework that the author has developed has been found to be quite useful in this regard. When dealing with 'change' situations, it can be useful to explore the participant's depictions of 'the past', the 'entities involved', the 'agent of change', the 'intentions of the agent', any 'forces

Table 6.2   *A framework for considering images used by participants that may connote tacit feel*

How is the past depicted? What does this tell us?
What entities are involved in the situation? What are they? What might they depict?
Who or what is the agent of change? How is it/he/she operating?
What are the intentions of the agent? What can it/he/she bring about?
What other forces are present?
What process is being used to bring about change?
What is the nature of any 'obstacles' to change?
What indications are there of any prevailing emotions?
What 'outcome' is depicted or implicit?

present', the 'process used', the 'nature of any obstacles', 'prevailing emotions' and the 'outcomes'. Table 6.2 lists these considerations, for ease of reference. It may be possible to identify patterns in the tone of the depictions used by a particular workgroup, and infer some basic tacit view of the issues.

A second imagistic approach could be the use of photo-elicitation. It will be recalled how photographs of organizational scenes can be used to structure the elicitation of knowledge (for example Gold, 1991). It may be possible to request participants to outline any metaphors that they could use to describe the scene/individual(s) depicted. One may find that the basic 'resonance' of the image is an interpretation of the fundamental pattern of experiences associated with the situation/individual(s) depicted. This pattern may have been implicitly learned, and thus be tacit mental material.

A propositional approach that utilizes metaphor is described by Akin and Schultheiss (1990). They request participants to outline a story of a 'notable success by your department, office or group' and a separate story of a 'personally meaningful success at work' (p. 14). In the first instance, they are asked to outline 'what were the circumstances?, what actually happened? (Who did what?), what was the outcome?, how did you know it was a success?'. Similarly, in articulating the story of a personally meaningful success, participants are asked to detail, 'when?, where?, what were you doing?, what else was going on?, and what were the results?' (p. 14, Table 1). If the emphasis was on the elicitation of episodic mental material, one might analyse the transcript in terms of key sequences, or episodes. Insights into tacit mental material may be obtained, however, through a search for metaphors. Metaphors are more likely to reflect non-conscious mental material. It can be argued that such metaphors are more likely to be tacit feel rather than skills, since there is little evidence of them being used in the course of skill acquisition. Akin and Schultheiss (1990) believe that 'an important interpretive device is to look for the metaphors embedded in the stories and the language in which they are told', to surface the 'taken-for-granted cultural images' (p. 14).

Examples of metaphors belying tacit feel may be apparent in the following extracts from interviews with owner-managers of high-technology small

Table 6.3 *Some example 'everyday' uses of metaphor that may signal tacit readings of situations*

'Like playing the currency market in a way, you know, the prices are fluctuating all the time and you have to be aware of where prices are going.'

'At the moment it is in its very early stages but with the new laws of recycling that have come from the East and Europe we see this as a big birth.'

'Be seen as a bit of a "soft touch".'

'There's not too much throat cutting.'

'He is running around like a cornered rat.'

'Bail out, I would have bailed out before that.'

Extracts from a series of interviews with owner-managers of high-technology small firms, concerning risk management, from a study conducted by Patrick Bentley and the author, from the University of Central England (Bentley and Sparrow, 1997)

firms, concerning their approaches to risk management. The extracts are from a study being conducted by the author with Patrick Bentley of the University of Central England Business School (Bentley and Sparrow, 1997). Table 6.3 details the extracts.

An examination of the extracts may give us a flavour of the 'world' in which these owner-managers live. The stereotype of small business entrepreneurs is of people battling to survive. Certainly the language in the extracts suggests that they may live in a world of chance, offering new opportunities, where people may have to ensure they are not seen as soft touches or they may find their throats cut. Escape may not be possible, if one finds oneself cornered. In such an environment, one may need to recognize that one may need to bail out. The hypothesis being put here is that such basic experiences have created tacit feel, through which the hallmarks of any such business situations are 'sensed' and responded to automatically. Searching for basic metaphors may, in general, give us clues about the tacit feel that participants have acquired.

A further propositional approach towards eliciting tacit mental material involves an identification of any underlying form (genre) of a transcript of a person's free account of a situation. These 'genres' can be argued to represent underlying scripts that characterize experiences in the context in question. Indeed, it may be that people subconsciously learn basic patterns in everyday human affairs. These 'root' stories may be the scripts that are recorded in the myths of the world. Myths, by definition, have a resonance with current experiences. It may be possible to classify myths in a way that reveals something of the basic patterns in human events that people implicitly learn. Spence (1921) developed an overall framework for myths. The classes of myth that he identified can serve as a useful template for interpreting accounts that participants may give of work situations. It can be argued that accounts that 'fit' the basic patterns encapsulated in a particular class of myth are tacit feel for the context in question. Spence (1921) identifies 21 classes of myth (p. 138). Table 6.4 lists the classes of myth, together with an outline of the hallmarks that a participant's account

Table 6.4   *Spence's (1921) classification of myths and some hallmarks of organizational accounts that may imply tacit feel schematized in each basic form*

Class of myth	Some hallmarks in accounts of organizational practices
Creation	Creating or starting something as something of a feat; willpower
Origin of man	The creation of a weaker, diluted version of something
Flood	Despite widespread devastation, something surviving
Place of reward	Things being polarized and labelled as wonderful
Place of punishment	Things being polarized and labelled as terrible
Sun	A source of warmth/light/comfort
Moon	Evidence of temperamental, rapid changes
Hero	Actions against the odds
Beast	Entities somehow having excessive (unnatural) powers
Myths of customs and rites	Procedures that are imporant traditions
Journeys through underworld	Trying to do things the usual way, but in the wrong/adverse context
Birth of gods	Something vast that has come about wondrously and should be cherished
Fire	Total, indiscriminate destruction; if attempts are made to use a power beyond one's right (e.g. stolen), then one may obtain only a temporary advantage, that will be taken away, subsequently
Stars	Metamorphosis; total and complete transformation
Death	What happens for not doing things correctly
Food of the dead	Once an approach is bought into, then it is irrevocable
Taboo	Rules that if broken induce disproportionate consequences
Dismemberment	Something that even though split up continues to exert some power between its residual pieces
Dualistic myths	References to things in opposition
Origin of the arts	Issues of passing things on, tuition, being an 'insider'
Soul	Cherishing and nurturing the essence of something to keep it alive

of a situation may have, to be considered to be in line with the particular class of myth.

The hypothesis here is that these basic forms of events unfolding are such inevitable patterns, even across cultures, that they have occurred frequently within the personal experience of most individuals. As such, they may have become tacit mental material. People may implicitly 'read' situations (including work situations) in these terms. Taken together, they may be major aspects of a participant's experiences at work. They may colour decisions and actions subconsciously. One may find that, in a very real sense, a particular organizational participant is 'living out' a 'journey through the underworld', for example where he has been sent on a mission, to achieve a particular outcome, but where his 'standard' set of approaches are not sufficient and he has to cope by living on his wits. People may well cast themselves into particular roles and 'live them' at a subconscious level. Perhaps any deviations from the script are tacitly sensed, and behaviour adjusted in order to secure a better 'fit'.

Analyses of any scripts that participants may be using can be undertaken along the following lines. Participants can be asked to prepare accounts of a particular organizational episode, or of a possible future scenario. They can be asked to emphasize the sequence of events, motives and outcomes, rather than detailed technical descriptions. They can be given perhaps 20 minutes or so to compose their accounts. The lengths of the accounts tend to vary very widely. Some participants find it hard to envisage outcomes. Others may find what may be read into their accounts potentially concerning, and may seek to censor their work. Others may find the experience quite liberating and really get into the flow of writing.

The accounts can be analysed using the framework presented in Table 6.4. Participants are asked to look for evidence of 'dualism' in their accounts; for idealized conceptions of outcomes, labelled as 'wonderful'; for heroic battling against the odds (that may mean that battles are waged, rather than alliances sought) etc. Participants can often reflect on their accounts in many of these terms. The insights can be quite profound as they interpret their actions or plans in these terms. It would seem that people may well cast themselves in these (and prospectively, many other) ways. The essential neatness and balance in these stories may be the foundations that people use to guide their decisions and actions. In the course of 'acting out' one's own role, of course, one has in effect cast other participants into roles within the overall script. Indeed, we may ourselves have been cast into our roles by other participants. What evidence is there of people taking on such roles in their lives?

There is a long history of accounts of interpersonal dynamics being based on the idea of a self as the ongoing product of immediate interpersonal relationships. Mead (1934) suggested that we take on roles and, as it were, conduct conversations between our self and other people (as we have defined them in relation to our role). Goffman (1959) proposed a 'dramaturgic' analysis of human behaviour, to reveal the efforts on the part of each one of us to present ourselves in such a way as to create and maintain a desired social identity. That organizational processes may, in general, shape the roles that participants play has been argued by Foucault (1979) and demonstrated by Kemp (1985), for example. The degree of awareness (level of consciousness) of such role assignment and execution would appear to be subconscious. Whether it is a process that we become skilled in, only tacitly read or both is unclear. The value of the insights that can come from 'surfacing' such decision and action tendencies is, however, clear.

Overall it is believed that the approaches towards the elicitation of tacit mental material detailed here can provide valuable insights into perceptions, in terms that elicitation of other kinds of mental material may miss. Because of the degree of overlap in the assessments that we can make of non-conscious mental material, they are recommended for use alongside assessments of semantic understanding, episodic memories, skills and unconscious interpretations, in the belief that their unique characteristics will pick up on some of the aspects of tacit feel that other approaches may emphasize less clearly.

Unconscious interpretations

In Chapter 2, it was noted that a lack of 'balance' in our own reactions to situations can tell us much about our ways of coping with situations, and how our unconscious processes may be working alongside our conscious efforts. When a person is having difficulty in dealing with particular situations, we may identify some of the ways in which they 'manage' their thinking to cope. The key insights that we shall seek to incorporate are derived from the work of Freud and Jung.

Unconscious processes

Freud suggested that there are four basic ways in which a person may try to deal with difficulties they are facing at the conscious level. He argued, for example, that where a person feels that the natural, spontaneous responses that might normally be used appear inappropriate or insufficient, energy may be invested differently. A person thinks instead of acts. It can therefore be useful in observing people's behaviour at work to consider those aspects where the person appears to elect to think excessively rather than act. A second balance that has to be struck concerns the controls one places on one's behaviour. Adulthood has the hallmark of 'moderation'. There is a reduction in the spontaneity and impulsiveness of youthful behaviour. If the responses are the product of an excessive incorporation of prohibitions, then the 'personality will be marked, not by moderation, but by rigidity. One who has such a personality lives a guarded, narrowly confined life. His stability is that of a person in a straightjacket' (Hall, 1954, p. 121).

This dimension of rigidity vs impulsivity can be particularly revealing in considering the behaviour of organizations. Where a person feels unable to deal with a situation as it is, he may 'try to alter reality and make it consonant with his wishes or ideals' (Hall, 1954, p. 119). Indeed, a person may have come to use particular mild transformations on a fairly permanent basis. These patterns express themselves as interests, attitudes, attachments and preferences. Within a work setting one may find 'ritual, tradition, custom, convention, uniformity, order, conservatism, habit and repetition' (Hall, 1954, p. 120) as more or less constant compromises to achieve stability. The extent and form of these protections from reality are worthy of note in examining work behaviour.

The final group of responses that may contribute to the achievement of a stabilized personality are those that are based on 'denial'. This involves 'pushing certain thoughts, feelings and experiences out of conscious awareness because they have become too anxiety-provoking' (Halton, 1994). As Klein (1959) identified, responses can include 'splitting' (the process of dividing feelings into differentiated elements) and 'projection' (locating feelings in others rather than in oneself). Employees may people their worlds with saints and sinners accordingly. Interestingly, psycho-analysts suggest, two processes reinforce and perpetuate this 'separation' of feelings into manageable forms. 'Projective identification' is an unconscious personal interaction in which the recipients of a projection react to it in such a way that their own feelings are affected: they unconsciously identify with the projected feelings. 'Countertransference' can occur so that other people's feelings are experienced as one's own. In exploring people's thinking at work, therefore, it may be that one can detect instances where a person is acting as a 'container' (Bion, 1961) for these various projections and introjections, or as a person whose actions are governed by splitting and projections.

The Jungian perspective on the unconscious was introduced in Chapter 1. The Myers Briggs Type Indicator distinguishes between introverted and extraverted attitudes, and between thinking and feeling orientations ('functions' in Jung's terms) and intuition and sensation orientations (functions). The ideal might be to have conscious access to the function or functions required or appropriate for particular circumstances but, in practice, the four functions are not equally at one's conscious disposal. They are not universally developed or differentiated in any individual. Invariably one is more developed, and the others less developed. What role do these relatively undeveloped functions play in each person's overall psyche? According to Jung, 'they remain in a more or less primitive and infantile state, often only half conscious, or even quite unconscious' (Jung, 1961, Vol. 6, par. 955). The argument is therefore that what a person thinks they are consciously or intentionally trying to do may accord with their mental access to the primary function. Very often, however, an outside observer might see the person's life differently. 'A man's unconscious makes a far stronger impression on an observer than his consciousness does, and his actions are of considerably more importance than his rational intentions' (Jung, 1961, Vol. 6, par. 982). Sharp (1987) suggests that it can be more revealing to ask oneself, not what one was thinking or trying to do, but to consider: 'What is my greatest cross? From what do I suffer the most? Where is it in life that I always knock my head against the wall and feel foolish?' (p. 34). These are the questions that can reveal the less developed attitude and functions that have contributed to the situation. In essence, therefore, as a person places an ever-increasing emphasis on their preferred attitude (introversion or extraversion) and function (sensing, intuition, thinking or feeling), they impoverish their respective counterparts.

Jung distinguished between this personal unconscious (effectively acquired during the individual's unique life experiences) and a 'collective unconscious' that has features and operates on elements that occur throughout all societies in the world. These 'elements' are fundamental.

They are 'archetypes'. They are the 'motifs' in mythology. They are fundamental pre-existing forms. The unconscious mind operates with archetypes.
Jung felt that there are three archetypes that 'have the most frequent and
most disturbing influence on the ego. These are the shadow, the anima and
the animus' (Jung, 1961, Vol. 9. Pt 2, p. 8). The shadow can be inferred
from the personal unconscious. It is often equated with the inferior attitude
and functions. The shadow 'projects' its characteristics onto other people
and objects. 'No matter how obvious it may be to the neutral observer that
it is a matter of projections, there is little hope that the subject will perceive
this himself. He must be convinced that he throws a very long shadow
before he is willing to withdraw his emotionally-toned projections from
their object' (Jung, 1961, Vol. 9. Pt 2, p. 9). The 'anima' refers to the
archetype of femininity. She is 'the much needed compensation for the risks,
struggles, sacrifices that all end in disappointment; she is the solace for all
the bitterness of life' (Jung, 1961, Vol. 9. Pt 2, p. 11). The projection of
masculinity is the 'animus'. It is a conception of power and logic/reason.
The source of much animosity at work may well be the conflict in
projections between participants. The 'abusive' terms in which pleas for
'sensitivity' can be greeted may reflect the primitive and stereotypical grasp
of the approach when thinking in a masculine way. Over-the-top statements
of the 'futility' of 'reason' abound when thinking in a feminine way.

   Do unconscious processes pervade organizations? Kets de Vries and
Miller (1984) suggest that it can be the fundamental unconscious processes
that predominate the thinking of the top echelon of managers that create
some of the uniformities of organizational culture. In particular, they
suggest that neurotic characteristics of these managers foster parallel
neurotic organizational styles. Each style has its 'specific characteristics,
predominant motivating fantasy and associated dangers' (p. 27) and 'has its
counterparts in the strategic behaviour, climate and structure' (p. 27) of the
companies. They elucidate five neurotic styles that are based on the
psychoanalytic and psychiatric literature: dramatic, depressive, paranoid,
compulsive and schizoid. Finding evidence of these coping strategies in the
thinking of organizational participants can help considerably in understanding decision-making.

The 'day residue' and characteristic behaviour

Given the basic premise that the unconscious may deal with information/
feelings that are not fully addressed by the conscious mind, we can
distinguish between fundamental approaches that are characteristic of the
individual in question, and more immediate matters that may temporarily
'spill over' from the day, that is, the 'day residue'. The unconscious may
have some basic uniformities, some 'preferences' that can be seen as hallmarks. Many of the issues outlined above concern these more fundamental
aspects of the unconscious. We can also identify unconscious work on more
transitory issues, the matters we have not dealt with appropriately in the

immediate period. We can, for example, consider evenings when we go to sleep, with certain issues unresolved. As Ullman (1996) puts it, 'when we come up with the resources needed to cope with what is novel in our lives, we succeed in enlarging our behavioural repertoire. When we cannot or, for one reason or another, avoid dealing with what confronts us, there results a lingering tension of greater or lesser intensity, depending on the significance of the issue' (p. 248). In order to understand the efforts being made by the unconscious, we have to try to identify the situation to which the unconscious processing relates. The unconscious uses a 'language so elegantly suited to transforming our feelings and concerns into a pictorial mode' (Ullman, 1996, p. 177) that we need to 'search for context' (Ullman, 1996, p. 60) if we are to understand it. The processes we use to explore unconscious interpretations need to work with both fundamental (characteristic) styles of operating, as well as residues from current contexts.

Important considerations

Before considering some of the important practical considerations in working with unconscious mental material, there are two important differences between the clinical psychotherapeutic context and approach and the organizational setting that need to be stressed. These concern the ownership and depth of the change process. The first important distinction to make is that there is no 'therapist' or 'patient' in the organizational context. This means that there is nobody in a position to exercise expert control over the processes. Nor is the guiding process quite so well informed. In clinical settings, a therapist may form views concerning important areas for the client to pursue, and guide them accordingly. In some instances, a therapist may, on the basis of their expertise, offer a client a particularly apposite interpretation. There is a clear appreciation that the two parties are working together (essentially in an equal or near equal partnership). In the self-managed reflective practice context, one only has one's diary or log of events to interact with. One has to be careful that one doesn't create concerns and affect self-esteem because one lacks any comparative information about how other people may be handling similar issues (Rich and Parker, 1995). In the organizational context, the role of other players is merely to offer a participant some possibilities and for the participant to consider the value and implications of the insight. The individual concerned controls the process, not the other players. The second distinction between the clinical and organizational contexts concerns the nature and scale of change at stake. In a clinical setting a client has made an expressed declaration that she wishes to change. There is a particular aspect of her behaviour that she wishes to address. The matter is of sufficient concern for the client to undertake quite a comprehensive (long) soul-searching and reconstruction process. In the organizational context, any 'dysfunction' may not previously have been expressed. It may be of concern, but not of sufficient gravity to warrant a protracted self-examination process. As such, the 'depth' of any search or change process in the organizational setting is likely to be less profound. This is not to imply that the issues that will be encountered, or the changes that may ensue are trivial. It is merely to note that the nature of participation, the time and the expertise available inevitably limit the depth of changes.

A major task facing those seeking to work with unconscious mental material concerns the means through which the information and feelings can be kept in the open for long enough for them to be explored. In organizational contexts, this is not a burden that can be placed on the individual participant. It is important to provide an alternative means of holding such information, so that it can be considered. Davis (1994), for example, refers to the MIT approach to metalogue (for example Isaacs, 1993) being used in an organization as a means to deal with the unconscious projection of feelings. He reports Isaacs using Bion's (1961) psychoanalytic notion of a 'container' as a means of dealing with emotion. People can be helped to reflect on their feelings, if they can be helped to contain the anxieties that the process stirs up. The interesting point about this approach is that the people in the meeting *imagine* a container that 'holds everyone's hostile thoughts and feelings. As everyone speaks out, putting their fears, biases and anger on the table, the hostility becomes neutralized; it sits there in the middle of the room in a safe place for all to observe and discuss' (Davis, 1994, p. 154). Sometimes several group members may unknowingly project their feelings onto a particular person. It can be useful for a facilitator to act as a temporary container. Indeed, Halton (1994) argues, 'The consultant's willingness and ability to contain or hold on to the projected feelings stirred up by these ambiguities until the group is ready to use an interpretation are crucial' (p. 17). Another variant on this notion of a temporary container can be identified in examining one of the learning tools outlined by Senge (1990). The 'left-hand, right-hand column' technique can be used by individuals. In a group meeting, individuals write down what they really think in the left-hand column of a piece of paper, and what they actually said in the corresponding right-hand column of the paper. Senge's aim is to help people get in touch with the biases and feelings that are hindering effective dialogue. In a sense, however, we can see that the approach can be construed as a psychoanalytic therapeutic process. The paper is operating dialectically by serving as a container for the feelings themselves. It is an example of an external representation supporting thinking (as outlined in Chapter 3) and an example of a psychoanalytic container.

It is crucial that one addresses ethical concerns. The freedom of participants at all times to proceed or withdraw from elicitation and interpretation processes is paramount. Ullman (1996) has articulated these 'safety' considerations in three guidelines concerning the rights of the 'dreamer' in offering dreams to dream groups for help in appreciation. The specific references to 'dreamers' and 'dreams' can be replaced with broader terms such as 'participant' and 'information'. Accordingly the guidelines read:

1 The [participant] has the option of sharing or not sharing the [information].
2 The [participant] controls the level of self-exposure.
3 The process is subject to the [participant's] control and can be stopped by the
   [participant] at any point, with or without any explanation to the group.
   (pp. 6–7)

The final set of considerations concerns the process of supporting each
participant in accessing and considering the role of their unconscious mental
material. It is useful to distinguish between the two basic forms of elicitation
and two interpretation processes. We can consider verbal (propositional) and
imagistic approaches to elicitation. We can distinguish between clinical/
analytical 'interpretations' of the meaning of unconscious tendencies, and
group 'appreciation' of the meaning of tendencies. All of the elicitation and
analysis procedures are premised on the notion that in a fluid, open
situation, a person may unwittingly communicate aspects of themselves.
Their interpretation of the situation will include some projection of themselves. They are often collectively referred to as projective techniques. The
major ways in which unconscious material can be captured are outlined
below. Some of the ways in which it can be analysed are considered later in
the chapter.

Eliciting unconscious tendencies in dealing with issues

PROPOSITIONAL APPROACHES TO ELICITATION OF UNCONSCIOUS MATERIAL
Three propositional approaches will be considered here: sentence completions, free association and cathartic (free-intuitive) writing. The first
focuses on free responses that a person may give to open questions. These
'sentence completion' tests invite people to express their 'real feelings'
(*Rotter Incomplete Sentences Blank*, 1966). In order to overcome some of
the control that a person may seek to exercise over the responses they give
(to make them more socially acceptable, for example), sentences are constructed to be extremely open. For example, one might have a sentence that
begins, 'The best way to overcome fear is . . .' The respondent is given few
cues concerning a 'correct' response, and thus may elect to give a genuinely
felt response. Other examples of this form of sentence might be: 'I would
like to be successful in my life but . . .' and 'If my father . . .' More focused
insights can be obtained if questions are constructed with particular purposes in mind. For example, Oppenheim (1992, p. 219) describes how
sentence completions such as '"When I grow up I want to become an
engineer," said Mary, "but it may be difficult for me because . . ."', and
other similarly constructed questions, could be used to assess awareness of
sexism. It is also possible to elicit propositional responses to cartoon-like
scripts. Brown (1947), for example, constructed basic cartoon panels with a
bubble coming from one character with a particular sentence within it. The
bubble coming from the other character was blank. The participant's task is
to enter what they consider the response might be from the other character.

In general, drawings are 'left rather vague and schematic to facilitate self-identification' (Oppenheim, 1992, p. 239).

Galton (1879) described what he termed a 'free association test'. The procedure involves the presentation of a series of disconnected words, to each of which the participant is told to respond by giving the first word that comes to their mind. The basic logic of word association is compelling. Brown (1961) notes how in free association, powerful emotional drives sweep the 'uncontrolled thoughts in the direction of the psychic conflict as logs floating on the surface of a great river are whirled about by the currents beneath the surface of the water' (p. 17). When used in the spirit being advocated here for organizations, the approach could offer much. It seems relatively easy to generate a list of words that focus on particular key features of an organization at a particular time. It may be that participants would be willing to share their insights into a pattern with each other in a group forum. The focus would be on considering why the immediate reaction to particular stimulus words tends to have a specific nature, and whether there are any consequences for the participant that they may wish to address.

The third approach towards gaining insight into unconscious tendencies through verbal (propositional) approaches is cathartic and free-intuitive writing. Here one writes in a way that allows emotions immediate expression. It involves recognizing that writing is a process and not just a product. Rainer (1978) suggests that a diary can be used 'for purging strong emotions through writing' (p. 53). Merely beginning to write down how one feels at a particular juncture can begin a process of access and self-disclosure. The speed of (spontaneous) writing can set up a form of information access that is quite different from that involved in introspection and conversation.

IMAGISTIC APPROACHES TO ELICITATION OF UNCONSCIOUS MATERIAL
While it is possible to gain insight into unconscious interpretations through propositional approaches, as we saw in Chapter 2 and Chapter 4, approaches that recognize the role of imagistic forms of thought may be more fruitful. There are three fundamental ways of using imagery to gain insights into the unconscious. These are using dreams, found images and graphic expression. Some of the key considerations in using each of these approaches are outlined below.

Using dreams to gain insight into the unconscious Before we can gain insight from dreams we must recall and record them. This is a straightforward process. Rainer (1978) suggests keeping a diary under the pillow or on a bedside table. Alternatively, a cassette tape recorder can be positioned within reach. Ball (1996) suggests that you note 'what happened, who or what was in the dream, what was said or done, what you as the dreamer felt about it, what emotions were present, and how everything hung together' (p. 13). It is generally considered important to 'record dream words in the diary. Speeches made to yourself within a dream are of utmost importance; they usually say something' (Ball, 1996, p. 175).

Rainer (1978) suggests that any 'odd, strange, unique, or intensely idiosyncratic image' (p. 174) deserves attention. Dreams with particular verbal messages (in the form of oral or written messages, poems, songs, advice, soliloquies or dialogue) should be examined closely. In particular, basic puns (wordplays) may be revealing. She suggests that multiple states of being are noteworthy, i.e. where one is watching oneself, or when it is the present and then the past or future, or when one changes in some way in the course of the dream (spontaneous transformations, being of particular interest). Similarly, attention is warranted on instances where one is self-reflecting in a dream. Transcendent images of 'dancing, flying, floating, birth, flying saucers, mystical or religious imagery' or 'positive figures' such as a guru, a teacher etc. are often revealing aspirations (p. 175).

Ullman (1996) suggests that it might be useful to consider metaphorical associations with specific aspects in dreams, such as animals (for example 'its physical characteristics, its general qualities, past experiences with it' (p. 187)), inanimate objects (for example aspects of 'its function or usefulness that may seem relevant' (p. 187)), colours, puns, *double entendres*, unusual images, incongruities, any absence of appropriate feelings, presence of inappropriate feelings, and images where much detail is offered (Ullman, 1996, p. 187). He also considers that the spatial positioning of elements may be important. Deeper, more unconscious aspects of a situation may be depicted through images of cellars, expanses of water or dark areas. Receptacles and intrusive objects may refer to the female and male sex organs. It can be useful to consider whether one of the characters in a dream/ image 'is' the person themselves (for example animals, a close friend, a child, a sibling). It may be that some of the unidentified characters represent aspects of the self (for example a trait, need or feeling the participant has about themselves). Group members can also be asked to look for 'any theme, tension or contradiction' (p. 179), 'conspicuous absences' (p. 179) or 'identifiable social stereotypes' (p. 179). Finally, any changes of images between 'scenes' can be considered (for example opening versus closing, responses or solutions to conflicts or tensions, or directions of change).

Using found images to gain insight into the unconscious   A second major way in which insights into unconscious thinking can be obtained via imagistic thinking is through exploring a person's 'interpretation' of pre-drawn (found) images. Here, we are interested in facilitating fluid and open expression in articulating the interpretations that are being sensed by the participant. There are at least two alternative ways in which 'articulation' can be cued. One is a more focused approach and the other a non-directive stance. In a focused approach, the participant is encouraged to explore a found image, and consider meaning as it relates to a particular question in their mind. Meaning is 'identified' and then further explored through the metaphorical link with the found image. This focused approach invokes a reasoning type of thinking in the course of considering the found image.

In contrast, an autistic type of thinking can be cued and retained in working with found images. This stance requires that the participant and the interviewer do not 'break' the free-flowing associative mental processes that an image cues. There are minimal guidance/support instructions. Alcock (1963), for example, merely encourages the participant to consider each image that is presented using phrases such as the following: 'Look at it any way you like and as long as you like. Just tell me what you see in it, if anything looks like anything to you – and when you have finished, please hand the card back' (p. 24).

Using drawing to elicit unconscious tendencies/preferences   The third way in which insights into the unconscious can be established imagistically is by inviting participants to express themselves through drawing. It is important to undertake some orienting preparation to get participants into the imagistic form of thinking. Some relaxation and guided imagery may be appropriate preludes. Instructions that generate an encouragement of free expression and seek to minimize any self-censorship in the drawing of images are necessary. 'Cavalier', 'simple', 'big', 'multiple' images that can be 'discarded', in contrast to 'careful', 'detailed', 'complete', 'draftsman-like' drawing that has to be handled 'carefully' and undertaken 'painstakingly', should be encouraged. It may be useful, however, to capture the 'sequence' of images if this is possible.

Analysing unconscious material

There are two broad approaches to the interpretation/appreciation of unconscious tendencies in the articulations and visual expressions of participants. The first approach is an individual, more clinical interpretation of the material. It may tend to consider the material in terms of established language and frameworks. The second approach is an exploration of the material in less professional language within a group setting. Its focus is on alternative appreciations of material as opposed to interpretation. The specific elicitation approach involved (free association, cathartic writing, dreams, found images, generated images etc.) is not considered to be a major factor in interpreting/appreciating material.

CLINICAL INTERPRETATION OF UNCONSCIOUS MATERIAL   A distinction that can be drawn within the first approach is between interpretations that focus on the general insights one might obtain into one's personality through exploring projective material, and insights into more immediate/ pressing matters that may be evidence of the 'day residue'. Some observations concerning both of these emphases are made below.

Insights into one's personality from unconscious projective material   There are many different overarching frameworks that can be used to secure insights into personality from projective material. The Jungian perspective discussed in Chapters 1 and 2 is one that I have found useful. One can often sense evidence of relationships between Myers Briggs (MBTI) indications and the images that participants draw or articulate. By way of example, consider the drawings generated by participants in the course of being presented with the particular scenario outlined in Chapter 4. Figures 4.1 to 4.5 are examples of the sorts of responses one might get to the scenario. It will be recalled that the participants are encouraged to express how they might feel about the challenge of undertaking the management of integration between an established and newly acquired plant.

Consider Figure 4.1. These two images were drawn by participants with an iNtuitive and Thinking preference (NT) in Myers Briggs (MBTI) terms. It seems notable that the issue connotes a need to build (create) a new structure in order to bring the two parts together. It looks and feels visionary and ambitious. We are looking up to it. Contrast these images with the ones reproduced in Figure 4.2. These were drawn by participants with Sensing and Thinking MBTI preference (ST). Again, these images involve the figuring out of a link between the parts. This time, however, the images suggest routine, basic, practical, 'mechanical' solutions to the problem. There is a neat, logical, interlocking process involved. The issue is cogs and jigsaws. One just needs to put the pieces together. Other common images are chain links, nuts and bolts, and various fabrication processes. Note the complete absence of people in both Figures 4.1 and 4.2. Consider now the image in Figure 4.3. Here we see people and living things. We see a person being pulled apart. We see somebody small between two adversaries. We see an all-embracing human solution to the issue. These are typical of the images of participants with an iNtuitive and Feeling preference (NF). Figure 4.4, in contrast, shows the practical human approach typified by a Sensing and Feeling preference (SF). There is a practical, interpersonal, mature response to this issue. Here are the two faces talking, communicating. Here is the manager's office, the place where the parties will come together.

It tends to be the preferences that participants have developed that come to the fore in the images that they generate. Ball (1996) has offered a useful framework of images that may evidence the various functions (Sensation, Feeling, Thinking and iNtuition) in the images of men and women. Each function has a common positive and a common negative image. When a distortion has occurred we tend to project the archetype with which we have the most difficulty. Where a person is broadly comfortable with the specific facet of a situation the image will be the positive one associated with the particular function. When they are troubled by the facet we may find the negative archetype of the function. In men, therefore, we may find kindly mother:ogre (sensation), youth:tramp (feeling), hero:villain (thinking) and priest:sorcerer (intuition). In women we may find kindly mother:destructive mother (sensation), princess:siren (feeling), amazon:competitor (thinking) and priestess:witch (intuition) (Ball, 1996, p. 69).

In a typical workshop participants are encouraged to consider their images as projections of themselves. It is also prospectively useful to ask participants to consider the other side of themselves. In part this can be inferred from the inferior functions. This is the side of ourselves that has withered as we have become more practised in our preference. In becoming more and more skilled at seeing the logic of a situation, we may have lost sight of how to handle the feeling aspects of situations. In being intuitive we have not practised our everyday practical sensing. When our preferred response is inadequate (constrained or insufficient) we find ourselves thrashing about trying to use only an almost childlike degree of development of the other side of us. It can be useful to look for any gross exaggerations of facets of the situation that a person's childlike inferior functions may have projected. Perhaps a person with a feeling preference sees the 'chaos' and 'impossibility' of a rational solution. Perhaps the person with a thinking preference sees the ridiculousness of the bickering participants. The intuitive person sees a set of pedestrian thinking in play, and the sensing person sees absurd aspirations in play.

A key facet of this underdeveloped form of thinking is a tendency towards splitting. It will be recalled from Chapter 2 that this polarizing in thinking can serve to simplify one's world, and thereby to respond to neat extremes rather than complex realities. The first drawing in Figure 4.5 may constitute evidence of splitting in response to the scenario. The exaggerated distinction between the parts of the organization is evident in the shark/minnow depiction. A second form of evidence of not coping well with the scenario may come from images that denote the anima (in a man's case) or animus (in a woman's case). Reference was made earlier to the comfort that men can derive from the projected notion of all that is feminine to them (anima), and similarly women can through their projections of all that is male (animus). Images that suggest these archetypes may signify that a man is trying to access his more sensitive side, while a woman may be attempting to become more logical. The second drawing in Figure 4.5 may be evidence of anima in a male participant's thinking.

A more complete impression of this other side of a person is captured through consideration of their shadow. Ball (1996) suggests that one way consciously to meet the shadow 'is to think of all the things we dislike most about people, add to that everything we find hard to deal with in man's treatment of his fellow man and try to imagine what sort of person this would be' (p. 16). She suggests that we may find evidence of the shadow in images, 'as someone we heartily dislike, are afraid of or envy, but whom we cannot ignore' (p. 27). It may be useful, therefore, after one has undertaken an initial analysis of material from a dominant and ancillary function point of view, to ask participants to undertake Ball's (1996) analysis of themselves and to write down some personal summary of it. It may then be useful to ask participants to look for aspects in a 'scene' (image) that they really dislike and explore these in relation to their impression of their shadow.

A final Jungian personality perspective that can be useful concerns the self. The self is the archetype of potential. It holds the secret of the integrated person. Ball (1996, p. 30) suggests that: 'because the true potential beckons from the future, the first experience [in dream form] may be a figure encouraging us to move forward'. Participants can be encouraged to consider their material for insights into this unrealized aspect of themselves. When images of this archetype are evidenced (for example 'a guru, god, a saintly individual, a cross, mandala or other geometric shape') (p. 31), it may mean that we are ready to face the process of becoming whole. When negative or destructive images occur connected with this part, we may be aware that we are neglecting the power of the self.

Insights into the day residue from unconscious projective material The central position of work in people's lives means that it is often the issues that participants are finding problematic at work that carry over into non-work time, and become the focus of considerable unconscious mental processing. Gabelnick (1993), for example, suggests that some people may find women as leaders paradoxical. A woman working professionally as a leader (or indeed as a group relations conference consultant) may be 'available' for a barrage of contradictory, irrational projections, and groups may benefit from an opportunity to study their projections and fantasies surrounding leaders.

Can insights into the unconscious day residue be valuable to organizations? Are there any basic approaches towards interpretation that can be used? The most important point to make is that there can be no pronouncements. It is easy for anyone to project their own interpretation of the significance of an element in an image onto the participant concerned. The only true test of the value of an interpretation lies in the resonance that the participant concerned senses as alternative possibilities are explored. Colleagues are not psychiatrists. They do not have professional views about the meaning of particular projections. The following approach is offered in a spirit of 'aspects that might be better prospects for consideration', and not as a listing of the 'most significant and revealing aspects of a person'. Indeed, the meaning of any image may be apparent to a participant instantly, or through considerations other than those listed here.

The most comprehensive analysis framework for considering visual material has been developed to support the interpretation of the Rorschach (1921) ink blot test. Alcock (1963) provides a comprehensive strategy for the classification of data. He notes that the nature of any notion of 'movement' within a person's projections may be noteworthy. It can be useful to distinguish between human-like, animal and inanimate object movements and forces (p. 39). With regard to any human movement, one may wish to consider the extent to which 'human figures are active in a social relationship, their sex being defined' (p. 42) and consider instances where movement is 'restrained'. The presence of animals in projections may indicate a low tolerance of frustration, the size of animal depicted may be of interest and their movements worthy of note. For example, 'a preponderance of violent, aggressive action by large creatures suggests too little control' (p. 44). One might be surprised to see higher numbers of references to animals or inanimate object movements than to human movements. This may have general implications for the degree of control that a person senses over their lives. Inanimate objects can be considered from four perspectives. First, one can consider instances where inanimate forces are affecting living things (wind, gravity etc.). Secondly, one may consider instances where inanimate objects move (such as explosions). Thirdly, manufactured objects driven by some propulsive power might be considered. Finally, instances of abstract forces may be interesting (for example the wind of adversity). Alcock (1963) assigns images into four basic groups. These are 'living objects', human or animal forms perceived as 'inanimate objects', the 'buffer group' ('the content of which is external to the perceiver and comparatively neutral in character, thus serving as a buffer against unwelcome affect that may be aroused by percepts more closely related to the human field' (p. 66), such as architecture, plants etc.), and the 'disturbing content' group (things with a 'strongly affective charge'). One might expect to find most references to the first two categories, but 'little in the buffer group is likely to indicate a personality vulnerable in human relationships' (p. 67). An emphasis on disturbing content may indicate that 'relationships are felt as traumatic' (p. 67).

Nossiter and Biberman (1990) report a study of the use of projective drawing to obtain insights into organizational culture. Participants drew an image that represented their overall organization, and then an image that represented their department/grouping. The authors asked participants to confine their images to drawings of animals. Animals were chosen 'because of their widespread use as a metaphor in virtually all world cultures, and because of respondents' subsequent familiarity with the notion of animal as metaphor in such diverse areas as religion, sports and advertising' (p. 14). Many of the potential insights that may have been obtained from the full spectrum of image groupings detailed above were excluded by this restriction. The authors nevertheless identified what they considered to be useful patterns in the responses of participants. They report differences in the forms of animals drawn. Two case study organizations were studied and some 'meaning' was gleaned from the images used. In the first case study, the overall organization was represented, in the main, through large animals (lion, bear etc.). They were regarded as 'powerful' and 'solid' animals. In contrast, the human relations department was depicted by a goat, teddy bear, bird, salmon, octopus; the marketing department by a dog, for example; and the engineering department by a rabbit, a caterpillar and a mustang. Collectively the images at the departmental level were regarded as signifying 'working together'. The analysis of the second case study organization was also revealing. The respondents chose a few more large animals to represent departments than they had chosen to represent the total organization. Nossiter and Biberman (1990) suggest that 'their perception of the company's total culture was weaker than their perception of their own department' (p. 15). Furthermore, the images used to depict the total organization included ants, sardines and spiders. The authors considered that the rapid expansion of the company and the subsequent cramped conditions may have contributed to these choices of image. The relative lack of overall control and generally weak culture were further indicated by strong 'collective' images at the departmental level (beavers, bees etc.).

Overall, there would appear to be a clear potential for reflective practitioners and organizations to explore the 'residue' of their practices through projective techniques. The individual interpretation of images can be aggregated to provide insights into general decision-making styles (for example in MBTI terms) and pressing issues/concerns in so far as basic interpretive frameworks allow.

GROUP APPROACHES TO APPRECIATION OF UNCONSCIOUS MATERIAL   Projective material can be considered by an individual with the aid of a group of colleagues (or other set of fellow participants). The claim for the value of this approach rests on the notion that possible meanings can be appreciated by like-minded people, and that it is appreciation rather than interpretation that is the key issue in non-clinical contexts.

Most of the work with groups has explored their contribution towards the appreciation of dreams. The principles involved are clearly generalizable to the appreciation of any projective material. Ullman (1996) maintains that a dreamgroup represents a very powerful resource in helping individuals appreciate their dreams. Groups are particularly useful in this regard because dreams address 'issues that are part of the common experience of all of us – issues pertaining to authority, concern over being for oneself or for others, independence versus dependence, activity versus passivity, issues around self-identity, and so on' (p. 36) and 'the imagery that finds its way into our dreams is social in origin. We may combine, distort, and alter these images in highly idiosyncratic ways, but, . . . the fact that we move about in the same social arena and share a common social heritage makes it possible and even likely that a member of the group could come to the meaning of an image that feels right to the dreamer' (p. 37).

It is possible to design a process where the potential of additional insights from groups can be realized. Groups are fulfilling two basic functions, in this setting. First, they are helping to bring about a more thorough searching or self-exploration. Groups can be more rigorous and rational than individuals sometimes choose to be. They may not let a person 'get away' with gaps or inconsistencies in their arguments. A person can be pressed for information in a particular regard by a group member. It may be a facet of an issue that the individual might not have considered (or allowed themselves to pursue). The second function that the group fulfils is to widen the pool of potential insights. As is the case in creativity, groups can 'spark off' ideas in each other. The potential set of insights into the feelings and metaphors within dreams is widened by using a group of participants.

Ullman has spent many years refining his process. It is one that secures a balance between the reluctance/hesitancy of an individual to disclose and the theoretical potential of a group. The process follows four distinct stages. Stage 1 involves the presentation and clarification of the material. It involves the individual in making an initial attempt to present an account of the material (dream or expressed image) and the group restricting their efforts merely to clarifying what the individual means. Stage 2 is the group's first real task. It involves the group in using their own knowledge to attempt to experience personally the images that the participant has volunteered. The group can be asked to invoke the feelings implicit within a dream/image by being asked, 'Does it connect with your own life, and if so, do the images evoke any specific feelings?', 'Do the context and changes in context evoke any specific feeling?', to 'consider each image', whether there are 'any impersonal outside events (for example Christmas) that might seem related to the dream and evoke a feeling?', to ask themselves 'How might I feel were I in the role of the dreamer and having the dream?' and 'Can I capture an overall mood of the dream?' (Ullman, 1996, p. 176).

Stage 3a is the participant's response to the group's work, reporting what is striking about the group's contributions. This can be difficult for the participant. Four common tendencies in responses are highlighted. There can be a 'tendency to accept a projection intellectually without having any genuinely felt sense of its relevance . . . a true response, in contrast to one accepted in this fashion, has an "opening up" quality. As it sinks in, it opens the dreamer up to further thoughts and insights about the dream. There is a gut reaction that cannot be denied, a feeling of something falling into place and paving the way for further discoveries' (p. 55). Participants may 'tend to orient their responses to general issues that have been on their minds for some time and that have been touched on by some of the comments of the group' (p. 162). Thirdly, they may 'tend to focus responses on the outstanding or most striking elements in a dream' (p. 162) and thus ignore many of its features. Finally, there may be 'disowning' strategies used by the participant. For example, the participant may display 'an attitude of helplessness', appearing to be quite unable to 'see' anything for themselves. This leaves them 'in the position of disowning a projection coming at [them] from the outside' (pp. 196–7). The existence of any of these tendencies in the participant's response can be drawn to their attention by the group. This is a key juncture in the process. The group has put their own experience at the disposal of the participant. Its members have in a real sense given of themselves. What they offered was on a 'take it or leave it basis'.

Stage 3b involves the linking of the unconscious material with context. The group will try to help the participant search for context in their recent experience that might help them appreciate the meaning of the dream/image. The group are urged to 'abide by the dictum that the question you put to the dreamer has to be obviously related to the dream (obvious to the dreamer) or to something the dreamer has shared' (p. 193), that is, not one's own speculations. It may be that a participant requires time to consider whether the orchestration is of real value to them in appreciating the unconscious material. It may be that the participant reports back to the group (at a later session) any 'subsequent' appreciation of the material. Very often, however, insights that are 'on the mark' are recognized immediately, both at an intellectual and a felt level.

One of the most important aspects of Ullman's process is the real attention paid to the rights of the individual, which operate through the series of protocols. They secure most from the group, while retaining a balance between the participant's and the group's disclosures. They keep other people's contributions as their own and not as impositions on the participant. They ensure that control of the process remains in the hands of the participant. The principles of the process can be of great value to facilitators in working with all forms of unconscious mental material.

References

Abelson, R.P. (1981) 'Social psychological status of the script concept', *American Psychologist* 36.7.715–79.

Abercrombie, M.I.J. (1960) *The Anatomy of Judgement: an Investigation into the Processes of Perception and Judgement.* London: Free Association Books.

Abrahamson, E. and Fombrun, C.J. (1994) *Macrocultures: Determinants and Consequences.* Academy of Management Review, 19.4.728–55.

Abramson, N., Lane, H., Nagai, H. and Takagi, H. (1993) 'A comparison of Canadian and Japanese cognitive styles: implications for management interaction', *Journal of International Business Studies*, 24.3.575–87.

Ackermann, F. (1992) 'Strategic direction through burning issues', *OR Insight*, 5.3.24–8.

Ackermann, F. and Belton, V. (1994) 'Managing corporate knowledge experiences with SODA and VISA', *British Journal of Management*, 5. Special Edition. 163–76.

Ackermann, F., Eden, C. and Cropper, S. (1990) *Cognitive Mapping: a User's Guide.* Strathclyde Business School, Working Paper No. 12, Management Science: Theory Method and Practice Series, March. University of Strathclyde.

Adams, J.A. (1971) 'A closed loop theory of motor learning', *Journal of Motor Behaviour*, 3.2.111–50.

Aiken, M. and Carlisle, J. (1992) 'An automated idea consolidation tool for computer supported co-operative work', *Information and Management*, 23.6.373–82.

Akin, G. and Schultheiss, E. (1990) 'Jazz bands and missionaries: OD through stories and metaphor', *Journal of Managerial Psychology*, 5.4.12–18.

Akin, O. (1984) 'An exploration of the design process', in N. Cross (ed.) *Developments in Design Methodology.* Chichester: John Wiley.

Akkermans, H. (1995) 'Developing a logistics strategy through participative business modelling', *International Journal of Operations and Production Management*, 15.11.100.

Alba, J.W. and Hasher, L. (1983) 'Is memory schematic?' *Psychological Bulletin*, 93.2.203–31.

Alcock, T. (1963) *The Rorschach in Practice.* London: Tavistock Publications.

Anastasi, A. (1976) *Psychological Testing* (4th edn). New York: Collier Macmillan.

Anderson, G. (1993) 'Emotions and work in a lifestyle occupation', *Journal of European Industrial Training*, 17.5.10–14.

Anderson, J.R. (1983) *The Architecture of Cognition.* Cambridge, MA: Harvard University Press.

Anderson, J.R. (1990) *The Adaptive Character of Thought.* Hillsdale, New Jersey: Erlbaum.

Anderson, J.R., Farrell, R. and Sauers, R. (1984) 'Learning to program in LISP', *Cognitive Science*, 8.2.87–129.

Annett, J. (1996) 'Imaginary actions', *The Psychologist*, 9.1.25–9.

Annett, J., Duncan, K., Stammers, R. and Gray, M.J. (1971) *Task Analysis.* Training Information No. 6. London: HMSO.

Ansoff, H.I. and McDonnell, E. (1990) *Implanting Strategic Management* (2nd edn). Hemel Hempstead: Prentice-Hall.

Antaki, C. (1994) *Explaining and Arguing: the Social Organization of Accounts.* London: Sage.

Anthony, D.L., Heckathorn, D.D. and Maser, S.M. (1994) 'Rational rhetoric in politics: the debate over ratifying the United States', *Rationality and Society*, 6.4.489–518.

Anthony, W.P., Bennett, R.H., Maddox, E.N. and Wheatley, W.J. (1993) 'Picturing the future:

using mental imagery to enrich strategic environmental assessment', *Academy of Management Executive*, 7.2.43–56.

Argote, L. (1993) 'Group and organisational learning curves: individual, system and environmental components', *British Journal of Social Psychology*, 32.1.31–51.

Argyris, C. (1990) *Overcoming Organizational Defences*. Needham Heights, MA: Allyn and Bacon.

Argyris, C. (1986) 'Skilled incompetence'. Reprinted in 'The logic of business decision making', *Harvard Business Review*, 64.5.74–9.

Argyris, C. (1993) 'On the nature of actionable knowledge', *The Psychologist*, 6.1.29–32.

Arnold, J., Robertson, I.T. and Cooper, C.L. (1991) *Work Psychology: Understanding Human Behaviour in the Workplace*. London: Pitman.

Ashford, S.J. (1986) 'Feedback-seeking in individual adaptation: a resource perspective', *Academy of Management Journal*, 29.3.465–87.

Ashworth, P.D. (1995) 'The meaning of participation in participant observation', *Qualitative Health Research*, 5.3.366–87.

Axelrod, R. (1976) *The Structure of Decision*. Princeton, NJ: Princeton University Press.

Babbie, E. and Halley, F. (1995) *Adventures in Social Research: Data Analysis Using SPSS for Windows*. Thousand Oaks, CA: Pine Forge Press.

Backoff, R.W. and Nutt, P.C. (1988) 'A process for strategic management with specific application for the non-profit organization', in J.M. Bryson and R.C. Einsweiler (eds) *Strategic Planning: Threats and Opportunities for Planners*. Chicago: Planners Press.

Bainbridge, L. (1979) 'Verbal reports as evidence of the process operator's knowledge', *International Journal of Man Machine Studies*, 11.343–68.

Ball, M.S. and Smith, G.W.H. (1992) *Analyzing Visual Data*. Newbury Park, CA: Sage.

Ball, P. (1996) *10,000 Dreams Interpreted*. London: Arcturus.

Balle, M. (1994) *Managing with Systems Thinking*. London: McGraw-Hill.

Bantel, K. and Jackson, S.E. (1989) 'Top management and innovations in banking: does the composition of top management teams make a difference?', *Strategic Management Journal*, 10.10.107–24.

Barrett, R.S. (1995) 'Employee selection with the Performance Priority Survey', *Personnel Psychology*, 48.3.653–62.

Barrick, M.R. and Mount, M.K. (1991) 'The big five personality dimensions and job performance: a meta analysis', *Personnel Psychology*, 44.1.1–26.

Barsam, H.F. and Simutis, Z.M. (1984) 'Computer-based graphics for terrain visualisation training', *Human Factors*, 26.6.659–66.

Bartlett, F.C. (1932) *Remembering: an Experimental and Social Study*. Cambridge: Cambridge University Press.

Bass, B.M. and Avolio, B.J. (1989) *Manual for the Multifactor Leadership Questionnaire*. Palo Alto, CA: Consulting Psychologists Press.

Baumgartner, H., Sujan, M. and Bettman, J.R. (1992) 'Autobiographical memories, affect and consumer information processing', *Journal of Consumer Psychology*, 1.1.53–82.

Bedard, J.C. and Graham, L.E. (1994) 'Auditors' knowledge organization: observations from audit practice and their implications', *Auditing: a Journal of Practice and Theory*, 13.1.73–83.

Bennett, N., Herold, D.M. and Ashford, S. (1990) 'The effects of tolerance for ambiguity on feedback-seeking behaviour', *Journal of Occupational Psychology*, 63.4.343–7.

Bennett, P. (1994) 'Designing a parliamentary briefing system: an OR look at the Commons', *Journal of the Operational Research Society*, 45.11.1221–32.

Bentall, R.P. (1993) 'Personality traits may be alive, they may even be well, but are they really useful?' *The Psychologist*, 6.7.307.

Bentley, P. and Sparrow, J. (1997) *Risk Perception and Management Responses in Small Firms*. University of Central England Business School.

Berger, J. (1989) 'Appearances', in J. Berger and J. Mohr (eds) *Another Way of Selling*. Cambridge: Granta. pp. 81–129.

Berman, M. (1996) 'The shadow side of systems thinking', *Journal of Humanistic Psychology*, 36.1.28–54.

Bernsen, N.O. (1994) 'Foundations of multimodal representations: a taxonomy of representational modalities', *Interacting with Computers*, 6.4.347–71.

Berry, D.C. and Broadbent, D.E. (1984) 'On the relationship between task performance and associated verbalisable knowledge', *Quarterly Journal of Experimental Psychology*, 36A.2.209–31.

Berry, D.C. and Broadbent, D.E. (1988) 'Interactive tasks and the implicit–explicit distinction', *British Journal of Psychology*, 79.2.251–72.

Betts, G.H. (1909) *The Distribution and Functions of Mental Imagery*. New York: Teachers College, Columbia University.

Bibby, P.A. (1992) 'Mental models, instructions and internalization', in Y. Rogers, A. Rutherford and P.A. Bibby (eds) *Models in the Mind: Theory, Perspective and Application*. London: Academic Press. pp. 153–72.

Bion, W. (1961) *Experiences in Groups*. New York: Basic Books.

Bitonti, C. (1992) 'The self-esteem of women: a cognitive phenomenological study', *Smith College Studies in Social Work*, 63.1.295–311.

Bitonti, C. (1993) 'Cognitive mapping: a qualitative research method for social work', *Social Work Research and Abstracts*, 29.1.9–16.

Black, M. (1979) 'More about metaphor', in A. Ortony (ed.) *Metaphor and Thought*. Cambridge: Cambridge University Press.

Blackler, F. (1995) 'Knowledge, knowledge work and organizations: an overview and interpretation', *Organization Studies*, 16.6.1021–46.

Blanning, R.W. (1984) 'Knowledge acquisition and systems validation in expert systems for management', *Human Systems Management*, 4.4.280–5.

Bohr, N. (1958) *Atomic Theory and Human Knowledge*. New York: John Wiley.

Boje, D.M. (1994) 'Organizational storytelling: the struggles of premodern, modern and postmodern organizational learning discourses', *Management Learning*, 25.3.433–61.

Boje, D.M. (1995) 'Stories of the storytelling organization: a postmodern analysis of Disney as Tamaraland', *Academy of Management Journal*, 38.4.997–1035.

Bonnardel, N. (1993) 'Expertise transfer, knowledge elicitation and delayed recall in a design context', *Behaviour and Information Technology*, 12.5.304–14.

Boon, J. and Noon, E. (1994) 'Changing perspectives in cognitive interviewing', *Psychology, Crime and Law*, 1.1.59–69.

Bougon, M.G. (1983) 'Uncovering cognitive maps: the "Self Q" technique', in G. Morgan (ed.) *Beyond Method: a Study of Organizational Research Strategies*. New York: Sage. Chapter 11.

Bougon, M.G. (1992) 'Congregate cognitive maps: a unified dynamic theory of organisation and strategy', *Journal of Management Studies*, 29.3.369–89.

Bougon, M.G., Weick, K.E. and Binkhorst, D. (1977) 'Cognition in organizations: an analysis of the Utrecht Jazz Orchestra', *Administrative Science Quarterly*, 22.4.606–39.

Bourne, L.F., Dominowski, R.L., Loftus, E.F. and Healy, A.F. (1986) *Cognitive Processes* (2nd edn). Englewood Cliffs, New Jersey: Prentice-Hall.

Bowen, K. (1983) 'An experiment in problem formulation', *Journal of the Operational Research Society*, 34.8.685–94.

Bower, G.H. and Mayer, J.D. (1991) 'In search of mood-dependent recall', in D. Kuiken (ed.) *Mood and Memory*. Newbury Park, CA: Sage. pp. 133–68.

Bowles, M.L. (1993) 'Logos and Eros: the vital syzygy for understanding human relations and organizational action', *Human Relations*, 46.11.1271–89.

Bowles, N. (1995) 'Storytelling: a search for meaning within nursing practice', *Nurse Education Today*, 15.5.365–9.

Bowman, C. and Johnson, G. (1991) 'Surfacing managerial patterns of competitive strategy: interventions in strategy debates', *American Academy of Management Conference*, Miami, Florida.

Bowman, L. (1991) *High Impact Business Presentations*. London: Business Books.

Boyatsis, R. (1982) *The Competent Manager*. New York: John Wiley.

Boyd, D. and Wild, A. (1993) 'Innovation and learning in construction project management', *Proceedings of 9th Annual Conference of the Association of Researchers in Construction Management (ARCOM)*, Exeter College, Oxford, 14–16 September.

Boyd, R. (1979) 'Metaphor and theory change', in A. Ortony (ed.) *Metaphor and Thought*. Cambridge: Cambridge University Press.

Brant, L. (1993) 'Mind maps: applications for the training session', *Transition*, Feb.20–1.

Brewster, C. and Tyson, S. (eds) (1991) *International Comparisons in Human Resource Management*. London: Pitman.

Briggs, J. and Monaco, R. (1990) *Metaphor: the Logic of Poetry* (2nd edn). New York: Pace University Press.

Broadbent, D.E., Fitzgerald, P. and Broadbent, M.H.P. (1986) 'Implicit and explicit knowledge in the control of complex systems', *British Journal of Psychology*, 77.1.33–50.

Brocklesby, J. (1995) 'Using soft systems methodology to identify competence requirements in HRM', *International Journal of Manpower*, 16.5/6.70–80.

Brook, J.A. (1986) 'Research applications of the repertory grid technique', *International Review of Applied Psychology*, 35.4.489–500.

Brown, A.S. and Mitchell, D.B. (1994) 'A re-evaluation of semantic vs. non-semantic processing in implicit memory', *Memory and Cognition*, 22.5.533–41.

Brown, J.A.C. (1961) *Freud and the Post-Freudians*. Harmondsworth, Middlesex: Penguin.

Brown, J.F. (1947) 'A modification of the Rosenzweig Picture-Frustration Test to study hostile interracial attitudes', *Journal of Psychology*, 24.247–72.

Brown, R. and McNeill, D. (1966) 'The tip of the tongue phenomenon'. *Journal of Verbal Learning and Verbal Behaviour*, 5.325–77.

Brown, S.M. (1992) 'Cognitive mapping and repertory grids for qualitative survey research: some comparative observations', *Journal of Management Studies*, 29.3.287–308.

Bruton, G.D., Oviatt, B.M. and White, M.A. (1994) 'Performance of acquisitions of distressed firms', *Academy of Management Journal*, 37.4.972–89.

Bryan, W.L. and Harter, N. (1899) 'Studies on the telegraphic language: the acquisition of a hierarchy of habits', *Psychological Review*, 6.345–75.

Bryant, J.W. (1983) 'Hypermaps: a representation of perceptions in conflicts', *Omega*, 11.6.575–86.

Bryant, J. (1987) 'Systems of perceptions: developments in hypermapping', paper presented at the International Symposium on Decision Management, Toronto, August.

Bryant, J. (1989) *Problem Management*. Chichester: John Wiley.

Bryman, A. and Burgess, R.G. (eds) (1994) *Analyzing Qualitative Data*. London: Routledge.

Bryson, N., Ngwenyama, O.K. and Mobolurin, A. (1994) 'A qualitative discriminant process for scoring and ranking in group support systems', *Information Processing and Management*, 30.3.389–405.

Buchanan, D. and Wilson, R. (1996) *Re-engineering Operating Theatres: the Perspective Assessed*. Occasional Paper 34. Leicester Business School.

Burgoyne, J.G. (1995) 'Learning from experience: from individual discovery to meta-dialogue via the evolution of transitional myths', *Personnel Review*, 24.6.61.

Burr, V. and Butt, T. (1992) *Invitation to Personal Construct Psychology*. London: Whurr.

Buzan, T. (1989) *Use Your Head*. London: BBC Books.

Buzan, T. (1993) *The Mind Map Book*. London: BBC Books.

Calori, R., Johnson, G. and Sarnin, P. (1992) 'French and British top managers' understanding of the structure and dynamics of their industries: a cognitive analysis and comparison', *British Journal of Management*, 3.2.61–78.

Campbell, J.P. and Dunnette, M.D. (1968) 'Effectiveness of T-group experiences in managerial training and development', *Psychological Bulletin*, 70.2.73–104.

Carroll, D. (1984) *Biofeedback in Practice*. Harlow: Longman.

Cascio, W.F. (1982) *Applied Psychology in Personnel Management* (2nd edn). Reston, Virginia: Reston Publications.

Chatman, J.A. and Barsade, S.G. (1995) 'Personality, organizational culture, and co-operation: evidence from a business simulation', *Administrative Science Quarterly*, 40.3.423–43.

Chatman, J.A. and Jehn, K.A. (1994) 'Assessing the relationship between industry characteristics and organizational culture', *Academy of Management Journal*, 37.3.522–33.

Checkland, P.B. (1988) 'The case for "holon"', *Systems Practice*, 1.3.235–8.

Checkland, P.B. and Haynes, M.G. (1994) 'Varieties of systems thinking: the case of soft systems methodology', *Systems Dynamics Review*, 10.2/3.189–97.

Checkland, P.B. and Scholes, J. (1990) *Soft Systems Methodology in Action*. Chichester: John Wiley.

Chikudate, N. (1991) 'Cross-cultural analysis of cognitive systems in organizations: a comparison between Japanese and American organizations', *Management International Review*, 31.3.213–19.

Child, J. (1984) *Organization: A Guide to Problems and Practice* (2nd edn). London: Harper and Row.

Chmiel, N.R.J. and Wall, T.D. (1994) 'Fault prevention, job design and the adaptive control of advanced manufacturing technology', *Applied Psychology: An International Review*, 43.4.455–73.

Clark, D.M. (1983) 'On the induction of depressed mood in the laboratory: evaluation and comparison of the Velten and musical procedures', *Advanced Behavioural Research and Therapy*, 5.1.27–49.

Clark, S. and Scrivener, S.A.R. (1993) 'The use of interactive computer techniques to capture and structure drawing surface activity', *Proceedings of The International Symposium on Creativity and Cognition*, 13–15 April, LUTCHI, Loughborough University.

Cleeremans, A. and McClelland, J.L. (1991) 'Learning the structure of event sequences', *Journal of Experimental Psychology: General*, 120.3.235–53.

Clegg, C., Warr, P., Green, T., Monk, A., Kemp, N., Allison, G. and Lonsdale, M. (1988) *People and Computers: How to Evaluate Your Company's New Technology*. Chichester: Ellis Horwood.

Cohen, M.D., March, J.G. and Olsen, P.J. (1972) 'A garbage can model of organizational choice', *Administrative Science Quarterly*, 17.1.1–25.

Cole, M., John-Steiner, V., Scibner, S. and Souberman, E. (eds) (1978) *Mind in Society*. Cambridge, MA: Harvard University Press.

Collier, J. (1967) *Visual Anthropology: Photography as a Research Method*. New York: Holt Rinehart and Winston.

Convoy, J. and Laird, J.D. (1984) 'Projecting what you feel: the effects of emotion on story content', paper presented at Eastern Psychological Association Meeting, Baltimore.

Cook, M. (1988) *Personnel Selection and Productivity*. Chichester: John Wiley.

Cooke, N.J. (1994) 'Varieties of knowledge elicitation techniques', *International Journal of Human-Computer Studies*, 41.6.801–49.

Cooke, S. and Slack, N. (1991) *Making Management Decisions* (2nd edn). Hemel Hempstead: Prentice-Hall.

Corbridge, C., Rugg, G., Major, N.P., Shadbolt, N.R. and Burton, A.M. (1994) 'Laddering: technique and tool use in knowledge acquisition', *Knowledge Acquisition*, 6.3.315–41.

Cortazzi, M. (1993) *Narrative Analysis*. London: Falmer.

Corter, J.E. and Tversky, A. (1986) 'Extended similarity trees', *Psychometrika*, 51.3.429–51.

Coshall, J.T. (1991) 'An appropriate method for eliciting construct subsystems from repertory grids', *The Psychologist*, 4.8.354–7.

Costa, P.T. and McCrae, R.R. (1993) 'Bullish on personality psychology', *The Psychologist*, 6.7.302–3.

Courtney, J.F. and Paradice, D.B. (1993) 'Studies in managerial problem formulation systems', *Decision Support Systems*, 9.4.413–23.

Covin, T.J., Kilmann, R.H. and Kilmann, I. (1994) 'Using organizational stories for the diagnostic phase of planned change: some possibilities and precautions', *Psychological Reports*, 74.2.623–34.

Cropper, S.C., Eden, C.L. and Ackermann, F. (1990) 'Keeping sense of accounts using computer-based cognitive maps', *Social Science Computer Review*, 8.345–66.

Crossan, M.M. (1991) 'Organisation learning: a sociocognitive model of strategic management', Doctoral dissertation, University of Western Ontario.

Crossman, E.R.F.W. (1959) 'A theory of the acquisition of speed skill', *Ergonomics*, 2.153–66.

Crutcher, R.J., Ericsson, K.A. and Wichura, C.A. (1994) 'Improving the encoding of verbal reports by using MPAS: a computer-aided encoding system', *Behavior Research Methods, Instruments and Computers*, 26.2.167–71.

Daniels, H., McGhee, S. and Davis, G.A. (1994) 'The imagery-creativity connection', *Journal of Creative Behavior*, 28.3.151–76.

Daniels, K., Johnson, G. and de Chernatory, L. (1994) 'Differences in managerial cognitions of competition', *British Journal of Management*, Special Issue, 5.June.21–9.

Davey, A., Olson, D. and Wallenius, J. (1994) 'The process of multi-attribute decision-making: a case study of selecting applicants for a PhD program', *European Journal of Operational Research*, 72.3.469–84.

Davis, J. (1994) 'GM's $11,000,000,000 turnaround', *Fortune*, Oct. 17. 154.

Dearborn, D.C. and Simon, H.I. (1958) 'Selective perception: a note on the departmental identifications of executives', *Sociometry*, 21.140–4.

Deary, I.J. and Matthews, G. (1993) 'Personality traits are alive and well', *The Psychologist*, 6.7.299–311.

Delbecq, A., Van de Ven, A. and Gustafson, D. (1975) *Group Techniques for Program Planning: a Guide to Nominal Group and Delphi Processes*. Glenview, IL: Scott Foresman.

Deldin, P.J. and Levin, I.P. (1986) 'The effect of mood induction in a risky decision-making task', *Bulletin of the Psychonomic Society*, 24.1.4–6.

Denham, P. (1993) '9-year-old to 14-year-old children's conception of computers using drawings', *Behaviour and Information Technology*, 12.6.346–58.

Dey, I. (1993) *Qualitative Data Analysis*. London: Routledge.

Dibella, A.J., Nevis, E.C. and Gould, J.M. (1996) 'Understanding organizational capability', *Journal of Management Studies*, 33.3.361–79.

Digman, J.M. (1990) 'Personality structure: emergence of the five-factor model', *Annual Review of Psychology*, 41.417–40.

Dillon, J.T. (1990) *The Practice of Questioning*. London: Routledge.

Dobson, M. and Markham, R. (1993) 'Imagery ability and source monitoring: implications for eyewitness memory', *British Journal of Psychology*, 84.1.111–18.

Donnellon, A., Gray, B. and Bougon, M.G. (1986) 'Communication, meaning and organized action', *Administrative Science Quarterly*, 31.1.43–55.

Drewer, J. (1972) *A Dictionary of Psychology*. Harmondsworth, Middlesex: Penguin.

Drummond, H. (1992) 'Another fine mess: time for quality in decision-making', *Journal of General Management*, 18.1.1–14.

Dulewicz, V. (1989) 'Assessment centres as the route to competence', *Personnel Management*, 21.11.56–9.

Duncker, K. (1945) 'On problem solving', *Psychological Monographs*. 58. whole no. 270.

du Preez, P. (1991) *A Science of Mind: the Quest for Psychological Reality*. London: Academic Press.

Durivage, A., St. Martin, J. and Barrette, J. (1995) 'Practical or traditional intelligence: what does the situational interview measure?' *European Review of Applied Psychology*, 45.3.171–8.

Eckersley, M. (1988) 'The form of design processes: a protocol analysis study', *Design Studies*, 9.2.86–94.

Edelson, M. (1990) *Psychoanalysis: a Theory in Crisis*. Chicago and London: University of Chicago Press.

Eden, C. (1988) 'Cognitive mapping: a review', *European Journal of Operational Research*, 36.1.1–13.

Eden, C. (1989) 'Using cognitive mapping for strategic options development and analysis

(SODA)', in J. Rosenhead (ed.) *Rational Analysis for a Problematic World*. Chichester: John Wiley.

Eden, C. (1993) 'From the playpen to the bombsite: the changing nature of management science', *Omega*, 21.2.139–54.

Eden, C. (1994) 'Cognitive mapping and problem structuring for system dynamics model-building', *System Dynamics Review*, 10.2–3.257–76.

Eden, C. and Ackermann, F. (1993) 'Evaluating strategy: its role within the context of strategic control', *Journal of the Operational Research Society*, 44.9.853–65.

Eden, C., Ackermann, F. and Cropper, S. (1992) 'The analysis of cause maps', *Journal of Management Studies*, 29.3.309–24.

Eden, C., Jones, S., Sims, D. and Smithin, T. (1981) 'The intersubjectivity of issues and issues in intersubjectivity', *Journal of Management Studies*, 18.1.37–47.

Ellis, H.C. and Ashbrook, P.W. (1988) 'Resource allocation model of the effects of depressed mood states on memory', in K. Fiedler and J. Forgas (eds) *Affect, Cognition and Social Behaviour*. Toronto: Hogrefe.

Ellis, H.C. and Ashbrook, P.W. (1991) 'The state of mood and memory research: a selective review', in D. Kuiken (ed.) *Mood and Memory: Theory, Research and Applications*. London: Sage. pp. 1–21.

Ericsson, K.A. and Simon, H.A. (1980) 'Verbal reports as data', *Psychological Review*, 87.3.215–51.

Ericsson, K.A. and Simon, H.A. (1993) *Protocol Analysis: Verbal Reports as Data*. Cambridge, MA: MIT Press.

Farrell, M.P. (1976) 'Patterns in the development of self-analytic groups', *Journal of Applied Behavioural Science*, 12.4.523–43.

Feinberg, R.A., Deruyter, K., Trappey, C. and Lee, T.Z. (1995) 'Consumer-defined service quality in international retailing', *Total Quality Management*, 6.1.61–7.

Felcher, M. (1995) 'Professors, get-me-dones and moochers: how car salespeople experience their customers', *Advances in Consumer Research*, 22.611–16.

Feldman, S.P. (1990) 'Stories as cultural creativity: on the relation between symbolism and politics in organizational change', *Human Relations*, 43.9.809–28.

Ferguson, E.S. (1977) 'The mind's eye: nonverbal thought in technology', *Science*, 197.4306.827–36.

Ferguson, J. (1970) *Socrates: a Source Book*. London: Macmillan for the Open University Press.

Fiese, B.H., Hooker, K.A., Kotary, L., Schwagler, J. and Rimmer, M. (1995) 'Family stories in the early stages of parenthood', *Journal of Marriage and the Family*, 57.3.763–70.

Finlay, K. (1996) 'Reliable and valid measurement of memory content and structure as a function of brand usage patterns', *Advances in Consumer Research*, 23.282–8.

Finney, M. and Mitroff, I.I. (1986) 'Strategic plan failures: the organization as its worst enemy', in H. Sims and D.A. Gioia (eds) *The Thinking Organization*. San Francisco, CA: Jossey-Bass.

Fiol, C.M. (1991) 'Managing culture as a competitive resource: an identity-based view of sustainable competitive advantage', *Journal of Management*, 17.1.191–211.

Fiol, C.M. (1994) 'Consensus, diversity and learning in organizations', *Organization Science*, 5.3.403–20.

Fiol, C.M. and Huff, A.S. (1992) 'Maps for managers: where are we? Where do we go from here?' *Journal of Management Studies*, 29.3.267–86.

Firlej, M. and Hellens, D. (1991) *Knowledge Elicitation: a Practical Handbook*. London: Prentice-Hall.

Fish, J. and Scrivener, S.A.R. (1990) 'Amplifying the mind's eye: sketching and visual cognition', *Leonardo*, 23.1.117–26.

Fisher, A. (1988) *The Logic of Real Arguments*. Cambridge: Cambridge University Press.

Fisher, R.P. and Geiselman, R.E. (1992) *Memory-enhancing Techniques for Investigative Interviewing: the Cognitive Interview*. Springfield, IL: Charles C. Thomas.

Flanagan, J.C. (1954) 'The critical incident technique', *Psychological Bulletin*, 51.4.327–58.

Flanagan, J.C., Miller, R.B., Burns, R.K., Hendrix, A.A., Stewart, B., Preston, H.O. and West, E.D. (1953) *The Performance Record for Hourly Employees*. Chicago: Science Research Associates.

Flint, N. and Sparrow, J. (1994) 'Interactive multimedia: creative catalyst or constraint?' *Knowledge-Based Systems*, 7.4.247–52.

Flint, N. and Sparrow, J. (1995) 'A graphic designer's considerations in multimedia application development', *Design Research Society Conference on 4D Dynamics*, De Montfort University, 21 September.

Floyd, S.W. and Wooldridge, B. (1992) 'Managing strategic consensus: the foundation of effective implementation', *Academy of Management Executive*, 6.4.27–39.

Forrester, J. (1971) 'Counterintuitive behaviour of social systems', *Technology Review*, January.53–68.

Foucault, M. (1979) *Discipline and Punish: the Birth of the Prison*. New York: Random House.

Fournier, S. and Guiry, M. (1993) 'An emerald green Jaguar, a house on Nantucket, and an African safari: wish lists and consumption dreams in materialistic society', *Advances in Consumer Research*, 20.352–8.

Fransella, F. and Bannister, D. (1977) *A Manual for Repertory Grid Technique*. London: Academic Press.

Freeman, R.E. (1984) *Strategic Management: a Stakeholder Approach*. Boston: Pitman.

Freud, S. (1900) *The Interpretation of Dreams, Standard Edition, Vols 4/5*. London: Hogarth.

Freud, S. (1909) (1974 edn) 'Five lectures on psycho-analysis, Lecture 3', in *Two Short Accounts of Psycho-Analysis*. Harmondsworth, Middlesex: Penguin.

Freud, S. (1915) (1946 edn) 'The unconscious', in *Collected Papers, Vol. 4*, London: Hogarth. pp. 98–136.

Freud, S. and Breuer, J. (1893) *Studies in Hysteria. Standard Edition, Vol. 2*. London: Hogarth.

Friedman, W.J. (1993) 'Memory for the time of past events', *Psychological Bulletin*, 113.1.44–66.

Gabelnick, F. (1993) 'Roles of women in the large group: enduring paradigms in a chaotic environment', *Group*, 17.4.245–53.

Gabriel, Y. (1995) 'The unmanaged organization: stories, fantasies and subjectivity', *Organization Studies*, 16.3.477–501.

Gagliardi, P. (1986) 'The creation and change of organizational cultures: a conceptual framework', *Organization Studies*, 7.2.117–34.

Galotti, K.M. (1989) 'Approaches to studying formal and everyday reasoning', *Psychological Bulletin*, 105.3.331–51.

Galton, F. (1879) 'Psychometric experiments', *Brain*, 2.149–62.

Gardner, P.H., Chmiel, N. and Wall, T.D. (1996) 'Implicit knowledge and fault diagnosis in the control of advanced manufacturing technology', *Behaviour and Information Technology*, 15.4.205–12.

Garfinkel, H. (1967) *Studies in Ethnomethodology*. Englewood Cliffs, NJ: Prentice-Hall.

Gaskell, G., Wright, D. and O'Muircheartaigh, C. (1993) 'Reliability of surveys', *The Psychologist*, 6.11.500–3.

Gawain, S. (1982) *Creative Visualisation*. New York: Bantam Books.

Geiselman, R.E., Fisher, R.P., MacKinnon, D.P. and Holland, H.L. (1986) 'Enhancement of eyewitness memory with the cognitive interview', *American Journal of Psychology*, 99.3.385–401.

Gentner, D. (1983) 'Structure mapping: a theoretical framework for analogy', *Cognitive Science*, 7.1.155–70.

Gerrardhesse, A., Spies, K. and Hesse, F.W. (1994) 'Experimental inductions of emotional states and their effectiveness: a review', *British Journal of Psychology*, 85.1.55–78.

Ghiselli, E.E. and Brown, C.W. (1955) *Personnel and Industrial Psychology* (2nd edn). New York: McGraw-Hill.

Gibson, D.C. and Salvendy, G. (1992) 'The dimensions of human knowledge in problem solving', *Studia Psychologica*, 34.4/5.297–321.

Glaister, K. and Thwaites, D. (1993) 'Managerial perception and organisational strategy', *Journal of General Management*, 18.4.15–33.

Glaze, A. (1989) 'Cadbury's dictionary of competence', *Personnel Management*, 21.7.44–8.

Goffman, E. (1959) *The Presentation of Self in Everyday Life*. New York: Doubleday Anchor Books.

Goffman, E. (1974) *Frame Analysis*. Harmondsworth, Middlesex: Penguin.

Gold, S.J. (1991) 'Ethnic boundaries and ethnic entrepreneurship: a photo-elicitation study', *Visual Sociology*, 6.2.9–23.

Goldberg, L.R. (1993) 'The structure of phenotypic personality traits', *American Psychologist*, 48.1.26–34.

Goldschmidt, G. (1991) 'The dialectics of sketching', *Creativity Research Journal*, 4.2.123–43.

Goleman, D. (1995) *Emotional Intelligence*. London: Bloomsbury.

Golembiewski, R.T., Proehl, C.W. and Sink, D. (1982) 'Estimating the success of OD applications', *Training and Development Journal*, 18.1.86–95.

Gordon, G.G. (1991) 'Industry determinants of organization and culture', *Academy of Management Review*, 16.2.396–415.

Green, A. (1995) 'Verbal protocol analysis', *The Psychologist*, 8.5.126–9.

Greenwald, A.G. and Banaji, M.R. (1989) 'The self as a memory system: powerful but ordinary', *Journal of Personality and Social Psychology*, 57.1.41–54.

Gregory, F.H. (1995) 'Soft systems models for knowledge elicitation and representation', *Journal of the Operational Research Society*, 46.5.562–78.

Grey, C. and Mitev, N. (1995) 'Re-engineering organizations: a critical appraisal', *Personnel Review*, 24.1.6–18.

Guptara, P. (1988) 'How to shape up for 1992', *Personnel Today*, 14 June.24.

Guthrie, W.K.C. (1967) *The Greek Philosophers: from Thales to Aristotle*. London: Methuen.

Guzzo, R.A., Jette, R.D. and Katzell, R.A. (1985) 'The effects of psychologically based intervention programs on worker productivity: a meta analysis', *Personnel Psychology*, 38.2.275–91.

Habermas, J. (1970) *Toward a Rational Society* (trans. by J.J. Shapiro). Boston, MA: Beacon.

Hall, A. (1994) *Abuse of Trust*. Leicester: Bookmart.

Hall, C.S. (1954) *A Primer of Freudian Psychology*. New York: World Publishing.

Halton, W. (1994) 'Some unconscious aspects of organizational life: contributions from psychoanalysis', in A. Obholzer and V.G. Roberts (eds) *The Unconscious at Work*. London: Routledge. pp. 11–18.

Hammer, K. and Janes, R. (1990) 'Interactive management', *OR Insight*, 3.1.11–13.

Hansen, C.D. and Kahnweiler, W.M. (1993) 'Storytelling: an instrument for understanding the dynamics of corporate relationships', *Human Relations*, 46.12.1391–409.

Harper, D. (1994) 'On the authority of the image: visual methods at the crossroads', in N.K. Denzin and Y.P. Lincoln (eds) *Handbook of Qualitative Research*. Newbury Park, CA: Sage. pp. 403–12.

Harri-Augstein, S. and Thomas, L. (1991) *Learning Conversations: the Self-organised Learning Way to Personal and Organisational Growth*. London: Routledge.

Hart, S., Boroush, M., Enk, G. and Hornick, W. (1985) 'Managing complexity through consensus mapping: technology for the structuring of group decisions', *Academy of Management Review*, 10.3.587–600.

Harter, J.J. and Bass, B.M. (1988) 'Superiors' evaluations and subordinates' perceptions of transformational and transactional leadership', *Journal of Applied Psychology*, 73.4.695–702.

Hartman, D.E. and Lindgren, J.H. (1993) 'Consumer evaluations of goods and services: implications for services marketing', *Journal of Services Marketing*, 7.2.4–15.

Hartog, D.N.D., van Muijen, J.J. and Koopman, P.L. (1997) 'Transactional versus transformational leadership: an analysis of the MLQ', *Journal of Occupational and Organizational Psychology*, 70.1.19–34.

Hatano, G. and Inagaki, K. (1986) 'Two courses of expertise', in H. Stevenson, H. Azuma and

K. Hakuta (eds) *Child Development and Education in Japan.* San Francisco, CA: Freeman. pp. 262–72.

Hayes, N.A. and Broadbent, D.E. (1988) 'Two modes of learning for interactive tasks', *Cognition,* 28.3.249–76.

Haygood, R.C. and Bourne, L.E. (1965) 'Attribute and rule learning aspects of conceptual behaviour', *Psychological Review,* 72.175–95.

Heisenberg, W. (1958) *Physics and Philosophy.* New York: Harper.

Heron, J. (1985) 'The role of reflection in a co-operative inquiry', in D. Boud, R. Keogh and D. Walker (eds) *Reflection: Turning Experience into Learning.* London: Kogan Page. pp. 128–38.

Hewitt, J. (1982) *The Complete Relaxation Book: a Manual of Eastern and Western Techniques.* London: Rider.

Hickson, D.J., Butler, R.J., Cray, D., Mallory, G.R. and Wilson, D.C. (1986) *Top Decisions: Strategic Decision Making in Organisations.* Oxford: Blackwell.

Hinkle, D. (1965) 'The change of personal constructs from the viewpoint of a theory of construct implications', unpublished PhD thesis, Ohio State University.

Hintzman, D.L. (1990) 'Human learning and memory: connections and dissociations', *Annual Review of Psychology,* 41.109–39.

Hochschild, A.R. (1983) *The Managed Heart: Commercialisation of Human Feeling.* Berkeley, CA: University of California Press.

Hodgkinson, G.P., Padmore, J. and Tomes, A.E. (1991) 'Mapping consumers' cognitive structures: a comparison of similarity trees with multidimensional scaling and cluster analysis', *European Journal of Marketing,* 25.2.41–60.

Hofbauer, T.H., Woo, C.C. and Martens, C.D. (1994) 'Decision support through facilitating the exchange of experiences in a distributed environment', *International Journal of Intelligent and Co-operative Information Systems,* 3.3.255–78.

Hoffman, R.R., Shadbolt, N.R., Burton, A.M. and Klein, G. (1995) 'Eliciting knowledge from experts: a methodological analysis', *Organizational Behaviour and Human Decision Processes,* 62.2.129–58.

Holyoak, K.J. and Spellman, B.A. (1993) 'Thinking', *Annual Review of Psychology,* 44.265–315.

Hom, H.L. and Arbuckle, B. (1988) 'Mood induction effects upon goal setting and performance in young children', *Motivation and Emotion,* 12.2.113–22.

Hu, Y.S. (1995) 'The international transferability of the firm's advantages', *California Management Review,* 37.4.73–88.

Huffman, C.M. and Weaver, K.A. (1996) 'Autobiographical recall and visual imagery', *Perceptual and Motor Skills,* 82.3.1.1027–34.

Hukkinen, J. (1995) 'Corporatism as an impediment to ecological sustenance: the case of Finnish waste management', *Ecological Economics,* 15.1.59–75.

Hull, C.L. (1928) *Aptitude Testing.* London: Harrap.

Hutchins, E. (1991) 'Individual and socially distributed cognition', *Cognitive Science 234.* Course Notes, Cognitive Science Department, University of California at San Diego.

HyperResearch (1995) *Qualitative Data Analysis Software.* Randolf, MA: ResearchWare.

Ingram, R.E. (1984) 'Toward an information processing analysis of depression', *Cognitive Therapy and Research,* 1984.8.5.443–78.

Ireland, R.D., Hitt, M.A., Bettis, R.A. and Auld de Porras, D. (1987) 'Strategy formulation processes: differences in perceptions of strength and weaknesses indicators and environmental uncertainty by managerial level', *Strategic Management Journal,* 8.5.469–85.

Isaacs, W.N. (1993) 'Dialogue, collective thinking and organisational learning', *Organisational Dynamics,* 22.2.24–39.

Isenberg, D.J. (1984) 'How senior managers think', *Harvard Business Review,* Nov.–Dec.81–90.

Iyengar, S. (1996) 'Framing responsibility for political issues', *Annals of the American Academy of Political and Social Science,* 546.59–70.

James, G. (1991) *Quality of Working Life and Total Quality Management*. AXAS Work Research Unit Occasional Paper No. 50, Nov.

James, W. (1890) *The Principles of Psychology*. New York: Henry Holt.

James, W. (1892) *Textbook of Psychology*. London: Macmillan.

Janis, I.L. and Mann, L. (1977) *Decision Making: a Psychological Analysis of Conflict, Choice and Commitment*. New York: Free Press.

Jemison, D.B. (1987) 'Value creation and acquisition integration: the role of strategic capability transfer', in M. Liebcap (ed.) *Corporate Restructuring through Mergers, Acquisitions and Leveraged Buyouts*. Greenwich, CT: JAI Press.

Jenkins, M. (1993) *Thinking about Growth: a Cognitive Mapping Approach to Understanding Small Business Development*. Working Paper SWP 12/93. Bedford: Cranfield School of Management.

Jenlink, P.M. (1994) 'Using evaluation to understand the learning architecture of an organization', *Evaluation and Program Planning*, 17.3.315–25.

Jennings, D. and Wattam, S. (1994) *Decision-making: an Integrated Approach*. London: Pitman.

Jerome, J.K. (1889) (1993 edn) *Three Men in a Boat*. Ware: Wordsworth Classics.

Johnson-Laird, P.N. and Bara, B.G. (1984) 'Syllogistic inference', *Cognition*, 16.1.1–61.

Johnston, R. (1995) 'The determinants of service quality: satisfiers and dissatisfiers', *International Journal of Service Industry Management*, 6.5.53–61.

Jones, R.M. (1970) *The New Psychology of Dreaming*. Harmondsworth, Middlesex: Penguin.

Jorgensen, D.L. (1989) *Participant Observation: a Methodology for Human Studies*. Newbury Park, CA: Sage.

Jung, C.G. (1910) 'The association method', *American Journal of Psychology*, 21.219–69.

Jung, C.G. (1961) *The Collected Works of C.G. Jung. 20 volumes. The Bollingen Series*. Trans. R.F.C. Hull. H. Read, M. Fordham, G. Adler and W. McGuire (eds). New York: Pantheon.

Kahney, H. (1993) *Problem Solving: Current Issues* (2nd edn). Buckingham: Open University Press.

Kaiser, M.K., Jonides, J. and Alexander, J. (1986) 'Intuitive reasoning about abstract and familiar physics problems', *Memory and Cognition*, 14.4.308–12.

Kamiya, J. (1968) 'Conscious control of brain waves', *Psychology Today*, 1.11.57–60.

Keaveney, S.M. (1995) 'Customer-switching behavior in service industries: an exploratory study', *Journal of Marketing*, 59.2.71–82.

Keirsey, D. and Bates, M. (1984) *Please Understand Me: Character and Temperament Types* (5th edn). California: Prometheus Nemesis Book Company.

Kelly, G.A. (1955) *The Psychology of Personal Constructs*. New York: Norton.

Kelly, G.A. (1969) 'The role of classification in personality theory', in E. Maher (ed.) *Clinical Psychology and Personality: the Selected Papers of George Kelly*. New York: John Wiley.

Kelly, G.A. (1977) 'The psychology of the unknown', in D. Bannister (ed.) *New Perspectives in Personal Construct Theory*. London: Academic Press.

Kemp, R. (1985) 'Planning, public hearings and the politics of discourse', in J. Forester (ed.) *Critical Theory and Public Life*. Cambridge, MA: MIT Press.

Kerr, M.R. (1995) 'Tacit knowledge as a predictor of managerial success: a field study', *Canadian Journal of Behavioural Science*, 27.1.36–51.

Kets de Vries, M.F.R. and Miller, D. (1984) 'Unstable at the top', *Psychology Today*, 18.10.26–34.

Kim, D.H. (1993) *Systems Archetypes: Diagnosing Systemic Issues and Designing High Leverage Interventions*. Cambridge, MA: Pegasus Communications.

Kim, D.H. and Senge, P.M. (1994) 'Putting systems thinking into practice', *Systems Dynamics Review*, 10.2/3.277–90.

Kinder, A. and Robertson, I. (1995) 'Friend or foe: getting the best out of personality questionnaires', *Selection and Development Review*, 11.1.1–4.

Klein, J.H. and Cooper, D.F. (1982) 'Cognitive maps of decision makers in a complex game', *Journal of the Operational Research Society*, 33.1.63–71.

Klein, M. (1959) 'Our adult world and its roots in infancy', in A.D. Colman and M.H. Geller (eds) *Group Relations Reader 2*. Washington, DC: AK Rice Institute.

Kochan, T.A., Katz, H.C. and McKersie, R.B. (1986) *The Transformation of American Industrial Relations*. New York: Basic Books.

Koehnken, G., Milne, R., Memon, A. and Bull, R. (1994) 'A meta-analysis of the effects of the cognitive interview', paper presented at the Biennial Conference of the American Psychology Law Society Meeting, Sante Fe, New Mexico.

Kogut, B. and Zander, U. (1993) 'Knowledge of the firm and the evolutionary theory of the multinational corporation', *Journal of International Business Studies*, 24.4.625–43.

Kohnken, G., Thurer, C. and Zoberbier, D. (1994) 'The cognitive interview: are the interviewer's memories enhanced too?' *Applied Cognitive Psychology*, 8.1.13–24.

Korminouri, R. (1995) 'The nature of memory for action events: an episodic integration view', *European Journal of Cognitive Psychology*, 7.4.337–63.

Koukouris, K. (1994) 'Constructed case studies: athletes' perspectives of disengaging from organised competitive sport', *Sociology of Sport Journal*, 11.2.114–39.

Kriger, M.P. and Solomon, E.E. (1992) 'Strategic mindsets and decision making autonomy in US and Japanese MNCs', *Management International Review*, 32.4.327–43.

Krosnick, J.A. (1991) 'Response strategies for coping with the cognitive demands of attitude measures in surveys', *Applied Cognitive Psychology*, 5.3.213–36.

Krueger, R.A. (1988) *Focus Groups: a Practical Guide for Applied Research*. Beverly Hills, CA: Sage.

Kuhn, T.S. (1970) *The Structure of Scientific Revolution*. Chicago: University of Chicago Press.

Kunz, W., Rittel, H.W.J. and Schwuchow, W. (1977) *Methods of Analysis and Evaluation of Information Needs: a Critical Review*. Munich: Verlag Documentation.

Kusterer, K. (1978) *Know-how on the Job: the Important Working Knowledge of Unskilled Workers*. Boulder, CO: Westview Press.

Kvale, S. (1996) *InterViews: an Introduction to Qualitative Research Interviewing*, Thousand Oaks, CA: Sage.

Lakoff, G. and Johnson, M. (1983) *Metaphors We Live By*. Chicago: University of Chicago Press.

Landfield, A.W. (1971) *Personal Construct Systems in Psychotherapy*. Chicago: Rand McNally.

Langfield-Smith, K. (1992) 'Exploring the need for a shared cognitive map', *Journal of Management Studies*, 29.3.349–68.

Lapadat, J.C. and Martin, J. (1994) 'The role of episodic memory in learning from university lectures', *Contemporary Educational Psychology*, 19.3.266–85.

Larkin, J.H. and Simon, H.A. (1987) 'Why a diagram is (sometimes) worth ten thousand words', *Cognitive Science*, 11.1.65–99.

Latham, G.P. (1989) 'The reliability, validity and practicality of the situational interview', in R.W. Eler and G.R. Ferris (eds) *The Employment Interview*. London: Sage.

Latham, G.P., Saari, L.M., Pursell, E.D. and Campion, M.A. (1980) 'The situational interview', *Journal of Applied Psychology*, 65.4.422–7.

Leplat, J. (1990) 'Skills and tacit skills: a psychological perspective', *Applied Psychology: An International Review*, 39.2.143–54.

Levin, M. (1994) 'Action research and critical systems thinking: two icons carved out of the same log', *Systems Practice*, 7.1.25–41.

Levinson, H. (1994) 'The practitioner as diagnostic instrument', in A. Howard (ed.) *Diagnosis for Organisational Change: Methods and Models*. New York: Guilford Press. pp. 27–52.

Linstone, H.A. and Turoff, M. (eds) (1975) *The Delphi Method: Techniques and Applications*. Reading, MA: Addison Wesley.

Lloyd, P. and Scott, P. (1992) 'Interpreting the protocols of creativity', *Proceedings of Creativity and Cognition Conference*, Loughborough University.

London, M. and Wohlers, A.J. (1991) 'Agreement between subordinate and self-ratings in upward feedback', *Personnel Psychology*, 44.2.375–90.

Lorenz, C. (1988) 'Nostrums fall from favour', *Financial Times*, 15 February.

Louis, M.R. (1980) 'Surprise and sensemaking: what newcomers experience in entering unfamiliar organizational settings', *Administrative Science Quarterly*, 25.226–51.

Lundgren, D.C. and Knight, D.J. (1978) 'Sequential stages of development in sensitivity training groups', *Journal of Applied Behavoural Science*, 14.204–22.

Maas, J.B. (1965) 'Patterned expectation interview: reliability studies on a new technique', *Journal of Applied Psychology*, 49.431–3.

Mackenzie, D. and Spinardi, G. (1995) 'Tacit knowledge, weapons design, and the uninvention of nuclear weapons', *American Journal of Sociology*, 101.1.44–99.

Majaro, S. (1988) *The Creative Gap*. London: Longman.

Mannix, E.A., Neale, M.A. and Northcraft, G.B. (1995) 'Equity, equality or need: the effects of organizational culture on the allocation of benefits and burdens', *Organizational Behavior and Human Decision Processes*, 63.3.276–86.

Markowitsch, H.J. (1995) 'Which brain regions are critically involved in the retrieval of old episodic memory?' *Brain Research Reviews*, 21.2.117–27.

Martin, P. and Nicholls, J. (1987) *Creating a Committed Workforce*. London: Institute of Personnel Management.

Matlin, M.W. (1994) *Cognition* (3rd edn). Orlando: Harcourt Brace Jovanovich.

Maule, A.J. and Hockey, G.R.J. (1996) 'The effects of mood on risk-taking behaviour', *The Psychologist*, 9.10.464–7.

Maurer, S.D. and Fay, C. (1988) 'Effect of situational interviews, conventional structured interviews and training on interview rating agreement: an experimental analysis', *Personnel Psychology*, 41.2.329–43.

McCaskey, M.B. (1972) *The Executive Challenge*. Beverley Hills, CA: Sage.

McCrimmon, M. (1995) 'After competencies, then what?' *Selection and Development Review*, 11.1.4–6.

McDaniel, M.A., Whetzel, D.L., Schmidt, F.L. and Maurer, S.D. (1994) 'The validity of employment interviews: a comprehensive review and meta-analysis', *Journal of Applied Psychology*, 79.4.599–616.

McKim, R.H. (1980) *Experiences in Visual Thinking*. Monterey, CA: Brooks-Cole.

McLinden, D.J. and Jinkerson, D.L. (1994) 'Picture this: multivariate analysis in organizational assessment', *Evaluation and Program Planning*, 17.1.19–24.

McMullin, R.E. (1986) *Handbook of Cognitive Therapy Techniques*. New York: Norton.

Mead, G.H. (1934) *Mind, Self and Society*. Chicago: University of Chicago Press.

Mechitov, A.L., Moshkovich, H.M. and Olson, D.L. (1994) 'Problems of decision rule elicitation in a classification task', *Decision Support Systems*, 12.2.115–26.

Memon, A., Holley, A., Milne, R., Koehnken, G. and Bull, R. (1994) 'Towards understanding the effects of interviewer training in evaluating the cognitive interview', *Applied Cognitive Psychology*, 8.7.641–59.

Menon, G. (1992) *The Accessibility of Information in Autobiographical Memory and its Effects on Judgments of Behavioral Frequencies*. Working Paper, Leonard Stern School of Business, New York University.

Mercier, J. (1994) 'Looking at organizational culture, hermeneutically', *Administration and Society*, 26.1.28–47.

Metz, C. (1994) 'The fictional film and its viewer: a metapsychological study', *Psyche-Zeitschrift für Psychoanalyse und Ihre Anwendungen*, 48.11.1004–46.

Millar, R., Crute, V. and Hargie, O. (1992) *Professional Interviewing*. London: Routledge.

Miller, J.P. (1994) 'The relationship between organizational culture and environmental scanning: a case study', *Library Trends*, 43.2.170–205.

Miller, W.C. (1987) *The Creative Edge: Fostering Innovation Where You Work*. Reading, MA: Addison-Wesley.

Mind Maps Plus (1995) *User Manual to Mind Maps Plus (v3)*. Blairgowrie: Cedar Software Limited.

Mintzberg, H. (1994) *The Rise and Fall of Strategic Planning*. New York: Prentice-Hall.

Monnickendam, M., Yaniv, H. and Geva, N. (1994) 'Practitioners and the case record: patterns of use', *Administration in Social Work*, 18.4.73–87.

Moody, J.W., Will, R.P. and Blanton, J.E. (1996) 'Enhancing knowledge elicitation using the cognitive interview', *Expert Systems with Applications*, 10.1.127–33.

Moore, C.M., Gargan, J. and Parker, K. (1987) 'Interpretative structural modeling', in C. Moore (ed.) *Group Techniques for Idea Building*. Beverly Hills, CA: Sage. pp. 78–90.

Morgan, D.L. (1988) 'Focus groups as qualitative research', *Qualitative Research Methods Vol 16*. Beverly Hills, CA: Sage.

Morgan, D.L. (ed.) (1993) *Successful Focus Groups: Advancing the State of the Art*. Newbury Park, CA: Sage.

Morgan, G. (1993) *Imagaization: the Art of Creative Management*. London: Sage.

Mostyn, S. (1994) 'How recruitment consultants view their clients', unpublished MBA dissertation, University of Central England Business School. Birmingham.

Motowildo, S.J., Dunnette, M.D. and Carter, G.W. (1990) 'An alternative selection procedure: the low fidelity simulation', *Journal of Applied Psychology*, 75.6.640–7.

Motowildo, S.J. and Tippins, N. (1993) 'Further studies of the low-fidelity simulation in the form of a situational inventory', *Journal of Occupational and Organizational Psychology*, 66.4.337–44.

Mulej, M. and Rebernik, M. (1994) 'There is hardly a (total) quality without systems thinking', *Systems Research*, 11.1.7–14.

Mullings, C. (1984) *Observation. CRUS Guide*. Consultancy and Research Unit, Department of Information Studies, University of Sheffield.

Murray, H.A. (1938) *Explorations in Personality*. New York: Oxford University Press.

Mussi, S. (1995) 'Causal knowledge elicitation based on elicitation failures', *IEEE Transactions on Knowledge and Data Engineering*, 7.5.725–39.

Myers, C. and Davids, K. (1993) 'Tacit skill and performance at work', *Applied Psychology: An International Review*, 42.2.117–37.

Myers, I.B. (1989) *Myers Briggs Type Indicator (Form G)*. Palo Alto, CA: Consulting Psychologists Press.

Nagay, J.A. (1949) *The Development of a Procedure for Evaluating the Proficiency of Air Route Traffic Controllers*. Civil Aeronautics Administration, Division of Research Report No. 83, Washington, DC.

Neisser, U. (1987) 'Introduction: the ecological and intellectual bases of categorization', in U. Neisser (ed.) *Concepts and Conceptual Development: Ecological Conceptual Factors in Categorization*. Cambridge: Cambridge University Press.

Neuman, G.A., Edwards, J.E. and Raju, N.S. (1989) 'Organizational development interventions: a meta-analysis of their effects on satisfaction and other attitudes', *Personnel Psychology*, 42.3.461–83.

Newton, D.P. (1994) 'Pictorial support for discourse comprehension', *British Journal of Educational Psychology*, 64.2.221–9.

Ngwenyama, O.K., Bryson, N. and Mobolurin, A. (1996) 'Supporting facilitation in group support systems: techniques for analyzing consensus-relevant data', *Decision Support Systems*, 16.2.155–68.

Nicholas, J.M. (1982) 'The comparative impact of organization development interventions on hard criteria measures', *Academy of Management Review*, 7.4.531–42.

Nikolinakos, D.D. (1992) 'Freud on dreams and Kosslyn on mental imagery', *The Journal of Mind and Behaviour*, 13.4.395–412.

Nisbett, R.E. and Wilson, T.D. (1977) 'Telling more than we can know: verbal reports on mental processes', *Psychological Review*, 84.3.231–59.

Nolan, R. (1994) *Cognitive Practices: Human Language and Human Knowledge*. Oxford: Blackwell.

Nonaka, I., Takeuchi, H. and Umemoto, K. (1996) 'A theory of organizational knowledge creation', *International Journal of Technology Management*, 11.7/8.833–45.

Norton, R.W. (1975) 'Measurement of ambiguity tolerance', *Journal of Personality Assessment*, 39.6.607–19.

Nossiter, V. and Biberman, G. (1990) 'Projective drawings and metaphor: analysis of organisational culture', *Journal of Managerial Psychology*, 5.3.13–16.

Novick, L.R. and Hmelo, C.E. (1994) 'Transferring symbolic representations across non-isomorphic problems', *Journal of Experimental Psychology: Learning, Memory and Cognition*, 20.6.1296–321.

Nutt, P.C. (1984) *Planning Methods for Health and Related Organisations*. New York: John Wiley.

Obholzer, A. and Roberts, V.G. (eds) (1994) *The Unconscious at Work*. London: Routledge.

O'Connor, P. (1996) 'Organizational culture as a barrier to women's promotion', *Economic and Social Review*, 27.3.205–34.

O'Driscoll, M.P. and Cooper, C.L. (1996) 'A critical incident analysis of stress coping behaviours at work', *Stress Medicine*, 12.2.123–8.

Oliver, R.L., Robertson, T.S. and Mitchell, D.J. (1993) 'Imaging and analyzing in response to new product advertising', *Journal of Advertising*, 22.4.35–50.

Oppenheim, A.N. (1992) *Questionnaire Design, Interviewing and Attitude Measurement* (2nd edn). London: Pinter.

O'Roark, A.M. (1987) *What Can the MBTI Say about Management?* Gainsville, FL: Center for Applications of Psychological Type.

Overholser, J.C. (1993) 'Elements of the Socratic method', *Psychotherapy*, 30.1.75–85.

Packer, T., Race, K.E. and Hotch, D.F. (1994) 'Focus groups: a tool for consumer-based program evaluation in rehabilitation agency settings', *Journal of Rehabilitation*, 60.3.30–3.

Palmer, S. and Dryden, W. (1995) *Counselling for Stress Problems*. London: Sage.

Parker, D.L., Webb, J. and Dsouza, B. (1995) 'The value of critical incident analysis as an educational tool, and its relationship to experiential learning', *Nurse Education Today*, 15.2.111–16.

Parsons, M.J. (1987) *How We Understand Art: a Cognitive Developmental Account of Aesthetic Experience*. Cambridge: Cambridge University Press.

Pascale, P. (1990) *Managing on the Edge*. Harmondsworth, Middlesex: Penguin.

Patrick, J., Spurgeon, P., Barwell, F. and Sparrow, J. (1981) *The Development of Training Techniques for Kiln Control*. Birmingham: University of Aston.

Patton, M.Q. (1987) *Creative Evaluation* (2nd edn). Newbury Park, CA: Sage.

Pearn, M. and Kandola, R. (1993) *Job Analysis: a Manager's Guide* (2nd edn). London: Institute of Personnel Management.

Pedler, M., Burgoyne, J. and Boydell, T. (1991) *The Learning Company*. London: McGraw-Hill.

Pellegrino, J.W. and Glaser, R. (1982) 'Analysing aptitudes for learning: inductive reasoning', in R. Glaser (ed.) *Advances in Instructional Psychology (Vol 2)*. Hillsdale, NJ: Lawrence Erlbaum Associates.

Persson, R.S. (1996) 'Studying with a musical maestro: a case study of commonsense teaching in artistic training', *Creativity Research Journal*, 9.1.33–46.

Peters, S. and Sparrow, J.A. (1994) 'Human resource management philosophies and management action', *International Journal of Contemporary Hospitality Management*, 6.6.v–viii.

Phillips, M.E. (1994) 'Industry mindsets: exploring the cultures of two macro-organizational settings', *Organization Science*, 5.3.384–402.

Piaget, J. (1951) *Play, Dreams and Imitation in Childhood*. New York: W.W. Norton.

Piercy, N. (1989) 'Diagnosing and solving implementation problems in strategic planning', *Journal of General Management*, 15.1.19–38.

Polyani, M. (1958) *Personal Knowledge: Towards a Post-critical Philosophy*. London: Routledge and Kegan Paul.

Porac, J.F., Thomas, H. and Emme, B. (1987) 'Knowing the competition: the mental models of retail strategists', in G. Johnson (ed.) *Business Strategy and Retailing*. Chichester: John Wiley.

Prasad, P. and Prasad, A. (1994) 'The ideology of professionalism and work computerization: an institutionalist study of technological change', *Human Relations*, 47.12.1433–58.

Proffitt, D.R., Kaiser, M.K. and Whelan, S.M. (1990) 'Understanding wheel dynamics', *Cognitive Psychology*, 22.3.342–73.

Rackham, N. and Morgan, T. (1977) *Behaviour Analysis in Training*. London: McGraw-Hill.

Radenhausen, R.A. (1989) 'Effects of mood induction on ratings of self and experimenter', *Journal of Clinical Psychology*, 45.1.134–8.

Raghuram, S. (1996) 'Knowledge creation in the telework context', *International Journal of Technology Management*, 11.7/8.859–70.

Rainer, T. (1978) *The New Diary*. London: Angus and Robertson.

Ramaprasad, A. and Rai, A. (1996) 'Envisioning management of information', *Omega: International Journal of Management Science*, 24.2.179–93.

Rapaport, D. (1945) *Diagnostic Psychological Testing*. Chicago: Year Book Publishers.

Rathus, J.H., Reber, A.S., Manza, L. and Kushner, M. (1994) 'Implicit and explicit learning: differential effects of affective states', *Perceptual and Motor Skills*, 79.1.163–84.

Read, H., Fordham, M., Adler, G. and McGuire, W. (1961) *The Collected Works of C.G. Jung. Bollingen Series 20*. Trans. R.F.C. Hull. New York: Pantheon.

Reason, P. and Rowan, J. (1981) 'On making sense', in P. Reason and J. Rowan (eds) *Human Enquiry: a Sourcebook of New Paradigm Research*. Chichester: John Wiley.

Reber, A.S. (1967) 'Implicit learning of artificial grammars', *Journal of Verbal Learning and Verbal Behavior*, 6.855–63.

Reber, A.S., Kassin, S.M., Lewis, S. and Cantor, G. (1980) 'On the relationship between implicit and explicit modes in the learning of a complex rule structure', *Journal of Experimental Psychology: Human Learning and Memory*, 6.5.492–514.

Reber, P.J. and Squire, L.R. (1994) 'Parallel brain systems for learning with and without awareness', *Learning and Memory*, 1.4.217–29.

Rebernik, M. (1994) 'De-memorising and changing of mental models as a precondition for TQM', *Systems Research*, 11.1.101–11.

Reddy, W.B. and Lippert, K.M. (1980) 'Studies of the processes and dynamics within experiential groups', in P.B. Smith (ed.) *Small Groups and Personal Change*. London: Methuen. pp. 56–84.

Rees, L. (1992) *Selling Politics*. London: BBC Books.

Reger, R.K. and Palmer, T.B. (1996) 'Managerial categorization of competitors: using old maps to navigate new environments', *Organizational Science*, 7.1.22–39.

Rentsch, J.R. (1990) 'Climate and culture: interaction and qualitative differences in organizational meanings', *Journal of Applied Psychology*, 75.6.668–81.

Reynolds, T.J. (1988) 'Laddering theory, method and interpretation', *Journal of Advertising Research*, 28.1.11–31.

Rhinesmith, S. (1992) 'Global mindsets for global managers', *Training and Development*, Oct.63–6.

Rich, A. and Parker, D.L. (1995) 'Reflection and critical incident analysis: ethical and moral implications of their use within nursing and midwifery education', *Journal of Advanced Nursing*, 22.6.1050–7.

Richmond, B. (1993) 'Systems thinking: critical thinking skills for the 1990s and beyond', *System Dynamics Review*, 9.2.113–33.

Rickards, T. (1990) *Creativity and Problem Solving at Work*. Aldershot: Gower.

Rieber, L.P. (1996) 'Animation as feedback in a computer-based simulation: representation matters', *Educational Technology Research and Development*, 44.1.5–22.

Risch, J.D., Troyanobermudez, L. and Stenman, J.D. (1995) 'Designing corporate strategy with systems dynamics: a case study in the pulp and paper industry', *System Dynamics Review*, 11.4.249–74.

Riskind, J.H. and Rholes, W.S. (1985) 'The Velten mood induction procedure and cognitive manipulation: our response to Clark (1983)', *Behaviour Research and Therapy*, 23.6.671–3.

Robbins, S.P. (1989) *Training in Interpersonal Skills: Tips for Managing People at Work*. Englewood Cliffs, NJ: Prentice Hall International.

Robertson, I.T. and Kandola, R.S. (1982) 'Work sample tests: validity, adverse impact and applicant reaction', *Journal of Occupational Psychology*, 55.3.171–83.

Robertson, I.T., Gratton, L. and Rout, U. (1990) 'The validity of situational interviews for administrative jobs', *Journal of Organizational Behaviour*, 11.1.69–76.

Robins, C.J. (1988) 'Development of experimental mood induction procedures for testing personality-event interaction models of depression', *Journal of Clinical Psychology*, 44.6.958–63.

Rogers, Y. and Rutherford, A. (1992) 'Future directions in mental models research', in Y. Rogers, A. Rutherford and P.A. Bibby (eds) *Models in the Mind: Theory, Perspective and Application*. London: Academic Press. pp. 289–314.

Rorschach, H. (1921) *Psychodiagnostics*. Berne: Hans Huber.

Rorty, R. (1989) *Contingency, Irony and Solidarity*. Cambridge: Cambridge University Press.

Rosch, E.H. (1973) 'Natural categories', *Cognitive Psychology*, 4.3.328–50.

Rosch, E.H. (1975) 'Cognitive reference points', *Cognitive Psychology*, 7.4.532–47.

Rothe, H.J. (1994) 'Elicitation and modeling of expert knowledge as a basis for building of expert systems', *Zeitschrift für Psychologie*, 202.4.321–48.

Rotter Incomplete Sentences Blank (1966) New York: Psychological Corporation.

Rouse, W.B. and Morris, N.M. (1986) 'On looking into the black box: prospects and limits in the search for mental models', *Psychological Bulletin*, 100.3.349–63.

Rugg, G. and McGeorge, P. (1995) 'Laddering', *Expert Systems*, 12.4.339–46.

Sampson, E.E. (1991) *Social Worlds, Personal Lives: an Introduction to Social Psychology*. San Diego: Harcourt Brace Jovanovich.

Samurcay, R. and Delsart, F. (1994) 'Collective activities in dynamic environment management: functioning and efficiency', *Travail Humain*, 57.3.252–70.

Sattath, S. and Tversky, A. (1977) 'Additive similarity trees', *Psychometrika*, 42.3.319–45.

Saville and Holdsworth (1990) *OPQ Manual*. Esher, Surrey: Saville and Holdsworth.

Schaef, A.W. and Fassel, D. (1988) *The Addictive Organization*. San Francisco, CA: Harper and Row.

Schank, R.C. (1982) *Dynamic Memory: a Theory of Learning in Computers and People*. Cambridge: Cambridge University Press.

Schar, S.G. (1996) 'The influence of the user interface on solving well-defined and ill-defined problems', *International Journal of Human-Computer Studies*, 44.1.1–18.

Schein, E.H. (1993) 'Legitimating clinical research in the study of organizational culture', *Journal of Counseling and Development*, 71.6.703–8.

Schenk, P. (1991) 'The role of drawing in the graphic design process', *Design Studies*, 12.3.168–81.

Schmidt, F.L. and Hunter, J.E. (1983) 'Individual differences in productivity: an empirical test of estimates derived from studies of selection procedure utility', *Journal of Applied Psychology*, 68.3.407–14.

Schneider, F., Gur, R.C., Gur, R.E. and Muenz, L.R. (1994) 'Standardised mood induction with happy and sad facial expressions', *Psychiatry Research*, 51.1.19–31.

Schon, D.A. (1991) *The Reflective Practitioner: How Professionals Think in Action*. Aldershot: Avebury.

Schuler, H., Diemand, A. and Moser, K. (1993) 'Film scenes: development and construct validation of a new personnel assessment method', *Zeitschrift für Arbeits und Organisationpsychologie*, 37.1.3–9.

Schutz, W.C. (1967) *Joy: Expanding Human Awareness*. New York: Grove Press.

Scribner, S. (1986) 'Thinking in action: some characteristics of practical thought', in R.J. Sternberg and R.K. Wagner (eds) *Practical Intelligence: Nature and Origins of Competence in the Everyday World*. Cambridge: Cambridge University Press.

Seger, C.A. (1992) *Implicit Learning*. Technical Report UCLA CSRP 92-3, Cognitive Science Research Programmes. Los Angeles, CA: University of California.

Senge, P.M. (1990) *The Fifth Discipline: the Art and Practice of the Learning Organisation*. London: Century Business.

Senge, P.M., Roberts, C., Ross, R.B., Smith, B.J. and Kleiner, A. (1994) *The Fifth Discipline Fieldbook: Strategies and Tools for Building a Learning Organisation*. London: Nicholas Brealey.

Sevastos, P., Smith, L. and Cordery, J.L. (1992) 'Evidence on the reliability and construct validity of Warr's (1990) well-being and mental health measures', *Journal of Occupational and Organizational Psychology*, 65.1.33–49.

Sharp, D. (1987) *Personality Types: Jung's Model of Typology*. Toronto: Inner City Books.

Shaughnessy, P. and Kivlighan, D.M. (1995) 'Using group participants' perceptions of therapeutic factors to form client typologies', *Small Group Research*, 26.2.250–68.

Sheehan, P.W. (1967) 'A shortened form of Betts' Questionnaire upon mental imagery', *Journal of Clinical Psychology*, 23.3.386–9.

Shepard, R.N. (1975) 'Form, formation, and transformation of internal representations', in R. Solso (ed.) *Information Processing and Cognition: the Loyola Symposium*. Hillsdale, NJ: Erlbaum.

Shepard, R.N. and Metzler, J. (1971) 'Mental rotation of three-dimensional objects', *Science*, 171.701–3.

Simon, H.A. (1947) *Administrative Behaviour: a Study of Decision Making Process in Administrative Organisations*. New York: Free Press.

Sinclair, S.A. (1990) 'Perceptual mapping: a tool for industrial marketing: a case study', *Journal of Business and Industrial Marketing*, 5.1.55–66.

Sinetar, M. (1991) *Developing a 21st Century Mind*. New York: Villard Books.

Singer, J.L. (1993) 'Experimental studies of ongoing conscious experience', *CIBA Foundation Symposia*, 174.100–22.

Sirigu, A. and Grafman, J. (1996) 'Selective impairments within episodic memories', *Cortex*, 32.1.83–95.

Sissons, K. (1989) *Personnel Management in Britain*. Oxford: Blackwell.

Smart, J.C. and Hamm, R.E. (1993) 'Organizational culture and effectiveness in 2-year colleges', *Research in Higher Education*, 34.1.95–106.

Smircich, L. (1983) 'Concepts of culture and organizational analysis', *Administrative Science Quarterly*, 28.3.339–68.

Smith, P.B. (1980a) *Group Processes and Personal Change*. London: Harper and Row.

Smith, P.B. (1980b) (ed.) *Small Groups and Personal Change*. London: Methuen.

Smith, P.B. (1980c) 'The outcome of sensitivity training and encounter', in P.B. Smith (ed.) *Small Groups and Personal Change*. London: Methuen. pp. 25–55.

Smith, S.M. (1988) 'Environmental context-dependent memory', in G.M. Davies and D.M. Thomson (eds) *Memory in Context: Context in Memory*. Chichester: John Wiley. pp. 13–34.

Sobol, M.G. and Lei, D. (1994) 'Environment, manufacturing technology and embedded knowledge', *International Journal of Human Factors in Manufacturing*, 4.2.167–89.

Sparrow, J.A. (1984) 'Ability assessment and job structure measures in occupational mobility', unpublished PhD thesis, Birmingham: University of Aston.

Sparrow, J.A. (1989) 'Graphical displays in information systems: some data properties influencing the effectiveness of alternative forms', *Behaviour and Information Technology*, 8.1.43–56.

Sparrow, J.A. and Bushell, M. (1996) 'Personal business adviser models of business strategy and operations', paper presented at the 19th Institute of Small Business Affairs Conference, 22 November, Birmingham.

Sparrow, J.A., Ingold, A., Huyton, J. and Baker, J. (1992) 'Experienced staff and tailoring food service', *International Journal of Contemporary Hospitality Management*, 4.1.4–11.

Sparrow, J.A. and Rigg, C. (1993) 'Job analysis: selecting for the masculine approach to management', *Selection and Development Review*, 9.2.5–8.

Sparrow, J.A., Robinson, G., Robinson, K. and Wood, C. (1993) *Quality Matters: GPs' Perceptions of Services Provided by Solihull Healthcare*. Birmingham: University of Central England.

Sparrow, J.A. and Wood, G. (1994) 'Constraints in meeting customer needs in food service', *International Journal of Contemporary Hospitality Management*, 6.1.61–7.

Sparrow, P.R. (1994) 'The psychology of strategic management: emerging themes of diversity and cognition', in C.L. Cooper and I. Robertson (eds) *International Review of Industrial and Organisational Psychology*. Vol. 9. Chichester: John Wiley. pp. 147–82.

Spence, L. (1921) (1994 edn) *Introduction to Mythology*. London: Senate.

Sproull, L.S. (1981) 'Beliefs in organizations', in P.C. Nystrom and W.H. Starbuck (eds) *Handbook of Organizational Design*. Oxford: Oxford University Press.

Squire, L.R., Knowlton, B. and Musen, G. (1993) 'The structure and organisation of memory', *Annual Review of Psychology*, 44.453–95.

Stacey, R. (1991) *The Chaos Frontier: Creative Strategic Control for Business*. Oxford: Butterworth-Heinemann.

Stacey, R. (1992) *Managing Chaos*. London: Kogan Page.

Stanley, W.B., Mathews, R.C., Buss, R.R. and Kotler-Cope, S. (1989) 'Insight without awareness: on the interaction of verbalization, instruction and practice in a simulated process control task', *Quarterly Journal of Experimental Psychology*, 41a.3.553–78.

Stephens, R.A. and Gammack, J.G. (1994) 'Knowledge elicitation for systems practitioners: a constructivist application of the repertory grid technique', *Systems Practice*, 7.2.161–82.

Sternberg, R.J., Wagner, R.K., Williams, W.M. and Horvath, J.A. (1995) 'Testing common sense', *American Psychologist*, 50.11.912–27.

Stevenson, W.B. and Bartunek, J.M. (1996) 'Power, interaction, position and the generation of cultural agreement in organizations', *Human Relations*, 49.1.75–104.

Stewart, V. and Stewart, A. (1981) *Business Applications of Repertory Grid*. London: McGraw-Hill.

Stone, K.F. and Dillehunt, H.Q. (1978) *Self-Science: the Subject Is Me*. Santa Monica, CA: Goodyear.

Strickland, L. (1994) 'Autobiographical interviewing and narrative analysis: an approach to psychosocial assessment', *Clinical Social Work Journal*, 22.1.27–41.

Stubbart, C.I. and Ramaprasad, A. (1988) 'Probing two chief executives's schematic knowledge of the US steel industry using cognitive maps', *Advances in Strategic Management*, 5.139–64.

Sujan, M., Bettman, J.R. and Baumgartner, H. (1993) 'Influencing consumer judgments using autobiographical memories: a self-referencing perspective', *Journal of Marketing Research*, 30.Nov.422–36.

Sutherland, G., Newman, B. and Rachman, S. (1982) 'Experimental investigations of the relations between mood and intrusive unwanted cognitions', *British Journal of Medical Psychology*, 55.2.127–38.

Taylor, J.W. (1961) *How to Create Ideas*. Englewood Cliffs, NJ: Prentice-Hall.

Teasdale, J.D. and Russell, M.L. (1983) 'Differential effects of induced mood on the recall of positive, negative and neutral words', *British Journal of Clinical Psychology*, 22.3.163–71.

Tenaglia, M. and Noonan, P. (1992) 'Scenario-based strategic planning: a process for building top management consensus', *Planning Review*, March/April.12–19.

Tesch, R. (1990) *Qualitative Research: Analysis Types and Software Tools*. London: Falmer.

Tett, R.P. and Jackson, D.N. (1990) 'Organization and personality correlates of participative behaviours using an in-basket exercise', *Journal of Occupational Psychology*, 63.2.175–88.

Thomas, L.H. (1994) 'A comparison of the verbal interactions of qualified nurses and nursing auxiliaries in primary, team and functional nursing wards', *Journal of Nursing Studies*, 31.3.231–44.

Thomas, S.N. (1986) *Practical Reasoning in Natural Language*. Englewood Cliffs, NJ: Prentice-Hall.

Titchener, E.B. (1909) *A Textbook of Psychology, Vol 1*. New York: Macmillan.

Tomlinson, C.M. and Johnson, L. (1994) 'Notes on the techniques adopted for knowledge elicitation', *Systems Research and Information Science*, 6.4.179–85.

Toms, M. (1992) 'Verbal protocols: how useful are they to cognitive ergonomists?' in E.J. Lovesey (ed.) *Contemporary Ergonomics*. London: Taylor and Francis.

Tonges, M.C. and Madden, M.J. (1993) 'Running the vicious circle backward and other systems solutions to nursing problems', *Journal of Nursing Administration*, 23.1.39–44.

Torrington, D. and Blandamer, W. (1992) 'Competence, pay and performance', in R. Boam and P. Sparrow (eds) *Designing and Achieving Competency*. London: McGraw-Hill. pp. 137–45.

Toulmin, S., Rieke, R. and Janik, A. (1979) *An Introduction to Reasoning*. New York: Macmillan.

Townsend, J. and Favier, J. (1991) *The Creative Manager's Pocketbook*. Alresford, Hants: Management Pocket Books.

Tsouvalis, C. and Checkland, P. (1996) 'Reflecting on SSM: the dividing line between real-world and systems thinking world', *Systems Research*, 13.1.35–45.

Tufte, E.R. (1983) *The Visual Display of Quantitative Information*. Cheshire, Connecticut: Graphics Press.

Tulving, E. (1972) 'Episodic and semantic memory', in E. Tulving and W. Donaldson (eds) *Organization of Memory*. New York: Academic Press.

Tulving, E. (1983) *Elements of Episodic Memory*. Oxford: Oxford University Press.

Tulving, E. and Thomson, D.M. (1971) 'Retrieval processes in recognition memory: effect of associative context', *Journal of Experimental Psychology*, 87.1.352–73.

Turban, E. (1988) *Decision Support and Expert Systems: Managerial Perspectives*. London: Collier Macmillan.

Twyman, M. (1985) 'Using pictorial language: a discussion of the dimensions of the problem', in T.M. Duffy (ed.) *Designing Usable Texts*. London: Academic Press.

Ullman, M. (1996) *Appreciating Dreams: a Group Approach*. Thousand Oaks, CA: Sage.

Valkenburg, P.M. and Vandervoort, T.H.A. (1995) 'The influence of television on children's daydreaming styles', *Communication Research*, 22.3.267–87.

VanGundy, A.B. (1988) *Techniques of Structured Problem Solving* (2nd edn). New York: Van Nostrand Reinhold.

Vaughan, F.E. (1979) *Awakening Intuition*. New York: Anchor Books.

Velten, E. (1968) 'A laboratory task for induction of mood states', *Behaviour Research and Therapy*, 6.4.473–82.

Vennix, J.A.M. (1995) 'Building consensus in strategic decision making: systems dynamics as a group support system', *Group Decision and Negotiation*, 4.4.335–55.

Voss, J.F., Greene, T.R., Post, T.A. and Penner, B. (1983) 'Problem-solving skill in the social sciences', in G. Bower (ed.) *The Psychology of Learning and Motivation, Vol. 17*. New York: Academic Press.

Voyer, J.J. (1994) 'Coercive organizational politics and organizational outcomes: an interpretive study', *Organization Science*, 5.1.72–85.

Waelchli, F. (1992) 'Theses of general systems theory', *Systems Research*, 9.4.3–8.

Wagner, R.K. (1985) 'Tacit knowledge in everyday intelligent behaviour', PhD thesis, Dissertations Abstracts International.

Wagner, R.K. (1987) 'Tacit knowledge in everyday intelligent behaviour', *Journal of Personality and Social Psychology*, 52.6.1236–47.

Wagner, R.K. and Sternberg, R.J. (1985) 'Practical intelligence in real world pursuits: the role of tacit knowledge', *Journal of Personality and Social Psychology*, 49.2.436–58.

Wagner, R.K. and Sternberg, R.J. (1987) 'Tacit knowledge in managerial success', *Journal of Business and Psychology*, 1.4.301–12.

Walker, D. (1985) 'Writing and reflection', in D. Boud, R. Keogh and D. Walker (eds) *Reflection: Turning Experience into Learning*. London: Kogan Page.

Walker, M.J., Huber, G.P. and Glick, W.H. (1995) 'Functional background as a determinant of executives' selective perception', *Academy of Management Journal*, 38.4.943–74.

Wall, T.D. and Lischeron, J.A. (1977) *Worker Participation: a Critique of the Literature and Some Fresh Evidence*. London: McGraw-Hill.

Ward, K. (1994) 'Internal Marketing at Rank Xerox (UK) Ltd.', unpublished undergraduate dissertation for the University of Central England, Birmingham.

Warr, P. (1990) 'The measurement of well-being and other aspects of mental health', *Journal of Occupational Psychology*, 63.3.193–210.

Warr, P. and Conner, M. (1992) 'The measurement of effective working styles during entry-level training', *Journal of Occupational and Organizational Psychology*, 65.1.17–32.

Watson, D. and Tellegen, A. (1985) 'Toward a consensual structure of mood', *Psychological Bulletin*, 98.2.219–35.

Watson, T.J. (1996) 'How do managers think? Identity, morality and pragmatism in managerial theory and practice', *Management Learning*, 27.3.323–41.

Wax, R.H. (1971) *Doing Fieldwork*. Chicago: University of Chicago Press.

Weekley, J.A. and Gier, J.A. (1987) 'Reliability and validity of the situational interview for a sales position', *Journal of Applied Psychology*, 72.3.484–7.

Weick, K.E. (1976) 'Educational organizations as loosely coupled systems', *Administrative Science Quarterly*, 21.1–19.

Weick, K.E. (1979) *The Social Psychology of Organising*. Reading, MA: Addison Wesley.

Weick, K.E. and Bougon, M.G. (1986) 'Organizations as cognitive maps: charting ways to success and failure', in H. Sims and D. Gioia (eds) *The Thinking Organization: Dynamics of Organizational Cognition*. San Francisco, CA: Jossey-Bass.

Weisbord, M.R. (1992) *Discovering Common Ground*. San Francisco, CA: Berrett-Koehler.

Weisinger, J.Y. and Salipante, P.F. (1995) 'Toward a method of exposing hidden assumptions in multicultural conflict', *International Journal of Conflict Management*, 6.2.147–70.

Weiss, J.W. (1994) *Business Ethics: a Managerial Stakeholder Approach*. Belmont, CA: Wadsworth.

Weiss, J.W. (1996) *Organizational Behavior and Change: Managing Diversity, Cross-cultural Dynamics and Ethics*. St Paul, MN: West Publishing.

West, M.A. (1990) 'The social psychology of innovation in groups', in M.A. West and J.L. Farr (eds) *Innovation and Creativity at Work: Psychological and Organizational Strategies*. New York: John Wiley. pp. 309–33.

Wetherall, M. (1994) 'Good art, bad art, social constructionism and humanism', *The Psychologist*, 7.11.508–9.

Wheatley, W.J., Maddox, E.N. and Anthony, W.P. (1989) 'Enhancing creativity and imagination in strategic planners through the utilization of guided imagery', *Organisational Development Journal*, 110.1.33–9.

Wickert, F. (1947) *Psychological Research on Problems of Redistribution*. American Air Force Aviation Psychology Program Research Report No. 14. Washington, DC: US Government Printing Office.

Wiersema, M. and Bantel, K. (1992) 'Top management team demography and corporate strategic change', *Academy of Management Journal*, 35.1.91–121.

Wilcocks, D. and Saunders, I. (1994) 'Animating recursion as an aid to instruction', *Computers and Education*, 23.3.221–6.

Williams, T., Eden, C., Ackermann, F. and Tait, A. (1995) 'The effects of design changes and delays on project costs', *Journal of the Operational Research Society*, 46.7.809–18.

Wilson, D., Hickson, D. and Miller, S. (1995) *A Step too Far: Expansionist Strategies and Decision Over-reach*. Research Paper RP9503, January, Birmingham: Aston Business School Research Institute.

Wohlers, A.J., Hall, M. and London, M. (1993) 'Subordinates rating managers: organizational and demographic correlates of self/subordinate agreement', *Journal of Occupational and Organizational Psychology*, 66.3.263–75.

Wood, C.C. (1992) 'A study of the graphical mediating representations used by collaborating authors', *Intelligent Tutoring Media*, 3.2/3.75–83.

Wood, C.C. (1993) 'The cognitive dimensions of sketching notations and media in creative design activity', *Proceedings of The International Symposium on Creativity and Cognition*, 13–15 April, LUTCHI, Loughborough University.

Wood, L.E. and Ford, J.M. (1993) 'Structuring interviews with experts during knowledge elicitation', *International Journal of Intelligent Systems*, 8.1.71–90.

Woodruffe, C. (1990) *Assessment Centres: Identifying and Developing Competence*. London: Institute of Personnel Management.

Woodruffe, C. (1992) 'What is meant by a competency?' in R. Boam and P. Sparrow (eds) *Designing and Achieving Competency*. Maidenhead: McGraw-Hill International. Chapter 2.

Woods, P. (1983) *Sociology and the School: an Interactionist Viewpoint*. London: Routledge and Kegan Paul.

Worthing, E.L. (1978) 'The effects of imagery content, choice of imagery content and self-verbalization on the control of pain', *Cognitive Therapy and Research*, 2.3.225–40.

WT Grant Consortium on the School-based Promotion of Social Competence (1992) 'Drug and alcohol prevention curricula', in J.D. Hawkins (ed.) *Communities that Care*. San Francisco: Jossey-Bass.

Yu, X.J. (1995) 'Conflict in a multicultural organization: an ethnographic attempt to discover work-related cultural assumptions between Chinese and American co-workers', *International Journal of Conflict Management*, 6.2.211–32.

Zeitz, C.M. (1994) 'Expert-novice differences in memory, abstraction, and reasoning in the domain of literature', *Cognition and Instruction*, 12.4.277–312.

Zmud, R.W., Anthony, W.P. and Stair, R.M. (1993) 'The use of mental imagery to facilitate information identification in requirements analysis', *Journal of Management Information Systems*, 9.4.175–91.

Index